The Captive Sea

The Captive Sea

SLAVERY, COMMUNICATION, AND
COMMERCE IN EARLY MODERN SPAIN
AND THE MEDITERRANEAN

Daniel Hershenzon

PENN

UNIVERSITY OF PENNSYLVANIA PRESS *Philadelphia*

THIS BOOK IS MADE POSSIBLE BY A COLLABORATIVE GRANT
FROM THE ANDREW W. MELLON FOUNDATION.

Published by
University of Pennsylvania Press
Philadelphia, Pennsylvania 19104-4112
www.upenn.edu/pennpress

Printed in the United States of America
on acid-free paper

10 9 8 7 6 5 4 3 2 1

Library of Congress Cataloging-in-Publication Data
is available.

ISBN 978-0-8122-5048-0

CONTENTS

Tracing the entangled histories of Christians, Jews, and Muslims who interacted in the early modern Mediterranean raises orthographic difficulties. In order to help the modern reader, I employed the modern spelling of place-names and proper names whenever possible. Spanish spelling in the period was erratic and place-names as well as proper names were often spelled in various forms, not only by different authors but also by the same author in a single document. The spelling of names and terms from languages written in non-Latin alphabets, often including sounds not in use in European languages, raises other problems. For example, the Muslim name "Musa" and the Jewish "Moses" are often spelled in early modern Spanish documents interchangeably as "Muxi" and "Muji." The vast majority of the people mentioned in these records were not asked to spell their names and did not choose the spelling used. Thus, when possible, I rendered Ottoman and Arabic names using modern spelling and transliterated them without diacritical marks except for the hamza (') and the ʿayn (ʿ), and macron over some long vowels. Unless otherwise indicated, all translations are mine. The bibliographic notes will easily allow researchers to find the records and trace the individuals mentioned despite the modernization of the spelling of these names.

The Captive Sea

Introduction

In 1608, Genoese naval forces took a thirteen-year-old Algerian girl named Fatima captive and sold her into slavery in Livorno, Italy. Her father almost succeeded in ransoming her that same year, but the ship that would have returned her to Algiers stopped in Corsica, where Fatima was forcibly converted and baptized as "Madalena." In an unrelated incident, also in 1608, Algerian pirates captured Diego de Pacheco, illegitimate son of the Spanish Marquis de Villena, and enslaved him in Algiers. While a captive, Pacheco was taken to Istanbul where, after attempting and failing to arrange his ransom, he converted to Islam. Piecing together these Mediterranean episodes from the archives leads to a third story beginning just a year after the capture of Fatima and Pacheco. In 1609, three Spanish Trinitarian friars were on the brink of departing for Spain with Christians they had redeemed from the Maghrib when the Algerian Governing Council detained them. All three friars and many of the captives they had redeemed would die in captivity. Meanwhile in 1613, the Sicilian squadron of Spain captured Muhammad Bey, a high-ranking Ottoman official from Alexandria. Negotiations over his ransom failed, and Muhammad died in his prison cell in Sicily.

At first glance, though they all occurred within a five-year period and in the same geographic area, these stories do not seem to have much to do with one another. Yet these different Mediterranean trajectories intersected and had strong effects on one another, whether through their ransom negotiations, for example, or in that one captive was taken as revenge for the imprisonment of another. These episodes overlap not only in how each individual was situated in relation to the other by captors and redeemers but also in the way that information about each case was transmitted across the sea. Because captives frequently contacted their kin, who in turn contacted pasha, king, and sultan, who then exchanged messages with one another, these cases had the potential to intersect in Spanish, Moroccan, or Ottoman political hubs as well as in the slave prisons. Such negotiations often led ecclesiastical redemption institutions and North African merchants to establish uneasy ransom coalitions. This was the case of the opening four episodes. Fatima's father set in motion the connections between the stories when he demanded the Algerian Governing Council secure her return. Algiers retained the Trinitarians and the captives they had ransomed as a riposte to Fatima's unsuccessful ransom and forced conversion. The friars tried to repatriate Fatima in return for their own liberty but failed. Subsequently they sought their freedom in exchange for the return of the bey, but Pacheco's father was also using all his influence in Madrid to get permission to exchange the bey for his son. This book is about the Mediterranean world that Fatima, Pacheco, the Trinitarians, and the bey inhabited, a world that captivity, commerce, and communication created.

In the early modern western Mediterranean, a wide range of individuals, networks, and institutions dealt with the trafficking of people—capturing, enslaving, smuggling, and ransoming—across and beyond the borders of Spain's Mediterranean territories, Morocco, and Ottoman Algiers and Tunis. According to a recent estimation, between 1450 and 1850 at least three million people—Muslims and Christians—lost their liberty at sea or on land and were enslaved. More than a million Christians were enslaved in the Maghrib (northwest Africa) between 1530 and 1780, and a million or more Muslims were enslaved on the inner sea's northern shores.[1] Records do not always clearly distinguish between Muslims from the Maghrib, from the Mashriq (Lebanon, Jordan, Palestine, and Syria), or from Anatolia, but as these calculations exclude the Spanish Balearic and Canary Islands, Sardinia, and France, the number of Maghribis enslaved in southern Europe must have been even higher. Of this number, few managed to obtain release through compensation, swap, or flight. The majority never knew freedom again and became an integral part of the society of their captors.[2] The widespread practice of captive-taking meant, then, that the sight of laboring captives and the recounting of stories about individuals who had lost their liberty to corsairs were common on the southern and northern shores of the early modern Mediterranean.

Piracy has always been endemic in the Mediterranean, but its increase at the turn of the seventeenth century marked the end of the age of large imperial clashes at the high seas. During the preceding century, the Ottoman and Spanish empires reigned in the Mediterranean, gripping the region after the conquest of Constantinople-turned-Istanbul in 1453 and Muslim Granada in 1492. Imperial competition reached an equilibrium of sorts with Ottoman control established in the Balkans, Syria (1516), Egypt (1517), and the Maghrib (1530–1570s), excluding Morocco, and the Spanish controlling Portugal, Naples, Sicily, Milan, Sardinia, and a number of garrison towns along the Atlantic and Mediterranean North African littoral. During the sixteenth century, Christian coalitions clashed with the Ottomans in a series of spectacular battles, but in 1581 the empires signed a truce and turned their attention away from the sea, the Ottomans toward Safavid Persia and the Spaniards toward northern Europe and the Atlantic world. To be sure, imperial structures and logics continued to shape life in the Mediterranean, but the sea was transformed from an offensive into a defensive frontier.[3] This moment ushered in a new age of privateering—*corso* (Spanish, Italian) or *course* (French), as the peoples of the Mediterranean called it. Christian and Muslim corsairs and freebooters stepped in to fill the vacuum imperial forces had left in the western half of the sea. Maghribi corsairs raided southern European shores—they even reached as far as Ireland and Iceland in the 1620s and 1630s—and attacked Christian ships on the high seas. Christian corsairs, pirates, soldiers, and royal fleets raided Maghribi cities and ships and captured and enslaved Moroccan and Ottoman subjects.

Unlike black slaves in the Atlantic world, the victims of the Mediterranean system of bondage knew their captors, not personally but rather on the basis of *longue durée* violent and peaceful exchanges. Moreover, the distances separating southern Andalusia from Morocco (less than nine miles), the Spanish Levant from Ottoman Algiers (about 200 miles), or Sicily from Ottoman Tunis (around 110 miles) were short. Algiers was closer to Majorca than was Madrid, and Majorca was closer to Algiers than was Istanbul. This proximity meant that throughout the medieval and early modern periods intense social, economic, and political interactions prevailed alongside violence, captive-taking, and enslavement.[4] Geography and history meant that this bondage system articulated alienation, or the condition of foreignness, differently than the bondage system in the Atlantic or sub-Saharan world.[5] Unlike black slaves in Africa, the Atlantic world, and Iberia, Mediterranean slaves generally maintained some contact, in the form of letters, with their kinfolk and communities.[6] In North African cities, priests and friars provided religious services for captives in prison churches. Muslims enslaved in Italy had mosques as early as the mid-seventeenth century, and even in Catholic Spain, Muslim slaves had private worship spaces during the seventeenth century. At the turn of the eighteenth century the Spanish king ordered the allocation of burial space to Muslims in any city where Muslim slaves resided.[7]

In the Mediterranean, captivity and slavery were not exclusive conditions but rather dimensions of a single process. Contemporaries used the terms "captive" and "slave" interchangeably to refer to the system's victims.[8] As "captives," slaves retained claims on kin living across the sea. In fact, masters interested in ransom money encouraged their slaves to write home. Ransoming might occur in various ways: the Trinitarian and Mercedarian orders and urban fraternities ransomed Christian captives; Muslim and Christian captives commissioned merchants to ransom them and transfer them home; Muslim and Christian rulers often negotiated the exchange of their subjects; and kin negotiated the exchange of their enslaved relatives. Even slaves with no prospect of paying ransom could send letters to kin and home authorities and receive correspondence in return. Captivity and enslavement were undoubtedly among the worst experiences of the early modern Mediterranean; numerous texts recount the hellish living conditions captives-turned-authors suffered. Yet the mechanisms of captivity, enslavement, and ransom prevented the full alienation or social isolation of enslaved captives in the Mediterranean. Geography and the intensity of exchange in the region left Mediterranean slaves comparatively better off than their counterparts in other places. This was the world of Diego de Pacheco, Fatima, the Trinitarians, and the old bey.

This book argues that piracy, captivity, and redemption shaped the western Mediterranean as an integrated region socially, politically, and economically. It explores the entangled experiences of Muslim and Christian captives and by extension the entangled histories of the

Spanish Empire, Morocco, and Ottoman Algiers in the seventeenth century. Adopting a sociocultural perspective and drawing on the history of commerce, the book demonstrates that a Mediterranean system of bondage entwined the lives of Muslim and Christian captives in spite of confessional differences. They were connected by a political economy of ransom, the result of the intermingling of the market, social obligation, religion, and politics.[9] Actors from across the sea—captives, merchants, friars, and rulers—shaped this political economy and interacted through an array of texts that captives created and distributed across the sea. Constant circulation of texts and people meant that the lives of Fatima, the Trinitarians, Pacheco, Muhammad, and others, which historians have so far studied in isolation, were interdependent. The history that emerges from their stories is both local and regional; it is a history *in* the Mediterranean and a history *of* the Mediterranean.[10] The book offers an analysis of competing Spanish, Algerian, and Moroccan projects intended to shape Mediterranean mobility structures. Simultaneously, it reveals the tragic upending of the lives of individuals by these imperial maritime political agendas and also how Christian, Muslim, and Jewish merchants subverted such plans.

Scholars often write the history of the early modern Mediterranean as either a story of religious enmity or a tale of canny merchants and thriving markets. These are sometimes mutually exclusive approaches, but in the context of the western half of the sea they can also operate as complementary elements arranged along a temporal axis.[11] Historians imagine the sixteenth-century western Mediterranean as a world sharply divided along confessional lines. In *The Forgotten Frontier*, historian Andrew Hess described the Ibero-African frontier not only as hostile but also as an empty region.[12] Even Fernand Braudel, whose work Hess was criticizing, and who famously and poetically claimed that the "Turkish Mediterranean lived and breathed with the same rhythms as the Christian, [and] that the whole sea shared a common destiny," stressed religious oppositions and the division of the sea into two blocs, Ottoman Muslim and Spanish Christian.[13] The transformation of the western Mediterranean into a religiously and imperially divided maritime space was the result of events and processes internal and external to the sea; the shift was slow and occurred over more than a century. It allegedly began with the Christian conquest of Muslim Granada (1492) and ended with the expulsion (1609–14) of the Moriscos (Spain's forcefully converted

Muslims and their descendants). At the turn of the seventeenth century, these events were complemented by the "northern invasion," when English, Dutch, and French merchants and fleets invaded the Mediterranean en masse, transforming it into an internationalized arena where homogeneous nation-states competed in the market. This was supposedly the time when Christians and Muslims living around the sea had lost their shared world.[14] According to this narrative, an international setting replaced an imperial world, foreigners substituted for local actors, and an impersonal market supplanted archaic religious violence. In short, after the northern invasion, Europeans modernized the sea,[15] a process that completed the region's disintegration or the sea's "death." The common rhythms that according to Braudel had orchestrated the lives of the sixteenth-century Muslim and Christian Mediterraneans were replaced by polyphony in the seventeenth century, and the confessional "shared destiny" shattered into various national destinies. Faruk Tabak has succinctly summarized the shift thus: "In historical studies that investigate the waning of the Mediterranean, the ecumenical setting of the golden age of the basin fades into the background, only to be supplanted by differential and singular settings from the seventeenth century."[16]

The history of piracy and captivity is no exception to these historiographical framings.[17] Studies of captivity in the Mediterranean, a theme that has recently drawn much scholarly attention, follow that trend. Rather than account for how Mediterranean ransom actors interacted and intersected, they focus either on urban and royal-ecclesiastical ransom institutions or, more recently, on small-scale ransom networks. An institutional perspective that is concerned solely with the Trinitarian and Mercedarian orders of redemption favors the nation ("Spain") and religion ("Catholicism") as its units of analysis and fails to account for the ways in which pressures from both Maghribi political actors and merchants who ransomed captives continually influenced Spanish ransom agendas.[18] This approach results in histories of Spanish, French, or Algerian captivity instead of a connected regional history of Mediterranean slavery.[19] When scholars focus on ransom intermediaries, the Mediterranean reemerges as a space defined by commercial exchange. They describe the redemption of captives as part of an "economy of ransom" that regulated religious violence and rationalized commerce with Muslims as a means of freeing captives.[20] This approach sheds new light on the related issues of transaction costs, credit mechanisms, and insurance and rightly avoids reading captivity and ransom in terms of a transhistorical clash between Islam and Christendom. However, in the context of the western Mediterranean this corrective emphasis risks divorcing ransom institutions and individual ransomers, which constantly interacted, and obscures the continuous importance of religion, political dynamics, and social obligation in shaping the market.[21]

This book seeks to go beyond both the northern invasion thesis and Hess's portrayal of the Mediterranean as a sterile, segregated space. It avoids the bifurcated approach that contrasts market exchange and religion by treating the Mediterranean as both a perspective and an object of study, employing a lens that makes visible not only social relations otherwise unnoticed but also a transimperial process of *region formation*.[22] Region formation includes the ways in which movement, practices, and relations became more intense across the sea, creating a regional unity in spite of political and religious rivalries that shaped the imaginaries of the peoples living in that region and that continue to shape much contemporary historiography.[23] Mediterranean region formation was the result of contacts between cross-boundary maritime practices and political attempts to limit and shape mobility across the sea. The process was uneven, and integration was unequally distributed across the western Mediterranean, being exceptional in its intensity and particularly noticeable in three "Mediterranean corridors," to borrow Julia Clancy-Smith's term.[24] The eastern corridor ran roughly from the coastline of Ottoman Tunis to Spanish Sicily and Malta; the central corridor stretched between Ottoman Algiers, Spanish Oran, the Balearic Islands, and Catalonia; and the western one linked Christian and Muslim cities in Atlantic and Mediterranean Morocco with southern Andalusia and Sanlúcar de Barrameda in Atlantic Spain.[25] I examine the process that made the sea palpable for the people living around its shores by reconstructing interactions and links across captives and kin, ecclesiastic ransom institutions, Jewish, Muslim, and Christian merchants, and Spanish, Algerian, and Moroccan rulers.

There are two reasons to focus on the interactions of various polities and nonpolitical actors rather than examine the Mediterranean designs of a single polity alone. First, region formation processes were never the result of a single cause. Even when rulers promoted regional projects, they were not alone on the stage, and their plans had to be adjusted to, and were even transformed by, the interests of other political actors as well as the meddling of commercial and social networks. Moreover, the states these Mediterranean rulers governed were not coherent organizations with clearly articulated and unified Mediterranean agendas. In the intertwined cases of Fatima, Diego, the three Trinitarians, and the bey, for example, two interest groups, each of which included Spaniards and Algerians or Muslims and Christians, envisioned opposing solutions to meet the conflicting needs of powerful forces on each side (Chapter 7). The first group included the Trinitarians, Ottoman sultan, Algerian pasha, and Spanish king, all of whom were interested in restarting the commerce of captives to the degree they cared less about Fatima's repatriation. The second group included members of the Janissary militia of Algiers, Christian converts to Islam, who refused to open the ransom market unless Fatima was freed and allowed to return home. Against the idea that by the end of the sixteenth century the market and nations had replaced religion and social obligation in the Mediterranean, this book shows how religion, imperial politics, and social mechanisms shaped the market into the next century too. By reconstructing the webs that linked captives, captors, masters, kin, and rulers, we can see the political economy of ransom and the processes by which these actors sought to mold it, as well as the intense communication across the sea their actions engendered. Circulation and exchange are important for the light they shed on captivity and ransom, but they are even more significant as indicators of region formation, or integration.[26] These multiple cross-maritime interactions do more than counter an image of a declining seventeenth-century Mediterranean dissolving into nation-states. They force us to rethink early modern Europe and its others and to question how transimperial maritime networks shaped Europe's seemingly bounded territorial identities.

The system this book reconstructs took shape in the last quarter of the sixteenth century. The Ottoman-Spanish truce of 1581 coincided with the northern invasion and marked the loss of the Mediterranean's economic supremacy over northern Europe and the Atlantic world.[27] The book shows how these events transformed the ways in which the sea connected Morocco, the Ottoman Maghrib, and Spain and changed how those who lived alongside the Mediterranean imagined the sea. When corsairs took the place of imperial fleets, the number of captives increased and the patterns of their circulation across time and space changed. In earlier periods, dramatic maritime battles like Lepanto (1571) had seen thousands of captives lose their liberty, but some had regained it quickly, often within a few short hours,[28] while many captives had changed hands in the cease-fire and peace treaties that followed such large-scale and violent encounters. After 1581, seldom did more than a few hundred soldiers or sailors aboard ship lose or regain their liberty within such short intervals. Most incidents involved the seizure, by corsairs, of small numbers of captives—a few fishermen or peasants, or dozens of travelers.[29] In other words, piracy transformed the circulation of captives across the imperial map, producing a longer-lasting and more stable population of captives than had large-scale naval battles before 1581.

The Captive Sea argues that these geopolitical and demographic changes had unexpected and significant consequences. They enhanced the importance of ransom networks, which Maghribi Jewish and Muslim merchants and Iberian Christian merchants had formed, while reinforcing the institutionalization of the Mercedarians and the Trinitarians, religious orders charged with redeeming Christians. Competition and collaboration between religious orders and merchants created an infrastructure that channeled the return home of captives. The weekly arrival of Christian and Muslim captives into port cities also revolutionized the production and transmission of information. Captives—captured, ransomed, and runaway—generated and distributed news in oral interrogations and any number of written modes: requests for help, letters to their kin, urban topographies describing places of imprisonment, intelligence reports, diaries, and letters of recommendation they wrote for other Christian captives who had converted to Islam and desired to return to Christianity but feared the Inquisition (Chapters 4–6). In this sense, this book claims that Mediterranean slavery was both a forced-labor system and a communication system.

Writing was central to the experience of captivity and powerfully mediated captives' social relations. The book draws on a vast and dispersed textual and visual production in the published and archival sources composed by Christians, Muslims, and Jews from Spain, Morocco, Ottoman Algiers, Italy, and France. In addition to narratives penned by freed captives, Inquisitorial sources, Trinitarian and Mercedarian records, pamphlets, maps, and plays, the book makes ample use of records that captives composed during their captivity, such as letters, requests, and intelligence reports. Literary and historical accounts of captivity often read captivity narratives in terms of testimony and representation, but this book also analyzes these rich

captivity-related archives as a social practice central to the experience
of captivity. Put differently, in addition to reconstructing the reality such texts represent, the book asks what captives, captors, and
redeemers did by writing and what the local and regional effects of
the production and circulation of such texts were. Read this way, previously identified and newly uncovered sources shed novel light on
Mediterranean bondage in terms of labor but also in terms of its functioning as a communication system.

The intensive circulation of people and information reshaped and
entangled communities around the Mediterranean, extending their
boundaries across the sea. Captivity brutally ruptured lives but simultaneously helped make the Mediterranean into an economic, social,
and political space. Captivity forced Maghribi women to negotiate
the exchange of their sons and husbands with their Christian counterparts; it allowed captives to maintain kinship ties at home; it facilitated the entry of Maghribi Jews and Muslims into Spain, from which
they had been expelled only a few generations previously; and thanks
to paper and information flows, it permitted Spanish and Maghribi
religious and political institutions to gain knowledge of enemy territory before the peace negotiations of the eighteenth century. Piracy,
captivity, and ransom allowed Mediterranean people to learn much
about their neighbor-enemies across the sea. Ironically, the redemption of captives, a form of mobility geared toward separating Christians from Muslims, extended the social and religious boundaries of
coastal communities and port cities in Spain and North Africa and
created new links between them.

The captivity of Muslims and the captivity of Christians formed
interdependent elements in a single Mediterranean system, but those
elements were not identical. The system was asymmetrical.[30] While
ecclesiastic institutions redeemed Portuguese, Spanish, French, and
Italian captives and urban fraternities redeemed Italians, during
the first two-thirds of the seventeenth-century Moroccan and later
Algerian rulers ransomed their subjects unsystematically and their
enslaved subjects had to rely mostly on their kin. Only in the last
third of the seventeenth century did Maghribi rulers begin rescuing
their subjects on a regular basis. The absence of comparable institutions on the Muslim side meant that the system offered Christians and
Muslims uneven chances of regaining their liberty.

The asymmetry is significantly more acute in the production and
archiving of records that documented the trafficking and ransom

of captives. In Spain, from the 1570s the orders of redemption systematically recorded their missions, thus establishing serial documentary corpora that contain names of ransomed captives, ransom prices, and detailed descriptions of ransom negotiations; the Council of State collected information about political events in the Maghrib; the Council of War methodically archived petitions for help that captives and their kin submitted to the crown, or copies or summaries of such petitions; parochial churches collected information about captives who had died or converted; and the Inquisition carefully kept transcripts of trials of renegades and sent detailed summaries to Madrid. In addition, a few former captives wrote learned treatises on the Maghrib and memoirs recounting their experiences. While there are no archival sections that contain captivity-related documents exclusively, captives and captivity narratives lie hidden throughout Spain's state archives, local archives, and manuscript collections.

Similar corpora for seventeenth-century North Africa do not appear to exist. Such records may have been produced in smaller quantities; perhaps they were not archived or have been destroyed—or perhaps they await discovery and study.[31] Moroccan archives offer only limited information on piracy, captivity, and ransom in the seventeenth century.[32] In Tunis the oldest register in the National Archives to have survived the Algerian sacking of the city in 1756 is the fiscal register, and the earliest records in this register—documenting the relations between the bey and the local population—date back only to 1676.[33] Thus, like the Moroccan archives, the Tunisian archives offer limited information on the seventeenth-century Mediterranean. Algiers may be an exception, as the pioneering work of Fatiha Loualich on seventeenth- and eighteenth-century social history suggests.[34] While Loualich's work focuses mostly on sub-Saharan slavery in the city, she references archival sources that discuss corsairs, Christian captives, and the ways in which such captives were assimilated into the social fabric of the city. Despite these important studies, there is little scholarly production on captivity and redemption in the early modern western Mediterranean based exclusively or primarily on Moroccan or Ottoman archival sources. The establishment of repositories containing documents from the Muslim western Mediterranean would make it possible to create a more complete history of captivity and ransom and of the sea in the early modern period. For now at least, the study of Mediterranean captivity must rely on European archives, which, fortunately for the historian, hold numerous records written by Christians, Maghribi Muslims, and Jews.

Our protagonists resist our desire for neat categorization, the academic's urge to label, as they constantly crossed political, religious, and geographical boundaries and subverted expectations of their fields of expertise and action. Thus, across seven chapters, *The Captive Sea* applies an integrative approach to the history of captivity, exploring it from various geopolitical scales and value regimes. The first three chapters introduce the main actors of this history: captives, redeeming friars, ransoming merchants, and Mediterranean rulers—Spanish kings, Moroccan sultans and governors, and Algerian pashas. Chapter 1, "The Social Life of Enslaved Captives," offers a broad comparative analysis of the slavery experiences of Muslims and Christians across the western Mediterranean. It examines the lives of captives, including capture, through social networks, occupations, informal economies, and religious conversion, along with modes of slave ownership. The chapter argues that the movement of Muslim and Christian slaves between masters and occupations by means of various forms of temporary and permanent exchange resulted in spatial and occupational mobility both in cities and across the sea and shaped the bondage of Muslims and of Christians as part of a single Mediterranean system.

The next two chapters examine what captives had to do in order to obtain their liberty and the individuals and institutions that helped captives return home. Chapter 2, "Ransom: Between Economic, Political, and Salvific Interests," focuses on ransomers: Trinitarian and Mercedarian friars as well as merchants. The chapter demonstrates the linkage of ransom to religion and to commerce between Europe and North Africa. Friars ransomed captives as a way of redeeming souls in danger of conversion to Islam, but in the process they exported bullion and goods to the Muslim Maghrib. Shrewd merchants could legitimize otherwise illegal trade with Muslims by ransoming captives. The chapter argues that ransom formed a locus of struggles between redeeming friars, ransoming merchants, and critics of conjoined trade with Islam and redemption, who advocated war instead. These three groups sought to manage interactions with Islam according to their respective visions—religious, economic, and political. Finally, the chapter shows the role Maghribi rulers played in shaping Spanish ransom procedures.

Chapter 3, "Negotiating Ransom, Seeking Redemption," turns to captives' experiences of engineering their return home and argues that they took an active part in planning ransom procedures. Coaxed by masters, captives contacted relatives, provided them with information about their place of captivity, urged their kin to collect money or exchange them for other slaves, and contracted middlemen or sought help from church institutions to execute their ransom or swapping. Risk accompanied every stage of ransoming, from planning to negotiation to execution. Captives, masters, and rescuers had to rely on exchange enclaves and the intervention of legal, religious, and political bureaucracies to complete the exchange successfully.

Chapters 4–6 advance our understanding of the production and circulation of information in the early modern Mediterranean as well as their social and political effects. They show (1) how central writing was to the experience of captivity, for literate and illiterate captives alike; (2) how captives became instrumental in the production of all sorts of information about current affairs in hostile territories; and (3) how, in addition to being mobile in cities and among cities in an imperially inscribed zone (Morocco and the Hispanic and Ottoman empires), captives made other geographical crossings—when captured and upon their return. All these factors ensured that captives not only actively produced news but also acted as major agents in the circulation of information. These chapters argue that the letters captives composed to advance their freedom created an infrastructure for the diffusion of social, political, and religious information linking people, communities, and institutions around and across the Mediterranean. Locally, such writing and communication operated as a survival strategy, allowing captives to improve their living conditions. At the Mediterranean level, this sharing of information extended the reach of institutions such as the Inquisition, the family, and political bureaucracies beyond territorial boundaries, thereby connecting the Spanish Empire, Morocco, and the North African Ottoman regencies.

Chapter 4, "Taking Captives, Capturing Communities," follows captives' letters to kin, friends, and church. It argues that captivity extended communal boundaries across the sea as captives were put in charge of channeling information about community members who had died, converted as captives, or suffered martyrdom. Their actions were crucial, allowing "chained widows" to remarry, bereaved kin to mourn the dead, and the church to exclude and excommunicate members who had converted or to canonize martyrs.

Chapter 5, "Confronting Threats, Countering Violence," examines how Christians and Muslims narrated violence exerted upon slaves. It argues that instances of aggression such as forced conversions, desecration of bodies, and executions, which other scholars have considered irrational and arbitrary, in fact reflected a system of reciprocity that operated on a Mediterranean scale. What had started as a local event, initiated by individual slave owners, quickly grew to involve people and institutions ranging from family members to North African political authorities to Spanish religious orders and political authorities.

Chapter 6, "Moving Captives, Moving Information," examines the role captives played in collecting, writing, and transmitting political information about the Maghrib to Spanish decision makers. It argues that by the turn of the seventeenth century—a time when the market for printed accounts of Mediterranean experiences is conventionally thought to have waned—Spanish politicians came to rely almost exclusively on captives and ransomers for information about Algerian plans to attack Spain or the arrival of merchant ships from plague-ridden Maghribi cities. This information circulated intensely in manuscript and also in print.

Chapter 7, "The Political Economy of Ransom," takes a closer look at the tightly connected failed attempts to ransom Fatima, Diego de Pacheco, the Trinitarians, and Muhammad Bey, whose stories began this introduction. This zooming-in highlights social and political tensions within and between the Spanish and Ottoman empires. By analyzing ransom as a transimperial political economy, the chapter shows how state centralization in Spain, partly articulated in relation to the practice of ransom, depended upon the outsourcing of power, not only to imperial units (local agents, historical territories, or cities) but also to former subjects previously expelled (Jews and Muslims) who were now residents of enemy territories (Algiers and Morocco). The chapter demonstrates how in the process Spain's paradigmatic religious others, Maghribi Jews and Muslims, against whom the monarchy defined its Catholicism, became instrumental for the redemption of Christian souls. The chapter illustrates the dynamism that characterized the Mediterranean bondage system and examines how the system's transformation at the end of the sixteenth century resulted in a new mode of region formation and in denser interactions and thicker links connecting the southern and northern shores of the sea.

In the early modern period, the western half of the Mediterranean was a hostile region but not an empty space. Ordinary Christians and Muslims, as well as political, religious, and social institutions, constantly made and unmade the links that intertwined Spain, Ottoman Algiers, and Morocco. Captors and captives, petty merchants and friars, and humble relatives interacted with one another, coaxed rulers to help in ways that required them to dialogue with their counterparts, and pressured rulers to avoid action, when inaction seemed to be safer for their enslaved kin. Intensive interactions meant that in the seventeenth century the people populating the lands encircled by the sea knew more about their neighbors on the opposite side, and received news about them more frequently, than people living in the region a century earlier. Fear of captivity and hate of pirates must have been a constant; however, they also turned the sea for Spaniards, Algerians, and Moroccans into a palpable scale, linking the local and the regional.

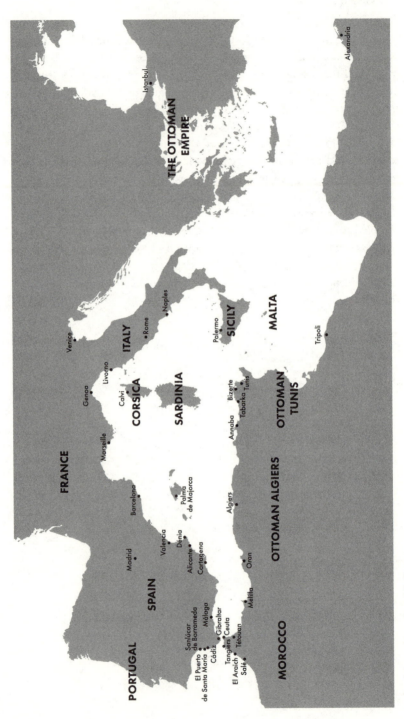

Map of the early modern Mediterranean

CHAPTER I

The Social Life
of Enslaved Captives

In 1574, Ottoman corsairs from Algiers took Jerónimo de Pasamonte captive. In his autobiography, Pasamonte, an Aragonese of the lower gentry, described his purchase when he was at death's door by an Ottoman galley captain, who had paid the low price of 15 ducats per head for Pasamonte and several others in similar condition. The captain took Pasamonte to Istanbul, where the Aragonese recovered from his wounds and worked in his master's garden, enjoying freedom of movement in the city. After talking with some captives who worked in the dockyards, he became convinced that working as a galley slave would increase his chance of running away and returning to Spain. Pasamonte persuaded his owner to sell him to Recep Pasha, who had been recently nominated as pasha of Tunis.[1] He traveled with his new master for more than fifteen years among Tunis, Biserta, Alexandria, the west of the Peloponnesus, Algiers, and Rhodes. When Hasan Aga's daughter married Recep Pasha's son, the father of the bride received Pasamonte as part of the marriage agreement. But Hasan Aga died two years later, and Recep Pasha's son inherited all of Hasan Aga's property, returning Pasamonte to the service of his previous master's family.[2] Pasamonte's hopes that as a galley slave he would escape had proved false, but eventually he arranged his ransom and returned to Spain.

Pasamonte's experience of continual occupational displacement and spatial mobility, which such displacements meant, was common to Mediterranean slaves. Not counting the occasion when the corsairs sold him to the galley captain, he changed hands at least four

times in diverse transactions: he was sold twice and, as part of a marriage agreement, moved between slave owners twice. On at least one
occasion, he himself proposed he be sold. While slaves' volition was
necessarily limited, their mobility across the Maghrib and the entire
Mediterranean brought them into constant contact with other captives and masters. Through these contacts they became instrumental in the production and distribution of information throughout the
Mediterranean.

Pasamonte's trials as a captive were far from exceptional. During the
early modern period millions of Christians and Muslims were taken
captive and enslaved in the Mediterranean.[3] Before 1700 the number
of Muslim and Christian slaves in the Mediterranean equaled, or was
even greater than, the number of sub-Saharan slaves in the Atlantic.[4]
Between 1530 and 1780, some 1,000,000 to 1,250,000 Christians
were enslaved in Morocco and the Ottoman Maghrib, while a similar
number of Muslims were enslaved in Christian Europe. Between 1450
and 1750, calculations have suggested, 300,000 to 400,000 Moroccans and North African Ottoman slaves passed through Portugal and
Spain. Between the beginning of the sixteenth century and the end of
the eighteenth century about 500,000 Muslims were enslaved in Italy.
In the seventeenth and eighteenth centuries in Malta alone between
35,000 and 40,000 Muslims (around half of whom were North Africans) were sold as slaves.[5] The sources do not always distinguish
between Muslims from different parts of the Muslim world, but
given that the figures above exclude the Spanish Balearic and Canary
Islands, Sardinia, and France, many more Muslims must have been
enslaved in southern Europe.[6] To early modern city dwellers, captives
were a common sight and their stories painfully familiar.

    This chapter offers a comparison of the employment patterns and
spatial mobility experienced by Muslim and Christian slaves, mostly
the men among them, in the western Mediterranean. The chapter argues that dynamism—understood as continual occupational
displacement that generated spatial mobility—rather than stasis
governed the lives of Christian and Muslim captives in the Mediterranean and that the experience of these slaves formed part of a single Mediterranean system of bondage. Sales, socialized exchanges
such as gifts or inheritances, short-term "slave rentals," and seasonal
cycles of labor created occupational mobility. Such disruption almost
always involved geographic displacement—within cities, from city

to city, across North Africa, or across the sea. Continual transformations meant that slaves' occupational trajectories only *began* with their initial insertion into the market. On a macrolevel, they suggest that the volume of the economy of slavery was much larger than historians have imagined, since many slaves changed hands more than once. Despite the multiplicity of experiences, Mediterranean slavery was largely a unified system, created by mobility and intensified by the connectedness of the lands surrounding the sea.

TAKING CAPTIVES

The similar experience of Christian and Muslim slaves began at the moment of their enslavement. They were launched violently into the Mediterranean system of slavery. They lost their liberty either in military raids and clashes or in maritime attacks by corsairs and official fleets—in modern parlance these captives would be deemed "prisoners of war." In contrast, sub-Saharan Africans enslaved in the Mediterranean were not captured by Spaniards, Algerians, or Moroccans but rather purchased by them. In other words, sub-Saharan Africans were already victims of the slave trade before their arrival in the Middle Sea.[7] This distinction is indicative of the relatively short distance that separated enslaved Christians and Muslims from their kin in contrast to sub-Saharan Africans enslaved truly far away from home. The short distance was reflective of the potential of communication with home.

A depiction of capture at sea is often found in Christian captivity narratives and "bureaucratic autobiographies," short petitions that captives, former captives, and their kin submitted to the Spanish crown in hope of receiving compensation.[8] Again and again, captive narratives recount how the watch spotted a sail on the horizon as the ship on which the soon-to-be-captives sailed on the Mediterranean. With the strangers identified as corsairs, the passengers anxiously populated the decks. As the captain and his crew increased speed to attempt escape, the passengers hid their precious belongings and rid themselves of all signs of distinction that might identify them as wealthy (and thus able to pay greater ransoms).[9]

Men, women, and children living along Iberian, Italian, and French shores and in Tunis, Algiers, and Morocco were all also potential prey for Muslim and Christian corsairs (privateers) and soldiers, who attacked and pillaged their villages or ship aboard which they sailed.

Privateering and captive-taking were activities with political, economic, and religious significance. Privateering was a political practice
allowing states to extend their naval might with no costs. Corsairs
were state-authorized pirates, who chased and attacked the enemies
of the polity to which they belonged and which issued them letters
of marque authorizing their activity. In return for these letters that
permitted them to act in ways otherwise considered piracy corsairs
had to pay a share of their booty to their home authorities. Corsairs
provided slave markets with slaves, and the commodities they captured were sold for low prices to merchants, who often belonged to
the states against which the corsairs fought and who redistributed the
stolen goods in markets back in their home states. However, conceiving of piracy and privateering in exclusively political and economic
terms ignores the point of view of the system's victims. The slaves
that corsairs captured or the communities to which these captives
belonged were not economic actors but rather piracy's poor victims.
From the latter's perspective the corsairs that captured them were
nothing but pirates. Finally, in the Mediterranean this lucrative activity was often justified by religious ideology. In Tunis, at least from the
early eighteenth century and despite the significant number of European converts to Islam among the corsairs' ranks, corsairs were perceived as practicing a jihad, and those among them who died during
raids were praised as martyrs.[10] In the eighteenth century, part of
the corsairs' proceeds was reserved for the cult of local saints. Many
Christian corsairs presented themselves as holy warriors in a crusade,
and Saint James, the patron saint of Spain, was believed to support
the attacks that Spanish soldiers of Spain's North African garrison led
against Muslims.[11]

    Muslim corsairs reached Galicia, Cantabria, Basque country, and
British shores. In 1631 they attacked Baltimore in West Cork, Ireland;
four years earlier, in 1627, they had raided Iceland.[12] Corsairs from
the Balearic Islands, Cartagena, and other Andalusian cities attacked
and enslaved Maghribis on a regular basis. The Maltese Knights of
Saint John and Tuscan Knights of Saint Stephen raided Greek Orthodox, Jewish, and Muslim Ottoman subjects in the eastern Mediterranean.[13] Muslims also captured Christians and were captured by
Christians in the Maghrib. Christian soldiers who manned the Spanish *presidios* (literally "garrisons" but also a term for prisons) in the
Maghrib risked, and often lost, their liberty in military encounters
with Janissaries or neighboring Berber tribes. Soldiers from Oran

became captives after defecting to escape the living conditions in the garrisons, where food shortages were common.[14] The defectors often planned to convert to Islam and settle in Algiers or escape from there to Spain, but those who made it to Algiers discovered that the pasha did not consider their conversion economically expedient and instead sold them as Christian captives.[15] Oran, the largest and most important Spanish garrison in the Maghrib, was a crucial conduit of Muslim slaves to Spain.[16] Records of Christian raids on neighboring tribes of "enemy Moors" during the first half of the seventeenth century describe hundreds of enslaved Muslim captives brought to Oran. On March 10, 1645, for example, Spanish soldiers returned to Oran with 106 male and female captives; nine months later, they captured a further 175.[17] While a few of those taken were quickly ransomed or exchanged for Christian captives and others achieved their release by converting to Christianity, the majority remained enslaved in the *presidio* or were later shipped to Málaga or Cartagena.[18]

The ratios of male to female slaves were different for Muslims and Christians. In the Middle Ages and the early modern period, there were always more female than male (Muslim) slaves in Iberia, with the gaps larger for Maghribi slaves than for sub-Saharans.[19] In early modern Granada, for example, about 70 percent of North African and Morisco slaves were female.[20] The shipments of slaves from Oran to Spain provide supporting evidence of this gap. Between May 3, 1661, and May 6, 1662, the governor sent 107 slaves, the majority of whom were women, children, and babies (the mean age was 17, the median 16).[21] Most Muslim slaves in Spain were taken captive in land raids, in which more women were captured than men; in maritime attacks the proportion of men captured was greater. Determination of the gender ratio for Christians enslaved in the Maghrib is not possible. Men were ransomed in larger numbers, but we cannot therefore deduce that they made up the larger portion of all those captured.[22] The ransom price for women was significantly higher than that for men. Many women were incorporated into local households or married to Muslims or renegades (Christians who "turned Turk") and thus never even entered the ransom market. Additionally, most Christians were captured at sea, but few women could be found aboard ships at the time.[23]

Female Christian captives have left few traces in the archives. The large majority of captivity narratives were written by men, and nearly all renegades' depositions were taken from men.[24] Thus we know a lot less about women's experience of captivity, and if we do have access to their voice, their words have been mediated by men. Only requests for help submitted by captives, many of whom were women, to the Spanish crown offer a revealing exception (Chapters 3 and 4). The knowledge gap is especially acute in regard to labor and social trajectories—we know nearly nothing about the labor conditions of women in Morocco and in Algiers. Therefore, while we have enough evidence to draw the contours of a Mediterranean bondage system in which the experiences of Christian and Muslim male slaves had much in common, at this stage of research it is impossible to paint a parallel picture for female slaves.

ENSLAVEMENT

Christians and Muslims who lost their liberty to corsairs on the high seas or during corsair attacks on their villages were deemed to belong to the captain and to those who had funded the raid.[25] On returning to their home port, corsairs had to submit a list of their booty, prepared by the ship's scribe, to the governor. In Algiers, Tunis, Livorno, La Valette (Malta), and Spanish coastal cities, the city's governor or the crown was entitled to a share that ranged from 5 to 10 percent.[26] By contrast, Christian captives taken in clashes between Ottoman Janissaries from Algiers and Christian forces from Oran became the sole property of the governor.[27] The captives were sold at public auction in the slave market, where they were made to parade before the trained gaze of potential buyers, who examined their bodies and teeth, while criers' voices roared, announcing ages, professions, origins, and prices.[28] This traumatic cacophony is a primal scene in many of the extant captive autobiographies.[29]

Two aspects of the public market were especially shocking for authors and their audiences. First, social distinctions collapsed in the slave market.[30] Pedro, one of the three protagonists of *Viaje de Turquía* (A Journey to Turkey [1557]), makes this point aptly: "the dress of the slaves is the same for good and for bad [people], like that of the monks."[31] Rich and poor and men of all estates were stripped of their class markers, threatening their social identity. Second, commodification at the slave market blurred racial distinctions. The former captive João Mascarenhas recounted how nobles, priests, and bourgeoisie found themselves "like new blacks [*nègres*] made to march from the ship to the customs house."[32]

Such accounts are usually silent on the active roles that captives played in this social effacement and on its temporal limits. Christian captives participated by seeking to hide marks of distinction and look poor, in order to lower their ransom. After a peace treaty between Spain and Morocco was signed in 1767, Algerian captives participated similarly when upon capture by Spaniards they claimed to be Moroccan, knowing that according to the treaty, the Spaniards had to free Moroccan captives.[33] Captive-authors do not connect the captives' active shedding of class, status, and national markers to the absence of these marks from the market. Being sold at the slave market transformed a human being into a commodity, temporarily masking the social and ethnic order of the captive's world before bondage. The social order was soon restored, however, as buyers were seeking not only laboring bodies but also valuable commodities for the ransom market, where wealth and status mattered more than health, age, and strength.

The initial sale was one of the most significant moments in the process of captivity, creating a contrast between the captives' past and present that was not re-created by subsequent exchanges and transfers. Unlike later exchanges, the first sale at the slave market was ritualized and publicly staged. Redeemed captives who recounted their experience in writing stylized that moment. Its public nature was reinforced by the presence of agents of the local political order, who took a share from each sale or capture. Nonetheless, the significance of the initial enslavement was only the first stage of a process that captives, their audiences, and scholars have overlooked, in which social death and rebirth recurred with each sale, resale, or other form of displacement.

As this chapter demonstrates, underestimating the social dynamics that underpinned the economy of slavery is not the only historiographical consequence of the emphasis on the initial sale and the public market regulated by the polity. Scholars have neglected the other markets that existed in the city and across the region. Slaves were peddled under the scrutinizing gaze of the state only when sold for the first time; subsequently they were variously sold and swapped in private or semiprivate spaces. Slavery and its economy were not centralized but spatially pervasive. Moreover, the overemphasis on enslavement's first stage at the expense of subsequent transitions has restricted our understanding of the lives of victims of piracy in the Mediterranean to two flat modalities: bondage-slavery and captivity. Yet enslaved

captives constantly moved between commoditization and singular-
ization. To be sure, the moment of sale transformed individuals into
objects, but they were soon inserted into a household or another kind
of host group where they were partly resocialized and rehumanized—
and rarely fully disconnected from their kin and communities—until
the next time they changed hands.[34] In reconstructing these occupational paths, we recognize that sale was not the only form of exchange
that defined the lives of slaves. Slaves also changed hands through
bartering, gift-giving, bequeathing, short- and mid-term rental, and
other social forms of exchange. Each of these transitions entailed not
only new masters or employers and altered labor conditions but also
a reframing of bondage by both its perpetrator and its object in terms
of future sale, enslavement for life, conversion and adoption, or ransom and liberty.

DOCUMENTATION OF MULTIPLE SALES

Notarial and administrative records documenting the sale and resale
of male and female Muslim slaves in the Christian Mediterranean
provide clear evidence of the frequency with which slaves changed
hands. In May 1571, immediately after the suppression of the rebellion of the Spanish Moriscos known as the Second War of Granada,
Alonso de Vega, a tailor from Guadix, paid Antonio Arias de Morroy,
a soldier from Toro, 40 ducats for eighteen-year-old Morisco Úrsula.
Two and a half years later, De Vega sold Úrsula for 90 ducats.[35] About
a century later, probably in the 1650s, Zaarca, a female member of
one of the Berber tribes residing within the vicinity of Spanish Oran,
was taken captive by the garrison's soldiers. David Maquer, a Jewish
resident of Oran, purchased Zaarca and resold her to Antoni Barceló,
a ship patron. Barceló sold Zaarca to Francesc Cotoner, a Majorcan
knight of the Order of Santiago, who in his turn authorized a merchant, Francesc Artós, to sell her in Barcelona in February 1659.[36]
Among the buyers and sellers of slaves, we find soldiers, captains,
knights, and merchants, as well as simple folk with humble occupations. Sales and resales were neither limited to wartime nor conducted
exclusively by individuals: while individuals bought and sold slaves in
times of peace, the Spanish fleet also sold its disabled or old slaves or
exchanged them for healthy new slaves.[37]

　　While notarial records and fleet documentation attest to the ubiq-
uity of multiple sales for a single captive, they disclose nothing about

the trajectories of enslavement from the victims' point of view. Here, autobiographies and inquisitorial depositions that recorded the first-person narratives of Christian ex-slaves prove extremely helpful. Sale-tan corsairs took Jacobo de Maqueda (as the scribe transcribed his name), a peasant from a little village near Calais, captive in 1620, while he was a child. The corsairs sold him into slavery, and within a year his master had sold him on to a Morisco merchant from Algiers, who sold him again, to a Tunisian Morisco who kept Maqueda as a field hand for twelve years.[38] When France and Tunis signed a peace agreement, the French consul in Tunis tried to have Maqueda freed, but his master refused his release. Soon afterward, under the threat of death, Maqueda converted to Islam, as a result of which he gained the trust of his master and other Muslims and joined the corsairs as a soldier. Taking advantage of his new situation, he fled from the rest of the crew during an attack on Ibiza and submitted himself to the Inquisition of Majorca, where he gave the deposition that describes his history. Maqueda's trajectory demonstrates how changing hands could lead to movement across space and between regimes of labor, religion, privilege, and affect. Maqueda's movements were particularly long-ranging—he journeyed more than 1,500 miles from Calais at the English Channel to Moroccan Salé in Atlantic North Africa, nearly 600 miles east to Algiers, and then 500 miles farther east to Tunis. During the time he spent in slavery in Morocco, Algiers, and Tunis, Maqueda probably learned some Arabic. His having two Morisco masters, one of whom was a native of Madrid, suggests that he might have also picked up Spanish. While his long hours of labor under the North African sun in the fields of the Morisco from Tunis might have marked his most onerous work and most isolated years, they also coincided with a period of stability; by contrast, Maqueda's time with the Morisco merchant would likely have carried a constant prospect of resale and concomitant worry about a harsher new master and the loss of tenuous new social ties.

The confession given by Castilian Bartholomé Martín de Castro at the Majorcan Inquisitorial tribunal in 1689 resembles the account given by Maqueda.[39] Taken captive at the age of twelve and sold in Algiers to a Turk who held him for eight months, Castro was then sold to his master's brother and remained in his service for one year. Around this time, having failed to arrange his ransom, Castro converted to Islam. Castro's new owner, a barber and tailor, freed him after only seven years, perhaps because the two men had brokered a *mukātaba*, a common agreement between slaves and their masters in the Ottoman Empire that provided for slaves' manumission after seven years of labor.[40] Castro's master would have seen this agreement as a means to incentivize Castro to work harder. Castro's case sheds light on the institutional framing of bondage. While he was negotiating his ransom with the brother of his first master, news of Castro's rich father arrived in Algiers from Spain. His master incarcerated him in the hope that pressure would advance a ransom deal, but his plans came to nothing, perhaps because Castro's father's wealth had been exaggerated. Disappointed, Castro converted to Islam, changing his confession and transforming himself him into a non-redeemable commodity, for no Christian would ransom a Muslim. If indeed Castro and his next master negotiated and arranged a *mukātaba* agreement, then Castro's final years of slavery followed a new path toward liberty. Rather than by ransom by his kin, Castro was to be freed in return for a certain number of years of labor and potentially be assimilated into his former master's household. Such agreements created a climate that fostered nonviolent and inclusive social relations.

Could slaves influence their movement between masters and occupations? While sources leave no doubt that they could and did, different source types reveal different interventions. Notarial records from Spain suggest that Muslim slaves often sabotaged their sales. Muslim slaves in fifteenth-century Valencia behaved violently or as if insane, claimed to be badly ill, or inflicted injuries upon themselves.[41] In his autobiography, Pasamonte maintained he had convinced his master to sell him, and he was not the only Christian captive who described influencing his own sale.[42] Both Christian and Muslim slaves might claim other political or religious affiliations in an effort to achieve their freedom: Muslim slaves in Valencia claimed to be Christians, and Christians in Algiers claimed to be French after the French signed peace agreements with the Algerians that obliged both parties to release all their captives.[43]

Pasamonte, like the Morisco slave from Guadix, was sold twice, while Zaarca, Maqueda, and Castro were each sold three times. Such mobility was not common to all occupations, and mobility did not necessarily, or even often, lead to liberty. For example, Muslims employed as royal slaves in the mercury mines near Ciudad Real in Spain labored to the end of their lives in miserable conditions with no mobility of the kind discussed here.[44] But in the rest of the Iberian Peninsula and in the Maghrib, as in the antebellum United States, there were at least twice as many resales as first-time sales of captives into slavery.[45] Each sale engendered new a social relationship between master and slave that was framed by the specific institutional setting and by idioms that regulated power, privilege, labor, affect, and prospects of freedom. Simultaneously, resales relocated slaves spatially and socially as they followed their new masters to new towns or neighborhoods and gave up social ties they had created. Maqueda's long trial as a field slave and his decision to convert in order to leave that position attest to the limited mobility options open to slaves like him. When Castro's second owner sold Castro to his brother, the siblings must have negotiated the deal in private. Pasamonte's second sale was likely similarly private, as probably were many other sales. Only by taking account of these multiple shifts can we understand the operation of the system of slavery as well as its meanings for slaves and masters.

EXCHANGING CAPTIVES: BETWEEN COMMODITIES AND GIFTS

Slaves were not only commodities but also property, and thus sale was not the only mode through which they circulated among owners, as Pasamonte's exchange as part of a marriage agreement suggests.[46] Diego Galán's owner passed him on to Mamí Napolitano in lieu of payment on a debt. Galán's autobiography states that his life improved under the new master, who provided him with more freedom, responsibility, and power. But such exchanges could just as easily mean a deterioration in conditions. In 1548 or 1549, Simón Gonzalves's owner, Caralym, demanded that he convert to Islam, threatening to give him to the corsair Arguiti as payment for a debt if he did not give up Christianity.[47] The fact that Caralym framed the exchange as a threat suggests that both master and slave knew the latter would suffer with the change in ownership. Masters could also use such threats to pressure slaves to work harder.[48] Gonzalves succumbed to the threat and converted to Islam, whereupon Caralym gave him two Christian slaves as a gift, an act that symbolized Gonzalves's progress toward liberty and assimilation into Caralym's household.[49] Gonzalves's depositions make apparent that the gift was part of a larger cycle of reciprocity that had begun with his conversion and concluded with his manumission.[50] Slaves, like other forms of property, were not understood in economic terms exclusively, even if they were often exchanged as part of commercial transactions.

SHORT- AND MID-TERM EXCHANGES

Even apart from changing ownership, slaves moved between masters and employers in short cycles, on a seasonal or even daily basis.
Whether owned by individuals or by the state, slaves worked in a variety of jobs under different supervisory arrangements. Slaves owned
by individuals carried out agricultural, domestic, or artisanal labor.
State slaves labored in mines, shipyards, and galleys. In the shipyard
alone, a slave's work might vary from preparing ships for the sailing season to producing ropes, oars, and sails. Galley labor came to
epitomize Mediterranean slavery, yet there were marked differences
between fleets. Mediterranean fleets relied on convicts and *bonevo-*
glie, or free oarsmen, as well as enslaved oarsmen, except in Venice, where *bonevoglie* manned all the galleys. Fearing revolts, some
fleets limited the number of slaves who could row on their galleys, but
slaves rarely formed less than a quarter of the oarsmen, and sometimes represented up to two-thirds.[51]

Seasonal cycles structured the lives of galley slaves. Slaves condemned to galley labor pulled the oar during the sailing season (early
April to late October) but in the winter were assigned to work in the
shipyards, in workshops on the galley, or in the homes or workshops
of residents of the port city who rented them.[52] In his *Topografía
e Historia General de Argel* (*Topography and General History of
Algiers*), Antonio de Sosa described how during the winter, Algerian
corsairs unable to employ the slaves they owned did their best to rent
them to others: "certain corsairs sometimes have their own particular captives, masters of shipbuilding, and they use them at sea to
arrange certain things. But once they are back in Algiers, these captives serve for nothing more than to help the foremen of the commonwealth (the city), and they are charged with building and provisioning
all the ships."[53] Renting galley slaves to the commonwealth was not
uniquely Algerian. During the winter, slaves bound to French galleys worked in Marseille in workshops on the galleys, producing hats,
shoes, gloves, and purses, or they were rented out to artisans and the
city's bourgeoisie.[54] Similarly, beginning in 1597, the Order of the
Knights of Saint John allowed its members to rent out their Muslim
slaves as long as they were too old or too weak to be employed as
oarsmen on the galleys.[55] Sosa expanded on the other end of this practice, noting that corsairs who did not own enough slaves to man their
vessels hired additional slaves from merchants in the summertime:

"The captain who does not own a quantity of Christians, enough to arm the vessel . . . can rent Christians from merchants who have them especially for hire. And from one merchant, he may rent two, four, six and eight and from another ten, twelve, twenty, thirty or however many he wants from among those who most please him and seem to be the most robust."[56] Mediterranean galley slaves, then, were not always galley slaves.

Slaves laboring in the city and the countryside had even shorter occupational cycles than galley slaves. In Spain, slaves might be rented by the day (*jornalero*) or for a longer period (*cortado*), and they might have some degree of autonomy and the freedom to find their employers. Renting out slaves was a way for masters to cover their investment, while slaves who were permitted to keep a small portion of their earnings used the opportunity to save money toward their ransoms or make purchases. When in April 1663 the king of Spain prohibited slave owners in the Valencian city of Alicante from renting out their Muslim slaves by the day, the slaves complained, arguing that their Christian counterparts in the Maghrib were allowed to work in order to advance their liberty.[57] While the archival record does not reveal whether the king relented because of this objection, the episode reflected a broad shared expectation of slaves across the Mediterranean that Christian and Muslim slaves would experience equitable treatment. Laugier de Tassy, chancellor of the French consulate in Algiers, described a similar practice in Algiers in the early eighteenth century. In an account he composed in 1724 he wrote, "Masters who have many slaves rent them to the *ru'asā'* [from Arabic, the plural form of *ra'īs* (adapted into Spanish as *arraez*), a corsair or a sea captain] for work in the arsenals or for sailing."[58] Renters, he added, confiscated part of the plunder their slaves received as salary instead of charging daily rent from the corsairs who hired them.[59] The dey, for example, took two-thirds of the proceeds received by slaves he rented out.[60]

Some accounts suggest a rigid distinction between slaves based on ownership and occupation and linked to captives' prospects of being ransomed. Miguel de Cervantes Saavedra, who spent five years as a captive in Algiers, was the most famous Christian captive in the Maghrib. The three chapters in *Don Quixote* based on his experiences form a unit known as the Captive's Tale, and here Cervantes distinguished between three types of slave: the ones who belonged to the pasha, the ones who belonged to private individuals, and the "stockpiled," the term he used for those "who serve the city in public works and in other employment for the general good."[61] As Cervantes told it, the stockpiled had no hope of ransom as they had no one with which to negotiate.[62] The records of the orders of redemption reiterate this tripartite division of slave ownership and the link between the nature of ownership and captives' prospects of ransom.

However, since ownership and occupation often changed over time, on a daily basis, or with the season, some slaves became "public" in winter and "private" in summer. Thus at least a few stockpiled captives who could afford their ransom could convince or cut a deal with someone to buy them and then release them in return for payment. Public ownership might limit captives' chances of regaining their liberty, but it did not necessarily prevent it. The ransom expeditions the religious orders sent to Tunis, Algiers, and Tétouan were dependent on the cooperation of Ottoman pashas and Moroccan governors, who issued passports that protected the friars on their journey and during their stay, and who, in return, imposed their own ransom agendas. Maghribi rulers forced the friars to buy their own captives and those of their confidants first, before buying the captives of others in the city (see Chapter 2). The representation of slave ownership as rigidly divided into three groups, then, largely reflects the dependent position of the redeeming friars vis-à-vis the pasha or the local governor.

SOCIAL STRATIFICATION AND INFORMAL ECONOMIES

Records of captives' social interactions—among themselves and with their overseers and masters—sometimes reveal an array of formal positions and power structures. The spatial mobility captives enjoyed, especially if they worked in cities, imposed shifting social environments upon them and meant their insertion into varied and interdependent formal and informal economies and social hierarchies. Even rowing in the galleys was extremely stratified labor with privileges and obligations, and it placed captives in complicated hierarchies of power.[63] As slave secretary (*scrivani* [Italian]) or pacesetter (*vogavan* [lingua franca] or *bogavante* [Spanish]), a slave had power in the galley.[64] The secretary kept the ship's log, while pacesetters established and coordinated the rhythm of the rowing, acting as the leaders of their benches. Social and occupational stratification within the galley did not end there: even among slaves who shared a galley bench, pulling the same oar, there were better and worse positions. The appearance of occupational sameness conceals a complex division of labor. Galán describes such complexity in his account of his time as a galley slave in Algiers:

> [Agustin] was a very good friend of mine because since we left Algiers, the Pasha ordered me to pull the back oar, [the same oar] as Agustin's, doing me a favor, because it was always the most distinguished soldiers and the most spirited guys who pulled that oar. And this position is free from punishments and repeated castigations that are common on the galleys when bad things are done, [when] the [Muslims] give so many blows to everyone except those who pull the back oar, [and] who sit in the first bench near the stern, that forms the back of the galley; and for that, they call the rower of that bench the stern rower [espalder]. And bogavante means "rows ahead," because he pulls the oar before the four or five or more who [also pull] the [same] oar; and they call the first bogavante, the second outrigger [postizo], the third tercerol and the fourth cuarterol. And I, they bestowed me with the dignity of the fourth, because I was a boy, [and] because the fourth works less than the rest.[65]

The distribution of slaves among and on benches was tied in with privileges, obligations, and opportunities. As Galán described, oarsmen pulling the last oar were exempted from the regular punishments to which others were subject. Additionally, even among oarsmen on a single bench there was a complex division of labor. The pacesetter worked harder than the rest, had greater responsibility, and received more privileges, but his importance to the functioning of the ship made his masters unwilling to negotiate his ransom. The cuarterol, the fourth man on the oar, had the benefits of a physically easier task. Despite the fact that the pacesetter enjoyed more privileges than the fourth rower, Galán thought his position preferable, befitting his young age and physical condition at the time and sparing him the beatings endured by other slaves. If, as Galán suggests, galley slaves perceived and experienced such close positions in the galleys as radically different, social stratification likely characterized other labors also.

Slaves' employment and its related division of labor facilitated the production of goods and services, theft, bribery, gift-giving, and trading.[66] In their free time, galley slaves produced stockings and other items, which they sold to their oar mates and overseers and to others when they returned to port.[67] While some slaves concentrated on production, others, whom the officers referred to as "merchants," specialized in buying and selling such goods. Informal and formal economies were related and interdependent. The fleet officers acknowledged how important the slave-merchants' economic activity was and were reluctant to give up slaves who traded. In 1645, a Spanish fleet officer who had been asked by the Council of War to hand over a Muslim "merchant" in return for another slave explained that "merchants" were crucial for the galleys to be functional, prevented the slaves from being lazy, and, by paying others to perform their work, enabled the slaves to have a little money with which they could better sustain themselves.[68]

Similar dynamics characterized the lives of slaves on the French galleys. In 1698, for example, when the French galleys wintered at the port of Marseille, a group of Muslim slaves and Christian convicts were employed in a galley workshop making shackles, handcuffs, shafts, and other implements for chaining slaves. Like the rest of the crew of the galleys where they worked in warmer weather, they had been sent to execute other chores in the winter, which in their case required some expertise, possibly developed prior to their enslavement. A Muslim slave stole the handcuffs the group produced and sold them to a convict, who sold them to another Muslim slave, who sold them to a third Muslim slave, who sold them to a merchant from the city.[69] The three slaves were attached to three different galleys, and the markup at the final exchange was 25 percent. This string of transactions suggests that cross-class alliances existed among slaves, convicts, and overseers from the same and from different galleys and also among all these and free people from the city. Slaves were not only inserted into production cycles but also part of illicit distribution and redistribution circuits that connected informal economies with formal economies, labor organized from above with illegal activity. Finally, the case reflects slaves' knowledge of their labor environments—the galleys—and of the cities in which they were enslaved. The galley slaves knew where, to whom, and at what price to buy and sell. In the process and in parallel to material circulation, slaves became crucial to the production and dissemination of information.

CONVERSION

Muslim and Christian slaves alike converted, and in a few cases were converted by force, to their enslavers' religion. Early modern descriptions of Algiers and other Mediterranean cities stressed the presence of renegades with a variety of ethnic and geographic origins. In his *Topografía e Historia General de Argel*, Sosa opens his discussion of renegades in Algiers with the following words:

> "Turks by profession" are all those renegades of Christian blood and parentage who have turned Turk of their own free will . . . there is no Christian nation on earth that has not produced renegades in this city . . . Muscovites, Russians, Ukrainians, Vlachs, Bulgarians, Poles, Hungarians, Bohemians, Germans, Danish and Norwegians, Scotsmen, Englishmen, Irishmen, Flemish, Burgundians, Frenchmen, Navarrese, Basques, Castilians, Galicians, Portuguese, Andalusians, Valencians, Aragonese, Catalans, Majorcans, Sardinians, Corsicans, Sicilians, Calabrese, Neapolitans, Romans, Tuscans, Genoese, Savoyards, Piedmontese, Lombards, Venetians, Slavs, Albanians, Armenians, Greeks, Cretans, Cypriots, Syrians, Egyptians, and even Abyssinians of Prester John as well as Indians from the Portuguese Indies, from Brazil, and from New Spain.[70]

In fact, the distribution of ethnicities and origins among converted slaves reflected to a large degree the geography of the Mediterranean. In Morocco, most renegades (called *elches* locally) were Portuguese; in Algiers and Tunis, the majority were Iberian, French, and Italian.[71] North African Ottoman cities also had a large contingent of Janissaries, Ottoman soldiers born into Christian families from the Balkans and Anatolia who had been forced as children to convert to Islam. Among the Muslim slaves who converted to Christianity in Iberia, Moroccan and Algerians formed a majority; in Italy converts were more likely to be Tunisians and slaves from the eastern Mediterranean.[72]

By forcing their slaves to convert to Islam or by having them baptized, slave owners manipulated their slaves' value and status (see Chapter 7). Some slaves converted of their own volition. By "turning Turk" or by being baptized and catechized, slaves could potentially improve their living conditions, advance manumission, assimilate socially, develop careers, or gain more freedom of movement, which might allow them to flee. Some conversions may have been sincere or might have become sincere with practice of the new religion. Historians cannot distinguish the sincere from the insincere, but history does show that conversion had social and political implications.[73]

Two sets of sources portray the conversion of Christian and Muslim slaves as a forced process, one in which captives had little or no influence. The first are depositions of renegades who returned to Spain submitted during their Inquisitorial trial, which often followed a similar script. They opened with their subject's initial objection to conversion and continued with the physical pressure exerted upon him and the punishments he suffered before he succumbed, his recitation of the *shahāda*, the Muslim profession of faith, and his being required to wear the clothing of a Turk. By framing their conversions in this way, renegades sought light punishment and social reintegration into a Christian community.[74] Another type of source, complaints and demands for redress that Muslim slaves or their friends sent to their kin or rulers in Morocco and Algiers, reports forced baptisms, mostly of slaves on their deathbeds and of children (see Chapter 5). These records suggest that Christians and Muslims alike were willing to bend canon law and sharia law, respectively, both of which forbade forced conversion.

At least one group of Muslim slaves was prone to be forced to convert. Most of the slaves captured during raids conducted by the military forces of Oran were members of the Berber tribes who lived in the city's vicinity and were converted soon after their capture and arrival in Oran. The majority of the converts were women and children, and given their age and command of Spanish, it is unlikely that they chose to be baptized.[75] This pattern was not repeated for Maghribi residents of larger cities of North Africa taken captive during maritime clashes, who were almost exclusively adult males and were sent to Spain, allocated to service in the royal galleys, or sold in the slave markets. Incidents of forced baptism for Muslims already enslaved in Spain were uncommon and their overall number was not high. Jesuits, Capuchins, and Dominicans who preached to and evangelized among the small and dispersed Muslim communities in Iberia usually avoided forced baptism—possibly because they feared Algerian or Moroccan riposte against their Christian captives.[76] In general, however, Spaniards and Portuguese suspected conversions of Muslims to Christianity were inauthentic, believed the converts continued to practice Islam clandestinely after their conversion, and spent limited effort on trying to convert adult Muslims.[77]

European consuls posted to the Maghrib contradicted claims about conversions to Islam being forced and often described the conversion of Christians as intentional, instrumental, and geared toward obtaining benefits. The Knight d'Arvieux wrote in his description of his 1666 diplomatic mission to Tunis, "As for what they say that the Muslims force the captives by tortures to become Mahommedans, that happens only rarely and it can be said to be extremely exceptional." Only the zealous want slaves to convert, he added, and even they never force anyone to convert. Sometimes, he claimed, Muslim women try to convince captives to convert and then marry them.[78] Tassy, chancellor of the French consulate in Tunis in the 1720s, asserted that Muslims objected to the conversion of Christians, calling the idea of forced conversion to Islam a "great" error and insisting, "their masters would be very angry if their slaves become Mohammedan despite the fact that they do not become free following their conversion."[79] He went on to clarify that Algerian slaveholders knew that if their Christian slaves converted, neither their families nor the church would redeem them. The reaction of the pasha of Algiers to Christian soldiers who defected—Spanish intelligence reports stated that the pasha preferred to enslave them and did not allow them to convert to Islam—suggests the French emissary was accurate.[80] French consuls and others agreed: Muslim masters deemed their captives too precious as commodities to allow them to convert, much less to force them to convert. The economic explanations these reports provide for the resistance of Muslims to the conversion of their Christian slaves resonate with what we know about Malta, notorious for its corsairs who enslaved Ottoman Muslims (as well as Orthodox Greek and Jews). The thriving ransom market of the island was so efficient that slaves rarely stayed long enough for successful evangelization to take place.[81]

The peace agreements negotiated among France, the Dutch Republic, and the Ottoman Empire and its North African regencies, however, established one context that incentivized forced conversion. These agreements obliged Algerians, Tunisians, and others to set free all French and Dutch captives they owned unless the captives had converted to Islam.[82] The French renegade Guillermo—known after his conversion as Murat—recounted to his Inquisitors in 1634 that the Muslim infantry captain who bought him forced him to convert to avoid the financial loss of freeing him.[83] While it is possible that Guillermo sought a light punishment for converting and reintegration into the Christian community on his return, it also seems possible that the strong incentive to force conversion these treaties inadvertently created did lead to coercion. Under these exceptional circumstances, Muslim slave owners forced their slaves to convert in order not to lose their initial investment.

Conversion did not necessarily lead to manumission but did nearly always generate new social bonds—occupational, conjugal, and fraternal. Royal or municipal slaves who converted to Christianity in Spain would often receive lighter tasks to allow them to perform their religious duties, but most did not experience any change in their labor conditions because of conversion.[84] As part of their conversion, however, they established new ties with often socially prominent godparents and with members of the religious order that was involved in their conversion. They also adjusted their relationship with their former masters, especially in cases of slaves owned by individuals.[85] Similarly, Christian slaves who did convert to Islam experienced social effects that went beyond the realm of the religious. The Knight d'Arvieux confirmed that captives in Tunis who converted transformed their status. They could pay their owners a monthly fixed fee determined by the Divan (the Governing Council) and wander freely, although they still belonged to their masters, who ultimately decided whether to grant their slaves manumission.[86] A few converts to Islam developed extremely successful careers in the fleet or in the political administration; in contrast, we have limited evidence of slaves who thrived professionally following, and as a result of, their conversion to Christianity.[87]

Slaves who converted to Islam were gradually inserted into their masters' families.[88] In a few cases, Muslim masters married their daughters or sisters to their converted slaves.[89] In other instances, male captives who had converted to Islam married female captives they had redeemed or freed female captives who had also converted.[90] Tunisian Romdhane Bey El Mouradi (1696–99) had a Christian mother, for whom, after her death, he created a Christian cemetery.[91] A rare case of a female renegade sentenced by the Inquisition was provided by Marquesa Dezcano, who was captured by Algerians in 1592, a year after her marriage in Sardinia. When she realized her husband was not going to free her, Dezcano converted and married another renegade.[92] Slave marriage is one of the topics on which we know even less in the case of Muslims enslaved in Spain. It is probable that Muslim slaves married other Muslim slaves, but unless they had converted, their marriages left no trace in church records, and we thus have no information about them.

Some slave converts to Islam became Janissaries, soldiers of the Ottoman militia, which constituted a kind of adoption. The new converts moved into the soldiers' barracks and became members of a male fraternity, referring to their fellow Janissaries as brothers.[93] Muslim slaves who converted to Christianity similarly created new social ties in being given to monasteries and becoming members of a social brotherhood.[94] At least in the short run, conversion did not bring about greater freedom, but it did create new social bonds.

Importantly, conversion did not necessarily result in a rupture with the convert's social past, especially not for former Christians. Converts did not have to give up their former families, and there is some evidence of renegades who brought their wives, children, or brothers to the Maghrib to live with them.[95] Archival evidence is even greater for renegades who maintained their family ties in Christendom through letter exchange, remittances, and occasionally even visits with their kin.[96] Correspondence was a medium that enabled renegades to maintain blood ties and friendships across the sea, while renegades who did well in their new life often sent money or supported their families (see Chapter 4).[97]

Conversion, then, had profound social implications. It resulted in the formation of new social ties, but it did not necessarily bring social rupture. While some renegades returned to Christendom independently or were captured, the majority, even if they continued to be in touch with their relatives, never returned, becoming instead part of the social tissue of the Muslim Maghrib. In that sense, conversion could be a strategy that enabled captives to improve their living conditions and might eventually remove them from the system of slavery. In one sense, conversion also increased mobility, but it did so within an imperially inscribed space. Baptized former Muslims had more freedom of movement within the city or even the region in which they lived, and eventually Christians in the Maghrib who converted to Islam gained full or nearly complete mobility. Conversion reduced, however, the chance that converts might cross the sea and return to their home communities.

SLAVE REBELLIONS

Some slaves took advantage of features of the system to stage rebellions, which facilitated their liberty and return home. One exceptional case brings into relief the potential inherent in the links between spatial and occupational mobility, social networks, and ease of communication. Damián Montenegro from Ragusa was one of a small number of slaves who in 1589 organized a spectacular slave rebellion in two galleys. Within a few hours, 420 captives were set free while 300 "Turks" were killed.[98] At least one printed pamphlet celebrating the episode, *Verdadera relación de la vitoria y libertad que alcançaron quatrocientos christianos captivos* (A True Account of the Victory and Freedom that Four-Hundred Christian Captives Achieved), circulated in Barcelona, the port to which the captives navigated after taking over the galleys.[99] These captives had spent months planning and preparing the rebellion, and they risked their lives by buying arms in various ports over a long period. Montenegro's testimony described the planning process:

> Damián Montenegro, Ragusan, says that having been in Constantinople in the bagnio of the Pasha, General of the Sea, he began negotiating that business [the rebellion] with Orazio Acquaviva Romano; and departing from Constantinople and arriving in Tripoli of Barbary, he continued to plan [it] with Orazio Acquaviva Romano and with Nicolo Rizzo, a Genoese renegade and servant of the Bey; and in the said Tripoli, the latter gave me two swords for my ship; and departing from there we arrived in Bizerte where I returned to deal with the same two and with one-eyed Pedro Napolitano; and [there] Orazio Acquaviva gave me a false eyebolt in order that I would prepare more like it; and departing from there we arrived in Algiers where he organized ten false bolts from the blacksmith of ra'īs Murat and bought five swords for my ship.[100]

Montenegro was a subject of the thriving Ragusan Republic in the Adriatic Sea, and his native tongue was probably the Slavic language spoken in the region. Yet in the prison cell in Istanbul he could plot with Acquaviva, a Roman whose mother tongue was probably the Roman dialect.[101] The fact that they made the plans in prison suggests that it was winter; they knew that when spring came, they would be placed in galleys, pulling a heavy oar and chained to their benches. Indeed, in the spring, they were set to row on galleys headed to North Africa. In Tripoli, Montenegro, who later commanded one of the rebelling galleys, met Rizzo, a Genoese renegade who led the rebellion on the second galley, who provided Montenegro with two swords. The plot's success, then, was partly based on the continuous relations some renegades maintained with their kin and members of their former confession. According to Alonso de Peña, an accomplice, Montenegro hid the swords Rizzo had given him underneath his galley bench.[102] When the two men met again in Bizerte, the next port visited by the galleys of Hasan Pasha, nearly six hundred miles from Tripoli, they must have first shared updates, informing each other about the state of their arms, their inventory of props, and their fellow conspirators on their galley. They advanced their plan by constructing a false eyebolt similar to those used by Muslims to cuff slaves—perhaps like those produced by slaves and convicts from the French galleys during the summers in Marseille. They carried the eyebolt with them to Algiers, their next stop, where they arranged for the manufacture of ten similar devices. They must have accumulated contacts with artisans across Maghribi cities who were willing to sell them their products and with couriers who took the props to the port. Which guards were willing to take bribes must have been common knowledge, shared by many captives. The arms and equipment were bought with money the captives had raised, probably through petty commerce. On the appointed date, the plot's leaders signaled their accomplices, attacked their guards, took over the galleys, and sailed for Barcelona, where they found their freedom.

According to Miquel Llot de Ribera, who compiled and published the above-mentioned pamphlet, the captives had been planning the rebellion for two or three years. While this time frame may have been an exaggeration, planning and preparing the rebellion must have taken weeks, probably months. It also required activating a widespread social network formed by renegades and captives and others, which captives were able to establish because of their mobility. These galley slaves had been doomed to row in what was often described as the hardest labor forced on captives, with death often the only way out. Given the superior mobility enjoyed by slaves laboring in cities, their opportunity to create long-distance networks must have been much greater.

CONCLUSION

Mediterranean bondage, then, was a system in which slaves, Christian and Muslim alike, constantly moved between masters and occupations and in space, across the region and within the city. Slavery in this system was not a condition but rather a dynamic. The lives of Muslim and Christian slaves resembled each other not only because they were structured along similar patterns of mobility but also because slaves labored in the same space, the Mediterranean, and were frequently in contact with their homes. These connections and their mobility allowed some captives to maintain kinship relations and the possibility of ransom, even if only a minority of captives regained their liberty this way.

This chapter has compared the labor conditions and manumission of Muslim and Christian slaves in the western Mediterranean and demonstrated that captives were mobile while unfree, both in space and in social categories. The next two chapters turn to exploring what slaves did in order to advance their freedom and which institutions and individuals assisted them in the process. These chapters move beyond comparison to look at how the Mediterranean system of bondage linked the slavery of Muslims with that of Christians. The mobility that characterized the lives of Muslim and Christian slaves was the key to connectivity, as it allowed for the development of extensive social networks, which transformed slaves into well-informed and efficient and rapid carriers of all sorts of news. The system of Mediterranean slavery transformed people into commodities, but it also made people into sources of knowledge and conveyers of information, a topic the rest of this book will take up.

CHAPTER 2

Ransom

*Between Economic, Political,
and Salvific Interests*

In the Christian Mediterranean world, visual and textual representations of captivity and redemption of captives were ubiquitous.
Trinitarians and Mercedarians, friars whose mission was to redeem
Christians from North Africa, published pamphlets and commissioned prints and artworks representing captivity and redemption
as part of propaganda campaigns.[1] These depictions detailed the
dangers implicit in the friars' redemption operations, stressed the
importance of the orders' apostolic mission, and enumerated the
miseries of those reduced to captivity: compelled to hand over their
fortunes, captives were sold into slavery, beaten, forcibly converted,
and worked to death. The ransoming expeditions of the orders of
redemption, as depicted in such texts and images, provided captives'
only chance of escape. Part of the altarpiece of the Mercedarian
convent of Valladolid in Castile, a high relief more than five feet tall
carved by Pedro de la Cuadra in 1599, depicts a ransoming scene
that could have taken place in Algiers, Tunis, or Fez (see Figure 1).[2]
On the left, a Muslim captor or "Turk," accompanied by his black
slave, sits on a cushion, counting golden coins on a table. The Turk
has a possessive arm around part of the pile of coins. Four captives
with heavy chains around their necks and reddish Phrygian caps
that allude to their near manumission stand behind the captor and
his slave. On the right stand two Mercedarian brothers. Negotiations over the price to be paid for the captives have already taken
place, but the Turk seems dissatisfied, and the Mercedarians are
adding money to the pile.[3]

Figure 1. Pedro de la Cuadra, *La redención de cautivos*, 1599. Museo Nacional de Escultura, Valladolid.

In this work, known as "La redención de cautivos" (The redemption of captives), de la Cuadra portrays the captives as mute objects, even as "dead bodies," as the Portuguese Antonio de Sosa described the figure of the captive in his renowned *Topografía e Historia General de Argel*, published in 1612.[4] First commoditized when sold at the slave market after their capture, the captives now experience a second commoditization. They have no agency or legal persona; in representations like this one, they cannot take care of themselves and are therefore grateful to the Mercedarians, who alone are able to redeem the wretched figures. To contemporaries, the function and message of the image were clear: good Catholics are urged to contribute alms to be used for the redemption of their fellow Christians.

Images such as "La redención de cautivos" obscure the complexities of captivity and the redeeming of captives in the early modern Mediterranean. For Spanish and other Mediterranean rulers, ransom was a foreign policy issue integral to practical relations between Islam and Christianity. Additionally, the freeing of their subjects held captive on the other side of the religious divide offered Christian and Muslim rulers an opportunity to heighten an image of devoutness.[5] For Spanish rulers, captivity was particularly troubling as it challenged the monarchy's early modern project of imposing ethnoreligious unity on Spanish territory and among Spanish subjects. Captivity transplanted Christians to Muslim territory, threatening their confessional identity, and forged Muslim slave communities in Spain. Muslim slaves were an economic asset, and the crown ultimately turned a blind eye to their presence; the presence of Christians in Muslim North Africa was a different story. Typically, Catholic kings were committed to redeeming their subjects from the Maghrib and responded positively to pleas for help. Philip II and successive Habsburg kings (1598–1700) and Bourbon kings (1700–1808) organized ecclesiastical redemption expeditions to North Africa, issued licenses to trade with the Maghrib to merchants who offered to ransom Christians, assisted captives financially, and in some cases agreed to give up royal slaves in order that they could be swapped with Christians. And yet, the crown's policy of supporting redemption through ransom and trade had its detractors in Spain. These critics grappled constantly with various actors involved in ransom, and redemption via the church became the most common form of ransom partly as an outcome of these conflicts.

The Trinitarians and the Mercedarians, two orders that became nearly indistinguishable because of their role in redeeming Christians, ransomed more captives than any individual or other institution in the Iberian Peninsula, indeed in the early modern Mediterranean and Europe.[6] However, throughout the period they had to compete with merchants who ransomed captives and had to defend themselves against critics who argued Spain should make war instead of paying. As the orders became well-funded royal ransom agencies at the turn of the seventeenth century, ransom became a locus for debates about the nature of interactions with Muslim North Africa. The textual and visual propaganda circulated by the orders of redemption was so successful that modern scholarship on captivity has at times ignored the other actors who labored in this space.[7] Nonetheless, new scholarship has begun to recover the host of agents that deliberated on, participated in, and tussled over the ransom market and the practice of ransom. The characterization of the Mediterranean as a space dominated by sacred violence that could be resolved exclusively by payment coordinated by the friars is misleading. The regulation the Spanish crown imposed on the friars' redemptive labor in the late sixteenth century caused the friars to extend their propaganda efforts, simplifying in turn historians' access to their participation in ransoming. However, that regulation did not eliminate the activities of small-scale ransomers who offered an alternative to ecclesiastic redemption, nor did it silence opponents of redemption.

Historians who focus on the role of the orders in shaping ransom procedures overlook the participation of Algerian pashas, Moroccan sultans, and their representatives and ignore the relations between ransom actors. The intra-imperial perspective that neglects other Mediterranean actors to portray an insular Spanish dynamic fails to explain the motivation of Spanish critics of redemption, shifting relations between friars and merchants, and changing patterns of ransom over the early modern period. In order to show the complexity of these processes, in addition to examining these relations and patterns, this chapter reintroduces to this history North African rulers, highlighting their role in limiting and giving form to ransom across the Mediterranean.

De la Cuadra's relief—whom it represents and whom it omits, as well as the claims it makes—helps structure this chapter. The discussion begins by examining not only the medieval and early modern history of the orders of redemption, their funding mechanisms, and the procedures for launching a ransom expedition but also how the friars understood their own redemptive labor. It then considers North African Jewish and Muslim merchants—who also ransomed captives on occasion yet whose involvement the artist chose to ignore—and their relations with the friars. Ransoming merchants and redeeming friars overlapped, collaborated, and competed for ransom funds and the opportunity to ransom particular captives. While they engaged differently in ransoming captives, their activities ultimately led Spaniards to be freed in exchange for goods or bullion and thickened the networks that linked Spain and North Africa. At this point, the chapter returns to a debate de la Cuadra's relief obscures and examines and contextualizes the arguments against redemption. Finally, it turns to the North African rulers with whom the friars had to conduct business and looks at their ransom agenda and how they imposed it, in part, on Spanish actors. The framing of the redemption of captives within this wider context sheds new light on the complex ways in which trade and religion were intertwined, the degree to which Mediterranean policy was a fraught topic in early modern Spain, and how Muslim actors participated in shaping the terms and outcome of the debates.

MEDIEVAL BEGINNINGS

Ecclesiastical ransom institutions were active in Iberia at least from the turn of the twelfth century.[8] In 1198 in Cerfroid near Paris, the Provençal John of Matha (1160–1213) established the Order of the Holy Trinity, the first order of friars to have the redemption of captives as its principal mission. While the crusaders' defeat in 1187 at the battle of Hattin outside Jerusalem likely prompted the order's founding, the community's concerns were soon redirected to the Iberian Muslim-Christian frontier.[9] In 1202, Matha established a second house in Marseille, and from there Trinitarian houses spread throughout France, Austria, the Crown of Aragon, Castile, and Portugal. In the Crown of Aragon, however, the Trinitarians encountered obstacles. Support from the French monarchy, the great feudal lords of France, and Pope Innocent III (1160 or 1161–1216) aligned the order against the Crown of Aragon, an ally of the Albigensians, who objected to French royal policy in Languedoc. The Trinitarians eventually gained a footing in the Aragonese kingdoms, but their status there was always weaker than in both Castile and France. The Mercedarians—members of the Order of Our Lady of Mercy, which Pere Nolasc (1189–1256) and Ramon de Penyafort (1175 or 1176–1275) established in 1218 under the patronage of the city of Barcelona and James the Conqueror (1208–1276)—dominated in Aragon. The first Mercedarian houses were established in the lands of the Crown of Aragon and, in the second half of the thirteenth century, with the support of the Crown of Castile, the order began establishing houses in Castile.[10]

Saving souls was an expensive enterprise. The Mercedarian and Trinitarian orders funded their activities from both public and private sources. Revenue from private property played a major role. During the Middle Ages, the Portuguese, Castilian, and Aragonese kings conquered numerous Muslim territories, which they granted to religious orders as well as to soldiers and settlers. The orders of redemption also acquired land independently and received land grants from individual patrons. Leasing of their lands provided a portion of the orders' funds.[11] Private giving, from estate bequests to alms found in begging bowls located in churches and elsewhere, also played a key role.[12] Following their ransom, redeemed captives had to remain with the friars and participate in fund-raising processions, at which they performed their past captivity, for six months to a year.[13]

While the foundation of the orders and the distribution of their sister houses across the Iberian Peninsula echoed political tensions involving the Aragonese king, the French king, the pope, and the French nobility, international politics alone do not explain the rivalry between the orders. Mercedarians and Trinitarians competed fiercely for ransom monies and begging rights. The Mercedarians accepted former members of other orders upon the approval of their chapter general, but not former Trinitarians.[14] From 1366, the rivalry manifested itself in disputes over areas for begging, which premodern kings regulated through royal permits. Such licenses were usually valid for one year or two and limited to a single diocese or a small number of dioceses. In 1363, the Trinitarians asked Peter the Ceremonious (1319–87) for a license that would allow them to claim the proceeds from begging bowls in churches throughout the Crown of Aragon. When the king granted the Trinitarians the coveted license, the Mercedarians demanded its annulment; the Trinitarians protested but to no avail. In 1384, however, the Trinitarians won back the privilege, but by then they had been overwhelmed by the Mercedarian presence in the Crown of Aragon. In 1388, John I (1350–96) issued a royal provision that restored the monopoly over begging in the Crown of Aragon to the Mercedarians.[15] The Trinitarians never regained their position, and by 1477 they had ended their activities in the Crown of Aragon altogether.[16] In Castile, however, the orders continued to quarrel about begging zones until at least the mid-seventeenth century and probably later still.[17]

Both orders had to protect their right to beg from forces other than each other. In 1306 the Mercedarians complained about charlatans who had obtained a royal begging permit by falsely claiming to have been captives.[18] The wording implied that these beggars had never experienced captivity, but the friars also tried to prevent people they knew to have been captives from begging. Nicolás Gil and Juan of Seville, who had obtained their liberty with the help of merchants rather than with the help of the Mercedarians, petitioned Peter the Ceremonious for begging permits in 1374. They asked the king not only for the right to collect alms but also for an explicit stipulation that the Mercedarians had no right to prevent them from doing so,[19] which suggests that the former captives had reason to anticipate such interference. The episode shows how the struggles between the orders and others involved in ransoming led the orders into conflict with captives they themselves had not ransomed. They never succeeded in preventing individual captives or their kin from begging or other ransomers from assisting captives altogether, but their efforts may in part explain their near monopoly on ransom.

EARLY MODERN TRANSFORMATIONS

Political developments in Spain and the Mediterranean over the long sixteenth century, reaching from 1492 to 1614, reshaped the geography of the world of ransom and relations among captives, friars, and merchants and made the ransom of captives a state prerogative. In January 1492, the Catholic kings occupied Muslim Granada. They guaranteed generous capitulations to the Muslim residents of Granada, permitting them to practice their religion openly and maintain traditional Muslim social, juridical, and cultural structures.[20] Three months later, the monarchs issued an edict requiring Spanish Jews to convert or leave the peninsula. For Muslims as well, evangelization and forced baptisms soon replaced peaceful colonization. When faced with the options of conversion, enslavement, or expulsion, the majority of the Muslims chose to convert. Repression continued nonetheless until the converts' descendants were expelled from Spain between 1609 and 1614.[21]

Seen from a Mediterranean perspective, the Iberian project of religious universalism only began with the fall of Granada. Two decades after the conquest of Granada, the Spanish monarchs sought to expand their Crusaders' fantasy of conquest, colonization, and

Christianization to Muslim North Africa, a goal they then pursued throughout most of the sixteenth century. The Portuguese conquered Tangiers, Agadir, and Safi between 1504 and 1508, and the Spaniards occupied Mers El-Kebir in 1505, the Peñón de Vélez de la Gomera in 1508, Oran in 1509, and Béjaïa, Tripoli, and the Peñón of Algiers in 1510. In the following decades they conquered, and lost, other cities, devised attack plans, and were intensively engaged in belligerent Mediterranean politics. Through the century, however, the project ran out of steam, and soon Spain had lost all its strongholds east of Oran. In 1577 Philip II abandoned his initial North African colonial policy, and in 1581 the Spanish and Ottoman empires signed a truce and turned their backs on the Middle Sea.[22] Both the Ottomans and the Spaniards continued to be involved in Mediterranean activities, but the big rivalry stopped playing out in Mediterranean military action. As a result, corsairs (privateers) replaced the large imperial fleets, and captive-taking became a common practice independent of spectacular maritime battles.[23] The number of captives increased and the patterns of their circulation changed, becoming more balanced and evenly dispersed across time and space.[24] After 1581, rarely did corsairs capture hundreds of soldiers at once, as they had during the previous decades of galley warfare; instead raids became much more common and most of them resulted in small numbers of captives—a few peasants, sea travelers, or sailors.[25]

The geopolitical and demographic shifts of the long sixteenth century turned captives into a group over whom Spanish kings, and other Mediterranean rulers, claimed royal authority and spiritual guardianship. From 1575, the Spanish crown tightened its regulation of the orders, increased the funds it made available for ransom, and bureaucratized ransom procedures. These steps were compelled in part by the completion of the conquest of Granada, which significantly increased the challenges and costs of freeing Muslims and Christians, as the Mediterranean now had to be crossed. To tackle the growing expense, the new royal governing councils filled the orders' collection tins, but financing ransom was accompanied by dictating the ransom agenda.[26] Whereas captives' kin were interested in freeing their loved ones and friars sought prestige by redeeming ecclesiastics, women, and children, the crown sought to save soldiers who could be reassigned to military service and the Royal Councils hoped to save subjects who fell under their jurisdictions.[27] Beginning in 1575, the Royal Council (Consejo Real) inspected the orders' finances, regulating the procedures that governed their rescue operations. From that date on, the Mercedarian and Trinitarian generals had to request that the Council of Castile authorize rescue expeditions and issue the passports that would allow friars to travel through Spanish lands and on to North Africa; the council also directed Spanish officials to assist the friars as required.[28] The monarchy imposed strict bookkeeping regulations, demanding that its appointed scribe accompany the expeditions and record the negotiations, the identity of the rescued captives, prices paid, and the sources of funds.[29]

Royal sponsorship did not bring to an end the quarrels of the Trinitarian and Mercedarian orders with each other and with other orders. In the seventeenth century, when a reform movement developed out of the Mercedarian order, approved in 1621 by the pope as a semiautonomous branch called the Discalced Mercedarians, the mother order sought to prevent the new friars from participating in the redemption of captives. The Mercedarians pressured the king to ask the pope to make the new order dispense with its fourth vow, to redeem captives. Although the king consented, eventually the Discalced Mercedarians joined the ransom efforts of the Mercedarians and Trinitarians.[30] As in the Middle Ages, such disputes often stood for struggles between much stronger political actors. In 1650, the pope nominated Phillipe le Vacher, French consul in Algiers and a member of the Congregation of the Mission, or Lazarists, as Apostolic Vicar of Algiers, a title that was not accompanied by apostolic powers (namely, he was not an ordained bishop) but permitted Vacher to provide captives with pastoral care without being a slave himself. The Trinitarians in Algiers refused to acknowledge Vacher's jurisdiction. The pope reproached the Trinitarians but, backed by the Spanish crown, they refused to obey the apostolic vicar's orders, even to the extent that the Trinitarians incited the captives against the French Lazarist.[31]

The transformation of ransom into an imperially sponsored enterprise was part of larger religious and political reforms related to the Counter-Reformation and Philip II's empire-building project.[32] In reshaping the religious life of the friars and regulating the redemption of captives, the monarch sought to achieve three goals: to strengthen his control of the orders as part of a process of centralizing and bureaucratizing royal power; to increase the number of ransom expeditions and, thus, of rescued Spanish subjects; and to heighten his image as a devout Catholic, for he was saving Christian souls in danger of conversion to Islam under duress.

FRIARS AND MERCHANTS: COMPETITION OVER THE
RANSOM MARKET

Pedro de la Cuadra's ransom scene depicted friars and Turks as protagonists, ignoring independent intermediaries who also rescued
captives and who overlapped and interacted with ecclesiastical ransomers. This representation is not completely unfounded. During
the early modern period, Trinitarian and Mercedarian friars were
responsible for the ransoming of most of the Spanish, Portuguese,
and French captives who were released, with Trinitarians and Mercedarians rescuing more captives than any other ransom institution
in Europe, including the Italian confraternities and Baltic, Danish,
and English ransoming bodies.[33] Moreover, redemption via the orders
had the advantage of being cheaper than the ransom services merchants provided. On average, the friars spent 60 percent of their funds
on captives who did not contribute a single maravedi toward their
ransom—mostly Spanish, Portuguese, and Italian soldiers, women,
and children. The remaining 40 percent was earmarked for the ransom of specific captives whose kin had contributed to the funds for
their ransom. Redemption via the friars was, however, slow: during
the seventeenth century, the friars did not frequent Algiers, Fez, or
Tétouan more than once every three years on average.

For these reasons, many captives and their relatives turned to individual ransomers for help. Indeed, at least for the period between 1574
and 1609, which has been closely studied, merchants ransomed more
Spaniards than did Trinitarians or Mercedarians.[34] These independent
ransomers, at first mostly Jews, had been active in Iberia at least since
the turn of the thirteenth century; over the course of the fourteenth
century, Christians and Muslims came to outnumber Jews in their
ranks.[35] Redeemers called *alfaqueques* (from the Arabic *al-Fakkāk*)
in Castile and *exeas* in the Crown of Aragon, often working for specific town councils, ransomed captives across the Muslim-Christian
and the Castilian-Aragonese boundaries. In the mid-thirteenth century, the office had been codified in the Siete Partidas, the Castilian
statutes, but the crown did not nominate a royal *alfaqueque*, who was
involved in coordinating the operations of municipal *alfaqueques*,
until 1410, and it annulled the royal office less than a century later,
reestablishing the independence of the ransomers.[36] The Muslim governors and residents of Granada and Valencia employed *al-fakkākīn*
who were sent to Aragon or Castile to ransom Muslims.[37] Merchants

began to join the ranks of both *alfaqueques* and *exeas* in the four-teenth century.[38] Individual and municipal ransom agents competed with Trinitarians and the Mercedarians for ransom funds, patronage, and clients, namely captives or their kin. *Alfaqueques* and merchants offered their clients similar advantages. *Alfaqueques* benefited from diplomatic immunity, and merchants took advantage of their com-mercial contacts across the borders. They knew the territory better than anyone else, and unlike the Trinitarians and Mercedarians they were willing to redeem small numbers of captives quickly rather than wait to collect larger sums for larger operations. Captives' kin knew that turning to *alfaqueques* or merchants increased the chance they would quickly be reunited with their relatives. At the same time, how-ever, ransom via *alfaqueques* was more expensive than ransom by the orders.[39]

The end of the Reconquista and the sixteenth century's geopolitical shifts also influenced independent ransomers, dividing Christian mer-chants from Iberia from Jewish, Muslim, and Morisco North Afri-can merchants and European consuls in the Maghrib.[40] These two groups were subject to distinct mobility regimes and developed differ-ent relations with the friars and with Mediterranean rulers. Iberian merchants' trade with and within North Africa never disappeared; indeed, direct and indirect Spanish commerce with the Maghrib continued to grow throughout the early modern period.[41] Officially, the crown had prohibited trade with the infidel, grounding its posi-tion in canon law and ideology, but in practice, trade with North Africa became routine for seventeenth-century Spain under a system of "permanent exception."[42] Individual merchants who wanted trad-ing licenses that would permit commerce with the Maghrib had to declare that they would not trade in war materials and would use their profits to ransom Christians rather than invest in goods for resale in Spain.[43] For some of these merchants the position of pirate, ransomer, or captive was a stage in a complex professional trajectory. Often they were former captives who had developed local connec-tions in the Maghrib and had mastered Arabic and Turkish during their captivity.[44] As Spaniards and Christians, they enjoyed freedom of movement in the Iberian Peninsula and hence easy access to fami-lies of captives who sought help rescuing their relatives and to whom these merchants could offer their skills and contacts.

In contrast, North African Muslim and Jewish merchants had limited access to Spain but could move more freely in and among

Maghribi cities and thus could ransom Christian captives that Christian redeemers could not. For example, Yehuda (Judas) Malaqui, a Jewish merchant from Chefchaouen in the Rif Mountains of northwest Morocco, one of the suppliers of the Spanish fort Peñón de Vélez in Morocco, was also an expert ransomer. Malaqui had Muslim associates, and to solidify his connections in the peninsula, he sent one of his sons to Málaga, where the son converted to Christianity and was baptized as "Juan Bautista de Padilla."[45] In 1589 Malaqui made an offer to the Spanish crown, hoping to become its exclusive ransom agent in the Maghrib and promising "to get all the Christian captives from all of Barbary and Algiers." Malaqui continued, "I offer to bring them to whatever part your highness asks me; for two-thirds of the price it would cost anyone else ransoming them, be they [from the Order of the] Holy Trinity or [from the Order] our Lady of Mercy."[46] Malaqui was confident about his abilities, repeatedly positioning himself in relation to the friars and claiming he could ransom captives they could not: "In the journey I have just executed, I brought nineteen captives, among them five women and four babies, two of whom are nursing at the breast, and these women and children I got out of the house of the king of Fez; and not one of those who ransom [captives] could ransom them for any price; and together with these I brought ten men with the intention that I would be paid [for ransoming them] from the alms of the redemption of captives of the [Holy] Trinity and the [Holy] Mercy."[47] Malaqui not only explicitly compared his skills and connections with the friars', but here he also asked to be paid from the alms allocated to the friars' redemption operations. His success in rescuing women and children, precisely the kind of captives in whom the orders were interested, convinced Philip II to employ him as a professional crown ransom agent, a position he occupied until at least late 1595.[48]

Jacob Crudo, a Jewish Tétouanite operating at the same time as Malaqui and with contacts in Algiers, Annaba (a port city less than 120 miles west of Tunis), and even Livorno in Italy, had a relationship with the friars more typical than Malaqui's.[49] He rented his house in Tétouan to the Mercedarians when they came to buy captives in 1590 and 1596, and he negotiated better prices and made deals on their behalf. In establishing these contacts, Crudo hoped to facilitate his immigration to Spain.[50] Indeed, in 1596 he moved to Seville but was arrested for wandering its streets, according to the Inquisition documents, "dressed in a Christian habit and dealing and trading out in the open, thus causing a great scandal."[51] Crudo presented warm letters of recommendation from the governor of Ceuta, the Duke of Medina-Sidonia, and two Mercedarian brothers to his Inquisitors, but the letters did not prevent the Inquisitors from expelling him, and by the end of the year Crudo was back in Tétouan dealing again with the Mercedarians.

The Jewish subjects of the Spanish colonies in North Africa developed working relations with the Mercedarians similar to those of Crudo. The Çaportas and the Cansino, the leading families of the Jewish community of Oran (the largest Spanish settlement in the Maghrib), frequently donated money to captives' relatives and actively rescued Christians, taking advantage of their social networks that stretched across the Maghrib.[52] The Çaportas and Cansino families facilitated the ransom of Christian captives until 1669, when Mariana of Austria, queen consort of Spain, ordered the expulsion of the Jewish community from Oran.[53]

Various factors turned North African merchants into valuable allies for the friars. While Christian merchants required a permit from the Spanish authorities to trade with Morocco or Algiers, Algerians and Moroccans needed a license to enter Spain. Over the course of the seventeenth century, the Spanish king issued only a few such licenses to North Africans. Jacob Crudo's visibility in the streets of Seville and the scandal his appearance provoked join the conversion of Yehuda Malaqui's son in marking the limits of North Africans' mobility within Spanish territory. Their limited access to the peninsula made it nearly impossible for Maghribi ransomers to advertise their skills to Christian captives' kin in Castile, Portugal, or Aragon and thus gain commissions. The friars had good reason to collaborate with these merchants in the latter's command of local languages and their connections in Muslim North Africa.[54] Additionally, as they were for the most part unable to enter Spain, Maghribi ransomers could not subvert the orders' suggestion that they offered the only path through which captives could be redeemed. Indeed, in cooperating with Maghribis, Trinitarians and Mercedarians could easily take credit for redemptions executed in practice by Jews and Muslims.

In contrast, the involvement of Christian merchants in the ransom market placed them in direct competition with the orders, with the latter occasionally complaining to the crown that these merchants were abusing trading licenses at captives' expense.[55] For example, in 1658 Trinitarian friar Francisco Diego de Pacheco, posted to Algiers, dispatched several complaints to the viceroy of Valencia about merchants from Alicante, Majorca, and Castile. One of these merchants was Jacinto Sevilia, who, according to the Valencian viceroy, was a liar and smuggler who engaged in illegal trade and never intended to ransom captives. The viceroy recommended the crown not renew Sevilia's permit to trade with North Africa,[56] and Pacheco seconded the viceroy, claiming Sevilia and others abused their licenses, exported war materials (such as gunpowder or tar) to the Maghrib, and invested the monies they collected from captives' kin in commodities rather than in freeing captives. The damage, he claimed, was great: the captives remained unfree, their kin lost the money they had raised for ransom, the Algerians received ammunition, and royal revenues were lost when untaxed goods were smuggled.

Nevertheless, two years later Jacinto Sevilia enjoyed the support of a Mercedarian, evidence the orders might favor the involvement of merchants in the world of ransom when it served their needs. In July 1660 Mercedarian Diego de Orozco requested the king renew Sevilia's license to trade with Algiers. Orozco had recently returned from Algiers, where he had freed 379 Spaniards. At that time, he and his fellow redeemers had observed twelve young Christian boys held captive. Fearing their youth would make them vulnerable to pressure to convert to Islam should they remain in Algiers and having exhausted the funds they had brought with them, the Mercedarians had left one of their members a hostage. In return, the authorities provided them with credit to redeem the boys. The redeemers knew the quickest way ensure the hostage was released was to commission Jacinto Sevilia for the task, but Sevilia's permit to trade would need to be renewed if he were to make the trip.[57]

In trafficking human plunder, corsairs, North African authorities, and slave brokers participated in an economy of booty.[58] Likewise—however friars, captives' kin, and merchants perceived the freeing of captives—in practice they were engaged in economic transactions. These dealings started months, sometimes years, before the actual ransoming, with captives' kin and friars begging for alms and seeking royal funding. By the time the redeemers were ready to embark, they would have collected large sums of money. For example, in 1591 Mercedarians asked for royal permission to take 24,000 ducats in cash and goods with them to Algiers without paying export taxes, a favor the king granted ecclesiastic rescue expeditions. Nearly two decades later, in 1609, the Trinitarian Bernardo de Monroy left the port of Valencia for Algiers with ten cases filled with 20,000 Castilian reales, twenty-two boxes of tarbooshes from Toledo, and various textiles.[59] In addition to paying the slave trader, Monroy and his fellow friars spent money on taxes, customs, transit fees, documents such as safe conducts, consular fees, and transport, as well as on commissions for middlemen, credit, and insurance. On top of these expenses, the friars had to pay a commission of 3 to 4 escudos for each ransomed captive.

Merchant-ransomers regularly charged captives or their kin a commission of 4 percent of the total cost of the deal, with war sharply increasing this rate. Merchants' licenses did not permit them to carry as much money to North Africa as the friars did, but they often left with 5,000 or even 10,000 ducats in cash or goods. On these sums they paid export taxes, 6 percent for insuring the transfer of bullion, 2 percent commission to the ships' captains, and 11.5 percent to North African governors upon arrival in their ports. The use of money was expensive. Merchant-ransomers could also borrow from European merchants in the Maghrib via letters of exchange, but the use of such bills might absorb up to two-thirds of their expenses.[60] Beyond payments to the large number of intermediaries involved and the cut agents reaped, ransoming entailed a significant export of bullion or commodities to the Maghrib, against which all critics of redemption protested.

Though the friars would have been well aware of the material and economic realities of the ransoming process, and were integrated into exchange networks and the market, they did not believe they were conducting business, nor did they seek to abolish slavery or manumit individual slaves.[61] They aimed to instruct, counsel, and encourage captives who suffered and experienced mistreatment, and their main goal in doing so was to minimize the conversion to Islam among captives.[62] Communal solidarity, which followed a reciprocal logic, drove their activities.[63] As Christians, they rescued fellow Christians, members of their confessional community but also members of their ethnopolitical community. The orders were associated with specific kingdoms (Castile, Andalusia, Aragon, or Portugal), and friars rescued Christians from their individual provinces.[64] In protecting the souls of Christians, their efforts increased the orders' religious prestige.

Merchants likewise could win religious esteem by ransoming their coreligionists,[65] and in their applications for trade licenses,

Christian merchants emphasized the risk that captives who were left unredeemed might convert. Nonetheless, commercial advantage and profit-making drove their labors. Christian merchants could benefit economically from illegal trade with Muslims in commodities deemed materials of war; and they might grease the wheels of commerce with the infidel by including ransom in their activities.[66] For North African Jews and Muslims, ransom facilitated commercial contacts with Spain and granted them entry to an empire that had expelled them a century before.[67]

REDEMPTION UNDER FIRE

As conjoined projects, the ransoming of Christians and trading with Muslims were fiercely criticized internationally throughout the early modern period.[68] In Spain, the crown, the *arbitristas* ("projectors" or "reformers"), the religious orders, former captives, and local authorities articulated their arguments and counterarguments in terms of moral duty and political economy. Political figures and *arbitristas* opposed redemption as inefficient. The crown transformed the orders into funded ransom agencies, and thus supported the practice, but in so doing, the king intensified commerce with the Maghrib, a practice to which he theoretically objected and against which he evoked canon law and other prohibitions, especially when merchants or local authorities petitioned him for permits to trade with North Africa. Finally, despite royal objection to such trade, the Spanish king tended to approve requests for such licenses and issued them repeatedly.

The earliest critics of redemption in the seventeenth century called for the North African corsairs' nests to be conquered rather than "medieval tributes" be paid,[69] but as the century progressed, the idea of military subjugation became unrealistic and later opponents sought humbler ends, such as the formation of a strong Mediterranean fleet to protect the coasts and make ransom payment less necessary. Spanish contemporaries saw the first two decades of the seventeenth century as an opportunity to relive Spain's sixteenth-century Mediterranean glory days. Spain expelled the Moriscos (1609–14), successfully sacked Tunis twice (1609 and 1612), occupied Moroccan El Araich (Larache) in 1610 and Mehdya (La Mamora) in 1614, and contemplated taking over Algiers, although that plan failed.[70] The eradication of Islam in Spain and the success of Christian attacks, some of which brought conquests, in North Africa had contradictory effects. Some Spaniards came to believe Spain could terminate corsairing for good, especially if the plan to conquer Algiers succeeded; at the same time many of the expelled Moriscos joined the corsairs, strengthening corsairs' cities such as Tétouan, Salé, Algiers, and Tunis. Moriscos' mastery of the Spanish language and of coastal topography resulted in increasing numbers of captives, both Spanish and other Europeans.[71] Again, the crown significantly increased the funds it made available to the orders of redemption.[72] In 1609 it also intervened to place new restrictions on the financing of redemption expeditions, demanding that the friars use more bullion and fewer commodities to ransom captives. The resurfacing of a crusader spirit together with the growing number of captives and increased bullion exports for ransom formed the context for the opposition to redemption in the early seventeenth century.

On May 31, 1612, the Duke of Osuna, viceroy of Sicily, wrote to the king arguing that the orders were draining the royal treasury, ransoming the weak, sick, and old as well as deserters (known as *bienvenidos*) from the North African Spanish settlements who had defected to Algiers, and funding Spain's enemies. If no rescue expeditions were sent to the Maghrib, he continued, the Muslims would themselves set free the helpless in order to avoid the expense of their maintenance. The Council of State thanked the duke but prohibited him from adopting any measures on the matter unless ordered by the king.[73] Osuna probably believed that Spain would soon conquer Algiers, a plan the king was entertaining at the time, which would reduce the number of captives to a minimum. Osuna's contemporary Miguel Martínez del Villar, regent of the Council of Aragon, went a step further in an *arbitrio*, a project proposal to reform the economy, titled *Discurso acerca de la conquista de los reynos de Argel y Bugía* (A Discourse About the Conquest of the Kingdoms of Algiers and Béjaïa), which he published in 1619.[74] As the title makes clear, Martínez del Villar called for the occupation of these cities, arguing that merely arming a patrol fleet would not solve the problem of captivity. To Osuna's economic arguments, Martínez del Villar added a moral one. Rescued captives were not only physically disabled and hence a financial burden but also introduced to Spain "abominable customs" that they had learned from their Muslim captors, a reference to homosexuality.[75] In their proposals, Osuna and Martínez del Villar combined arguments about efficiency, reduced numbers of captives, and the moral impurity embedded in ransomed captives. By the end of the second decade of the seventeenth century, Spain had lost military momentum and the idea of occupying Algiers likely sounded obsolete. Probably for this reason, as far as the archives disclose, neither the crown nor the orders responded to Martínez del Villar's *arbitrio*.

Less than a decade later, Guillermo Garrett, a captain and an *arbitrista*, launched a focused call for the reform of Spain's Mediterranean policy. At the 1626 Valencian *cortes* convened at Monzón in Aragon, Garrett argued that "preventive redemption" in the form of a squadron to defend the Spanish coasts, protect royal subjects, and capture Muslims who would be enslaved as oarsmen would be a better use of funds than redemption itself.[76] Like Osuna and Martínez del Villar, Garrett accused the orders of spending too much money, funding the crown's enemies, and ransoming disabled and defector captives. The novelty of his proposal was found in his suggestion that the money currently allocated for the ransom of captives could be added to the funds for the fleet.

The orders immediately replied to Garrett's proposal, identifying it as a threat to their mission. Gaspar Prieto, general of the Mercedarian order and present in the *cortes*, responded in some anger, expounding on the importance of the orders and terming the critics "unauthorized men, merchants by profession and especially idiots."[77] By calling them out as merchants when addressing the king and leading political figures, the majority of whom were members of the nobility, Prieto allied himself with his audience against these who stained their hands in exchange. Prieto stressed the antiquity of the institution of redemption, highlighted what he perceived as fallacies in Garrett's project, and insisted that not even the pope could reroute funds earmarked for redemption, and yet he implicitly accepted part of Garrett's critique by proposing improvements to the orders' ransoming procedures. In the following years, Trinitarians and Mercedarians composed several replies to Garrett's *arbitrio* reiterating Prieto's arguments.[78] In 1629, the Trinitarian provincial of Castile responded vehemently, silencing an *arbitrista* supported by the count-duke Olivares, who was promoting large-scale taxation reforms at the time.[79] Perhaps owing to the friars' efforts, the *arbitristas'* proposals never became reality.

Other critics sought ways to redeem Christian captives yet to do so efficiently. Like others before him, captive and Jesuit José Tamayo y Velarde warned that Spanish silver used to redeem Spanish captives supported and strengthened the corsairs of Algiers and Morocco.[80] His solution was to make Algerians and Moroccans pay the same price for Muslims enslaved in Spain that Spaniards paid for Spaniards held captive in the Maghrib. To adjust the monetary imbalance created by the redemption of captives, Tamayo y Velarde recommended, the king of Spain should prohibit his subjects from manumitting Muslim slaves, refuse to free Muslim corsairs enslaved in the royal fleet, and tighten Spain's maritime borders, making sure Muslim slaves did not escape to the Maghrib. Once these measures were implemented, he claimed, it would be easy to pressure Algerians and Moroccans to pay the same sums of money for Muslim slaves that Spaniards paid for Christian captives. Tamayo y Velarde began writing his *Compendiosa Relación de costumbres, ritos y gobiernos de Berbería* (Compendious Account of the Customs, Rites and Governments of Barbary) during his captivity in Tétouan in 1645, a few months before he was ransomed. He never published the text, and thus the degree to which it circulated, if at all, and actively participated in the debate remains unclear. Yet it presents us with a more nuanced perspective on the disagreement about the redemption of captives.

Political opposition to the friars persisted, and arguments against redemption intertwined with calls for the reform of Spain's Mediterranean naval power resurfaced in the 1650s and 1660s, but the international political context was now different. When, in 1654, the governor of Ibiza suggested that the Spanish Armada bombard Algiers, he had in mind the recent success of France, which had used its naval power to force Algiers to release all French captives.[81] In 1661, the Dutch, frustrated by failed diplomatic negotiations, proposed a Spanish-Dutch armada patrol the seas and attack Algiers.[82] While Spain did not implement any of these plans, until well into the eighteenth century various parties continued to propose more like them as an alternative to ecclesiastical ransom.[83]

The criticism of redemption did have its effect on the friars, who found themselves claiming economic efficiency, in clear contrast to how they perceived the redemption of captives. For centuries Trinitarians and Mercedarians had gone to court against each other, spending considerable sums on this legal competition. Now the two orders united to oppose their detractors. The friars engaged Garrett's critique of their efficiency directly. Here the bookkeeping practices Philip II had imposed on them came in handy. In reply to the accusation that during their expeditions Trinitarians and Mercedarians spent too much money on travel, food, and accommodation, the friars argued that the accounts of the royal notary disproved Garrett's figures and that "the [expenses] are not even a tenth of what the captain [Garrett] claims."[84] Prieto and his followers acknowledged some ineffectiveness by pointing out how the redeemers might increase efficiency. The critics had succeeded in forcing the Trinitarians and the Mercedarians to represent their redemptive labor in terms of economic efficiency, a portrayal that stood in tension with the orders' official self-presentation.

Commerce with Islam in general, and not only the redemption of captives, was also under fire. The crown expressed the sharpest opposition to trade with the Maghrib, and yet it constantly issued permits allowing merchants to practice such trade. In some cases the very royal officers who objected to commerce with the Maghrib and punished participating merchants were themselves involved in such trade. For example, in 1588, the Valencian viceroy Francisco de Moncada y Cardona ordered the city crier to announce in the city's squares and markets: "It has been a while since a few merchants from this city and kingdom have in Algiers agents and correspondents for the purpose of buying there goods and other things that the corsairs, enemies of our saintly catholic faith, take and rob from ships of Christians, which they capture in these seas; what these [merchants] buy in the best conditions and in a price lower than the just one, they later send back to this kingdom and other parts of the coasts of Spain in order to resell it in great profit and much gain."[85] The accusation was moral. The "goods and other things" he mentioned were the *galima*, or spoils, seized by corsairs on first taking over a ship, often in the form of clothing and foodstuffs. Since canon law and trading permits prohibited even licensed merchants from returning from North Africa with goods for sale that they had purchased there, those who did so traded illegally. The viceroy does not explicitly refer to such prohibitions in this text but claims that such trade is unjust as it comes at the expense of Christians. When, in 1631, Valencian viceroy Luis Fajardo de Zúñiga y Requesens caught three French merchants with a cargo of codfish, sardines, and conger eel bought cheaply in Algiers having been previously stolen from Christians, the viceroy punished them severely, even though the merchants had also ransomed fourteen captives on the same trip.[86] Yet the viceroy himself had ordered and received wool from Algiers in 1629.[87] At least three other Valencian viceroys were involved in such trade: Rodrigo Ponce León (viceroy from 1642 to 1645), Manuel de los Cobos (viceroy from 1659 to 1663), and Antonio Pedro Álvarez Osorio Gómez Dávila y Toledo (viceroy from 1664 to 1666) purchased slaves, dates, feathers, and barley in North Africa.[88]

The case of Majorca illustrates the tensions between military, economic, and moral priorities. From the island, debates over commerce involving the Maghrib suggest that the moral arguments advanced by both the king and the Universitat de la Ciutat i Regne de Mallorca, the representative Majorcan body, overshadowed economic interest.[89] The crown evoked canon law and other legal prohibitions and claimed that trade with Islam strengthened the power of the monarchy's enemies. Additionally, such business was counter to political reason and the public good and insulted the church and the monarchy's moral principles. Majorcans benefited from thirteenth-century papal and royal privileges that allowed the islanders to trade with Muslims in times of peace and war and that the king did not have the power to revoke. However, despite that constitutional right, the Majorcan authorities framed their appeal in terms of the common good and the king's moral duty toward his subjects in time of dire need. The Universitat de la Ciutat i Regne de Mallorca claimed it could not provision the island owing to the island's poor fiscal condition and had to commission merchants for the task. It added that since buying grain and other products was less dangerous in the Maghrib than in Sardinia, the commissioned merchants would rightly refuse to provision the island if they were not allowed to trade with the Maghrib. If the king were to prevent Majorcans from purchasing wheat and other commodities in North Africa when harvests failed, he would be acting tyrannically and against public interest.

When the debate is inspected closely, it becomes clear that both parties dissimulated. The Algerian Mediterranean was undoubtedly more dangerous to Majorcans than the Sardinian Mediterranean, but wheat and other commodities were much cheaper in Algiers or Tunis than in Sardinia or Sicily. Examination of the membership of the Universitat de la Ciutat i Regne de Mallorca reveals that many participants belonged to the same merchant families—the island's representatives were lobbying for their kin, and the public interest they evoked stood for their own economic interest. The king, in turn, referenced canon law to ground objections to trade with Islam, but the real goal was for the crown to ensure its subjects purchased provisions only from imperial territories—Sicily or Sardinia—to the benefit of the royal treasury. The trading permits the crown granted to individual merchants not only appeared in accord with canon prohibitions in being both exceptional and time limited but also strengthened the image of the king as a devout ruler, for they involved an obligation to redeem Christians. Those claims were also valid for the permissions the Majorcans obtained, equally exceptional and requiring renewal several times over the course of the seventeenth century. Moreover, licensed merchants had to pay a 10 percent tax on goods exchanged, and these merchants also often ransomed captives from the cities with which they traded. The result? Majorcan authorities were able to ensure the provisioning of the islands; local merchants and the royal treasury reaped hefty profits; and, technically, canon law was not transgressed.

Both parties advanced moral arguments: the king was protecting the souls of fellow Christians, whereas the islanders appealed to the principle of distributive justice that governed political life in the Spanish Empire. Ostensibly, the negotiations embodied an opposition of state norms and cross-boundary (maritime) practices characteristic of frontier regions such as Majorca. Moreover, this opposition seems to overlap with another: while the king supported the orders even though the redemption of captives required the export of bullion and goods to enemy territory, he sought to prevent merchants from trading with the Maghrib even though these merchants ransomed captives. Such arguments prove, however, to be in part a smoke screen put up to hide economic interests and in part a fashioning of Christian guardianship.

MAGHRIBI RULERS' SHAPING OF SPANISH REDEMPTION

Moroccan and Algerian actors participated in the shaping of human trafficking with its ties to Christian notions of salvation. In de la Cuadra's relief the Mercedarians are negotiating with a Turk, who, unhappy with their initial offer, represented by the pile of coins on the table, apparently asks for still more in return for the captives. The sculptor reminds viewers that it takes two to ransom, a seller and a buyer. The sellers in this system, Algerian pashas and Moroccan sultans and governors, participated in negotiating the price. But Maghribi actors did much more than set the price for captives. Beyond the interaction depicted, they determined which captives were available for ransom and forced slave swapping on the orders when it seemed advantageous. On at least one occasion the sultan of Morocco played the orders off against each other. Thus early modern ransom procedures also involved North African actors—rulers, on whom the following discussion expands, and merchants (Chapter 7). Ransom and its transformations cannot be understood as an exclusively Iberian Peninsular problem; account must be taken of Maghribi pressures on the system. And once Moroccan and Algerian perspectives are incorporated into the analysis, the degree to which ransom was a multilateral process becomes clear.

The Spanish crown was not alone in institutionalizing ransom, with North African actors participating in the process directly. The coordination of operations vis-à-vis the Moroccan and Ottoman authorities was more complex than securing funds and obtaining the necessary permits from the Spanish crown. An official from one of the Spanish garrisons in the Maghrib or a friar sent for the purpose from Spain had to travel to the city where the orders planned to ransom captives and purchase a safe conduct from its governor. This document prevented corsairs of the issuing authority from attacking the friars, although an Algerian safe conduct was no protection from Moroccan or Tunisian corsairs, and vice versa. The pass stipulated the number of slaves that the orders committed to buy from the governor and his men, thus imposing something of a Maghribi ransom agenda on the orders.[90] The orders often found themselves forced to purchase captives in whom they were not interested so that they would be allowed to buy the captives they wanted. For example, slave traders backed by the local authorities insisted that the orders first spend their monies on the purchase of captives who negotiated their ransom independently (*cortados*) and whose price exceeded the ransoms negotiated collectively by the friars. Maghribis also favored selling the old, the sick, deserters who had defected from the Spanish colonies in North Africa, and Protestant captives, which gave ammunition to the critics of ransom and was not in all instances in accord with the orders' religious mission.

Apart from their dealings with friars, Maghribi rulers successfully conditioned the continuation of redemption through the swapping of Muslim slaves for Christians. In the first two thirds of the seventeenth century, such exchanges (Chapter 3) were carried out mostly by individuals and only rarely by state officials. Catholic kings, like their Muslim counterparts, were reluctant to give up their slaves, and they agreed to do so only when the slaves in question had no personal history of combat and were too old or sick to pull the oar. Louis XIV of France (1638–1715) avoided such exchanges at all costs.[91] When the

Spanish crown agreed to give to captives' kin who had petitioned one of the crown's slaves the slave in question, the crown often demanded alternative slaves in lieu of the ones it agreed to release for purposes of swapping. And yet, at irregular intervals Algerian pashas or Moroccan sultans initiated negotiations with their Spanish and Italian counterparts over the exchange of captives.[92] In 1612, for example, Muhammad al-Shaykh al-Ma'mūn (1566–1613), ruler of Fez and one of three sons of Saadian sultan Ahmad al-Mansūr (1549–1603), negotiated with the Portuguese governor of Tangiers the return of several of his subjects, in exchange for Christian captives.[93] Murat Aga, an Algerian official, cut a similar deal in 1629, bartering five Turks for Christians in the Spanish fortress town of Oran.[94] In 1632 and 1633, the Algerian Agas Idris and Ahmed and the pasha Hüseyin negotiated the exchange of an Algerian Janissary with the Grand Duke of Tuscany.[95] In 1634 a local Moroccan leader whose name the sources do not reveal negotiated with the governor of El Araich the swap of two Muslims for seventy Christians.[96]

A shift toward more systematic and frequent exchanges appears to have occurred, however, from 1664, as Moroccan sultans of the Alaouite dynasty (1631–present) increasingly engaged in slave swapping, and in the eighteenth century their Algerian counterparts followed suit, creating a new fiscal category, endowment for Muslim captives, appearing in the Algerian *waqf* (inalienable charitable endowment) income registers (Chapter 3).[97] Money for the ransom of corsairs and other captives was collected in mosques, and a portion of the corsairs' booty was allocated for the purpose.[98] From the second half of the seventeenth century, then, Moroccan sultans and Algerian pashas imposed their ransom agenda on the Spaniards more forcefully than ever. This shift partly reflected the increasing power of Alaouite sultans in comparison with their Saadian predecessors (1549–1659). It probably also echoes pleas from below that the sultan rescue his enslaved subjects. Exchanges of captives between Morocco and Spain became common during the last quarter of the seventeenth century and between Algiers and Spain after 1738. In such exchanges rulers, both Christian and Muslim, performed their piety, molded their image as spiritual guardians, and responded to pressure from below to take care of their subjects. For Mediterranean Muslim rulers—Moroccan and Ottoman sultans—ransoming was one of several resources on which they could draw to support their claims to religious authority across the sea and to the caliphal title.[99] Thus when Alaouite sultan Mawlāy Isma'il ibn al-Sharif (1672–1727) established control over large swaths of territory reconquered from the Spanish presidios, he asserted his power by ransoming his Muslim subjects and imposing on the Spaniards exchange rates that favored Muslims. In 1689, when the sultan conquered El Araich, he demanded one thousand Muslims in return for the hundred Spaniards he had taken captive.[100] His eighteenth-century successors continued bartering slaves at exchange rates unfavorable to Spain, giving a Christian in return for a Muslim *and* an additional ransom fee or merchandise. They framed the redemption of Muslim captives in religious terms: in 1765 Sultan Muhammad ibn 'Abdallāh al-Khaṭīb (1710–90) asked King Carlos III (1716–88) to liberate fifteen Moroccan slaves, explaining that Islam obliged him to care for Muslim captives.[101] The majority of the roughly three thousand Muslims the sultan had ransomed were not Moroccans but rather Ottoman subjects. By redeeming Muslims from Ottoman Algiers, Tunis, or Tripoli Moroccan sultans sought to reduce the prestige of the pashas of Algiers and improve the diplomatic relations between Morocco and Tunis and Tripoli.[102] Competition over religious authority across the Mediterranean with the Moroccan sultan contributed to the Algerians' restarting slave swapping as late as in 1738. In most cases the Algerians enacted a one-to-one exchange with Spain.[103] During this century, friars were increasingly likely to transport Muslim slaves as well as silver and merchandise for exchange for Christians.

The increasing power of the Alaouites manifested itself in other ways too. Mawlāy Ismā'īl al-Sharīf's overwhelming power in the region allowed him to choose with which Spaniards he would negotiate, and the Trinitarians considered his favor worth the dispute with the Franciscans. Maghribi rulers could also privilege one order over another, thus influencing relations among Trinitarians, Mercedarians, and members of other religious orders, such as the Augustinians and the Franciscans, who were occasionally involved in redemption. For example, in 1677, Sultan Mawlāy Ismā'īl expelled the Franciscans, who had provided spiritual services and often redeemed captives, from his territories. Moreover, he allowed the Trinitarians to take over the new monastery that the Franciscans had built in Fez in 1673. The Franciscans blamed not the sultan but rather the Trinitarians, who had committed to pay the Moroccan ruler 1,500 pesos annually for the right to take the place of the Franciscans.[104]

The claims of the friars' critics referred specifically to the accommo-
dations the friars made to the Maghribi rulers: violation of the terms
stipulated in the redeemers' passports; the purchase of independently
negotiating *cortados* or defector *bienvenidos*; and the asymmetrical
exchange of slaves. As friction between Algiers and the redeemers
over the first two of these points intensified in the eighteenth century, Mercedarian Pedro Ros Valle wrote a treatise that reiterated
many of these critiques. But his conclusions were novel. Instead of
calling for more aggressive means to replace redemption, he proposed
that reforms could make redemption more efficient and might avoid
such abuses. For example, he suggested Spanish warships accompany
the friars and that their money remain onboard until the completion
of the redemption. Some of his suggestions were implemented in the
final Spanish redemption expedition, which the Trinitarians and the
Mercedarians codirected in 1768–69.[105]

CONCLUSION

Critique of the redeeming of Christians with money and goods was
almost as old as the practice itself.[106] It is tempting to read redemp-
tionist visual propaganda in light of debates over Spain's Mediterranean policy, with de la Cuadra's work, for example, clearly seeking to
encourage the faithful to contribute money for the freeing of Christians. However, such visual imagery also seems to respond to accusations of the kind Garrett and others made regarding the "quality" of
the captives the friars had redeemed. In the relief, the captives located
in the upper left corner look miserable, as if entirely dependent on
the Mercedarians. And yet they are in the prime of their lives, young,
healthy, and strong, precisely the kind of captives that redemption
opponents wanted to be saved. From this perspective, the image's
argument concerns the relationship between the friars and their mission, on the one hand, and the empire and its needs, on the other. In
risking their lives in the Maghrib and ransoming captives, the friars not only engaged in good works but also contributed to imperial
state-building, rescuing the nation's most able.

Contextualized and interpreted in this way, the relief hints at the
degree to which redemption and trade with Islam were predicated
upon one another. It also suggests how contentious these intertwined
practices were in early modern Spain. Redemption and trade became
the locus of struggles involving king, reformers, merchants, and friars,

all of whom sought to impose their definitions of the ransom of captives. The friars claimed a spiritual mission intended to rescue souls in danger, but they engaged in trade with Muslims. *Arbitristas* insisted that the friars were nothing more than failing merchants who wasted precious financial resources, bolstered the enemy, and, worse, threatened the moral purity of the nation. Finally, in condemning trade with Islam and redeeming his enslaved subjects, the king fashioned himself as a just ruler and obscured the links between redemption and trade. In reality, the king accepted trade with the Maghrib, taking his cut and contributing to its intensification by financing redemption. At stake were not only the efficiency of redemption, its morality, or a monarch's obligations to his subjects. Religious and economic arguments served the parties in their attempts to define redemption, but the debate stood for larger questions regarding Spain's Mediterranean politics, the nature of its relations with North African Islam, and the shaping of Spanish policies by Maghribi rulers.

CHAPTER 3

Negotiating Ransom, Seeking Redemption

Only a minority of captives succeeded in laying down a path to freedom. Yet virtually all captives—from the young and healthy to the old and sick, from children in danger of forced conversion to breastfeeding mothers and entire families—persistently sought ways to terminate their captivity. Steeped as they were in their precarious condition, freedom-seeking captives actively participated in this risk-fraught endeavor. In their attempts to engineer ransom, captives produced and transmitted precise information about their imprisonment to kin and home authorities while fabricating and spreading misinformation in their places of captivity. These captives cut deals with masters, pleaded with sovereigns for assistance, and begged relatives to collect alms and to commission ransom experts.

In crying out for help and in seeking assistance from individuals and institutions, captives transformed themselves into hubs within an information and exchange infrastructure partly of their own design. In turn, these hubs tightly netted together North Africa, the Mediterranean, and Europe. Information about captives—including places of captivity, ransom prices, and arrangements with ransom intermediaries—crisscrossed land and sea, carried by redeeming friars, merchants, consuls, and freed or fugitive captives. These networks were made denser by masters' encouraging their captives to contact relatives and by all captives' planning their own ransom, not necessarily successfully.

Ransom was a hostile and fleeting business prone to failure at various points. In contrast to usual commercial practice throughout

North Africa and Europe, those party to ransom agreements were not relatives or colleagues but rather potential enemies.[1] There was no trust based on long-term shared experience or mutual knowledge. While masters encouraged their captives to seek ransom, having lacked information about the captives at the time of their purchase, the masters often had expectations too high to allow them to cut a deal. Additionally, the communication channels captives depended on were unreliable. Even once masters agreed to a figure for the ransom, rulers might still reject the captive's petition for assistance or kin fail to collect the necessary money. Moreover, some ransom dealers refused to provide credit or stole the money captives' relatives sent them. Worse, some captives who achieved their freedom through loans from ransom dealers might find themselves in debtors' prison if they could not repay the advance. At the same time, the difficulty of enforcing loans across geographical and imperial boundaries made getting credit harder. Nonetheless, some captives achieved their freedom. In light of the physical violence and religious hatred that captivity generated, how could trust be established? What mechanisms enabled such deals and enforced their realization?

Part of the answer lies in the measures rulers and communities took to ransom their enslaved subjects and prevent merchants and captives from cheating one another, measures that thickened circulation of information and the infrastructure that facilitated it. This chapter addresses the related issues of trust and enforcement by examining ransom as it unfolded for captives, captors, and ransomers. Focusing on moments of friction, it explores the strategies captives employed to cope with uncertainty, how captives and masters collaborated, and how communities and rulers from across the religious divide vouched for the fair execution of ransom deals. Trust in this system was not an unconditional sentiment between captors, captives, and ransom agents of all confessions but a social relationship grounded in and guaranteed by an array of royal bureaucracies, frontier enclaves that provided safe space for exchanges, and legal instruments. The attempts of individuals to free themselves and the institutional support they received to achieve their freedom had unintended consequences. Geared toward separation of Muslims and Christians, these operations instead reproduced the very links they sought to eliminate and wove endless new ties between Spain, Morocco, and the Ottoman Maghrib.

SETTING THE PRICE

Some slave owners had little interest in ransoming their slaves. When Jerónimo de Pasamonte, who served as a galley's pacesetter, first solicited his ransom, his master refused, saying that he needed him in his galleys.[2] Diego Galán did not even receive an explanation; his master simply yelled at him, "Even if they offer me a thousand ducats, I won't sell you."[3] But other owners were interested in a deal. The first step was to set a ransom price. Over the seventeenth century ransom prices fluctuated. Serial information about prices is fragmentary, available in Trinitarian and Mercedarian sources alone, and hence concerns only the captives that members of the orders ransomed. During the sixteenth and seventeenth centuries ransom prices in Algiers ranged from 1,000 to 2,000 reales (see Table 1),[4] fantastic sums for Spanish wage laborers, whose annual wage around 1600 was likely 330 to 400 reales.[5] Scholars have suggested that variables such as age, sex, status, wealth, and professional skills determined a captive's value.[6] An eighteenth-century list of Christian "captives of importance" held in Algiers that was found in the dey's palace by nineteenth-century French colonists reflects these variables by listing captains and skippers, doctors and barbers, and priests.[7] And yet value was rarely an inherent quality of commodities, particularly in the case of captives, who were at once objects and subjects.

Captives had an advantage over their masters in that they had more information about how much money they could collect and pay. Masters interested in a deal had to search for hints and spy on captives to obtain this information and price them accordingly.[8] Captives therefore manipulated these qualities, pretending to be poor or rich, healthy or sick, trained or lacking in professional skills. Captives' accounts suggest that in order to gain an advantage, both parties tried to demonstrate reluctance to reach a deal. Jerónimo Gracián, confessor of Saint Teresa, who was held captive for two years in Tunis, described a fellow captive in his prison cell telling him, "Even if the Pasha talks about it, don't think for a second about dealing with the ransom or talking [about it]. Rather, answer that you're ready to die here and that there is nobody in a Christian land who remembers you, because there is no other way of winning back your liberty."[9] Gracián interpreted this advice as a recommendation to feign disinterest at home as a negotiating tactic, which he took. Similarly, the orders instructed the friars not to show interest in the captives they

Table 1. Average prices for captives ransomed by Trinitarians and Mercedarians from Algiers, 1575–1692

Years	1575–94	1609–26	1627–44	1645–59	1660–75	1676–86	1687–92
Price (in reales)	1,000	1,800	1,350	2,000	1,350	1,680	1,900

Source: José Antonio Martínez Torres, *Prisioneros de los infieles: Vida y rescate de los cautivos cristianos en el Mediterráneo musulmán (siglos XVI–XVII)* (Barcelona: Edicions Bellaterra, 2004), 144.

most desired to redeem in negotiation.[10] The Mercedarians and the Trinitarians strongly discouraged captives from negotiating independently at all, feeling they were superior negotiators. They claimed they would not redeem *cortados*—their term for slaves who had "cut" their own deals, always at prices higher than those the friars would have negotiated collectively. However, the authorities in the Maghrib often included *cortados*, at the price the captives themselves had negotiated, in transactions that liberated the captives the friars particularly wished to free. Similarly, Italian Jews who ran communal organizations that specialized in the ransom of Jews held captive in Malta expressed anger when captives negotiated a ransom fee independently of the organizations' agents.[11] The advice to pretend to have little interest in the commodity seems to be a universal truth for bargaining. However, in the case of ransom negotiations, as the commodity being exchanged was the freedom of one of the parties to the transactions, pressure from the captor to cut a deal was hard to resist; many captives succumbed and agreed to an exceptionally high price.

Many captives negotiated a price knowing full well they could not arrange the sums of money they promised. They did so aware that their master's hope for payment might incentivize him to treat them better, at least for a time. Others tried to negotiate a sum they genuinely thought they could raise. Laurent d'Arvieux, the French emissary sent to Tunis in 1666, claimed that well-to-do Spaniard captives refused to pretend they were poor because they were too arrogant.[12] Even if he exaggerated, his description stresses the active role captives played in fixing their own ransom price. Feigned detachment might convince a master to drop the price to an amount that interested the captive, but given that masters knew captives had an incentive to dissimulate, reaching that point might take a while. Time was

the only resource available to captives, but they also had greater interest in speeding negotiations to end their hardships. In general captives' prices decreased the longer they remained in captivity, at least
among those the orders redeemed,[13] and their owners might wish
to raise cash quickly for any number of reasons. In his autobiography Gracián claimed the pasha decided to sell him for a fair price
because of an acute need for money. But the letters he sent from Tunis
suggest his grasp of the pasha's finances was tenuous. In June 1594,
he excitedly wrote to his mother that the best circumstances for an
agreement were when the pasha ended his triennial term, and further
letters betray a similar confidence in November and December of that
year.[14] However, the pasha did not sign the deal that set him free until
the spring of 1595.

The case of João Mascarenhas suggests the complicated manip-
ulations a captive might attempt. Mascarenhas was held captive in
Algiers from 1621 to 1626. While recovering from an illness, possibly during one of the plagues that occasionally ravaged the region, he
persuaded a Morisco doctor to tell his master he was about to die.[15]
Mascarenhas was taking a chance. Plagues could lead to a sharp rise
in ransom prices, as happened in Algiers in 1691, when slaves' average price skyrocketed.[16] But a dead captive was worth nothing, and
his owner agreed to the price Mascarenhas offered.[17]

Mascarenhas's master may have been particularly ineffective in
gathering information about his captives. Emanuel d'Aranda, a captive in Tunis in 1640, mentions a merchant who provided mail services and surreptitiously read captives' letters to get information about
their value.[18] He also described slaves who served masters as informers, getting new captives to reveal information about themselves that
the informers then passed on to their masters, who went shopping in
the slave market and later negotiated profitable ransom deals.[19] At the
same time, there were always longer-standing captives who warned
new captives not to share personal information with anyone. The way
d'Aranda describes it, dissimulation was the norm. Captives could
not even trust members of their own confession. Moreover, during
the negotiation process, things could easily get out of control as in
cases of ill-intended or sincere misidentification and in the spread of
rumors.

In the absence of reliable information, masters trusted rumors,
even though they were often false. The Flemish Jean-Baptiste Gramaye, held captive in Algiers between 1619 and 1625, noted that a

fellow captive might "make of you someone who you are not: from a priest they make you a bishop; from a gentleman, a duke; from a soldier, a captain; from a mercenary, a merchant."[20] Jerónimo Gracián described such an experience, saying that some Christian captives "maliciously" lied about him to the pasha of Tunis, alleging that Gracián was an archbishop on his way to Rome for elevation to a cardinalate rather than a simple priest. The pasha then demanded 30,000 golden escudos for Gracián's freedom because of his supposed status.[21] At a later date, another anonymous party spread a rumor among the Janissaries that Gracián was an Inquisitor who had had some of the militia's soldiers burned at the stake in Spain. The Algerians almost put him to death because of this hearsay. Subsequently, a corsair told the pasha that Gracián was so important that in return for his freedom, the pasha could bring about the release of ra'īs Murat, a corsair held captive in Naples.[22] Finally, in what Gracián later insisted was nationalistic retaliation for the Spanish occupation of Sicily, a Sicilian merchant "insinuated in the town square" that Gracián was a rich person—"they would pay at least six thousands escudos for him."[23] The numerous rumors spread about Gracián border on the absurd, as he recognized: "If in Christian land, I was so criticized and passed over that I was not even worthy of being the cook of any religion in the world, in the land of Moors, I was promoted to be a great archbishop on his way to Rome to become cardinal and in a few days to become the *gran papaz* which is what [the Moors] call the pope."[24] Despite their limited trustworthiness, rumors regarding captives' identities could have an immense influence on captives' ability to negotiate a reasonable ransom agreement.

Employing a network of informers and reading captives' letters were probably secondary recourses for masters. For many captors, it was enough to examine their slaves' *hexis*, or bodily dispositions.[25] The slave owner's trained gaze easily read the captive's body, which often betrayed a performance of poverty. When Aranda, for example, tried to convince his owner's wife he was a simple soldier, she replied, "say whatever you'd like; nevertheless you're not like Grégoire"—referring to her Galician gardener, who had been a fisherman in his village, a slave with "the right body for work."[26] Many captives described slave masters inspecting their bodies and teeth in the slave market, estimating and calculating their potential exchange and labor value.[27] Given the brutalities of poverty, the exercise was illuminating.

Factors beyond the captives' own condition, such as political circumstances, could also radically alter their value. Peace agreements between European and North African polities obliged them to set free each other's enslaved subjects, so long as those subjects had not publicly converted to their captors' religion. When conditions seemed ripe for peace, prices fell.[28] Algerians and Tunisians forcibly converted Christians when the state signed peace agreements to avoid liberating them. While the orders and others had no interest in redeeming converted captives, the latter continued to provide manpower for their masters. At the same time, captives knew that the threat that they might convert could lead the friars to take extra measures to free them, even if initially the friars had not intended to redeem them or had lacked the means.[29]

Sometimes, masters and captives plotted together to manipulate the latter's value by conjuring up disease or potential conversion. Laugier de Tassy, the French consul in Algiers in the 1720s, reported that captives pretended to be badly ill or expressed a desire to convert to Islam, declarations masters strongly backed up in order to increase the captives' price when negotiating with the friars. They would then give the captives a percentage of the monies they raised.[30] Here again captives had an active role in the ransom process, as competitive negotiation could ultimately become a collaborative endeavor by masters and slaves, improving both their positions.

Captives, captors, and ransomers could also influence captives' value in cases of slave swapping. In theory, slaves of similar standing were exchanged one for another, but sometimes one party would inflate the value of its slaves. In 1589, for example, Spaniards held captive in Algiers sent a complaint to the Council of War about the king's approval of several ransom deals, which included the trading of Christians and Muslims. The captives expressed fury over the rates of exchange on which the deals were based.[31] In the complaint, they argued that the crown freed rich Muslims in return for poor Christians—in other words, that the king paid too much and got too little: "In Barbary, they have been making a profit by giving a poor Christian for a wealthy Moor from your Majesty's slaves and even if it is true that one engages in good works when a captive leaves [captivity] in return for a Moor, one causes damage to the rest of the captives. [B]ecause following that the [Moors] raise the ransom saying that such a poor Christian won them a Moor that was worth that much . . . and as a result ransoms cost a lot."[32] The crown, the captives argued, was inflating ransom rates and sabotaging their chances of returning home. In response, the king ordered a halt to such exchanges, citing the reasons listed in the captives' complaint. Their grievances demonstrate that the king's actions could have an immediate effect on the ransom market in Algiers and thereby on slaves' lives, but they also show that captives could attempt to control the rates on which exchange was based and could do so from captivity. Captives were victims of the system, but they were not therefore without the power to manipulate and even influence that system.

Volition and strategizing join environmental (for example, the plague) and political (for example, peace agreements) factors in influencing captives' value and determining prospects for their ransom. In spite of the deficiencies of the market, and in particular the lack of information, parties did come to understandings. Once a ransom fee had been agreed, captives and sellers could start to collaborate, hastening on the ransoming process by facilitating communication between captives and their families.

COMMUNICATING CAPTIVITY

Captivity and attempts to arrange ransom generated an immense amount of paperwork. Excluding cases of captives who fled their masters and those of captives freed when the galleys on which they rowed were seized, rescue necessitated communication with one's kin, home authorities, and individual or institutional ransom agents.[33] Thus masters encouraged and even pressured their slaves to write home. Writing was a common practice for Christian and Muslim slaves, alluded to by both archival records and literary sources. A vita of an Augustinian monk written in 1648 mentions a Sevillian noblewoman who had a North African Muslim maid. According to the story, the maid's mother kept writing letters to her daughter in which she promised to ransom her.[34] It is likely that the noblewoman, her maid, and her maid's mother never existed, let alone were engaged in an epistolary exchange, but the monk's decision to plot these events in his vita is telling for the volume of slaves' letters that crisscrossed the sea. This kind of correspondence followed the routes of even the most humble of slaves, regardless of gender or religious identity, who were able to engage in this practice of writing (independently or with the assistance of scribes) and paperwork. These letters accomplished various functions: planning ransom; maintaining status in a home community (see Chapter 4); enacting kinship and political ties across the sea to improve living conditions as a slave (see Chapter 5); and transmitting strategic information and intelligence (see Chapter 6). However, the possibility of ransom, the desire to unite with kin, and greed were their principal impulses, with generating a ransom deal often their main function. For example, a letter sent by an Algerian enslaved in Majorca to his home in 1692 listed nine of his relatives and indicated how much he hoped each of them would contribute toward his ransom.[35] Poor kin in Spain would petition their rulers for begging licenses, in order to allow them to collect money to be used to pay the ransom. Soldiers asked the crown to commit the salary their capture had prevented them from collecting, and also requested grants.[36] Relatives were the conduit for transferring the funds to the Trinitarians or Mercedarians, although some journeyed themselves or hired an intermediary to conclude the ransom. Kin might look for the slave who had been promised in exchange for their captured relative. Writing and conveying information was nearly always a prerequisite for planning and executing ransom. Given the volume of captivity in the period, thousands of captives must have written and sent such letters.

The stories recounted in petitions made to rulers always began with the moment of capture.[37] Descriptions of life in captivity were sparse and conveyed either the captive's misery or his heroism. After their Algerian captor had allowed him to return to Spain to find money for his wife's ransom, for example, captive Miguel de la Varrera emphasized his unhappiness and that of his pregnant wife when, in 1672, he petitioned for an alms-collecting patent that would allow him to raise the funds he needed.[38] In 1692, the Algerian Bive Muhammad Rex complained in a letter about his Majorcan mistress's starving, beating, and chaining him at night.[39] The widow Elvira Garcia stated in her 1594 petition that her only son, held captive in Morocco, was being mistreated for refusing to convert.[40] The mention of the risk of forced conversion to Islam might have reflected masters' attempts to scare their captives into urging their kin to send them money, but Garcia likely hoped the magistrates would recognize the merit and the pressing necessity of her petition because of this threat to a Christian soul.

Some captives described at length the variety of services they had rendered to the crown during their time in captivity. For instance, in 1612 Simón Méndez recounted in his petition how as a captive he had established a position at the court of the Moroccan contender to the sultanate Mawlāy Shaykh, and he had received from the latter favors and valuables, which "he spent on ransoming [other] captives and helping their needs and in accompanying them on their way out of captivity, and he provided the agents of your majesty with many reports about matters concerning the service of your majesty the favors he received."[41] These words hinted that Méndez sought the king's help as an obligation because he had been captured while performing services for the king. Such petitions were based on an ethic of distributive justice that authors shared with their monarch.[42] In their petitions, soldiers in particular referenced the likelihood that they could provide future service. In the case of soldiers captured during their military service, this promise sealed the story line that framed their petition.

Masters, slaves, kin, and officials all contributed to the making of any petition, which like other bureaucratic autobiographies was a polyphonic artifact generated over time and by various voices.[43] In the case of ransom based on an exchange of slaves, a master would dictate to the petitioner the name, description, and place of enslavement of the slave he hoped to ransom. Diego López de Acosta, for instance, wrote a letter to Tomas Velásquez de Oliver explaining that his master would exchange him for a Muslim slave. He directed Velásquez de Oliver to buy "in Sanlúcar [de Barrameda in western Andalusia] a Turk who lives in the street of the Bretons, and his owner is called Nicolás Rubin," information doubtlessly dictated to him by his master, who must have received it from the "Turk" he referenced.[44]

The need to authenticate petitioners' claims often extended the paper trail, generating more communication and thereby maintaining the networks through which the original was transmitted. While official guidelines regarding which records might heighten the merit of a petition were never issued, petitioners often provided documentation such as letters, testimonies, and reports—and the more, the better. Comments on such supporting material as well as their tone attest to the importance of these records, which also reflect how captives and their families tried to accommodate the logic of bureaucracy.[45] Magistrates expressed doubts about poorly supported petitions, such as that of the Franciscan Antonio Castro, who in 1587 submitted nothing but the *memorial* unfolding his story and the help he requested.[46] The better-supported claims usually achieved the desired outcome, whether in convincing captives' kin to send money, provide credit, or start collecting the necessary ransom.

The power to authenticate claims about captivity emerged from varying combinations of testimonies of free and unfree individuals, personal letters, and institutional documentation. Since captives and their kin were the source of petitions and their supporting information, magistrates might have good reason to doubt their truthfulness. To verify the initial information, they required additional information, thus generating cycles of information gathering and transmitting that often failed to provide the required authentication. The case of Christian captive Gaspar Méndez and Muslim slave Hamad Musa, who hoped to be exchanged one in return for the other, demonstrates one such cycle. Probably in the 1580s, Gaspar Méndez was taken captive and enslaved in Morocco. He sent Juana de los Santos, his wife, information about his place of detention and the name of a Muslim slave, Hamad Musa, in exchange for whom Méndez's captor— Hamad Musa's wife—was willing to free Méndez. The problem was that Hamad Musa, an oarsman on a royal galley, had been identified and registered at the time of his capture as a corsair; for this reason the Spanish fleet officers refused to release him to Juana de los Santos. De los Santos's claim that Hamad Musa was a simple person (baxo), not a corsair, and therefore no threat to Spaniards, was not enough to convince the royal administrators, and she had to contact her husband and urge him to find witnesses who would testify to Hamad Musa's true identity. A group of Christian captives provided a deposition, but fearing that such an arrangement might not satisfy the royal officials, de los Santos made sure that Luis de la Guerra, a Portuguese Trinitarian held as a hostage in Tétouan, vouched for the witnesses' declaration. In addition to presenting these statements, de los Santos claimed that Luis de Matienzo, a Mercedarian who had spent time in Tétouan, could identify Luis de la Guerra's signature.[47] Thus the plan involved various free and enslaved Christians and Muslims and many documents. Authority was distributed, on the one hand, among captives, friars, spouses, and fleet officers and, on the other hand, among textual artifacts such as Méndez's initial letter, the slave registry of the fleet officers, legal depositions by witnesses, the testimony of a reputable witness who vouched for the deposition, and a signature vouching for the authenticity of the handwriting of the testimony of a witness.

That the subjects of the magistrates' observation and evaluation were also their sources of information might trap crown and petitioners in epistemological loops of information, doubt, more information, and more doubt. Interactions among captives, kin, and bureaucrats and the administrative cycles they generated reappear throughout the centuries: captors identified and registered the captives; captives informed their wives, sisters, or mothers about their captivity and listed the moves necessary for their release; and wives took a range of steps involving the most powerful men in the realm to prove the veracity of their claims. These negotiations were mediated by a host of records, all originating in captives' initial letters.

CREDIT AND HOSTAGES

Most ransom deals required captives, or the agents who assisted them, to pay the full agreed ransom before they could leave captivity, but captives might also be released upon a promise to pay their ransom after they arrived home. The fair execution of such agreements had to be vouched for by either the ruler or institutions from the captive's homeland or by merchants based in the city in which the captive in question was imprisoned. Emanuel d'Aranda's owner agreed to send some of his slaves on a ship to Livorno in Italy as long as they would remain in prison until he received their ransom.[48] The Algerian owner of Melchor Zúñiga, a captive-turned-redeemer, as well as an acute observer of life in Algiers in the first half of the seventeenth century, allowed Zúñiga to leave to Spain after the latter provided guarantees that vouched for his return. It took Zúñiga two years to collect the money for his ransom, as well as for the ransom of other Spaniards enslaved in Algiers, but then he returned to Algiers, paid his debt to his owner, and was formally freed.[49] These agreements carried a higher price, given the risk that captives would fail to return: d'Aranda's owner offered to give him his liberty for 25 percent less if he paid immediately rather than being conditionally released.[50] Captives who negotiated a conditional release often had to pay at least part of their ransom before they left their place of captivity. Their manumission documents (*l'instrum de la libertà*) would be dispatched to them only after they had paid their debt in full. The Venetian communal organization dedicated to the ransom of Jewish captives objected to such deals and in principle refused to serve as guarantor for the obligation taken by redeemed captives. The logic behind this decision was that the organization could not hold captive a person who had paid part of his ransom and had left his place of captivity, even if formally he was not yet free. Thus, in theory and often in practice, the organization expected family members to vouch for such debts. And yet the organization's officials understood that evading payment entailed risking the relationship with the authorities in Malta (where most of those they liberated had been enslaved), and not paying the outstanding ransom when families did not pay was never considered.[51] Christian captors also set free Muslim captives, taking their word that they would pay the ransom later. In his history of Oran written in the first decade of the seventeenth century, Diego Suárez Montañés describes how a Turkish military officer captured by Spanish soldiers was released by the governor of Oran, Martín de Córdoba, on his word that he would pay his ransom just a few days later.[52]

There were alternative, sometime complementary, ways to arrange credit. The case of Miguel de la Varrera, who left his wife as a hostage while he sought to pay the negotiated ransom for her, was not unusual. Similarly, Bárbara Truiol, from the island of Menorca, described in a petition sent to the Council of Aragon in 1665 how she, her husband, and their children had been captured by corsairs and taken to Tunis. Her husband and three-year-old child stayed as hostages, while she and the rest of their children returned home to seek the funds to pay their ransom.[53] In 1597, an old, one-armed Muslim slave in Melilla negotiated his ransom for 600 ducats. He received permission to leave the garrison for eight months to collect the money. Four Muslims had to wait for his payment to arrive before they too were allowed to leave Melilla.[54] Similar agreements were negotiated between Muslim slaves and slave owners in seventeenth-century Oran.[55] Such alternative forms of credit were not limited to specific social classes, and testimonies like Truiol's provide some of the oldest evidence of the capture of women, although husbands left their wives hostage more often.[56]

The redeeming friars often left hostages as a form of credit, as in the case of the Mercedarians left behind to redeem four young Christians in 1661. Mercedarian friar Luis de Matienzo stayed in Tétouan from 1578 until 1583 as security for a 12,000-ducat loan that his fellow friars received and immediately spent on the ransom of captives.[57] In the 1580s, the Portuguese Trinitarian Luis de Guerra, whom we encountered above vouching in the case of Juana de los Santos and her captive husband, had stayed in the city as a pledge on behalf of the Trinitarian order.[58] The most common scenario in which friars left hostages was that, having exhausted their ransom funds, members of the orders on a ransom mission discovered children or women in danger of conversion to Islam. Given that the orders traveled to Maghribi cities on average only once every three years, the commitment the hostage made was significant.

SLAVE SWAPPING

Many captives obtained their liberty in return for another slave, as part of an exchange of people. Captives' kin and the ransomers they had commissioned and on occasion the friars carried out such exchanges.[59] In some cases, especially those involving captives from humbler backgrounds, the exchange in fact increased the demand for slaves and could involve more than one merchant or ransom intermediary. In January 1677 Alonso Bermúdez from Huelva purchased a Muslim slave from an unidentified Spaniard, hoping to trade the slave for his brother, Pedro Bermúdez, who was held captive in Tétouan. Since Alonso Bermúdez knew nobody with the right connections, he authorized Joseph Manuel, also from Huelva, to take the Muslim slave to Cadiz and commission there a merchant with contacts in the Maghrib.[60] A third merchant in the process, commissioned by Pedro's Tétouanite owner, likely took Pedro to the Spanish garrison in Ceuta or to Tangiers for the exchange of slaves. Purchases such as Bermúdez's, which occurred solely for swapping, indicate that profit and labor were not the only forces driving the Mediterranean bondage market. There were individuals who purchased slaves only in order to exchange them for their relatives held captive. Moreover, enslavements of Christians and Muslims were, in some cases, interdependent. When Spaniards who were part of such ransom coalitions petitioned the crown for one of its slaves, they might agree to provide another slave in his place, intensifying this interdependence and pointing to the self-perpetuating nature of these violent practices and exchanges. While those party to such deals were seeking to resolve a violent outcome of piracy, in so doing they perpetuated that very practice: one slave was to be exchange for a second, who in turn was exchanged for a third.

Common law (*Derecho consuetudinario*) required individual slave owners to hand over their slaves to petitioners in return for a payment that replicated what they had paid for the slaves. When slave owners refused, the courts, which supported the custom, took the side of captives' kin and forced slave masters to sell their slaves without any markup on the original price.[61] For example, in 1675 Amaro López, a resident of Ceuta taken captive and imprisoned in Tétouan, turned to the governor of Ceuta, the Count of Torres Verdas, for help. López's Muslim master was willing to let him go only in exchange for a Muslim slave who was owned by another resident of Ceuta. López offered to pay the latter what he had originally paid for the slave, but to no avail. He appealed to the count, who forced the Christian slave owner to accept the original purchase price in payment for the slave.[62]

Melchor de Zúñiga described a similar custom. Algerian women who needed a Christian slave owned by other Algerians to exchange for their enslaved husband, son, or brother asked the slave owner to sell them the slave in question for the price the owner had originally paid for the slave. When slave owners refused to sell their slaves, the women would plead with the divan for help. The authorities would then order the slave owner to sell the slave, and if the owner resisted, he was forced to give up his slave without any monetary compensation.[63] According to captive Tamayo y Velarde, writing in 1645, the authorities severely punished slave owners who refused to give up their slaves in such cases.[64] To support this agenda, Algerian rulers could evoke Maliki legal scholars (both the Maliki and the Hanafi rites were practiced in Algiers), who debated this issue for centuries and backed up this practice in fatwas they issued. For example, in his *Al-mi'yār al-mu'rib* (The Clear Standard), the most influential collection of fatwas in the early modern Islamic west, Ahmad ibn Yahyā al-Wansharīsī's (1430 or 1431–1508) cites two fatwas on the question of just price for a Christian slave to be used in exchange for a Muslim issued by twelfth-century Andalusian judge Ibn Rushd and thirteenth- and fourteenth-century Moroccan jurist and theologian Ibn al-Hājj al-'Abdarī. The fatwas and their inclusion in *Al-mi'yār al-mu'rib* testify to the continuous relevance of the issue for Muslims in Al-Andalus and later in the Maghrib. Tellingly, al-Wansharīsī lists the fatwas in the chapter on sales rather than together with other fatwas concerning captives in the chapter about war. The reason was that at stake was not only the issue of Muslims' liberty but also the question of usury, prohibited in Islam. In the earliest fatwa, Ibn Rushd responds to a problem similar to one that unfolded in Oran in 1675. A Christian owner of a Muslim captive agrees to set the captive free only in return for a Christian enslaved in Muslim territory. The Muslim owner of the Christian slave refuses to give up his slave, even for a price higher than the slave's current value. For Muslims, the problem in such an exchange, of exchanging an object for more than its value, is that the markup could be perceived as prohibited usury. Despite this worry, Ibn Rushd determined that the owner of the Christian slave should give him up in return for more than what he paid or the slave's current value. The price should not be determined by the Christian's physical condition but rather in accord with the wealth of the Christian's family and the ransom his family would have paid had it redeemed the slave for cash. In contrast, Ibn al-Hājj objects to paying the owner of the Christian more than his slave's value. Instead, the owner should receive the original sum he had paid for the slave and the maintenance expenses he accrued while owning the slave. One could read these disagreements as two ways of evading the prohibition on usury, but even if this was not the case, these fatwas show that Maliki law supported slaves and their kin in a way similar to Christian law.[65]

Women were often involved in such exchange trading, interacting with the most powerful men in the realm in so doing. For instance, in the 1580s, Fatima Algajon of Fez petitioned Ahmad al-Mansūr, Saadi sultan of Morocco, for assistance in redeeming her son ʿAbdallāh, who after his capture by Spanish forces had been put to the oar on the royal galley La Quimera. The sultan gave the Spanish slave Hernando Esteban to Algajon as a gift, in order that he could be exchanged for ʿAbdallāh. Algajon prompted Esteban to write to his wife, Catalina Díaz, and ask her to obtain ʿAbdallāh, which she did by promising to provide the royal fleet with a stronger replacement.[66]

A similar story of an exchange led by women illustrates the bureaucratic trajectories of the petitions Spaniards submitted to the crown. In this case, the sultan of Morocco had captured a ship in 1593. Diego García, an eighteen-year-old cabin boy who had become a galley slave at the time of capture, wrote to his mother, Elvira García, a poor widow from the city of the Port of Santa Maria, near Cadiz. García did all she could to ransom her son but without success. Two years later, a Moroccan widow whose son Ahmed was enslaved on the Spanish royal galley La Granada contacted García, offering to ask the king of Morocco for Diego and then trade him for Ahmed. García immediately addressed the Spanish king through his Council of War, recounting the sufferings of her child and asking him to facilitate the exchange.[67] The Council of War contacted the contador, the person in charge of the books listing the slaves working in the galleys, and asked him to ascertain Ahmed's status. The council could thus determine the Muslim slave's role on the ship on which he was held, the circumstances of his capture, and his current age.

The Spanish crown was reluctant to accept this kind of deal, and throughout the early modern period it issued orders to the royal fleet that prohibited the concession of galley slaves to individuals.[68] The crown had three reasons for its resistance: (1) the royal fleet was in constant need of slaves; (2) Spanish bureaucrats feared that Muslim ru'asā' (the plural form of ra'īs) would revert to their earlier practice of attacking Spanish ships and coasts and capturing Spaniards; and (3) although the crown prohibited the handing over of enslaved Muslim corsairs to Christian petitioners hoping to save their kin, it might support, and even initiate, such exchanges when powerful nobles or officers were to be redeemed. The somewhat confusing classification system of Muslim slaves developed by the bureaucrats of the Spanish fleet reflects these reasons. The fleet officers distinguished between "corsairs" or "sea captains" on the one hand and "Moors of ransom" (moros de rescate) and "Moors of value" (moros de consideración) on the other. Somewhat ironically, these petitioners were granted the slave they asked for only if he was not classified as "a moor of ransom," in which case the crown kept him for future exchange of rich or important figures. For example, on December 11, 1653, the crown ordered the fleet officers to keep aside eighteen Muslim captives "of value" and exchange them only for ecclesiastics or special individuals.[69] Yet the order as well as the abundance of royal objections to petitions by individuals requesting to be allowed to exchange royal galley slaves for their enslaved kin attest to the persistence and pervasiveness of concessions of royal slaves to petitioners.

If the fleet officers decided that the slave in question was a corsair or of value, they would recommend that the king deny the favor. Problems arose when petitioner and contador disagreed about a slave's status, sometimes as the result of an incorrect or questionable assessment of the Muslim slave at the time of his capture or when he was delivered to the fleet officers. Captains who caught Muslims sometimes falsely claimed they were corsairs in order to receive a greater bonus.[70] When petitioners' requests were refused because of the standing the crown attributed to the requested slave, petitioners tried to trace others who knew the slave in question and could testify to his status.[71]

Barring objections, petitioners could advance to the next step, which involved a twofold exchange. If and when the crown finally agreed to concede its galley slaves, it demanded other slaves in their place. While the slaves that petitioners sought were usually old, weak, and sick—or at least that was how petitioners portrayed them in their requests—the slaves that the crown demanded in their place had to be young, healthy, and strong. For example, in 1644 the Algerian oarsman Haci Mahmud, who offered the crown an alternative rower in exchange for his liberty, described himself as "seventy years old . . . broken and unable to pull the oar" and the slave he would provide as "young and strong."[72] In cases like these, successful ransoming did not decrease the number of slaves in the system and in fact intensified the administrative and economic connections that sustained it.

In exchanges like that of Elvira García's son, some likely had a happy end. In her case, Elvira first obtained a young slave whom she offered to the galley's officers in return for Ahmed. Having secured Ahmed, she obtained the necessary permission to exchange him. In their reply to the query from the Council of War regarding Ahmed's status, the fleet officers indicated that according to their books Ahmed "was not an ra'is, nor of importance, nor of ransom." The officers had in effect given a green light to the exchange, and Elvira was able to trade Ahmed for her son Diego.

Slave swapping, redemption by friars, and ransom by merchants were complementary modalities of ransom. While not including slave swapping, the 1624 Mercedarian expedition to Morocco illustrates the point. The friars' first and only stop on Maghribi soil was often the Spanish presidio of Tangiers. Instead of leaving Tangiers and traveling to Tétouan, they invited Tangier's governor and officials from Tétouan to come together at their residency in Tangiers, where negotiations were completed. Additionally, in anticipation of the friars' visit and acting on behalf of the Spanish king and the Mercedarians, the governor of Tangiers arranged the ransom of seventy-one captives held in the city of Salé. The governor paid the entire ransom for a small number of captives; for others he paid part of the ransom while the captives themselves paid the remainder, either from their own sources or from credit they obtained from local merchants; and for others yet, the governor paid part of the ransom and local merchants paid the remainder. In a few cases, the governor negotiated directly with the slave's captors, while in some instances he negotiated with merchants who had bought the captives from their initial owners.[73]

RISKS

Ransom dealers had a bad reputation among captives, who accused merchants, state agents, and on occasion even friars of misusing or embezzling captives' money or of facilitating their arrest for unpaid debt upon their return home.[74] Emanuel d'Aranda claimed, as we have heard, that a merchant provided slave owners with information about captives' financial status, having read the letters he carried. In a letter of July 1594 Jerónimo Gracián warned his friends against dealing with merchants lest they steal the funds,[75] and in a further letter sent the same year, he added, "Based on my experience I know there is no greater damage to captives than giving money to merchants, and only because of that there are innumerable captives who will never leave their captivity."[76] Although Gracián would be redeemed through a merchant, merchants did try to take advantage of captives' helplessness. The Spanish captive Jerónimo de Pasamonte claimed he received his money from a merchant only after he had threatened the merchant with a knife.[77] Even a merchant with good intentions might fail his client. For example, when Gaspar de los Reyes ransomed himself in 1670 after twelve years of captivity, he struck agreements with other captives before he left for Spain, promising to liberate them upon his return. Once in Spain, he collected the money the captives' relatives had saved for them and negotiated new deals with others in Málaga, promising to ransom their family members who were being held in Algiers. Before leaving Spain for Algiers, he invested all the money in Málaga's famous sweet wine, planning to sell his investment at a great profit. Unfortunately, upon arriving in Algiers, he discovered seven French ships unloading their wine cargo. Wine prices collapsed. The merchant had lost the money and could not execute the agreements for which he had been paid.[78] Similar scams are reflected in the letters Haci Ahmed bin al-Haci, dey of Algiers, exchanged with the Spanish authorities in 1695 and 1696 regarding a Neapolitan merchant who had committed to ransoming Algerians from Naples but had failed to do so.[79] The presence of charlatans who had neither the contacts nor the skills they claimed was another reason for distrusting ransomers.

State officials also abused their power and at times took advantage of captives. In 1579, Spanish soldiers held captive in Istanbul drafted a complaint to the Spanish crown. It addressed the behavior of Giovanni Margliani, a Milanese operating in Istanbul as an ambassador for the Spanish king, on whose behalf Margliani had negotiated a truce with the Ottomans.[80] The captives claimed that Margliani had misused the money he had received from the crown for their ransom, for instead of spending it on their rescue, he had used it to ransom Milanese captives.[81] Further, the viceroys of Sicily and Naples, representatives of the crown, had offered them insufficient assistance within the Habsburg Italian lands. Ransomed Spanish captives who traveled west to return home usually stopped in Sicily, Naples, or other Spanish Italian territories. Upon their arrival, the newly released who had been soldiers expected the authorities to provide them with financial support that would allow them to pay their debt to the intermediaries who had ransomed them. The prisoners in Istanbul called on the king to order his viceroys to assist the captives more efficiently: "[His majesty] would be served by ordering the viceroys of Sicily and Naples that whenever a slave is liberated . . . [the viceroys], without delays and excuses, find out the debt [the crown] owes such a man . . . [and] order that he be paid so that he could pay his creditor, because it happens that it takes six months and sometimes even a year to verify the said sum [owed to the captive]."[82] The authors of the petition wrote on behalf of captured soldiers to whom the crown owed salaries for their years of service prior to their captivity. The soldiers who managed to pay their own ransom did so by borrowing large sums from intermediaries; if they were unable to repay their debt, they might find they had won their freedom only to land in debtors' prison.

Designated spaces of exchange, legal instruments, and Mediterranean rulers protected captives from crooked ransomers and ransomers from crooked captives seeking to avoid settling their debt. Trading zones located in the Ottoman Empire, the Spanish and Portuguese forts of the Maghrib and the Atlantic coast of Morocco, or Italian free ports provided safe spaces where the captives could be sure they would not be sold back into slavery immediately upon paying the intermediary and where intermediaries could assume they would be compensated upon the release of captives they ransomed. When the merchant who held Jerónimo de Pasamonte's money first refused to hand it over, Pasamonte went to the Venetian *bailo*, or embassy, in Istanbul, where "they provide justice."[83] He turned to more violent, though effective, means only when political tensions between Spain and Venice barred his entry. Tabarka, an island near Tunis that the Spaniards leased to the Genoese, was also such a haven.[84] The island's location—only 80 miles from Tunis, 216 miles from Mazara del Vallo

(Sicily), and 317 miles from Algiers—and the fact that the Algerian and Tunisian authorities respected its autonomy while benefiting from the functions it fulfilled made it a perfect space for the exchange of Muslim and Christian captives.[85] The Spanish ambassador in Genoa stressed Tabarka's value in 1582 and again in 1603 in reports he sent to Madrid: "the only benefit of that place is the ransom of Christians, [since] the corsairs of Bizerte, Annaba, and all the coast of Barbary go there."[86] Spanish forts and towns in North Africa also provided safe spaces for intermediaries to exchange the captives they ransomed. Ceuta, only fourteen miles from Algeciras in Spain, and Moroccan Tétouan, located only twenty-eight miles from Ceuta, filled similar functions for the western tip of North Africa. In 1646, for example, Algerians who hoped to ransom their kin enslaved in Spain bought Diego Hernández, a Christian captive, for that purpose. They hired Sid Ahmed, an Algerian residing in Tétouan, and ordered him to take Hernández to Ceuta to meet Domingo Alvales, a Christian intermediary representing Hernández's wife. Alvales had to hand over to Sid Ahmed the relative of the Algerians and in return receive Diego Hernández.[87] A decade later, Diego López de Acosta, held captive in Algiers, was trying to engineer his exchange for a Muslim enslaved in Sanlúcar de Barrameda. He sent instructions to a Spanish friend and asked him to buy the Muslim slave: "Send him to Ceuta with heavy guard, and make him write [to me telling me] to leave [Algiers] to Tétouan in order that the exchange will be executed there *as is the custom* [my emphasis]."[88] De Acosta's reference to custom highlights the institutionalization of the unwritten protocols that governed the exchange and transfer of captives to and from such cities. He clearly wrote with the expectation that captives knew about such conventions and expected them to be respected and operative.

Ransom did not always confer immediate freedom. Some recently freed captives were transformed back into prisoners immediately upon their arrival in home territories. They discovered that authorities in towns and garrisons bound under the jurisdiction of the captives' rulers protected and served the needs of slave owners and go-betweens. Livorno serves as a good example. According to Emanuel d'Aranda, in the 1640s and probably earlier, the Grand Duke of Tuscany had made an agreement with Algerian authorities promising to imprison ransomed captives who had recently arrived from Algiers until they collected enough money to pay the debts they owed their captors.[89] Although such a formal agreement may have been exceptional, the practice it represented was quite common. Merchants who ransomed captives could order their imprisonment upon arrival in a Christian settlement until they paid their debt. The authorities usually cooperated. Pedro Brea, who ransomed several captives from Tunis in 1595, left two in the prison of the castle at Trapani, on the west coast of Sicily, because "they owed him 175 ounces [a coin worth 329 reales]."[90] Gaspar Discle, a squire from Oran who was captured by the Algerians in 1593, recounted a similar story in his petition for help. In 1596, using money his wife sent after selling their property and a loan he took from Valencian merchants, he bought his freedom, or so he thought. Soon after his return to Spanish Oran, the merchants demanded his imprisonment because he could not pay his debt.[91] The Franciscan Antonio Castaño showed awareness of this dynamic in his application for a begging license made in 1591, immediately upon his return to Spain after his ransom. Expressing in his petition his unease at not paying his debtors on time, he claimed that if he were not to raise the money, "he would be forced to return to captivity."[92] While captives ransomed by the orders of redemption typically had no financial burden to repay, if they failed to participate in the friars' processions, which were essentially a fund-raising exercise, for a designated period they might be arrested.[93] In 1718, Trinitarians in Cartagena asked the authorities to force captives who refused to participate in the procession to do so.[94] Two centuries earlier, the Trinitarian Diego de Gayangos complained about such an omission, and on June 9, 1519, he received a writ from the king that ordered the arrest of the former captives Gayangos had redeemed who had failed to fulfill their obligation to the Trinitarians.[95]

Debtors eluded capture on both sides of the Mediterranean. In September 1608, for example, Mawlāy Zaydān, the sultan of Morocco, directed a letter to Philip III through the Duke of Medina-Sidonia asking the Spanish monarch to help a Jewish Moroccan merchant. Abraham Ben Waish had loaned ransom money to Spanish hidalgos captured in Morocco, but they had never repaid him.[96] We do not know whether the Spanish king acquiesced, but clearly Zaydān thought he might. Exactly one year earlier, the Inquisition had responded positively to a similar request from Abraham de Loya and David Hocico, Moroccan Jewish merchants who had asked for passports to enter Spain in order to sue Portuguese nobles formerly held captive in Morocco to whom they had loaned ransom money that had never been repaid. The Inquisition acknowledged their legal rights in the matter and issued passports for them.[97]

Maghribi legal institutions also sought to enforce agreements between captives and intermediaries. For example, a legal trial preserved the freedom of Jerónimo Gracián when the pasha accused Gracián and Askenazi, the ransoming merchant, of cheating him. Askenazi and Gracián won the legal case after presenting the qadi (a judge presiding over matters in accord with Islamic law) with a letter of manumission dated April 11, 1595, which the qadi accepted.[98] The case of Gaspar de los Reyes shows other political-legal institutions in Maghribi cities that ensured, at least in some cases, the execution of ransom agreements, even when none of the parties involved was Muslim. After he lost the money entrusted to him to ransom captives, de los Reyes decided to convert to Islam. The governor and the divan insisted he pay his debt first and only then convert, even though he was a Christian who had staked, and lost, the money of Christian captives.[99]

After their expulsions in 1492 and 1609, Jews and Muslims were, at least theoretically, not permitted on Spanish soil, so Jewish and Muslim intermediaries could have had great difficulty in pursuing delinquent former captives who returned to Spain. But Mediterranean rulers nonetheless enforced their agreements much of the time, probably in part in the interest of imprisoned subjects who would have no access to intermediaries if cheating were rampant. Further, Spanish kings relied on commerce with Maghribis to sustain their strongholds along the North African coast, and Moroccan rulers were interested in the flow of commerce with European merchants. Mawlāy Zaydān, for example, sent a letter to Phillip III that reflects the friendly policy toward merchants his father, Ahmad al-Mansūr, had enacted soon after he won the sultanate in 1578.[100] Zaydān asserted, "The merchants of the Christian congregation . . . wherever in these provinces of ours . . . come with the protection of custody and guard . . . and with this they and their goods are safe, surrounded by our help . . . and they, in all our kingdoms, travel safe from troubles and dangers," and he requested that his own subjects, whether Jewish or Muslim, receive the same courtesy.[101]

CONCLUSION

Like others ransomed captives, Jerónimo Gracián played an active role in his ransom by negotiating his price and by contacting relatives and urging them to collect money and commission a merchant to help him. Bitter accord had almost ended his ransom, as we have seen, but Gracián chose to close his tale of captivity with a vignette stressing that even the least trustworthy Muslim corsairs respected ransom agreements. In his autobiography, he recounts that in the summer of 1595 he boarded a ship in Tabarka, ready to leave for Genoa. At the time, a galley belonging to ra'īs Murat, a famous North African corsair, was at anchor in the port. Its sailors, who had observed Gracián, informed their captain that Gracián was about to depart and urged him to order them to capture him again. According to Gracián, the corsair replied, "What do you want of this wretch? Didn't he pay his ransom? Let him go free!"[102] Gracián seals the paragraph with the words, "and these good works I owe Mataarraez," referring to ra'īs Murat. This conclusion, which we might interpret as merely stylistic, nevertheless reflects a decision to represent the system of ransom in a particular way—denying its institutional aspects and suggesting it was based on the good works of exceptional personalities. However, the documents relating to Gracián in the Archivo Histórico Nacional in Madrid reveal that legal instruments, not friendly trust, prompted ra'īs Murat to allow Gracián to continue on his way. Ra'īs Murat detained Gracián and demanded the safe pass issued to him in Tunis. Only after affirming its validity did he sign it, allowing Gracián to continue his passage home.[103] Gracián's description of his ransom offers an example of how an individual author helped mask the networks that facilitated his own rescue and return home. The few traces captives left in the archives often reflect moments at which the system failed—for example, freed captives' petitions to the crown to help them pay their debts and intermediaries' complaints about freed captives who escaped without paying their debt. Ironically, then, the more efficient the system, the fewer traces it left.

As this chapter has described, the early modern Mediterranean ransom world was populated by merchants who transferred money that relatives sent across the Mediterranean, middlemen who provided credit, Muslim slaves and the Christians slaves for whom they were exchanged, and captives and the temporary hostages they left in their place. Despite political violence, religious hatred, and all the suspicions associated with captivity, trust among captives, captors, and middlemen of different faiths was crucial to the functioning of that world. Trust took various forms and developed over time in trajectories of captivity and ransom. It began with masters accepting their captives' claims regarding their identity and hence their value and continued as captives sought credit or left their kin behind as hostages. Masters and intermediaries had to trust the captives to whom they provided credit. But, as we have seen, trust by no means took the form of unconditional empathy with the religious other. Rather, trust was a socially grounded, highly conventionalized, mutually recognizable, and institutionally guaranteed sentiment that implied certain rules of conduct.

The trust that underlay ransom agreements greased the wheels of news transmission across the Mediterranean. Virtually all captives participated in that system by seeking to negotiate ransom. Their efforts, found in letters to relatives and rulers, their kin's petitions to the authorities, and a host of legal documents intended to authenticate their petitions' claims gathered, fabricated, and circulated information. As subsequent chapters demonstrate, this infrastructure distributed information of many kinds, extending the power and hold of institutions across the sea and into enemy territory.

In the Spanish context, this network of ransom with its unique procedures had implications for the Habsburg desire for a religious, cultural, and legal cleansing of the peninsula. Lauren Benton, who developed the term "legal regimes" to describe homologous legal spaces, implicitly assumes in her discussion of Spain that with the expulsion of the Jews and the Muslims, Spain lost the legal pluralism by which it had previously been characterized.[104] But when Spanish captives, Maghribi captors, and Jewish, Muslim, and Christian ransom agents negotiated deals, they bound themselves to mutual legal agreements and thereby subverted the desired political boundedness of their legal regimes. An institutional umbrella, formed both by embassies and port cities and by the intervention of royal, religious, and legal bureaucracies, guaranteed the flow of transactions and made trust in the system across lines of faith possible. Spanish bureaucracies cooperated with that network and acknowledged the legal validity of the agreements reached within it, both implicitly, by conceding begging licenses, and explicitly, by facilitating entry to Spain for those who had been exiled many years earlier.

CHAPTER 4

Taking Captives, Capturing Communities

Maritime piracy made captives of home communities and families as well as of formerly free individuals. Social bodies that lost members to piracy became dependent upon those held captive in North Africa for information about those parts of the community, over which the captives had a near monopoly. Captives knew, for example, who among their fellow captives had died, had converted to Islam, or had been martyred, and how. News of such events not only affected the communal status of those who died or converted but also had the potential to reconfigure gender roles and social relations in the captives' families and within communities in Spain. In this sense, captives had access to extraordinarily important, even privileged, information. Captive correspondents became communal gatekeepers. They might transform a dead person into a saint, a "chained" widow into a bride, a native into a foreigner, or a Christian into a Muslim or vice versa. Their agency as informants enabled them to maintain a standing in their home communities and ensured that Spain's religious and political bureaucracies would continue to recognize that status. Sharing information was thus one way in which captives exerted political and social influence and maintained status within their communities. The geographical distance between kin and friends did not necessarily cut them off from one another; instead, captivity extended communal boundaries across the sea and onto another continent.

This epistolary exchange also influenced captives' immediate social milieu. Captives' evident ability to change other captives' confessional standing by reporting conversions and their power to make this ability evident placed them in a position of power vis-à-vis renegades, Christians who had converted to Islam. The potential impact of their words at home could be used to manipulate converts and to improve their own living conditions. In this sense, writing and circulating information was for captives primarily a survival strategy.

As I argued in Chapter 3, writing, sending, and receiving letters was part of the experience of captivity, with masters interested in hefty ransoms, especially in the case of enslaved Christians, encouraging their captives to contact their kin. In February 1676, Franca Pudda from the village of Iglesias on the southwestern tip of the island of Sardinia (then part of the Spanish Empire) wrote to her captured husband, "All [the other wives in the village] received greetings and letters from their husbands and I have received no letter nor greeting with which to console myself."[1] As Pudda's complaint suggests, captives were expected to write home.

Even illiterate captives were able to have their words put down on paper. When Inquisitors in Tenerife asked Juan de Herrera of Puerto de la Cruz if the handwriting and signature in the letter from 1679 he had received from Algiers belonged to the captive Domingo de la Luz, Herrera replied in the negative, saying that Luz was illiterate but noting that sending letters in "a foreign hand . . . is common among those who want to write letters but do not know how."[2] Other evidence that illiterate captives could still correspond appears in a letter by Jerónimo Gracián from Tunis in June 1594, in which he told his mother that God made him spend so much time in captivity so he could help the other poor captives by writing letters on their behalf in order to advance their ransom.[3] The testimony Inés Hernández Sardiña gave in 1670 before the Inquisitorial tribunal at Gran Canaria demonstrates an additional element of such correspondence:

> Inés Hernández Sardiña . . . [said] that after Francisco Márquez arrived from his captivity to the Puerto de la Cruz . . . he went to see her. . . . And he took out a linen bag in which there were many other letters and gave this witness [Inés Hernández Sardiña] the letter . . . and then she opened the letter in the presence of everyone who was there and gave it to one of the women, named María Fonte, present at the visit so she might read it; and among the news it contained, one bit was that Gaspar de los Reyes had turned Moor. . . . And all the people present stood amazed by the news they heard read aloud in the said letter.[4]

With a clear and resonant reading of the text, the human voice mediated publicly between the literate and the illiterate, or between the oral and written news. The scribe, the person deciphering the letter for the addressee, and additional listeners all shared the information the author sought to convey.

Through their letters, captives did more than mitigate the emotional trauma of captivity or separation from family.[5] Their first object was to advance their ransom—to direct family members to collect alms, hire intermediaries, and execute deals. Even when letters did not address the issue of ransom directly, release was often a subtext. Captives informed kin and friends about their hardships, expressed their fear of being forgotten, and shared their desire for and excitement about news from home. Tomás Báez de la Fuente, held captive in Algiers in the 1620s, wrote to his family that "when he held the[ir] letters in his hand, he shed so many tears he could not contain and he nearly started crying aloud like crazy in front of the redemptors and other Christians of this land."[6] Such descriptions, common in captives' letters, were informative and evocative at the same time. While directly addressing husbands and wives, children and parents, the information always held a call for action, which often necessitated extending the letters' journey, as they were forwarded on to political and religious institutions. But ultimately the captives also hoped that the letters would help overcome the distance from their family, enabling them to keep in touch with their home communities. Letters were a poetic tool used to craft co-presence and activate moral obligation.

THE FAMILY, THE VILLAGE, AND THE COMMUNITY OF SAINTS

The news that stunned the listeners in Inés Hernández Sardiña's telling, reinforcing their sense of community and producing an effect of contemporaneity, had to do with the conversion of a community member and, therefore, his forfeiture of his belonging to that community.[7] Early modern Spaniards identified themselves as members of several overlapping social groups: a family, a town or village community, a community of the kingdom, and a confessional community. Captivity affected membership in all of these groups. Identifying as Roman Catholic was a necessary, though insufficient, condition for membership in a town and in the community of the kingdom. Urban membership or urban citizenship (*vecindad*), as Tamar Herzog has argued, "was constituted on its own, at the moment people acted as if they felt attached to the community."[8] In principle, citizenship allowed members to use communal property and become involved in local political affairs, and it required them to reside in the town and pay taxes. Equally important was that citizenship reinforced the status of "natives" (*naturales*), that is, members in the community of the kingdom who were, for example, legally permitted to hold office or migrate to Spanish America. Captivity itself only limited and modified captives' membership in each of these communities; it did not necessarily eliminate that membership.

Once captured by corsairs, however, captives could no longer continue to claim membership in a local community by the usual mechanisms, that is, by having their cattle graze the common pastures, for example, or by voting. Instead, letters to kin and friends and to diocesan, Inquisitorial, and papal institutions became the mechanism for claiming communal membership. At the same time, the loss of liberty and enslavement had the potential to transform, limit, and reverse communal and gender roles. A breadwinner who was once the protector of the family had become an economic burden on that same family. Since men were captured more often than women, free women—wives, sisters, and mothers—were more likely to be tasked with collecting alms and transacting ransoms than were free men. And yet, as disruptive as captivity may have been, correspondence allowed many captives to maintain socially meaningful ties with their communities. The authors of such letters reported conversions to Islam or deaths of captives, events that influenced the status of the converts and the dead as Catholics, citizens, or natives of the crown. When captives' letters conveyed testimonies of captives who had died as martyrs to the Church and were, thus, candidates for canonization, they could influence another community, that of canonized saints. Captives' boundary work was important. For example, news about the death of a captive allowed his widow to remarry and to manage property, while all the family could now mourn the deceased; news of the conversion of a captive, by contrast, stained his family's honor. By writing, captives continued to play a central role in their communities by maintaining communal boundaries from the community's edges.

The reports that traveled in captives' letters were as much representations of events, narrative constructs, or sources of information as they were realizations of social relations and actions that could promote and pronounce social change, influencing the writers, their subjects, and their correspondents.[9] No libraries or special collections systematically archive these letters. These vital items of news and rumor must thus be caught at the margins: in investigations by the Inquisition, autobiographies, petitions for help, and other documents.[10] While it is impossible to establish the number of letters written and sent, the dossiers into which they were appended, copied, or summarized suggest a remarkable volume. The few letters that survived and the hundreds, likely thousands, of references, summaries, and verbatim copies of others in these dossiers make it clear that writing and sending letters were extremely common practices among captives, including renegades.[11] Analysis of the writing practices that echo through these letters offers a new way of understanding captivity, the diverse strategies that captives employed in order to survive, and linkages between North Africa and the Spanish Empire.

UNRELIABLE NETWORKS

Though captives had privileged access to information, the uncertainty of delivery significantly mitigated the power that captives wielded through their reports. In the letters that survive, captives constantly complained that correspondence had gone astray. To overcome the risk of lost letters and ensure their news would arrive, writers often shipped copies of the same letter with different carriers; addressees replied with helpful reports on the routes taken by the letters they had received.[12] That captives never gave up on writing suggests, however, that many letters reached their destinations in North Africa or in Europe.

In an attempt to control the circulation of information, captives, like merchants, employed common protocols geared toward tracing letters' routes and recording their sequence. To this end, they often opened their letters with an account of the correspondence they had most recently sent or received and by summarizing the information it contained, as if trying to keep track of the flow of communication.[13] For example, in a letter friar Gaspar Merino wrote from Algiers in 1641 to his uncle, friar Tomás de Aquino, the author indicated, "With this one, I have written ten (letters) to you, Father, and I have received no response."[14] To facilitate the tracking of letters, writers also described the long routes over which their letters were to be sent. The author of an unsigned letter from August 10, 1655, from Algiers addressed to Señor Manuel Jorge described how a previous letter to the same addressee was carried west from Ottoman Algiers to Spanish Ceuta, a distance of some 620 miles. It is unclear if the letter reached its addressee, but in order to do so, it should have been sent north from Ceuta on a ship to Spain. The same Inquisitorial dossier documents the path of six letters written by Spanish captives that the renegade Jusepe Brexa carried 222 miles across the Mediterranean from Algiers to Costa Blanca, which lies between Alicante and Valencia, after he escaped an Algerian embarkation. In Costa Blanca Brexa began a long journey north on foot. He first walked about 62 miles from Denia, in the province of Alicante, to Catarroja, a village six miles from Valencia, where he submitted himself to the *familares*, the Inquisition's lay collaborators, who then accompanied him, still on foot, six more miles to Valencia. The Valencian Inquisitors took him into custody and later copied the letters he carried into his sentencing file;[15] the archives do not reveal if the letters ever reached their addressees. With mail routes on land and at sea so complex, letter writers probably often did not know if their correspondence had reached its destination.

Muslim captives in the Spanish Empire also participated as couriers and recipients in mailing networks just as did Christians. The records are sparse, but we know that when the Algerian Muhammad Bibi, enslaved in the coastal village of Blanes, forty miles northeast of Barcelona, was liberated in 1687, he carried a letter to the son of a Catalan neighbor of his former owners who was enslaved in Algiers.[16] Bive Muhammad, an Algerian enslaved in Majorca in 1692, sent a letter home in which he listed family members and the sums he hoped they could contribute to his ransom fee.[17] Sometimes Muslims employed their contacts to deliver messages and queries on behalf of Christians. In 1584, one the Inquisitors of the Valencian tribunal asked a Morisco collaborator and a spy to send a letter to Algiers to find out if a relative of the Inquisitor was held captive there.[18] Non-Muslims also served as mailmen for Muslims. Juan Bautista, registered in the Inquisition records as a Polish sailor, carried letters that Muslims enslaved in Majorca in 1635 wrote to their relatives in Annaba and Tunis. Captured by agents of the Inquisitorial court, he failed to deliver them.[19] Merchants who traded with the Maghrib on a regular basis, the French consuls in Algiers who often traveled to Majorca to ransom Muslims, Trinitarians and Mercedarians, and captives' kin traveling to North Africa to ransom their family members all carried letters on behalf of Muslims enslaved in the villages or cities from which they had departed. Couriers did not have to share the religious faith of the sender or recipient of the letters they carried.

DEATH ANNOUNCEMENTS

In a letter written in Marrakesh in 1643, the author informed his addressee, Beatriz Lópes, that his godfather, who had been held captive with him, had died of malaria; in a letter dated July 14, 1668, Lucas Delgado, captive in Algiers, informed his wife, Paula Batista, of the death of Domingo Álvarez and added that the deceased's wife should pray for her dead husband's soul; in 1668 Bartolomé Estacio, captive in Algiers, wrote to Lucia Rodríguez confirming her husband's death in Algiers and recounting the burial, as he described "how her husband died . . . [when] he got sick where there was nobody to attend him," and continued, "Two days later, among us the captives, I was the first to assist with alms for his burial."[20] Estacio's letter, sent to San Cristóbal de la Laguna in Tenerife, enabled Lucia Rodríguez and other bereaved family members to launch the required social and administrative protocols and released them from the obligation to beg for alms for the ransom of their enslaved kin, an obligation that burdened captives' families financially. Diocesan bodies in the Canary and Balearic Islands, and probably in other regions along the Spanish littoral, collected and archived news of deceased captives that could release their widows and kin from these kinds of obligations.[21]

Such information could be crucial. The death of a married captive could turn a wife into a widow who was now free to remarry and could take control of valuable matrimonial assets: the gift her husband had given her upon their marriage (*arras*), her dowry, half the property the couple had accumulated during their married life (*ganancias*), and other matrimonial gifts. In practice, although not legally, widows also claimed *vecindad*, citizenship in a village or a town that, as we have seen, came with communal rights. Only a husband's death, and not his long absence, could make a wife a widow, heightening the significance of captives' monopoly of information about the deaths of fellow captives. In the decades after the Protestant Reformation, the Catholic Church had further regulated the sacrament of marriage. A woman seeking the status of widowhood or dispensation to remarry had to prove her husband's death to a bishop's provisor; otherwise her remarriage would make her a bigamist—a canon and civil offense subject to prosecution by the Inquisition.[22] In transmitting this kind of news, then, captives' communications reached beyond their direct addressees in the local community, acting as indirect correspondence with church institutions.

The case of the Majorcan Caterina Minguet, wife of the captive Josepe Lozano, who received a dispensation that allowed her to marry the ship patron Ginés Irles, shows these protocols in action. The permit was issued after Minguet had presented letters from her brother-in-law, captive in Tunis, who reported that Lozano had voluntarily converted to Islam and now served as a Tunisian corsair. When freed captives confirmed the information from her brother-in-law, Minguet denounced her husband to the island's Inquisitorial tribunal. She received dispensation to remarry after she provided additional testimonies, according to which Lozano had been captured by the knights of San Stefano, enslaved as an oarsman on a Florentine galley, and eventually died on his bench. But Irles and Minguet had lied, fabricating the extra testimonies. Lozano had indeed been enslaved and had been put to the oar on a Florentine galley, but he was still alive. When a French slave whom Lozano met at the prison in Livorno, which belonged to the Florentine duchy, told him his wife had remarried, Lozano contacted his mother, who reported the fraud to the Inquisition. In 1634, Minguet was sentenced to spiritual penitence, and Irles and his false witnesses were sentenced to hundreds of lashes and years of slavery on the galleys.[23] The case shows how information from captives could release chained widows but also unlawfully facilitate a remarriage of an already married women. As the fate of Minguet and her accomplices proves, killing off one's enslaved husband in writing was a risky business, as information circulated constantly and was all too likely to reach the enslaved "deceased." Even from their galley bench, chained and pulling a heavy oar, captives could counter such frauds—if they received word about them—and send alternative information, on the basis of which deceivers and false witnesses could be punished.

Confirmation of a husband's death had significant implications not only for wives but also for household structures and the community's spatial organization. Often a widow stayed in the home of one of her married children. If her children were still young, a widow might move with them to her parents' home or live with another married couple to whom she was related, which transformed nuclear families into extended families. If a widow remarried, her children with her deceased husband would stay with their grandparents. Beyond the redistribution of family members across various households, the transformation of wives into widows was often associated with financial difficulties. With no male breadwinner to support the household, poor widows who owned little or no property had to beg for their own alms or work as servants. Widows in rural areas experienced such great poverty that fiscal censuses might classify them as "poor," exempting them from tax contributions.[24] News about a captive's death, then, had the potential to restructure households, redistribute rights over personal and communal property, and transform the social, occupational, residential, and gendered experiences of family members.

The Moroccan and Algerian worlds resembled the Christian world in this regard. The death or conversion of a Muslim captive had significant implications for his wife, household, possessions, and inheritance. While the handful of extant letters written by Muslim captives do not provide enough examples to allow reconstruction of the practice on the Muslim side, fatwas, legal treatises, and notarial formularies from Al-Andalus, Morocco, and Mudejar communities in Aragon and Castile clearly point to the importance of such news. Andalusi and Moroccan muftis, who followed the Maliki School of religious law and issued fatwas regarding Muslims who were captured, argued that even when no information about the status of a Muslim captive was available, he must not be considered *mafqūd*, namely, absent but not necessarily dead. This decision was meant to protect the captives' marriage and property, and specified that a wife could not remarry unless she could provide certified documentation recording that her husband had died in battle or as a captive. In the meantime, a wife (and other potential inheritors) could not use, transfer, or alienate her captive husband's possessions. Wives of Muslims baptized by force could not remarry, but their husbands' property was turned into a pious endowment (*waqf*, or *habous*, the term used in the Ottoman Maghrib) that sustained the wives. If the husband had converted voluntarily to Christianity, his wife could divorce him, and his property was moved to the public treasury as a pious endowment.[25]

In Algiers, where the Hanafi rite—dominant in the Ottoman world—was practiced alongside the Maliki rite, the situation was similar. The parallels are evident when we look at those most likely to become *mafqūd*, namely ship captains, corsairs, and sailors, whose occupation entailed a high risk of death or captivity with no witnesses to confirm it. These individuals employed strategies to circumvent the rigid letter of Islamic inheritance law and to exert as much control as possible over the transmission of their possessions after their death.[26] The steps they took highlight corsairs' and sailors' awareness of how precarious their lives were, but they also make evident the limits of the strategies they employed. Without confirmed information regarding their death (or conversion), their inheritance could not be redistributed before a predetermined period had passed—according to Maliki jurists, between seventy-five and eighty years, according to Hanafi a full century, and according to Berber custom about seventy years.[27] In other words, the absence of verified news of a corsair's death could be disastrous for family members and potential heirs. Muslim captives were practically the sole source of such information, which can only have shored up their continuing significance and standing in their home communities across North Africa and the Ottoman world.

COMMUNITY AND CONVERSION

Families and institutions were also eager to learn about renegades, Christians who had "turned Turk." Inés Hernández Sardiña's description of a group of people listening to a captive's correspondence read aloud and standing speechless on hearing of Gaspar de los Reyes's conversion to Islam is indicative of that audience's recognition of a special threat to the community.[28] The letter warned that de los Reyes's conversion was complete and that he had no regrets; the renegade had joined the corsairs and was about to use his knowledge of the Canary Islands to sack villages and enslave Christians. The converts who joined the corsairs' lines naturally retained their mastery of the language of their community of origin, so they might pass as natives and thus more readily control access to villages. Villages of Mediterranean islands and littorals lost more members to corsairs than did inland communities, and renegades were more likely to be among their numbers.[29] Families, governors, and fleet officers expected captives to send a warning if they heard of renegades who had joined the corsairs' fleet and were constantly on the lookout for such news.

Conversion was not simply a security issue, however. Renegades had left the Christian community—and membership in that community was a condition for citizenship and, in turn, membership in the community of the kingdom.[30] Writers and intermediaries framed renegade conversions as a decisive deed and thus a betrayal of Christianity. But converts' religious faith—and, more importantly, their social belonging and loyalty to Christendom if and when they returned, as many did—was a hotly debated subject for captives, renegades, families, and the Inquisition. At stake were issues of belonging, family honor, and money.

RUMORS

Conversion was not a private affair and keeping it a secret was practically impossible. Rumors about captives who turned Turk, either voluntarily or by force, spread quickly in the cities where they converted, as several former captives in Algiers and sailors testified during the 1677 Canary Islands Inquisitorial investigation into the conversion of Augustinian friar Juan de Payba. Payba had been ransomed but returned to Algiers a year later, converted to Islam, and married the sister of his former master. In Inquisitorial depositions, witnesses testified that all the Christian captives in Algiers knew of his conversion almost immediately.[31]

In his account of his own captivity and freedom written in the 1630s, Diego Galán suggested that captives' awareness of how quickly the news of conversion crossed the sea often deterred them from converting to Islam. Certainly, he felt such circumstances held true in his own case: "The angel confronted me with my parents' honor and [with the fact] that there are no secrets in this world and that as soon as I arrived back in my place and in Toledo, someone who knew me in Algiers and in Constantinople would appear, and that would be shameful."[32] Galán implied that the decision to convert was motivated by the freedom it could provide, rather than by faith or theological conviction. However, even if Galán could have leveraged his conversion to Islam to provide him with freedom of movement that would enable him to escape, the cost would have been too great, for he would have dishonored his family and would have faced the Inquisition.

Seeking to maintain their reputation, some families summoned witnesses and provided countertestimonies to fight reports of captives' conversions. When word of Clemente Jordán's conversion and marriage to an Andalusian Morisca in Algiers arrived at his hometown in the Canary Islands, the local Inquisitorial tribunal sentenced him in absentia for apostasy. Tomás Báez de la Fuente, who was held captive in Algiers with Jordán, rushed to report in a letter of February 27, 1629, that "the wife of Clemente Jordán, father of Francisco Clemente, does not have a husband anymore nor his son a father, because [Jordán] is already [a member of] these pertaining to the devil's, because he left the Catholic [faith] and is following the one he should have followed."[33] His family, alerted to this challenge to its reputation, protested and appealed. The family lawyer framed the issue in terms of honor and dishonor—"that the innocence of [Jordán's] ancestry will not suffer infamy in law and in practice for being a very large and extensive family that has many priests, monks and persons imbued with dignity."[34] The family insisted on reopening the investigation and was willing to spend large sums on the collection of additional evidence in Algiers. The Inquisitors consented, and the parties agreed that Mercedarian friars in Algiers would continue inquiries. Eventually the process was suspended and Jordán was not condemned, a result that left the family satisfied. Like Galán's case, Jordán's case demonstrates the interplay between honor and conversion and the power held by captive informants. Captives could also use their knowledge of renegades' conversions to personal ends, promising to keep a conversion a secret in return for favors or punishing renegades by informing their relatives about their conversion.

PRESERVED FAMILIAL TIES

In spite of the specter of shame, conversion did not necessarily sever families. Renegades who fared well in their new lives often wrote home regularly, sent money to their families, or supported them in other ways.[35] Some renegades who settled in the Maghrib even received frequent visits from their kin, although probably only the wealthiest could make this happen. Simón Pérez, for example, a Genoese who married an Andalusian woman and lived in Cadiz, frequently visited family in Algiers, usually for several weeks at a time. His uncle, Mamí Genoese, a rich Algerian renegade, secured safe passes for these visits. In late December 1618 or early January 1619, Pérez went to meet Mamí but stayed for only seventeen days, an unusually short visit, because his uncle was on a trip and his uncle's second wife was unknown to him.[36] The Sicilian Pere Pelegri also had a brother in Algiers, who after several years in captivity converted and made a fortune. Pelegri frequently visited his brother, who supported him financially.[37] Whatever the exact nature of the visits, these and other cases show that the relations between renegades and their

Christian relatives were not limited to letter exchange; they might also meet in person.[38]

The most famous encounter between a renegade and his family involved a celebrity of Mediterranean history, Cigalazade Yusuf Sinan, the commander in chief of the Ottoman navy, or Kapudan Pasha. Cigala, as European sources called him, starred in intelligence reports and letters from all the leading information hubs in Italy and Spain—Venice, Naples, Sicily, and Majorca, among others.[39] In September 1598, his fleet appeared in Sicilian waters just off the coast of Messina, where he had been born. He sent two letters ashore—one to the viceroy and another to his aged mother, Lucrezia, whom he had not seen in thirty years. He asked the viceroy for permission to bring his mother onboard. The next day, mother and son, along with a few other relatives, met on Cigala's *capitana*, the fleet's flagship.[40] While these encounters demonstrate continuity in the relations between renegades and their families after captivity and conversion, they also mark the limits of that continuity. Cigala's case was exceptional, for usually Christian family members visited their converted kin, not the other way around. Renegades could not return home without risking investigation and punishment, and they certainly could not merely visit and then return to Barbary. Only Cigala's military power and notoriety allowed him to arrange the encounter.

To maintain ties with their families, and before being welcomed back into Spanish society, people said to have converted had to assure their families of their affection, convince them that they had been falsely accused, or argue that they had converted under duress. Francisco Girbau, or Hasan, as he was called after his conversion, never stopped writing to his family in Blanes, near Barcelona.[41] When he wrote to his father in July 1689, Girbau did not know if news of his conversion had already reached home, but he was already seeking to limit the damage. He opened his letter with a complaint about not receiving letters from his family, expressing the worry that their absence might be a reaction to news of his conversion to Islam. He wrote: "For the love of God do not distrust me this way; God, our lord is merciful, he will give me a way to exit this evil despicableness, and if by any chance Juan Yslas is around, he will tell you everything about the life I have[.] [D]o not believe news from anyone else, [since] all are lies, you should not forget me, that God, our lord knows what is in my heart, and the desire [I have] to go and see you."[42] He pleaded with his family not to believe anyone but the witness he has designated, not because he denies that he has converted but because only Juan Yslas could explain the "evil despicableness" of his present circumstance. His conversion is discursively implicit, referenced without use of the common expression "to turn Turk" (or Moor). He claimed that while he lived according to Muslim custom, he remained Christian in his heart, a state to which only God is a witness. And yet he acknowledged "the pain and shame you will feel for this bad news, when you will receive it," telling his family that he is "thinking about you everyday."[43] He recognized that even if his parents and siblings believe him, his cousins will hold him condemned to hell, and his sisters will suffer as a result. It is unclear if he wants to shame his cousins for thinking the worst of him or for ostracizing his sisters, as he imagines they will. Whatever his goal, Girbau clearly expected that his relatives would soon hear about his conversion and that their reaction could result in the restructuring of social and gendered roles for his kin. His family's honor was threatened, different lines within the wider family faced separation, and his closest kin might be socially isolated. He hoped his extended family might at least be united in believing him a Christian in his heart.

Francisco Verdera's September 2, 1606, letter to his aunt in Majorca resembles Girbau's. Another convert in Algiers, Verdera similarly expressed his suspicions that his aunt has ceased writing to him because of his conversion: "I don't know what the reason is, if it is because I turned Moor; The whole world knows that I was forced to do so."[44] Like Girbau, Verdera fears that someone has sent word of his conversion without fairly representing the conditions under which he converted. He also puts forward a character witness, Juan Maltés, a ship's captain who traded regularly with Algerians and who witnessed the duress that Verdera experienced.

In addition to the captain's speaking for him, Verdera wanted his friend to repay a debt: "and for the love of God, ask patron Juan Maltés to do me a favor regarding that money he owes me . . . and send me many biretta caps [tarbooshes], the good ones, and [ask] that he send them to the prison of St. Roque [in Algiers]."[45] It appears that Verdera had a small business selling tarbooshes, or fezzes, popular in Algiers. The fact that Verdera did not think his second request cast doubt on Maltés's credibility as his witness suggests it did not. Verdera expected to be able to maintain a network at home even after his conversion; he may have felt that his aunt's support hinged on her belief that his conversion was insincere.

Once news arrived in Spain, information of the kind that Verdera and Girbau attempted to control passed along webs of kinship and friendship and through the Inquisition. Verdera's letter survives because another nephew of the recipient kept it for almost forty years, at which time it entered the Inquisitorial record as part of a postmortem trial of the writer.[46] Rumors about conversion served as a weapon of the weak, used by captives against other captives, who had converted.[47] By proposing to send word about conversions back home, captives threatened to sever renegades' affective ties and communal status. Letters like Verdera's and Girbau's suggest that news *could* travel quickly across the sea. Simultaneously, the letters point out that information about family and community members taken captive was scarce and fraught with doubt, and yet also much desired.

FACING THE INQUISITION

Renegades were better off than captives who had not converted, even if they were not yet manumitted. And yet despite their conversion and improved living conditions, more than a few renegades, like both Verdera and Girbau, hoped to return home and reintegrate into their Christian communities with minimal punishment by the Inquisition. To do so, however, they would have to face the Inquisition and prove that their conversion had been superficial or insincere. Renegades frequently sought letters from Christian captives in support of such endeavors. In believing that such captives had the capacity to communicate legitimacy and enable absolution before the Inquisition for their conversions, renegades endowed those captives with tremendous power. Renegades might have been motivated by an authentic sense of guilt or shame, perhaps prompted by the despising gaze of their former coreligionists who had remained faithful. But they might have been driven also by a desire to return home, and for Spanish, Portuguese, and Italian renegades, to return home was to be investigated and likely punished by the Inquisition. In pleading for favors from captives, they may have been seeking ways to account for their conversions should they return to face the accusations of secular and ecclesiastical authorities, as well as of their families, neighbors, and friends.

Such letters might attest to their "true" Christian nature by arguing they had converted under duress or recounting how, despite their conversions, they kept helping Christians in need. This type of correspondence, which the sources alternately describe as certificates (*fees* or *patentes*), testimonies (*testimonios*), signatures (*firmas*), or simply letters (*cartas*), were not unlike letters of recommendation or insurance policies for renegades who wished to leave the Maghrib. Gracián described the practice in his *Peregrinación de Anastasio* (Pilgrimage of Anastasio, [1605]): "There are many renegades whose heart is touched by God and who wish to escape to a Christian land to save their soul; and the only reason for which they stay is out of fear of the Inquisition saying that it would punish them unless they carry some testimony of a man of credit and renown who would testify that they had left for Christian land out of their free will and desire for Catholic belief."[48] Gracián says little about the exchange involved, portraying the concession of such documents as disinterested. Renegades sincerely avowed their former creed and asked Christian captives to testify to the inner changes that they had experienced; in their testimony, captives tended simply to describe the reconversion of the renegade. In this instance, then, Gracián characterized the concession of these certificates as not reciprocal, as in a gift exchange, but as a unidirectional transaction, with testimony given and nothing received in return.

Nonetheless, an incident recounted in Gracián's *Tratado de la redención de cautivos* (Treaty of the Redemption of Captives [1609]) hints at the exchange that might be implicit in the provision of a certificate. He writes that Tunisian captors had circumcised a large number of French boys by force and that he provided one of them a certificate "with which he escaped and arrived in Cagliari [Sardinia]."[49] In the lines immediately following, Gracián records that he convinced another renegade to obtain a boat from his master, enabling the escape of twenty Christian captives. While he does not specify why he gave the first renegade a certificate, the juxtaposition with the subsequent story and the fact that the boat-obtaining renegade, who would have faced death in Algiers for his subterfuge, could expect grave punishment by the Inquisition if he arrived home without the certificate suggest an exchange of some kind.

The issuing of such certificates, and the implicit exchanges they involved, made its way into literary works of the Spanish Golden Age, shedding further light on the dynamics involving renegade petitioners and captive witnesses. For example, in his play *The Bagnios of Algiers* (1615), Cervantes describes Hazén, a renegade, entering a scene where Lope and Vivanco, two captives, stand talking.[50] Upon

seeing Hazén, Lope asks Vivanco to lower his voice so that the renegade—a potential traitor and an enemy—will not hear their conversation. But Hazén surprises them with a request that marks him as a
repentant Christian:

> With just your two signatures I'll happily set foot on Spanish shores;
> I'll have a favorable wind, a calm sea with smooth waves. I want
> to return to Spain, and to one to whom I must confess my childish
> and ancient error. . . . [He gives them a handwritten note.] It states
> here that it is true that I have treated Christians very affably, with-
> out Turkish cruelty in word or deed; that I have aided many; that as
> a child I was compelled to turn Turk; that, though I go roving, I'm a
> good Christian underneath. Perhaps I'll have a chance to remain in
> what for me is the Promised Land.[51]

Here, explicating what Gracián left implicit, Cervantes calls into
question the impartiality of captives' testimony. Hazén does not hum-
bly ask for a letter but demands that Lope and Vivanco confirm what
he has already put in writing. He employs the interiority trope that
Gracián also uses, explaining that, although he roves foreign lands,
he is "a good Christian underneath." Yet he also says that his behavior affirms his internal condition. He has "treated Christians very
affably, without Turkish cruelty in word or deed . . . [and has] aided
many." This last assertion is an explicit reference to a quid pro quo
between renegades and Christian captives—renegades hoping to
return to Christianity would help captives with goods and services in
return for absolution in the form of a certificate for the Inquisition.
The captives' response affirms the reciprocal nature of the exchange:
Lope, now happy to assist Hazén, tells him, "When the sinner mends
his ways, he pays an advance on his salvation. We'll happily provide
the signatures you ask of us, for we have witnessed that all you say
is true, Hazén, and that you are honest. May heaven grant that your
course be as smooth as you desire."[52] Hazén's down payment is his
vow to "try to raise a mutiny on my galliot" once they leave the Algerian port—to organize a slave rebellion at sea and help the captives
enslaved on the galliot take over the ship and escape to Spain.
    Letters of recommendation were both account and artifact: a tool
with social relevance. First, these letters offered evidence of the religious subjectivity of converts to Islam: they transform—or have the
potential to transform—a Muslim into a Christian. But beyond that,
as a material artifact the letter formed an object in an interaction of
exchange. The testimony itself—because of the qualities associated

with it—was exchanged for other goods or services. Similar references abound in Inquisitorial documentation and trial summaries (*relaciones de causa*).[53] The Maltese Marcos de Bono, for example, captured at the age of nineteen, was sold into slavery in Cyprus, then under Ottoman control, and later taken to Istanbul. During his deposition before the Inquisition in 1634, he explained that he had never actually converted to Islam. Instead, he said, he had taken advantage of the fact that he "knew how to speak the Morisco language [likely Arabic] from having spoken it often in his land" and pretended to be a Muslim.[54] He used his linguistic skills to avoid slavery and joined the forces of the Janissaries. While stationed in Tunis, he became acquainted with Christian captives to whom he recounted his adventures. When he explained that, whatever his position might suggest, he had never converted to Islam, they took him to the local church and introduced him to the chaplain. At de Bono's request, the chaplain at the captives' prison wrote him a certificate saying he was a good Christian.[55] The story suggests that even a captive who had never converted—for de Bono may have been telling the truth—might seek a certificate to support his case in any investigation. It also suggests such a certificate could have the desired effect: later, when he escaped to Majorca, de Bono presented the document to the island's Inquisitors and they absolved him, punishing him only lightly. Such letters were occasionally copied into Inquisition registers, but even when they were not, court transcripts provide details, as the accused often described the circumstances under which they received these certificates.

We have already encountered Jusepe Brexa as a letter carrier, a Neapolitan who was captured by corsairs, converted to Islam in Algiers, and spent seven years in North Africa before escaping to the Iberian Peninsula in the autumn of 1655. Fortunately for historians, Brexa submitted himself to the Inquisition's *familares* in a small village in Valencia and eventually found himself before the region's Inquisitorial tribunal, which ordered the six letters he carried with him be copied into the trial record. In five of them, the authors, who must have also had the Inquisitors in mind as secondary recipients of their letters, asked the letters' official addressees to assist Brexa, often supporting their requests for leniency by explaining how helpful he had been to them. For example, in a letter to an acquaintance, captive letter writer Diego Antonio de Tarfan asserted that Brexa had been converted by force but always meant to "go to a land of Christians" and asked the recipient to serve as a mediator with the Inquisitorial tribunal. The letter also requests Brexa be compensated for his service with shelter and money to buy clothes:

> Because here [in Algiers], being a young boy, his owner turned him Moor by force, [and] his intentions [were] always to go to a land of Christians. And so if he should fall in the hands of the Inquisitorial tribunal your honor would always serve as a mediator, and if by any chance he would be in need of money to buy clothes, your honor would do it as if it were me, and if it would be necessary during the time when he would not have a shelter to protect him, and during the days he may like to stay in that city, your honor would provide him with accommodation in your house, and if it would be necessary by any chance that he would like to go elsewhere, Your honor would help him with that.[56]

Brexa may not have performed his good works in the hope of obtaining such letters in exchange; the letter writer and the Inquisition both treated his actions not as part of an exchange but as signaling his character. As in those other letters, the subject's Christianity is framed in terms of the substance of his interior life: Brexa was forced to turn Moor and always desired to return to Christendom and to the Christian life. But his testimony alone would be insufficient, and he had to express his religiosity through good works that thus came to resemble gifts and that were used in exchange for the written evidence he was able to provide to the Inquisitors. This explanation does not mean, however, that converts and captives constructed and construed their actions in terms of gifts and countergifts. On the contrary, as the behavior required of Brexa matched the basic idea of charity and good works, participants could deny any inherent reciprocity.

All letters were not of equal value. Missives from clerics and church officials carried particular weight, and the higher a captured ecclesiastic's rank, the more valuable were his letters. Beyond the prestige associated with their office, priests and monks might hear confession, which the Inquisitors recognized as a means of determining a renegade's righteousness and sincerity. "The Captive's Tale" in *Don Quixote* refers to "renegades [who] used to bring with them certain signatures of *principal* captives when they had the intention of returning to a Christian land."[57] Gracián indicates that rumors among renegades misattributed to him the rank, first, of a cardinal and, subsequently, of an important Inquisitor, leading to a deluge of requests for certificates.[58]

Owing to the intensity of the circulation of news—written and reported—renegades and captives could not falsify such documents without risking sanctions. On occasion, the Inquisition contacted the recommending captive to make sure the certificate was sincere. The French renegade who arrived in Sardinia with Gracián's letter, for example, was first detained by the Inquisition, which wrote to Gracián to confirm the veracity of the certificate.[59] Captives who successfully claimed distinction—based on rank, title, or wealth—could employ such letters in their favor regardless of their reliability. At the same time, a letter's success in securing Inquisitorial absolution or mercy for its subject enhanced the status of its author; its failure to convince, however, damaged the author and the value of his letters. Writing letters of recommendation, then, could be a way of establishing social distinction among captives. That the Inquisition occasionally authenticated a letter's author reinforced hierarchies among captives as well as the value of the certificates that ranked individuals could provide. In other words, the practice of writing such letters allowed a Spanish institution, the Inquisition, to influence captives' lives in a Muslim prison in a hostile land across the sea.

The case of converted captive Juan de Nicolao, a native of Ragusa (Dubrovnik), suggests the low value Inquisitors and secular authorities put on some letters. Nicolao escaped from an Algerian corsair ship in 1563 and arrived in Almería in Andalusia, where the mayor, who suspected that Nicolao was a renegade because of his clothes, interrogated him. Nicolao presented a letter of recommendation to which several captives who had rowed with him had put their names. None of the captives was identified as a person of status; the letter had no specific recipient; and Nicolao was not named but instead termed a foreigner. The missive first testifies to Nicolao's Christianity, again understood in terms of both belief and behavior: "Sirs, (may) our grace favor and help, in all that would be possible, this youth who is carrying the present (letter), because he is a good Christian and always behaved well to Christians, and although he said, on the foist [a light ship], that he wanted to become a Moor, he is not actually a Moor, nor does he behave like one." The authors then ask the unspecified addressee to provide Nicolao with a job and to help him financially until he gains independence. Their tone is assertive, and they attempt to create a presence and eminence that the letter otherwise lacks:

> Therefore, Your Honor, as I have it said, help him, and this [Nico-
> lao's Christianity] you can take as truth, because here we are, Bar-
> tolomé delBaeça [*sic*] and Gavriel de Espinosa and Juan de Gibraltar,
> by faith and testimony of truth, because should things be different
> than what is hereby written, we will pay with our lives. And there is
> no more to add other than that you should help him with all the alms
> that you can, because he deserves it and because he is a foreigner, so
> that he could live until he finds work. I am entrusting myself to Your
> Mercifulness, Bartolomé delBaeça and Gavriel de Espinosa and Juan
> de Alcántara Miguel de Limán.[60]

Again and again the writers claim co-presence—"because here we
are," "I am entrusting myself to your mercifulness." But the more frequently they reiterate these assertions, the less convincing they sound.
The authors signed their names, but they had neither title nor renown.
While the letter appears in the file, the mayor required several witnesses who had known Nicolao in Algiers also to testify on his behalf
before he would release the apparent renegade.

The letter's failure—its rhetoric that seeks to compensate for the
very weaknesses of rank and status and the anonymity of its authors
and recipient—brings into relief both the performative aspects of such
documents and the properties of Mediterranean connectivities. By
writing in the voice of a witness who could testify to a renegade's religious character, captives enacted a legal persona of which captivity
and slavery had not deprived them, underscoring the fact that natal
alienation—the deprivation of all ties to one's home community—
did not define Mediterranean bondage as it defined some other slave
systems.[61] Even in their absence, captives retained their political and
social standing in their home communities, including their legal
privileges. This particular facet of Mediterranean bondage could be
utilized by captives to mitigate the conditions of their captivity: communal ties were a source of power in exile. Individuals and information circulated rapidly in the Mediterranean, but people in Spain,
France, and Italy still knew less about what was going on in North
Africa than those present in North Africa. Thus distance allowed captives not only to draw on the authority they had in their home communities but also to exert real influence in these same communities.

In producing written testimonies, captives performed two roles.
First, they claimed the authority to determine the religious identity
of another. Within these inscribed institutional contexts and situ-
ational features, their words could make a Christian of a Muslim.
Such letters shaped strategies that—far beyond serving the needs of

renegades—enabled Inquisitors and others to negotiate their fragmentary knowledge of the Maghrib and of the life of Christian captives. There were still limits to the authority a document conveyed,
however. Inquisitors and others sought to qualify and verify the
knowledge embedded in such letters, which explains the value that
renegades placed on letters from priests. As Gracián's case suggests,
in some instances Inquisitors attempted to contact the authors of such
letters and ensure their missives' authenticity and truthfulness. Second, in personal letters at least, captives were maintaining and acting upon social and familial ties in Christendom that had persisted
despite the distance and disconnect imposed by the experience of captivity. Moreover, Christian captives were able to impress upon renegades the durability and effectiveness of these connections, which in
turn induced renegades to participate in the exchange of aid and help
Christian captives escape and survive.

MARTYRDOM AND SAINTHOOD

As we saw in Chapter 1, Muslims rarely forced Christian slaves to
turn Turk, but the majority of captives who were put under such pressure seem to have succumbed. The few who resisted, dying as witnesses to their faith, became martyrs. Captives who witnessed their
deaths held the power to shape the most exclusive community in the
Christian world, for they could transform the dead into martyrs and
martyrs into saints.[62] Captives were instrumental in constructing narratives of martyrdom and in participating in the canonization of executed Christians. In a few cases, captives preserved the remains of
their fellow captives who had died as martyrs, venerating them as
relics and sometimes constructing local cults around them; in some
cases, these relics migrated to Christendom.[63]

Captives played the main role in this process, from the moment of
death, through the acquisition of body parts, to shipping the remains
to Christendom. Captives were generally the first to brand a death as
martyrdom. For example, in August 1622, as news of the death of the
Trinitarian Bernardo Monroy, the shepherd of the Christian community who was locked in solitary confinement in his last years, spread
through Algiers, five hundred captives gathered around one of the city
towers shouting, "Saint, confessor, and martyr!"[64] Such declarations
were by no means authoritative and were subject to later contesta-
tion and debate, but they often became rough fodder for canonization

dossiers, legitimated by the very fact that they had to be acknowledged and countered in order to be discredited. The captives hurried to claim parts of Monroy's corpse and his personal effects, including pieces of his habit, hair, and beard. A witness reported that two Augustinian captives cut "four large bones of his arms . . . a finger of his right hand and the entire jawbone with the moles and teeth."[65] They likely had to steal such items at night, as renegades or captors might block the gathering of the relics.[66] Their actions were not spontaneous, for they were part of a recognized protocol that followed the death of a potential candidate for sainthood. The Augustinians collected testimonies from the captives who had witnessed Monroy's death for later consideration by Church authorities.[67]

Often it took years to procure the relics, let alone ship them to Christendom.[68] The possessors of Monroy's exhumed remains did not send them to the Trinitarian provincial of Castile in Toledo until 1634, a full twelve years after Monroy's death; they accompanied the relics, along with a certificate vouching for their authenticity signed by a captive-chaplain.[69] The papal nuncio in Madrid had approved a "particular and private cult" of Monroy's relics in 1623, which suggests he thought Monroy would be canonized.[70] However, in 1634 Urban VIII tightened up the procedures required for canonization, and Monroy's case came to a halt.[71]

Canonization required much more than relics or the chanting of captives. In the sixteenth century in response to Erasmian criticism of the sanctity of Catholic saints in light of the laxity of canonization procedures and Calvinist attacks on the Catholic notion of sanctity at large, the papacy had redefined the criteria and complicated the process, going so far as to freeze canonizations from 1525 until 1588, when Pope Sixtus V elevated Diego of Alcalá (c. 1400–1463) to sainthood. The Church's new strictures required each candidate to pass through two hearings—one conducted by a bishop and one by a postulator—and witnesses had to answer a standard set of questions and submit depositions that would be examined twice.[72] These standards placed even greater weight on the statements of captives, who might be among the only witnesses of the last years and death of candidates whose lives ended in North Africa.

Captives administered the initial interrogations for the canonization of Franciscan missionary Juan de Prado, who had been executed by Saadian sultan al Walīd ibn Zaydān (1631–36) in Marrakesh on May 24, 1631. The news of his death had spread rapidly, and less than a week after the execution, the papacy had already been informed of the event. The curia nominated a friar to collect testimonies and send them to Rome. Isolated in a Moroccan prison (though still able to send and receive mail), the friar delegated the responsibility to the sultan's personal doctor, a Christian captive, who in turn appointed an alternate in his stead, described as "slave and captain of the other Christian slaves" in Marrakesh, to interrogate captives on the basis of a questionnaire sent from Rome.[73]

Even a well-documented dossier did not make a winning candidate. As far as Rome was concerned, the keys to canonization were the foundation of a religious order, a career as a missionary, a pastoral life, involvement in charitable activity, or mysticism. Only two of the fifty-five saints canonized after the conclusion of the Council of Trent in 1563 and during the seventeenth century were martyrs.[74] Men like Juan de Prado, missionary in Morocco, and Bernardo Monroy, shepherd to Christian captives in Algiers, made strong candidates. Yet neither was canonized. Monroy's case stalled with the reforms of Urban VIII;[75] Juan de Prado was eventually beatified but only in 1728, nearly a century after his death.[76] Contemporaries could not have known, however, that so few beatifications would occur. Thus by testifying for martyrs captives acquired significant social power and a crucial role in shaping cult and memory, extending the boundaries of Christendom across the sea.

CONCLUSION

Captivity extended Spanish communities, especially communities along the Mediterranean littoral, across two continents and the sea that separates them. Community members who fell prey to Maghribi corsairs and were enslaved in North Africa maintained their membership in their home communities by writing home and by reporting on other community members who either died or converted in captivity. For most captives, writing had a number of practical purposes.[77] Testifying, snitching, complaining, and recommending were all survival strategies, part of a larger repertoire of actions that in their entirety constituted captivity. Archival references to the practice of writing—the texts captives wrote; copies and summaries of those texts or references to them—abound. Spanish literature across genres also alludes to captives' writings. These literary references could have provided models of captivity writings and their uses for early modern

Spaniards while blurring the line between textual and cultural norms, between literary representations and the harsh reality of captivity.

Communities and families in Iberian port cities and coastal towns that had been reconfigured by piracy and captivity were neither exclusively face-to-face communities nor imagined communities.[78] Rather, they were constituted through social claims embedded in texts that ideally produced co-presence and contemporaneity while extending social, political, and religious communal boundaries from afar. The texts captives wrote served them locally, in maintaining or bettering the conditions of their captivity, but simultaneously they also operated on a Mediterranean scale. Prison letters from the Maghrib reshaped families and kin groups, excluded converts from the community of the faithful, and allowed for the potential inclusion of martyrs in the community of saints. Although their mobility was constrained and compelled, through their writings captives maintained the boundaries of several overlapping communities. Writing and the transmission of written texts across the sea required a confidence in the structures that connected writers and addressees, and the Maghrib and the Spanish Empire. When writing to their kin or to political or religious institutions, captives assumed that their messages had a good chance of reaching their destination, and indeed many did. At the same time, the distance separating the Maghrib from the Habsburg's Spanish Empire meant that people living in southwestern Europe knew a lot less about the Maghrib than the captives imprisoned there. The extant records testifying to these dynamics largely pertain to Christian captives, but Muslim captives also maintained kinship ties and their communal status by writing letters and by asking their sovereign to intervene on their behalf and to improve the conditions of their enslavement, as we shall see in the next chapter.

The massive presence of Christians in the Maghrib and of Muslims in Europe made captives into a principal source of information. By informing their kin about the conversion of friends or attesting to renegades' Christian faith, captives served as ambassadors of the Inquisition in the Maghrib and perhaps helped overcome the anxiety provoked by the conversion of Christians and the threat—real or imagined—it posed for Christian communities. In that sense, captivity enabled the reshaping of spatial and social boundaries, the reconfiguration of the near and the far, and the extension of the power of political, religious, and social institutions—crown, church, and family—across the sea and into a hostile land.

CHAPTER 5

Confronting Threats,
Countering Violence

On December 13, 1603, Vicente Colom, a Spaniard enslaved in Algiers and a spy for the Spanish crown, recorded a meeting of the divan, the Algerian ruling council. Those present, Colom reported, had decided that four Christian priests from among the Spaniards held captive in Algiers should be seized and then burned to death. Supported by all those present at the council's meeting, their execution at the stake was to be an act of retaliation: a certain "Turk" had "entered the Divan" with a letter in his hand and had asked for revenge for his brother, who had been "burned in the galleys of Spain."[1] Yet the planned execution never took place. The next day, a larger divan meeting convened, and the corsairs who formed a major faction on the council unanimously objected to the act of revenge. They considered the precedent a danger to themselves, as they often fell into Christian hands in the course of their business.[2] To substantiate their opposition to vengeance, the corsairs could have referenced the foremost early modern Maghribi jurist, Ahmad ibn Yahyā al-Wansharīsī, who more than a century earlier had cited an earlier fatwa in a similar scenario, determining that it was illegal to kill Christian captives as to do so might result in the killing of Muslim captives.[3] The early seventeenth-century incident suggests the dynamics of the demands and the threats of religious violence that this chapter explores: an unidentified Muslim slave was executed in the Spanish royal galley on which he rowed; his oar mates sent word home demanding revenge; and immediately upon hearing the news, the brother of the executed "Turk" went to the governing council waving the letter he had received with the news and demanding vengeance. Whereas in similar instances the council had taken revenge and had abused or executed Christian captives, in this particular case the corsairs, fearing they would become the next victims in a blood feud, objected to the killing of priests, and the revenge pattern was halted.

Despite the Spanish identity of the reporting spy, his account offers access to a Maghribi perspective on the events recorded. Violence against both Muslim and Christian slaves of the kind Colom describes was common across the Mediterranean, and yet it violated the norms that governed slaves' lives. This chapter focuses on such tense moments and argues that while violence was disruptive, not to say destructive, for its victims, it generated communication between political powers that were at war, affected slaves, go-betweens, and political actors, and over time solidified the very norms that were violated, reducing friction as a result. Violence, as Colom's account suggests, was reciprocal in that the threats that Maghribi authorities and slave owners made against Christian slaves and the punishments the latter suffered often came as responses to complaints Muslims enslaved in Spain had made. The lives of Christian captives in the Maghrib depended upon the living conditions and treatment of Muslims enslaved in Spain, and vice versa. The violence slaves suffered formed part of a larger chain of challenges and counterblows that occurred on a Mediterranean scale.[4]

In sending word home about violence and in asking their rulers to use their power to protect them, captives generated tense diplomatic interactions across the sea before the signing of peace agreements between Spain, Algiers, and Morocco in the eighteenth century and underscored the role of violence as a mediating force. European and North African powers shared understandings and expectations about the treatment of captives. When small or midlevel political or religious actors, ranging from slave owners to local governors and priests, violated these norms, they brought into relief the *doxa* that managed the lives of slaves in the Mediterranean and the implicit rules that were to be mutually respected. These violations influenced all the parties involved: suffering slaves, mediating friars, and violent rulers. By sending reports of grievances home and demanding redress from their rulers, slaves sought to better their living conditions or at least make them tolerable. When their rulers acted upon the slaves' requests, slaves often succeeded in improving their situation. But the impact of threats and religious violence—in particular forced conversions and the desecration of cadavers and of religious images—as well as the demands of slaves to be allowed to practice their religion freely had effects that went beyond the lives of individual slaves. Through the submission of such grievances, Muslim slaves defined themselves in relation to religious privilege. When, in response, Muslim rulers forced conversion on their Christian slaves or deprived them of ritual burial, these rulers reciprocated religious violence with their Christian counterparts, thereby recognizing slaves as subjects whose relation with the ruler was defined by religion rather than, for example, economic objects. At the same time, by responding to their subjects' needs and struggles to improve their living conditions, rulers were making political claims, which when acknowledged solidified their sovereignty. In the process, rulers' demands made the go-betweens, Trinitarians, Mercedarians, and other ecclesiastics, into de facto diplomatic agents channeling information of various kinds. Finally, these violent dynamics of reciprocity and revenge resulted in a Mediterranean consensus about the religious privilege to which slaves were entitled and eventually in the codification of this consensus.

Two types of early modern captivity narratives depict violence against slaves cast in confessional terms: one, which circulated in printed form, is found in chapbooks and martyrologies composed by Spanish, Portuguese, French, and Italian ecclesiastics writing about Christian captives, and the other is in the letters Muslims enslaved in Spain wrote to their families in the Maghrib and in oral testimonies given by redeemed Muslim slaves, which depicted the violation of ransom agreements, brutal executions, and religious violence against captives. While both forms were common, they have been little studied. Literary historians have been reluctant to explore works like the 1631 Sevillian chapbook *Relación de el riguroso martyrio que el padre fr. Ioan de Prado de la provincial de San Diego de Sevilla* (An Account of the Rigorous Martyrdom of the Father Friar Ioan de Prado) perhaps owing to their status as popular texts printed cheaply and distributed widely or their poor literary quality.[5] Historians have likewise dismissed their claims of religiously motivated violence visited upon Christian captives, redeemers, and missionaries because of their propagandistic nature.[6] The letters and testimonies of Muslim slaves have been little examined not least because they were rarely recorded and archived. And yet the handful of surviving originals, multiple copies, and summaries all capture how, on learning of violence against Muslim captives, relatives submitted complaints to

North African rulers, who, in response, warned their Spanish counterparts to amend the situation or face retaliation. These extant textual traces are important not only for what they depict but also for their role in setting in motion processes they document.

There are three manifest differences between the sources Christian and Muslim slaves generated: first, in their reversal of the religious identities of perpetrator and victim; second, in their intended audience and goals; and third, in their distribution and exposure among contemporaries. Whereas chapbooks and martyrologies were printed and meant for wide circulation, with the goal of animating the faithful and encouraging them to donate alms for the redemption of captives, letters and testimonies from Muslim slaves addressed their kin or state officials and circulated orally or in manuscript form, while their goal was to stop the mistreatment of slaves. The records of Muslim complaints more often reveal their outcome, since they tend to be in the form of official state documents. Moreover, the instances of violence against Muslim captives that have left an archival mark were those in which Christians acknowledged their responsibility or at least were willing to entertain the idea they might have been responsible.

There are also striking similarities between these representations of violence. Both sides portrayed their own actions as just and responsive and those of their opponents as unjust and provocative, and both denied cyclical reciprocity by claiming that violence originated in their opponents' unwarranted behavior. On these counts, these texts were mirror images. By juxtaposing these sources and pairing them with others, this chapter explores the generative nature of violence against slaves and exposes the links between seemingly isolated instances of violence (which authors of Christian martyrologies sought to conceal).

CHRISTIAN CAPTIVES IN ALGIERS: RELIGIOUS PRIVILEGES AND FREEDOM OF MOVEMENT

Acts of violence against captives and broken ransom deals were not rare, though they violated the standards by which captives expected their masters to abide. The religious privileges enjoyed by Christians held captive in the Maghrib and by Muslims held captive in Iberia and Italy were not identical. Yet both groups enjoyed such privileges, and these and the norms guiding them were acknowledged on both sides of the sea, even if no treaty or agreement ever codified them.[7] Indeed, the records refer to them rarely, and they manifested themselves only when violated. Therefore, reconstructing the norm requires analyzing its exceptions and thus reading sources for what they imply or take as given. Notations by enslaved captives about excessive curfews, religious repression, and arbitrary executions never identified explicitly the norms that were being violated.

Vicente Colom, who reported the incident that opened this chapter, meticulously recorded such moments in his diary. On August 19, 1602, for example, he related that the Algerians had "decreed curfew laws [imposing] chains and handcuffs and death penalty for any Christian walking around day or night."[8] It is unclear when the curfew was canceled and the regular routine reestablished, but four and a half months later, on January 8, 1603, he mentioned the imposition of other harsh laws: "They issued a cruel edict [ordering] the destruction of all the churches [and] forbidding [priests to say] mass under a death penalty; And they ordered that the . . . legal authorities in this land pay a visit to all the prisons and break and destroy all the [religious] images they could find."[9] A Valencian priest caught saying mass a few weeks later, on January 25, 1603, was severely punished by one hundred blows "only for saying the mass. [A]nd the [Algerians] were on the verge of burning him."[10] This curfew was continued for such a long period that the chronicler commented on its exceptional duration: "and although they say that in the past the [Muslims] imposed curfews, none was maintained for so long and none lasted so much time as this one does."[11] Colom never states exactly how long the curfew lasted, but an entry in his diary from May 18, 1603, referring to recently published and implemented curfew laws suggests that the January restrictions were annulled less than four months after their imposition. The new laws ordered "all the Christians to be chained and every two [captives] to walk in pairs chained one to the other and that they shave their beards and hair and that they don't wander around very early, late, or on Friday the prayer day, but rather be locked up."[12]

The careful recording of shifts in the rules marks these variations as violations of captives' expectations. Colon's logging of these episodes suggests that at least a majority of Christian captives in the Maghrib could normally roam unchained early and in the evening and when they were not working and that they could openly practice their religion in one of the few churches operating in Algiers. Suspension of these privileges seems to have been common, but usually these interludes were short, rarely more than a few weeks long. Colom's diary implies that when Muslim authorities wanted to change this routine and violate the daily order, they had to follow legal and administrative procedures. The divan—the governing council—had to convene, and the Janissaries, corsairs, and governor debated the issue before a decision was made. Such procedures do not exclude the possibility of unofficial violations of religious freedom or cruel behavior by individual slave owners; as a rule, however, norms governed the treatment of slaves, and their violation had to follow institutional procedures.

Why would Muslim slave owners bestow religious privileges on their slaves or feel obliged to respect norms regarding the right treatment of slaves? The Chevalier D'Arvieux, the French consul to Tunis and later to Algiers, explained in 1666 that owners treated slaves fairly because of their economic value: "the Turks have an interest to be careful with [their slaves]: among [the Turks], these [slaves] are commodities, they buy them in the best deal they can, and sell them at the most expensive price they can. They would risk losing their money if they were to treat their slaves so badly as to make them ill and even cause their death."[13] At the same time, on occasion Maghribi governors did execute slaves in response to news that Muslim slaves were mistreated in Spain and in order to prevent the repetition of such mistreatment, an act this economic reductionism cannot explain.

Colom rarely offers explanations for the violations he records, except by implication. He juxtaposes encroachments with events that the Algerians could have interpreted as strategic threats and reasons for stricter security, and he allows his readers to fill in the gaps. In the two and a half weeks preceding the curfew of January 19, 1602, for example, rumors about Spanish agents sent to the kingdom of Cuco—a nearby enemy of Algiers—rapidly spread across the city, terrified the population, and "caused great commotion."[14] On January 3, 7, and 18, Colom reported that the Spanish agents were heading to Algiers and communicating with captives and renegades there.[15] The curfew on May 18, 1603, seems to have had a different cause. It followed the army's departure from the city for its biennial demonstration of military might during which it collected taxes in the towns, villages, and encampments that surrounded Algiers (*Maḥalla* [Arabic]); the curfew could then have been, as Colom's account seems to suggest, a protective measure taken in light of the absence of a strong military force.

DEPRIVING MUSLIM SLAVES OF RELIGIOUS PRIVILEGES:
A CHRONICLE OF VIOLENCE FORETOLD

The decision not to take revenge for Spanish violence in December 1603, as recounted at the start of this chapter, followed a similar incident in May 1603. At that time a number of Muslim slaves escaped from the Spanish Empire's Sicilian galleys, anchored at the time at Cartagena, in the south of Spain. On arriving in Algiers, the runaways reported that the Spaniards had captured the galley of Murat Frances, a renegade and corsair, and that in Murcia in Spain, six renegades from Murat's crew had been burned at the stake. Enraged, at the next meeting of the divan renegades in Algiers demanded the burning of six captive priests.[16] As they would repeat in December, the divan elected not to cede to such demands, but in this case Colom's diary does not explain why.

The Majorcan Jeroni Contestí, a former captive in Algiers, would report another incident of threatened execution in 1615, when he returned to Majorca as a renegade. He submitted himself to the Inquisitorial tribunal on the island and told his story. He had been taken captive a year earlier and had been sold into slavery in Algiers. He had managed to negotiate a ransom deal, which was nearly carried through. While he was already on a boat that was about to set sail and return him to his island, the divan ordered his arrest. According to his description, the divan was reacting to news from Majorca that the Majorcan owners of three Morisco slaves from Andalusia had threatened them with death by burning if they refused to convert to Christianity. In response to the news, Contestí was detained together with another Majorcan captive, Bartolomé Vidal, and the two were forced to convert to Islam in retaliation.[17]

Contestí told this story before the Inquisitorial tribunal of Majorca while being investigated. It is quite possible that during these long, stressful hours facing his Inquisitors, he was more interested in inventing a convincing story about his conversion, one that would lead to his absolution, than in relaying the events the way they had truly happened. And yet the fact that Contestí chose to outline the story of his conversion with reference to the interactive and mutual nature of violence within the context of captivity suggests that it was an at least reasonable account, one that his Inquisitors were likely to believe. It thus demonstrates the discursive effects of these practices of violence. In other words, his case reflects not only the logic of violence but also its symbolical and rhetorical effects.

These documents support a number of hypotheses about religious violence within the context of Mediterranean captivity. Eruptions of violence in Algiers and other Maghribi cities were linked to violence or potential violence against Muslims enslaved in Spain and were dominated by a logic of challenge and riposte.[18] The episode began when Spaniards behaved in a way that Maghribis perceived as a violation of the conditions that their subjects enslaved in Spain deserved. A rejoinder followed, sometimes elevating the price—for one Muslim executed, three Christians might be executed and so on. Majorcan captives paid for violations of religious freedom that happened in Majorca, and captives from Gibraltar paid for actions taken against Muslims in Gibraltar. Priests often paid with their lives for executions of Christians who had converted to Islam or of Moriscos who returned to Islam in the Maghrib and thus were perceived by the Inquisition as renegades. Those who demanded redress often shared the identity of the initial victims—Moriscos sought revenge for violence exerted on Moriscos, renegades for violence exerted on renegades. Commonly, Maghribis targeted their responses, attempting to link their punitive actions to the event that elicited them. They did so by carefully selecting the slaves they punished and making sure they shared local, confessional, or ethnic identity with the perpetrators of the violence exerted upon Muslim slaves. What started as a local event could quickly turn into a Mediterranean affair. Even when the episode was local and private, initiated by individual slave owners, it immediately involved various institutions, ranging from the family or kin group applying for vengeance through the North African political authorities to other reactions from Spanish religious orders and political authorities. Religious violence, then, stressed local, confessional, and ethnic identities and articulated links at specific levels, such as the local, imperial, and Mediterranean. While the reality would have been messier, not to mention bloodier, the model suggested a tit-for-tat response.

Trinitarians, Mercedarians, Franciscans, and other friars produced pamphlets and images portraying violence against Christians that made no mention of Spanish retaliation, even though the friars themselves acted as go-betweens, mediating these violent exchanges. The tension between these images of violence, on the one hand, and productive collaboration, on the other, captures the friars' difficulty in catering to the interests of all of the various interest groups, which included Christian donors back home and in Latin America, Spanish authorities, non-ecclesiastic ransom agents who offered competing services, Spanish critics of the project of redemption and of the export of bullion and goods to North Africa, and, finally, the authorities in the Maghrib.[19] In order to convince the faithful and the Spanish crown to give the alms necessary for redemptions, each order published and circulated pamphlets that stressed the victimization of Christian captives as well as the risk the friars took in negotiating with Algerians and Moroccans. However, the redeemers also needed to maintain efficient working relations with the Maghribis if they were to be able to ransom Christians and thus justify their mission to both their critics and the crown. The friars operated as diplomats in an age that preceded formal diplomacy and the signing of peace treaties between Spain and Algiers. They had to maintain the impression that they had better working relations with the Algerians than any other redeemers, that their expertise earned them the right to be Spain's exclusive ransom agents, and that merchants who competed against them ought to be prohibited from traveling to North Africa.[20]

Documents from the second half of the century provide more details about continued violence, the political interactions it initiated, and their discursive construction. In January 1663, for example, Alonso de Jesús, a Franciscan friar posted in Algiers, was sent back to Spain with a message for the Council of Aragon from the Ismail Pasha, the Algerian governor. The friar reported that the divan had elected "to burn all the priests and images, destroy the churches, and [order] that the [members of the orders of] redemption be enslaved."[21] Was the Franciscan surprised by these atrocities? Did he demand that the crown retaliate? On the contrary, he explained that the pasha was reacting to letters he had received from Muslims enslaved in Andalusia. The slaves claimed that six other Muslim slaves from the city of Puerto de Santa María near Cadiz, six from Sardinia (then under Spanish rule), and one from the Andalusian town of Alcalá de los Gazules had been arrested shortly after paying the ransom fees that their masters demanded. In addition, the slaves reported that Christians were desecrating the bodies of Muslim slaves in Sanlúcar de Barrameda. This exchange demonstrates not only that Muslim slaves kept in touch with home but also that members of different slave communities within the Mediterranean territories of the Spanish Empire interacted, informing one another of their situation. The Algerian governor, according to de Jesús, demanded that the "mocking of the bodies of the Turks" stop at once.[22] De Jesús acknowledged the injustice of the precipitating actions and asked that the Spanish governors immediately correct the situation by allowing the Muslim slaves in their jurisdiction to bury their dead according to their custom, "because what they ask is just." The Council of Aragon stepped in rapidly and ordered that such actions be stopped and that manumitted slaves not be arrested.

While participating in and intensifying a cycle of violence, the Algerian retaliation was also a communicative action, a warning that order in Algiers would be reestablished only if the Spanish monarchy maintained acknowledged living standards—some religious freedom and fair execution of ransom deals—for its Muslim slaves. The records suggest that these incidents were not isolated, for similar episodes constantly recurred. Documents from 1644 shed light on the early stages of these chronicles. Yusuf of Tlemsen (about sixty-two miles southwest of Oran), the slave of a Sevillian noble, was arrested and put to work as a galley slave almost immediately after his manumission, without having committed any crime and in spite of carrying manumission records that proved he was a free man on his way back to the Maghrib. In the complaint he submitted to the Spanish Council of War on March 9, 1644, he demanded his immediate release, adding, "In Barbary, they never detain Christians who paid their ransom; and by detaining in Spain the Moors who had paid their ransom, [the Spaniards] create a situation in which in Barbary they would do the same with the Christians, a thing that would result in notable damage to many Christians because there are many more Christians than Moors who are ransomed."[23] Yusuf's complaint suggests that Muslim slaves were able to master the Spanish legal and administrative repertoires and employ them in moments of acute need. That facility is a sign of the degree to which captivity, slavery, and ransom linked Spain and North Africa. More importantly, it demonstrates the role that Muslim slaves played in making visible to the Spaniards the interactive nature of such violations and links these violations had established. Certainly his description might have been biased, providing an anti-Spanish perspective, and yet by referring to how Maghribi authorities allowed freed Christian slaves to return to Christendom— "in Barbary, they never detain Christians who paid their ransom"— Yusuf implicitly expressed that the Spaniards should let him go, not from kindness but because of institutional norms inherent in Mediterranean slavery that he expected his Spanish interlocutors would share. He reminded the magistrates of the Council of War how such

incidents end. While it is impossible to determine whether the Spaniards let him go because of his implied threat to write home to ask for
help, the record does show that they gave him his freedom without his
taking such a measure.

Yusuf's complaint and its success shed further light on the early
stages of the dynamics that preceded Maghribi threats. First, communication between the Maghrib and Spain flowed continuously, and
both Muslim and Christian slaves could send messages to their kin
about their situations. Second, Yusuf and the council alike expected
that once the right people in Algiers heard of Yusuf's troubles, Christian captives would face obstacles in achieving ransom. Beyond that,
the case reflects that Mediterranean slavery was an *interdependent*
but *asymmetrical* system: namely, it offered Muslims and Christians
uneven chances of recovering their liberty. Yusuf's statement that
Christians were ransomed in greater numbers was probably accurate
because Christian slaves could rely on institutions for ransom: the
Trinitarian and the Mercedarian orders ransomed Portuguese, Spanish, and French captives, and Italian urban fraternities ransomed Italian captives.[24] Similar institutions did not exist in Morocco or the
Ottoman Maghrib, and Muslims enslaved in the Habsburg's Spanish
Empire, France, or Italy had to rely on their relatives and, in some
cases, on deals their rulers struck with their Christian counterparts.[25]
Having achieved ransom, Yusuf used this asymmetry as an asset,
pointing out that violations of ransom procedures would dispropor-
tionately affect Christians.

Sometimes on-the-spot negotiation did not achieve the desired
effect for Muslim slaves. In April 1692 Bive Muhammad Rex, as
he is called in the Spanish sources, a Muslim slave held in Majorca,
whom we met in Chapter 3, failed to solve his problem by negotiating directly with his owners. He sent a letter to his relatives in Algiers
in which he complained about his miserable living conditions and the
bad treatment he was receiving from his mistress, the wife of a fisherman, who starved him, chained his neck at night, and interfered with
his practice of his religion.[26] Muhammad knew what he was doing.
His relatives addressed the governor of Algiers, who closed all the
churches in Algiers and ordered every slave from Majorca chained.[27]
The governor also asked the Trinitarians to write to Spain and make
sure Madrid urged the Majorcan local authorities to improve Muhammad's living conditions. Their letter described the conditions experienced by Christian slaves in Algiers prior to these measures:

> We [the Trinitarians] have recently arrived [in Algiers] and in the last
> short days we have enjoyed many favors of the gentleman governor
> and of all of these [Algerian] gentlemen. . . . [The Algerians] allow
> the slaves to attend the churches, to frequent the saintly sacraments
> and on holy days the owners send them to carry out the obligation
> of Christians, they do not force anyone to leave the Christian reli-
> gion, they treat them uniformly well, and if one of them complains to
> the governor about his owner mistreating him, they punish him and
> make him [the owner] sell him [the slave] to another.[28]

The Trinitarians explained that by mistreating Muslims in Spain,
depriving them of their religious rights and trying to force them to
convert, the Spaniards were "giving an excuse to these *señores* [the
Algerians] to do the same with these [Christian] poor slaves and with
us."[29] The friars sealed their letter with an animated appeal to the
viceroy of Majorca that he must order Muhammad's mistress "to
treat her slaves with love and charity in order that they [the Algeri-
ans] treat the Christians in this city [Algiers] in the same way."[30] The
viceroy of Majorca moved Muhammad to the viceregal prison to get
him away from his mistress and forced Muhammad's owners to pay
the Muslim slave a real per day for a period. In return, Muhammad
had to write a letter recounting how fairly he was now being treated.[31]
Having the written evidence circulate back to Muslim sovereigns was
evidently equally important to concluding this correspondence to
everyone's satisfaction.

As in the case of Yusuf, Muhammad's example demonstrates
how, in contrast to the public image of Algiers embedded in the
propaganda of the orders of redemption and left to us by the Trinitarians and the Mercedarians, representatives of the orders actually
worked in tandem with the Algerian authorities. While there is no
doubt that the lives of captive Christians and Muslims alike were
miserable, the descriptions provided by the Trinitarians, who passed
on the threats of the Algerians to the Spaniards, appear to provide
a more balanced picture of captivity. In their comments on the messages from the Algerians, the Trinitarians insisted that the Algerians
treat the Christians, both captives and ransomers, fairly. The Trinitarians understood that threats to the status quo that the Algerians
occasionally imposed made sense within the context of Mediterranean slavery. The friars' actions were an attempt to retain their position with the Spanish court as near exclusive or at least privileged
and royally funded redeemers. In order to maintain that standing,
they had to prove successful in ransoming captives, and that success

was predicated upon the friars convincing the Maghribis that the former could assist the latter in taking care of mistreated Muslims enslaved in Spain.

DESECRATION OF CADAVERS AND FORCED CONVERSIONS

In 1696, the dey of Algiers, Haci Ahmed bin al-Haci, used the Trinitarians again to address the Spanish Council of State. Algerians enslaved in Spain had appealed for his help, complaining that their masters and other Christians had desecrated the bodies of deceased Muslim slaves and had forcibly baptized others. The Trinitarians passed on an apparently verbatim translation of his letter, which survives. His listing of the injustices his subjects suffered included excessive labor demands and sick captives being forced to deny their own religion. He also complained about improper disposal of their bodies, including their being discarded in the sea tied to a stone, left in filthy streets, and thrown from castles. He concluded, "Why are you doing this when that is how one treats a dog?"[32] The dey's letter sheds light on a missive of 1663 from the Algerian governor in which the author claimed the divan had burned bodies. While it refers to a much later case, the detail the dey provides suggests that the 1663 message refers to the prevention of a religious burial according to traditional rites. Other captives and authors of Christian propagandistic texts made similar accusations, such as Jerónimo Gracián, who was held captive for two years in Tunis between 1592 and 1594. His *Tratado de la redención de cautivos* (1609) claimed that galley slaves' bodies were thrown in the sea when they died and that the bodies of slaves employed in the city were left in a rubbish dump.[33] Other accounts describe the desecration of bodies prior to disposal. The accounts suggest a general understanding that slaves deserved religious burial.

The dey's letter also accused Christians of baptizing dying Muslim slaves against their will. A few other accusations of forced baptism by Christians exist. In 1608, Fatima, an Algerian girl ransomed from Livorno, was baptized in Corsica when the ship that returned her to Algiers stopped to provision; in 1658, Algerians enslaved in Málaga sent letters to Algiers complaining about forced conversions; in 1668, a baby girl was baptized in Gibraltar against her parents' will; at an unknown date between 1689 and 1695, four boys and four girls from Algiers were converted by force, having been ransomed according to custom; and in 1696, crowds in Ibiza tied the hands of two "Turks" who refused to convert and threw them into the sea.[34] Finally, in 1723, another Muslim girl was baptized, in Cartagena and against her mother's will.[35] While Christian propaganda frequently described forced conversions imposed on Christian slaves in the Maghrib, evidence suggests the dey's claim of asymmetry was accurate.[36] The source of Muslim objection to forced conversion was the Quranic Sūrat al-Baqara.[37] However, beyond theological prohibitions conversion devalued Christian and Muslim captives. Converted captives were difficult if not impossible to ransom, as kin and redeemers were reluctant to pay for their freedom. The pasha of Algiers referenced this problem in 1608, according to a Spanish intelligence report, when he denied the request of soldiers defecting from Oran that they be permitted to convert to Islam upon their arrival in Algiers, saying that he preferred having them as Christian captives rather than as free Muslims.[38] The Chevalier d'Arvieux, who in 1666 negotiated the ransom of French captives in Tunis on behalf of the French king, wrote in his account of his diplomatic mission that charges of forced conversion by torture were unfounded and that such cases were "extremely exceptional."[39]

The dey claimed that Christian captives were treated in Algiers "like our vassals without preventing them from going to their churches and seeing their priests, and when they are sick, the priests attend to them at the hospital."[40] He demanded punishment of the priests who violated such norms for his own subjects and warned the council that he would exact punishment on the Christians in Algiers if the situation did not change: "and therefore we address you as a friend in order that later you will not say that you did not receive a warning before and after; because we will impose the same extortions and travails on the religious priests and all the captives which are in our kingdoms . . . and we will shut down the hospitals and force . . . the Christian captives to turn Moor."[41] The threat seals the letter that opened with the complaint. It suggests the communication protocols in place at the time: North African authorities issued warnings about their intentions, tied them to injuries Muslims slaves had suffered from their Spanish masters, and then imposed stricter curfews and executed captives. Such interactions indicated that the standards for the treatment of slaves were conceded by all parties. While Trinitarians often participated in the production of propaganda that presented violations of these standards as the result of irrational behavior by Algerians and other Maghribis, they acknowledged the validity of the dey's demands and urged the Spanish authorities to amend the situation.

Violence against captives offered both Spanish and North African rulers an opportunity to claim, measure, or demonstrate their power. It also mediated the political relations between the authorities where the slaves were held and the slaves' home authorities. Regardless of where slaves labored, their fate was directly tied to that of slaves across the sea. For this reason, eighteenth-century Italian cities often allocated a space where enslaved Muslims could pray.[42] The *bagno*, or slave prison, of Livorno offers an early example. From the time of its establishment, in 1598 to 1604, the Livornese prison contained a mosque. Because Livorno belonged to the Grand Duchy of Tuscany, the presence of four mosques and imams in the *bagno* by 1680 can be credited to Tuscan policy. No abstract ideal about freedom of religion underlay this policy; Tuscany expected that Florentines, as well as other Christian subjects enslaved in the Maghrib, would receive equal treatment if they permitted these institutions in turn. A letter that five Muslim slaves in Livorno sent to the authorities in Tunis in 1680 stressed that they had been able to attend services at mosques and follow Muslim burial rites, that they had received generous food portions, medical services, and salaries, and that they had been allowed to practice petty commerce. The slaves, four imams and the head of the merchant slaves (*capo de' mercanti schiavi*, who represented the slaves' economic interests), even described the Livornese authorities imposing sharia on Muslims by punishing slaves caught drunk. The authors concluded with a request, pleading with the Tunisian authorities to provide captive priests and friars and Christians in general with conditions equal to theirs, saying they would otherwise lose the privilege they were enjoying.[43] The authorities of Livorno had coaxed the slaves to write this letter upon receiving a warning from the Tunisian bey, who threatened to mistreat Christian captives should the Livornese continue to physically abuse Muslim slaves. In his turn, the bey was reacting to letters he had received from other Muslims enslaved in the Livornese prison.[44] The numerous concessions to the other's religion that such letters reference or demand reflect the relationship of religion and political power. Rulers claimed power by acceding to their subjects' pleadings and by intervening on their behalf. When a ruler's interventions violated norms—by executing or forcefully converting slaves, for example, whereby he removed valuable goods from networks of exchange—that ruler brought into relief the tension between the market and religion inherent in the Mediterranean system of bondage. In responding to forced baptisms of Muslim slaves and desecration of their bodies by forced conversion and shutting down of churches, Maghribi rulers were marking slaves as religious subjects, rather than exchangeable objects, defined in relation to the norms of religious privilege and conduct.

Violence against slaves varied across the region and had a complex history. Between 1609 and 1614, Spain had expelled the Moriscos, Spanish Muslims who had been forcefully baptized by the turn of the sixteenth century and their descendants. Yet recent excavations reveal that during the seventeenth century private worship spaces were available to Muslim slaves who labored in Spain after 1614. Probably at the turn of the eighteenth century, Muslim slaves purchased a building in Cartagena that they used as a mosque, with the permission of the bishop (*diocesano*); the slaves also had an adjacent space where they had buried their dead. It is unclear when exactly the mosque was established and how long it was in use. Although local magistrates often interrupted prayers, the mosque continued to operate at least until some point between the late 1720s and early 1730s, when the Inquisitorial tribunal of Murcia ordered its closing. The episode left its mark in the archives because when the news of the mosque's closing reached Algiers, the pasha immediately issued and dispatched a warning to Spain, carried by a Trinitarian friar. The pasha demanded the reopening of the mosque, that Muslims be allowed to pray there, and that local magistrates be prohibited from disturbing the worshipers' peace. If the Spaniards would not amend the situation, he added, Christian priests in Algiers would suffer and local churches would be shut down. The Inquisitorial tribunal of Murcia discussed the case, but unfortunately the archive does not provide us with evidence of its decision on the matter.[45]

Cycles composed of violence, threat, and sanction seem to have led to the expansion of the privilege to pray in a mosque or be buried according to custom. The threat by Dey Haci Ahmed bin al-Haci described earlier led the Spanish king to issue in 1696 an order forbidding the mistreatment of Muslim slaves or the desecration of their bodies. The king also ordered the governors of Spanish territories in which Muslim slaves lived to allocate burial space for them—"in all cities and towns (*lugares*) inside and outside of Spain."[46] Previous writs had responded to specific and local situations, but this order was general. The degree to which local governors obeyed the injunction remains unclear, and yet the order is indicative of what appears to have been a trend that eventually resulted in the return of burial spaces and, in fewer instances, Muslim worship about a century after the expulsion of the Moriscos.

Thus, in addition to making diplomats of redeeming friars, chains of violence that crossed the Mediterranean had at least three effects. First, by making threats or exerting violence perceived as a violation of the norm, rulers claimed and established political power that was defined in relation to religious privilege. Second, this process helped constitute enslaved captives as subjects defined by their religious practice, as opposed to only by their economic value. Finally, norms were reinforced, gradually formalized by mutual threats; in other words, what started as negative reciprocity (with negative effects on the reciprocating parties) turned into positive reciprocity.[47] Violence and violations of norms and privileges came to guarantee those same norms and privileges.

JUST AND UNJUST VIOLENCE

The unjust punishment of Muslim slaves, attempts to convert them by force, and desecrations of slaves' bodies produced an obligation to reciprocate with violence. The countering responses of Algerians occurred not only weeks, or even months, after the events that provoked them but also across geographic and imperial boundaries. The link between cause and effect had to be made visible in order to be effective; in other words, the Algerian reprisal had to be associated with the action from which it resulted.[48] Symmetry required reprisal, with those in Algiers or elsewhere in the Maghrib who demanded retaliation sharing a religious, cultural, or professional identity with the Muslims who had been unjustly punished in Spain. Renegades demanded vengeance for renegades, and other groups, such as Moriscos, displayed the same kind of loyalty. Punishment was enacted against slaves who shared a geographic or other identity with the perpetrators of violence on the other side of the sea. In enacting revenge for violence against renegades or Moriscos in Spain, Maghribis singled out priests because the Inquisition typically perpetrated these crimes, and for Maghribis priests emblematized Inquisitors. Vengeance and the violence that preceded it had to be carefully linked to each other to make causal relations evident.

In their exchanges with the Spanish authorities, Maghribi rulers portrayed their actions as always dependent upon initial Christian violence: violence began in Spain and only then moved to the Maghrib, and it was not cyclical. Christian representations of the Algerian violence wielded against Christian slaves made the same claim in reverse. However, publicity and propaganda were not the only media through which Christians responded to such events. In some cases, Spaniards engaged in a direct dialogue with North Africans about what constituted just violence. Such give-and-take followed an exchange of violence in 1630 that was commemorated in a play by Juan Pérez de Montalván.[49] An Algerian woman named Zahra Izanbgue had purchased a Spanish captive, Pedro Guiral, in the hope of exchanging him for her husband, the captive and shipwright Hasan, held captive in Naples (at the time, a Spanish imperial territory). Five years of negotiation ensued. Guiral's father requested shipwright Hasan from the king, and his request was approved.[50] However, instead of receiving the slave he requested, the royal magistrates mistakenly provided him with two other slaves.[51] When news that Hasan had been burned by Christians reached Algiers, Guiral was executed and religious images found in captives' churches were burned. The circumstances of Hasan's death are unclear. At least one Muslim slave reported that Hasan was burned alive; another source suggests that he died a natural death but then his body was burned and never buried. Christian captives in Algiers claimed he had died a natural death and been given a proper religious burial.

The case haunted Spaniards for at least two decades. In 1648, Isidro del Castillo y Aguilera, an ex-captive who developed a strong friendship with his former captors, assisted an Algerian envoy in convincing the authorities in Madrid to resume ransom operations in Algiers (after nearly forty years during which Spain had reduced to a minimum its redemptive efforts in Algiers; see Chapter 7). A letter discussing the latest round of violence against slaves that he sent to his former captors began by explaining that Spaniards had distrusted the Algerians since the execution of Pedro Guiral. The letter responded in part to a recent incident in which authorities in Madrid had sentenced to death by strangulation three Muslim slaves charged with murdering Spaniards. Algerian authorities, acting on a letter from a Muslim slave, had avenged the murders on Christian slaves. And yet Algiers sent an envoy to Spain to discuss the events, proposing to negotiate future ransom deals, and the Spaniards received the envoy ceremoniously and commenced negotiations. In his letter, del Castillo y Aguilera accused Algiers of often retaliating too quickly and on the basis of unfounded rumors, "only because one Moorish slave writes whatever he fancies and feels like, without an additional report or account. . . . And a government like the Divan of Algiers, [bringing together] so many great and noble men, is moved to action because of one fraudulent account of a slave, who due to the deprivation of his liberty, passionately writes whatever he fancies."[52] He emphasized the gulf between the ruling class at Algiers and slave-informants in order to cast doubt on the veracity of information Muslim slaves sent to the Maghrib. Additionally, he accused Algiers of retaliating unjustly, namely, without following legal procedure, while by contrast, the three Muslim slaves executed by Spanish authorities had been assigned a lawyer and procurator, investigated, and sentenced, and they had confessed to the crime of killing two Christian children and one Christian woman. To bolster his argument, he told his addressee that the Algerian envoy in Madrid had interviewed Muslim slaves who confirmed del Castillo y Aguilera's version of the events. The legality of the procedure in Madrid distinguished it from the Algerian vengeance, which was inappropriate. He suggested that the Algerian authorities acted without such legal procedures, allowing unfounded rumor to guide their actions.

Like other Spanish observers del Castillo y Aguilera claimed that Algiers always responded to news of this sort with unmeasured and unjust violence. The case reported by Colom that opened this chapter suggests otherwise. The corsairs, fearing a feud-like cycle of bloodshed of which they would be the victims, opposed retaliating the killing of the Turk in the Spanish galleys. Melchor de Zúñiga, captive in Algiers in the 1630s, whom we met earlier through his comments on the exchange of slaves, provides supporting evidence to Colom's account. De Zúñiga claims that whenever the Algerian authorities announced their intention to punish a Christian captive or a merchant, wives of Algerians enslaved in Spain immediately staged a protest in front of the divan. Shouting, the women claimed that should the Christians be punished, their husbands and sons enslaved in Christendom would pay with their lives.[53] This report is important. It stresses the crucial role women played in generating responsive violence—like Zahra Izanbgue, the wife of Hasan, did—*and* in preventing it. The account reminds us that Algiers, but also Spain, were not homogeneous entities but that measures taken were rather the effect of struggles between different individual and institutional actors. Against small-scale instigators, who demanded vengeance, and were often backed up by the local authorities, coalitions of humble actors, in this case women, could be formed demanding to end the bloodshed, not for humanistic reasons but out of love or fear of what might happen to their loved ones.

Beyond the specificities of how del Castillo y Aguilera framed Spanish and Algerian violence, his letter reflects a discourse of violence to a large degree embedded in oral testimonies, letters, pamphlets, and diplomatic exchanges and produced, replicated, and circulated by Christian and Muslim captives, redeemers, and political actors. Spaniards and Algerians constantly accused one another of unjust violence that in turn justified violence. Each side compared and contrasted its conduct with the other's, and both Christians and Muslims claimed that their opponents started any given episode and that the latter's unjust behavior was thus not part of a larger chain of challenges and counterblows but a justified response to provocation.

The nature of the evidence, which typically provides only one side's description of a single event, usually does not allow us to investigate whether violent episodes consisted of a single initial blow and a single response. A few cases suggest, however, that continuous challenges and ripostes produced larger cycles of violence. In 1589, for example, unidentified Muslims in Tétouan—a city densely populated and ruled by Moriscos for most of the seventeenth century—threatened to burn three Christian captives from the city of Gibraltar and to do the same with all future captives from Gibraltar.[54] Two friars, probably Trinitarians or Mercedarians who were in Tétouan on a ransom mission, served as couriers for the Muslims and sent the news through Ceuta to Gibraltar.[55] According to the message, the Muslims were reacting to word that the Inquisition and the governor of Gibraltar intended to burn Hamad Melexi, an enslaved Morisco originally from a village near Marbella in Andalusia. Melexi was a corsair whom the Spaniards had captured and enslaved numerous times but who repeatedly fled back to North Africa.[56] The Inquisition claimed Melexi had reconverted to Islam in North Africa, making him a punishable renegade, and that he had captured and enslaved many Christians. The governor of Tétouan announced that Christian captives would pay for any punishment of Melexi. The documents disclose nothing about Melexi's Spanish past or about his family, or about his ultimate fate, but the belligerent activity with which the Inquisition charged him suggests the episode was motivated at least in part by the suffering the Inquisition had caused the Moriscos. Hence, the case suggests an extended series of brutal challenges and counterblows.

In another incident that suggests a long cycle of violence, the Morisco Monfadal, a royal official in Tétouan, had twelve captives executed as punishment for an attempt to escape on the Feast of Saint Thomas (December 21) in 1594. The surviving captives wrote home and protested. On January 16, 1595, the *corregidor* of Gibraltar in turn wrote to the king lamenting his difficulties in preventing the relatives of the killed captives from killing Muslim slaves from Tétouan as revenge. He urged the king to contact the Moroccan sultan and demand that Monfadal liberate other captives as compensation or be punished.[57] Like the 1589 case, this case suggests the existence of ongoing cycles of violence. Since all parties involved had an interest in veiling the reciprocal nature of this dynamic in order to portray themselves as in the right, it seems possible that other incidents were part of such long cycles. Such masking drew on the unwitting collaboration of Algerians and friars who provided discursive descriptions of the sea as a boundary, as a body of water separating Christendom from the Maghrib, rather than as a space that enhanced communication.

CAPTIVITY, VIOLENCE, AND THE MAKING OF THE MEDITERRANEAN

Grievances and threats, embodiments of violence within the context of captivity, served captives locally but at the same time operated on a Mediterranean scale. Writing down complaints and sending them across the sea required assumptions about the structures of mobility that connected the Maghrib and the Habsburg Spanish Empire that writers and addressees shared. Like their Christian counterparts, when Muslims wrote to their kin or to rulers, they assumed that their messages had a good chance of reaching their destinations, and indeed many did. Captivity and slavery, then, did not cut Muslim slaves off from their communities, families, and rulers. Even in the absence of formal diplomatic agreements, they could mobilize their communities of origin to protect them from a distance.

Frequent violation of the religious privilege that Muslim and Christian slaves considered their right and the dynamics that ensued shaped the respective roles of captives, redeemers, and rulers. Violence defined captives as religious subjects and not only or not always as economic objects to be traded. By pressuring their slaves to convert, rulers removed these captives from networks of exchange. Demanding the burial of slaves according to custom had a similar effect, despite the fact that such claims concerned the dead, for debates over whether opposing parties had respected such customs influenced negotiations over ransom, complicating the significance and function of slaves in the Mediterranean. While underscoring captives' religious subjectivity, religious violence against captives could be deployed by Mediterranean rulers to invoke or strengthen their political power and to allow them to emerge as protectors of religious practice. In that sense, debates about captivity and violence were a medium for the articulation of the religious, economic, and political aspects of Mediterranean slavery, each in relation to the other. Repeated debates about what constituted unjust violence not only shaped the actors involved but also solidified their expectations, slowly minimizing friction and violence. Over time these dynamics codified captives' and rulers' expectations, making violations less common and hence limiting violence.

The final point of this chapter is that violence against captives generated, rather than disrupted, communication: slaves wrote to their families; kin pleaded with their rulers; Maghribi governors sent messages to Spain; redeeming friars delivered those messages; royal officials contacted local officials ordering investigations; local officials reported back to Madrid; and, having decided how to react, the Council of War and Council of State informed the pasha and the divan of their decision. In what might be termed "diplomacy from below," captives took the initiative, demanding that their sovereigns take action.[58] In the process, Trinitarians and Mercedarians were transformed into de facto diplomats, going beyond their official mission of redeeming captives. The friars claimed responsibility for communication between Maghribi powers and Spain more than a century before these powers signed peace treaties. In putting these dynamics in motion, slave owners, Mediterranean rulers, captives, and redeemers drew and redrew Mediterranean structures of mobility and directed a traffic in humans that routinely remained implicit.

CHAPTER 6

Moving Captives, Moving Knowledge

Viceroys, captains-general, fleet officers, and other imperial administrators of Habsburg Mediterranean territories constantly sought fresh
information about Maghribi cities, corsairs, and politics, information
produced by experts and carried by reliable transmitters. One consequence of Spain's military weakness in the Mediterranean throughout
most of the seventeenth century was the impairment of state bureaucrats' ability to gather such information. In the absence of institutionalized espionage networks, captives, friars, and merchants played
a central role in producing, collecting, transmitting, and receiving
information about issues related to maritime conflict. The oral news
they delivered and the written accounts they penned made captives
and others instrumental in shaping and maintaining Habsburg imperial boundaries in the Mediterranean. With limited ability to govern
information flows, royal administrators had to rely largely on these
information entrepreneurs.

This chapter charts the history of the cultural lenses through
which the Spanish Empire perceived the Maghrib, namely the forms
of knowledge and the practices that mediated the encounter between
Spain and Muslim North Africa. It does so by examining the kinds
of information royal bureaucrats had at their disposal, the identity of
those who provided them with that information, and the ways in which
administrators sought to regulate and verify information. Simultaneously, the chapter offers new ways of thinking about captivity by
showing that captives—Muslim and Christian; detained, ransomed,

and runaway—could be both active producers of knowledge of the enemy and passive bodies inscribed with useful information.[1]

Scholars have suggested that the signing of the Ottoman-Spanish truce in 1581 meant that Spain turned its attention to northern Europe and the Atlantic and lost interest in information about the Maghrib and its cities.[2] However, in contrast to the conventional narrative, after 1581 Spaniards received more information about North Africa than ever before—even if its form and media changed. Spanish printed treatises about the history, geography, and ethnography of the Maghrib composed in the last third of the sixteenth century were the earliest and best-known form of information created by captives. The authors' objective was generally to contribute to Spain's colonial enterprise in North Africa, but after 1581, treatises describing the Maghrib as a target for expansion were immediately obsolete in Spain. As Spain's military presence retreated from the Mediterranean corsair activity increased, and captives arrived in port cities in small numbers on a daily or weekly basis, bringing news about the places of their captivity. Anyone eager to extend the knowledge found in the published treatises of the turn of the century could turn to newly ransomed captives. Spaniards, then, continued to produce, gather, transmit, and receive political, military, and topographic information about the Maghrib and its cities during the seventeenth century, although this body of knowledge was not available in printed form.[3]

In the first two decades of the seventeenth century, as Spain sought to revive its Mediterranean heyday by conquering strategic North African cities, captives generated two important forms of information. First, between 1600 and 1610, Spanish captives in Algiers chronicled the city, sometimes on a daily basis. They sent their accounts to the viceroy of Majorca, who distributed them to other imperial officials. Second, in the following decade, captives, renegades, and others compiled topographic narratives of Algiers. These authors promised the Mediterranean viceregal courts and captaincies-general that their narratives would deliver the key to the conquest of the Maghrib. In addition, throughout the century, information also traveled in letters captives sent to their kin, missives that viceroys, captains-general, and imperial administrators gathered. The officials also interviewed and interrogated freed Christians and captured Muslims, eager to extract information either group might have about the Maghrib.

Captivity was an early modern maritime practice that effectively connected communities across the Mediterranean. It facilitated the traffic of goods and ideas as well as people. While scholars have understood the increasing numbers of captives at the turn of the seventeenth century and the violence that accompanied that growth as a sign that the sea had lost its earlier characteristic unity, this chapter argues that the system of captivity instead created greater unity—through mobility (forced and unforced) and information flows—than peoples in the Mediterranean had experienced during the sixteenth century. To be sure, captivity had divisive effects on the Mediterranean and on the experiences of individuals and their communities. Indeed, much of the information captives carried portrayed the Mediterranean as a divided space separated into self-contained political entities—the Habsburg Empire, the Ottoman Empire, and the Moroccan sultanate—and as religiously torn and divided. But captivity was more than a violent system of domination separating peoples; it produced a multiplicity of links between Europe and North Africa.

THE MAGHRIB IN PRINT

Spain's position in the late sixteenth-century western Mediterranean and in the Maghrib contains an apparent paradox: on the one hand, Spain had a greater presence in the region than any other Christian power and therefore had a particular need for information; on the other hand, studies of the Maghrib were poorly received in Spain, for Spaniards showed little interest in works on the topic. Iberians published a number of the earliest studies of Morocco and Algiers, including Luis del Mármol Carvajal's *Descripción general de África* (General Description of Africa, [vol. 1, 1573; vol. 2, 1599]); Diego de Torres's *Relación del origen de los xarifes y del estado de los reinos de Marruecos, Fez, y Tarudante* (An Account of the Origins and History of the Shereefs and of the State of the Kingdoms of Morocco, Fez and Taroudannt [1586]); and Antonio de Sosa's *Topography of Algiers* (1612).[4] These works provided extensive discussions of the history, geography, and ethnography of the Maghrib. Only the famous *Description of Africa* by al-Hasan ibn Muhammad al-Wazzan al-Fasi (Leo Africanus) was considered more authoritative.[5] While English and French authors appropriated large sections of these books, Spanish readers demonstrated little interest in them and their authors enjoyed a limited reception at home. Completed in 1526, al-Wazzan's celebrated treatise was not subsequently published in Spanish. It appeared in Italian in 1550, in Giovanni Battista Ramusio's collection of "discoveries," and quickly became an authoritative source throughout Europe for information about Africa. A series of Italian editions was joined by editions in French (1556), Latin (1556), English (1600), and Dutch (1665), reflecting worldwide interest and garnering worldwide attention, but no Spanish publisher seemed to have believed the work would interest Spanish audiences, and it was never translated into Spanish.[6] Spanish readers curious about al-Wazzan's work had to rely on Spanish Africanists who appropriated long sections of the text.[7]

Their experience of captivity had given Mármol Carvajal, de Torres, and de Sosa direct experience of Morocco and Algiers and knowledge of the languages required for further study. Mármol Carvajal had arrived in North Africa in 1535 as a soldier, whereupon he spent almost eight years as a prisoner.[8] De Torres had also been held captive in Morocco but for a shorter period. In 1546, he had joined a friend's relative who served as a ransomer in Morocco.[9] After four years in Morocco, he decided to return to Spain but was detained for the debts of his friend's relative. After spending more than a year and a half in captivity, de Torres was ransomed, but he remained in Morocco for another year and only returned to Spain in 1554. De Sosa, a doctor of canon and civil law and of theology, was held captive in Algiers for ten years, from 1571 to 1581.[10] He wrote his treatise during his imprisonment and drew heavily on al-Wazzan's work, which a Morisco from Fez had loaned him, as well as a biography of Saint Paulinus, bishop of Nola.[11] His conversations with other captives, renegades, and Muslims were also vital sources of information about Algiers.

Our three authors promoted an expansionist colonial agenda. Mármol Carvajal expressed his desire to contribute to Spain's colonial enterprise in the dedication of his book to Philip II, stating that he hoped his work would be "not less pleasant than beneficial for the conquest of the barbarous African people, our neighbors as they are our cruel enemies."[12] In his original dedication to Don Sebastian, king of Portugal, de Torres expressed similar wishes.[13] To encourage conquest of the country, these authors stressed its wealth and the potential utility of its resources for colonial Spain and Portugal. Although less pronounced, an imperialist agenda likewise reverberates through de Sosa's work.[14] Their timing proved unfortunate: after the Spanish victory at Lepanto in 1571 and the Portuguese victory in the Battle of

Alcazarquivir in 1578, the Habsburgs and Ottomans signed the peace treaty in 1581 that led Spain and Portugal to turn their attention away from the inner sea.[15]

Bad timing may explain why all three authors struggled to bring their work to print. Mármol Carvajal published the first volume of his *Descripción general de África* in 1573, seventeen years after he completed its writing. In spite of the treaty of 1581, which invalidated the expressed purpose of his manuscript, in 1584 he applied for another royal publishing privilege. While he received permission to reprint the first volume and to publish the second volume for the first time, he later said he had been unable to find a publisher because of the length of the book.[16] Spain's abandonment of conquest in the Mediterranean may well have been the stumbling block for this particular work, for more generally the number of books printed was constantly on the rise.[17] In 1599, about four years after his royal privilege had expired, Mármol Carvajal applied for its renewal. Acknowledging his failure to find a publisher, he published the second volume at his own expense.[18] That he found any success at all may have been a side product of the good reception of his book on the rebellion of the Moriscos in the Alpujaras.[19]

De Torres never lived to see his work in print. He had begun writing his *Relación del origen de los xarifes y del estado de los reinos de Marruecos, Fez, y Tarudante* after his return to Spain in 1554 and finished the text sometime before 1575. While he went so far as to pen a dedication, there is no archival indication that he took any steps to secure its publication. It was not until several years after his death that his widow, in dire need of money, petitioned the king and managed to publish the work.[20] Given that its call for the conquest and economic exploitation of Morocco had been obsolete since 1578, his widow's ability to find a publisher at all could seem surprising.[21]

De Sosa's *Topography of Algiers* was also printed posthumously, in 1612, about thirty years after its completion, under the name of his editor, Diego de Haedo.[22] Haedo was the nephew of a bishop in Sicily who had come into possession of the manuscript by unknown means sometime after 1581, although he may have been given it by de Sosa himself.[23] Haedo clearly did not rush the text to the printing press. The first known permission for publication he received was dated 1604 and his printing license from the Royal Council was dated 1610.[24] Haedo continued to be misidentified as the author of the manuscript until the 1970s.

The last two decades of the sixteenth century were not the right moment for expensive printed scholarship that called for colonial expansion in North Africa. Publishers and audiences did not detect the texts' colonial agenda, and if they did, they did not identify with it. Its imperial intentions outdated by the time it was published, neither Mármol Carvajal's nor de Torres's work circulated widely, and neither was reprinted in Spain before the twentieth century. Mármol Carvajal's book had some success, and nobles, royal functionaries, and artisans are known to have owned copies.[25] It was translated into French in 1667, and a handful of early modern works refer to his *Descripción general de África*. A few English authors who wrote about Algiers also acknowledged debts to both Mármol Carvajal and de Sosa.[26] De Torres's work was translated into French in 1636, and this translation was reprinted in 1667 with Mármol Carvajal's book as its third volume. Today only about two dozen copies of de Torres's treatise are extant.[27]

De Sosa's book was much better received, partly because it was published later, in 1612, by which date Spain seemed to be reliving its past Mediterranean glory with the conquest of important port cities in Morocco, the expulsion of the Moriscos, and plans and attempts (ultimately unsuccessful) to conquer Algiers.[28] De Sosa's success led Golden Age authors such as Lope de Vega and Gonzalo Céspedes y Meneses to appropriate sections of the *Topography of Algiers* for their novels and plays, and in the 1630s the former captive Diego Galán reproduced full sections of the text in his captivity account.[29] However, excluding a single 1619 *arbitrio* calling for the conquest of Algiers, de Sosa's work was never read for its vision of expansionism,[30] with Trinitarians and Mercedarians, for example, referring to it in their textual discussions of captives' travails.[31]

The suspension of Spain's Mediterranean imperial agenda in the last two decades of the sixteenth century *and* its belligerent effects influenced these works' future reception. The imperial retreat after the treaty of 1581 had allowed corsairs to take over the maritime space; captive-taking subsequently soared, and captives brought an abundance of information about North Africa to the Iberian Peninsula. De Sosa's *Topography of Algiers* described an intellectual community in Algiers of which he had been a part. Its members, sixty-two learned captives who included ecclesiastics, jurists, lawyers, and doctors, participated in discussions of faith and the nature of captivity. De Sosa also referred to intellectual discussions with Muslims and renegades. Even if de Sosa's book did find a limited readership owing to a resurgence of interest in Algiers, the reports of a parallel intelligence community—formed by captives-turned-spies, rather than around an intellectual agenda—are what would dominate the information about Algiers available in seventeenth-century Spain. A large corpus of material that included intelligence reports, chronicles, personal letters, and interviews and interrogations was mined by government officials for knowledge of the Maghrib.

REPORTS, LETTERS, AND INFORMAL CHRONICLES

A letter dated September 4, 1604, and sent by the Valencian viceroy, Marquis of Villamizar, to the Spanish Council of State sheds light on the nature of correspondence from Maghribi cities and on the relationship between high officials and captive field agents: "A person held captive there [in Algiers] meticulously provides me with extremely detailed reports of everything that happens there; and in order for Your Majesty to see them, I send His Majesty the very precise accounts I have from that person. That person wishes to leave the position he holds and it seems to me so useful to have him there."[32] The viceroy implies that he had the power to free this person and that captive agents in Algiers were dependent upon him for their freedom. As we shall see, captives risked their lives gathering and transmitting information, and their operators, the persons to whom they reported, would in return advance their ransom. A letter sent in 1637 to Fernando de Borja y Aragón, the viceroy of Valencia, by an old resident of Alicante who was being held captive in Algiers reinforces the impression of the power exercised by operators over their captured field agents. The captive, who informed the viceroy about nine Algerian galleys about to attack the Valencian city of Calpe, opened his letter by stressing how bad his health was and how much he desired to return to Valencia in order to serve the viceroy; in other words, he begs the viceroy to reciprocate by redeeming him and promises to continue his service upon returning home.[33] Further examination of the correspondence between commanding officers and their agents also suggests that in some cases the latter had some power over their patrons.

Between 1602 and 1614, and probably also before and after these dates, Majorcan and Valencian viceroys enjoyed the services of at least four Spanish captives who meticulously chronicled their experience in

Algiers and sent the viceroys their reports. Whereas the majority of the extant texts written by captives position their authors as humble supplicants begging their king for help, these reports generate their creators as authoritative informers with knowledge superior to that of their interlocutors. These chronicles are among the best sources for the history of Algiers during this period, which makes their neglect by scholars particularly surprising.[34] Their detailed lists of events, often only loosely related, form a narrative whose protagonist was the city of Algiers, with its rhythms and the fears, joys, and expectations of its inhabitants—all transmitted from the perspective of Spanish captives and spies.

Vicente Colom composed the earliest extant report. Colom first appears in the archive in 1601 as a commercial agent in Algiers dispatching taffeta, furs, gum arabic, dates, wax, and more to the Valencian merchants for whom he worked.[35] In circumstances that remain unclear, he began documenting the city in August 1602, or perhaps earlier, an activity he pursued almost up until his death on September 22, 1607. Juan Ramírez, a playwright and theater director captured along with his wife and company on August 24, 1602, authored a number of reports up until 1604. Colom's successor as an informer, second lieutenant Juan Baptista Soriano, offers the names of other captives who assisted him in his task. When Baptista Soriano stopped spying is unclear, but his extant account spans the period from September 19, 1607, to October 11, 1608. An anonymous captive from the Valencian city of Denia penned the next surviving account, which covers the period from the beginning of September 1613 to March 1614. The information the spies provided about disagreements and debates in the divan suggests they were either present in person or had informers in attendance. Each of the chroniclers has a unique tone and emphasis, but all were extremely disciplined in their writing, sometimes documenting even quotidian happenings. Baptista Soriano, like the anonymous chronicler from Denia, hardly missed a day. Some of his entries are extremely short, and he might laconically report, for example, "Monday, 1st of the said [month], offered nothing."[36] But other entries, especially in earlier reports by Ramírez and by Colom, are longer, filling a page or more.

From their perch in captivity in Algiers, the chroniclers recorded and commented on a swath of political and economic dynamics and events, both local and international. All showed an interest in Algerian plans to attack Spain or its Maghribi holdings and in preparations for an attack by the Spanish. Colom was especially alert to the arrival of news about the movements of the Spanish armada and meticulously noted the state of the Algerians' knowledge of Spanish imperial plans. The idea of attacking Algiers was popular in Spain at the time, and these plans were never really secret. Rumors circulated regularly across the sea. Algerians constantly feared invasion from Spain, and the Spaniards, for their part, had a near-obsessive interest in Algerian preparations to resist. Events related to the Berber kingdom of Cuco also garnered interest because at the beginning of the seventeenth century Spain had negotiated a joint attack on Algiers with its ruler.[37] The chroniclers also reported the return of corsairs to the port and recorded their prizes, and they wrote of debates between the French consul, the pasha, and the Janissaries that followed the arrest of free French merchants.

The frequency with which the chroniclers sent their reports is unclear, so it is difficult to gauge how valuable they were. The surviving chronicles archived at the Archivo General de Simancas near Valladolid cover long stretches of time: Baptista Soriano's covers more than a year, Juan Ramírez's nearly eleven months, and the anonymous reporter from Denia's more than six months. If they finished their reports and then sent them to Spain, instead of sending them piecemeal, the information would have lost a good deal of its potency by the time it arrived. The cramped handwriting and unusual spelling filling all the folios of the last chronicle, written by the anonymous source from Denia, could suggest that it was penned by a single author and sent in one piece to Majorca. Nonetheless, the Majorcan viceroy described receiving the report to the island in a few short pieces, indicating that it was most likely a secretary who united these pieces to prepare the surviving copy. Moreover, captives had the incentive and the means to send news quickly. They might ransom a reliable fellow captive and send a message with him. For example, in June 1603, Spanish captives in Algiers arranged the release of a captive from Nice named Ricart and sent him to meet the Majorcan viceroy to deliver information about Cuco and Algiers in the form of letters, part of Colom's chronicle, and an oral testimony. The viceroy compiled a letter from these various elements that he sent on to Madrid.[38] It is likely, then, that pieces of information later gathered together in the chronicles were first sent periodically, while the longer reports that covered a full year or more reiterated details and rendered longer-term trends.

The record suggests entrepreneurial captives appointed themselves secret agents more often than operators nominated them to the position. Testimonies submitted to the viceroys of Sicily and Naples from ex-captives who served as imperial secret agents in Istanbul spoke of their professional formation.[39] The Sicilian Juan Leonardo Saya was captured in 1589, taken to Algiers, and moved with his master to Istanbul.[40] Saya ransomed himself but remained in his master's employ, taking care of the garden and summerhouse.[41] As he explained in April 1604 to the viceroy of Naples, the Count of Benavente, Saya took advantage of the foreign tongues he had learned during the years he had spent as a slave and leveraged this position to become an agent in the Spanish intelligence network in Istanbul. He hid secret agents arriving from Naples in his master's garden, spied, helped Christian captives escape, and ransomed captives.[42] Captivity was a source of valuable connections for both captives and ex-captives. Hernán Pérez, who spent thirty-five years as a captive in Istanbul and returned to Christendom in 1613, included numerous letters of recommendation, all signed by important individuals, in the petition for help he submitted to the king. During his time in captivity he established connections with the patriarch, the English and French ambassadors in Istanbul, various Spanish spies posted there, and captains and soldiers he had rescued from captivity.[43]

The way in which Baptista Soriano took on the role of informant when Colom died in the line of duty is indicative of this dynamic. In the summer of 1607, the viceroy of Majorca sent a confidante, a Muslim slave, to Colom with a letter. The Muslim's cover story was that he had ransomed himself, but the Algerians suspected he was a spy; they tortured him until he admitted that he had delivered a letter from the viceroy to Colom, which exposed Colom's spying. Colom died under torture without giving up the names of others in the network. A letter sent to the king by Juan de Vilaragut, the Majorcan viceroy from 1606 to 1610, describes Baptista Soriano's succession to Colom's position and depicts Baptista Soriano's nomination as the result of the viceroy's own careful selection. The viceroy wrote that after Colom's death he had sought information "about the persons that have remained there and who could do what Colom did and enlighten us about what happens there, and a few Christian captives who arrived in the port told me that no one suited better the job than the second lieutenant Juan Baptista Soriano . . . and so I wrote to him about that matter assuring him on behalf of your majesty that he would be generously compensated."[44] De Vilaragut's letter reflects the striking extent of the links between Majorca and Algiers. News circulated constantly, and word of his agent's death immediately reached the viceroy, who promptly inquired about a suitable replacement and sent a letter to the candidate asking whether he might be interested in the role and listing the benefits the position offered; the viceroy then received the candidate's acceptance of his offer. This intensive and fluent exchange took place between two cities that were mutual sources of fear and menace. The letter also reveals the viceroy's desire to demonstrate to the king the effectiveness of his ties in Algiers, for its author created the impression of an efficient Majorcan intelligence apparatus that sought out and generated spies as required.

De Vilaragut clearly had more than one contact in Algiers, and when the need arose he was able to plant agents in the city. However, careful examination suggests he had less flexibility to choose an ideal candidate than he implied. The captives with whom he had inquired told him that Baptista Soriano was an appropriate and worthy candidate because his networks in the Algerian Council of State duplicated Colom's and because he had assisted Colom for a long time.[45] In a way, then, Baptista Soriano was the obvious candidate and had inserted himself into office long before Colom died. Baptista Soriano's connections with free Christians and other captives, and, most importantly, with powerful renegades and Muslims, were the main reasons he obtained the position. The viceroy was simply setting his seal to an arrangement already in place.

The viceroy's letter throws light on functional and relational characteristics of the cooperation of operator and agent. Developing and maintaining spy networks required that gifts be exchanged, and Baptista Soriano's first request to the viceroy was that he be given "two dozen colored Toledo hats [tarbooshes] made of fine woolen cloth," half of the "best brand" and half "of a lesser one," to use to compensate friends and bribe informants.[46] Baptista Soriano built up his network not only by distributing such goods but also by the show of power associated with his prompt receipt of such items on assuming Colom's position. At the same time, to maintain the impression in Madrid that he was in control of intelligence on the Maghrib, the viceroy had to be able to gather information from Baptista Soriano and therefore needed to comply with Baptista Soriano's requests.

Several entries in Colom's diary offer a glimpse of the weight of Spanish intelligence networks and also their fragility. On August 26,

1602, Colom recorded the arrival of a renegade sent to Algiers from Cuco. The Algerians tortured the renegade until he admitted that he had been sent to meet a Portuguese captive employed as a gardener. By torturing the gardener, whose name Colom does not supply, the Algerians extracted the identity of other group members, a Genovese called Paolo and a Portuguese priest called Salvador de la Cruz. Torturing these individuals produced the names of another Genovese and another Portuguese. The Algerians executed all six of the spies they had identified by flaying them alive.[47]

MAPPING ALGIERS IN WORD AND IMAGE

In addition to drawing on a network of spies, imperial officials gained information from the unsolicited submissions of a number of ex-captives, renegades, and others with frontier experience who produced urban topographic narratives.[48] These authors convinced imperial officials of their expertise, provided them with plans, pointed to how Algiers might be conquered, and expected to be remunerated for their efforts. The texts they compiled provided descriptions of varied detail for the spatial organization of the city and for its military might, with some including visual aids, maps, or plans. Other reports were a product of royal responses to this topographical information, for imperial officials taken with the potential of the material these adventurers relayed commissioned other individuals to travel to the Maghrib and verify their data. These subsequent reports were disseminated among governors-general and other military officials, copied, and distributed within limited circles. A report arriving in Sanlúcar might be reproduced and then travel on across the Spanish littoral as far as Valencia; likewise, reports from Majorca were sent to Barcelona, Valencia, and Madrid.

Topographic reports resemble chapters of de Sosa's *Topography of Algiers*, but although the authors may have consulted his work, they also always added to it. For example, they might give updated information on the number of Janissaries posted in the city or on the way the city's space was populated. In some cases, the textual panorama is so rich that it could be used to draw a visual map; a report submitted by Rodrigo Pardo in 1618, for example, is spread over twelve single-side folios. Pardo, who had enlisted in the Spanish army as a child, was fourteen when Algerian corsairs took him captive in 1610. He claimed that his master then forced him to convert and conscripted him into the Janissary militia, where he served more than three years before escaping to Spain. Pardo's experience of Algiers was short in comparison to that of others who produced similar texts, but his conversion and time as a Janissary offered him an insider's perspective. Beyond that privileged position, Pardo must also have had a talent for spatial perception and an extraordinary ability to translate his observations into writing. Urban topography was a driving factor for his documentation, and he outlined how space was inhabited and functioned socially. In minute detail he described the city's gates, underground water supply system, towers, casbah, and main streets, as well as the surrounding forts,[49] with details that included their respective distances as well as their locations vis-à-vis one another. His information had the potential to be very useful to an invading force.

Pardo's report did not need images. An account by escaped captive Símon Catena and engineer Pablo Pedro Floriano artfully combined complementary text and image, narrative and plans. Catena, a Sicilian, had been taken captive in 1596 and spent eighteen years as a slave in Algiers. In December 1614 he escaped to Spain, where he met Floriano; together they compiled a report on the city indicating how the Spaniards might take it over. It seems likely Floriano drew the plans, which included various elements of the landscape, from Catena's descriptions. The index of forts and gates permits the reader to relate the plans to the written text quickly and easily.[50]

The intent behind topographic reports such as those by Catena and Floriano and by Pardo was always strategic and specific: that Algiers might be conquered. Thus they all pointed out what they claimed was the simplest, cheapest, and safest way to take the city. Catena claimed the secret to easy conquest was a tunnel that ran underneath the city, in which he had hidden for three days prior to his escape: "A cave which is near the port and it goes underneath the grand mosque. . . . [I]t runs a large distance in the city. . . . [I]t is about eighteen feet high and fourteen wide and in the middle there is a man-made channel that becomes the aqueduct through which the waste and sewer liquids of the city are washed out."[51] Catena suggested that the Spanish crown send fifteen or twenty galleys with a total of eight thousand men. Based on Floriano's expertise, he recommended explosives be placed in the tunnel. He was confident everybody in the city would run to the mosque at the sight of invading galleys, as it provided the best panorama of the coast: "The people who go there, go so quickly, that it is certified that the city depopulates, and the first who go are the soldiers."[52] If the invaders blew up the tunnel at this point, the explosives would kill many, cause the walls to fall, and leave the survivors terrified and unable to protect themselves. This plan, then, was based on Catena's direct experience of the city and an understanding of its rhythms, fleshed out with in-depth knowledge of explosives and substantiated by the evocations of his engineer friend.

Others boosted their authority as experts by making reference to connections with insiders who promised to hand over the city to the Spaniards. The Catalan Maties Murillo was captured in 1612 by Algerian corsairs as he returned home from Flanders, where he had fought for fifteen years. He escaped after only a few months and three years later compiled a long report about Algiers. Murillo claimed that he had befriended Hasan Masul, a Catalan renegade and Janissary division captain who missed his family, was disenchanted with the life of a Muslim, and promised to take advantage of his position and "hand over" Algiers to the Spaniards. According to Murillo, the Spaniards should arrive with thirty galleys and four thousand men at Algiers, march to the New Gate, break through with explosives, and proceed to the casbah. The attack would not end there, but the key to success, according to Murillo, was taking over the casbah.

In this instance, as in other cases, the crown wanted to verify the facts before risking a fortune in the execution of a plan. The topographies might be accurate, but the plans were often unfounded. The crown thus decided to send engineer Pedro Pablo Floriano to investigate and verify the feasibility of Catena's plan. Floriano's report claimed Catena's scheme was groundless, but he presented an alternative, which the crown, so it seems, also did not pursue.[53] In response to Murillo's suggestions, Prince Philibert, Grand Admiral of Spain, sent a second lieutenant disguised as a merchant to Algiers to see whether Hasan Masul was indeed inclined to help the Spaniards.[54] Philibert's messenger found Hasan reluctant to speak about anything other than trade.

Pardo, Catena, and Murillo employed different strategies to convince the crown and to ensure their plans appeared authoritative. Catena provided a graphic representation of the narrative and evoked his friend's professional background as an engineer and the son of the foremost engineer in the Duchy of Milan. His plan's reliance on fear as its strategic hinge was echoed in his preference for the subjunctive over the indicative, a grammatical mode reflecting feelings rather than facts. Taken together, these spurious rhetorical tactics de-authorized his ambitious plans. Catena acknowledged the need for further investigation to support his plan; it was his idea that Floriano be sent to Algiers in person. The crown's amenability to his suggestion is indicative of interest in an invasion. The promise from the two compilers that "everything they offer would cost nothing to His Majesty nor risk anyone beyond their own lives" likely helped their cause.[55] They nonetheless sought compensation for their efforts and expenses, even though their plans came to nothing.

Pardo's authorial personality was singular, as his status as a Janissary provided him with a privileged perspective on the city unlike that of the average captive. He had become a Janissary early on, undoubtedly had mastered Turkish, and probably knew some Arabic; from a Spanish point of view, those characteristics would have made him appear an authority on Algerian military matters. But the very features that made him a valuable insider were associated with his conversion to Islam, which cast a shadow of doubt on his moral persona, his intentions, and the reliability of the information he was producing. At the same time, he had risked his life by escaping from Algiers and, again, by risking Inquisitorial punishment in Spain for his conversion to Islam. In light of this potentially dangerous situation, Pardo stressed the mitigating circumstances of his conversion and emphasized his escape with three other renegades, after they had taken over the Muslim crew of a settee, and return to Alicante.

Beyond his authorial persona, Pardo constructed a careful and balanced description of the city, identifying himself as a credible witness. In presenting his exceptionally detailed narrative, he explicitly acknowledged the limits of his knowledge. He specifically distinguished between what he had seen for himself and what he had heard from others. Thus, depicting the casbah, he reported: "and as there is no entry to it and only those [I] mentioned above . . . are allowed in, [I do] not know in detail the defenses and fortifications it has. But [I] heard from people."[56] Even as Pardo measures and quantifies, his narrative goes beyond a mere formal description of a grid to portray a living social space, with the kind of detail that reflects intimate knowledge. His description of the casbah's moat, for example, first provides strategic information: "The Casbah and the city have a moat that should be more or less twenty feet wide in some parts and about twelve in others." But then the text unfolds in other directions. As a defensive structure, he adds, the moat no longer functions: "It is weak and has little defensive importance . . . and it is in the process of turning into a place in which the children play and where the households placed against the wall throw their waste and in some parts there are orange and other trees."[57] Pardo was clearly a keen observer, sensitive to the social pulse of urban topography and to the sense of place attached to the urban space.[58] His account also differs from de Sosa's *Topography of Algiers*. While de Sosa repeatedly claimed that he "knew everything that occurred in Algiers," he also described how he was "locked in a dungeon . . . and shackled to a stone" and how he had to rely on others—Muslims, Jews, renegades, and captives—for his knowledge of the city.[59] In contrast, the reports of Pardo, Catena, and Murillo were based on firsthand experience of moving regularly around the city, which enabled them to claim expertise. The numerous reports of this kind produced in the first two decades of the seventeenth century, then, reflect continuity with the printed elaborated books written by de Sosa, de Torres, and Mármol Carvajal.

PERSONAL CORRESPONDENCE FROM CAPTIVES

Personal media in the form of the letters captives sent to their relatives were also important in providing a vehicle for the transmission of threats facing the community of which both author and addressee were members. A central shared concern stemmed from the conversion of other captives to Islam. The problem was not only social or religious, with the potential loss of fellow faithful, community members, or relatives (see Chapters 4 and 5). Equally or more disturbing was the prospect of the convert joining the corsairs' ranks, and given his mastery of the language or dialect and of the local coastal topography, he constituted an alarming risk to his former community. Letter writers warned their kin, asking them to watch out for and be careful of attacks from recently converted corsairs. We can recall here the letter Francisco Marques delivered to Inés Hernández Sardiña, in which the author recounted the conversion of Gaspar de los Reyes, warning his addressees that the latter had become a corsair and that, as a result, "they should not trust any sail." This piece of news was so striking that "all the people present stood amazed."[60]

When the information pertained to a concrete plan by renegades and others to raid the community, captives urged their kin to inform the magistrates immediately. In a report dated October 13, 1617, the viceroy of Majorca briefed the king about news he had received from two islanders held captive in Algiers: "In letters to their wives and mothers

written in Algiers the seventh of this month, Juan Maltés and Esteban
Gia, Majorcan slaves, told them to inform the magistrates of this city
that they might have certain knowledge of a renegade who is prepared
to come and attack one of the villages with fifty high deck ships and
the magistrates should be alert because there are renegades who speak
the language."[61] These cases highlight the role of captives in producing and sending unsolicited information to the authorities. Information
circulated through such media did not lead to, nor was it the result of,
direct relations between officials and informers; it was also not conditioned on an exchange of favors. In these cases, the viceregal authorities responded to the information rather than initiating its gathering
and transmission. However, knowing the potential strategic value of
such letters and assuming their recipients were not always aware of
their implications or did not always bother to report them, the Majorcan viceroys often collected and inspected letters that islanders received
from Algiers, whether or not they were from a known captive. A letter
accompanying the long report on Algiers that the viceroy sent to the
king on June 26, 1603, references this practice: "And [I also decided] to
collect all the letters sent from Algiers by Christian captives to individuals from here of which I am aware and to send them to your majesty
so that your majesty would better understand what is being reported
there."[62] In the context of this practice, captives served as passive bodies
that might carry valuable information of which they and their addressees were not aware. Once the information was in the viceroy's hands,
he could apply it to protect the king's subjects or, alternatively, advise
the king on how best to attack the enemy.

STIRRING NEWS, COMMUNAL REACTIONS

In his reports, Colom disclosed an Algerian hunger for information
and how news could animate communities.[63] For example, Colom
communicated the return to the port of Algiers of the corsair ra'is
Murat, on August 24, 1603, with three hundred Christians he had
just captured. While he had taken a hefty prize, the corsair claimed
that he had made his way back to Algiers earlier than initially planned
because he had spotted a large number of galleys near Ibiza that, he
assumed, were preparing to attack Algiers. Even without confirmation of the existence of an armada, the news "caused great fear."[64]
The Algerians were aware of the Spanish plot to conquer the city, and
the news quickly inflamed the public, causing great turmoil.

As uncertain as its truth-value may have been, news—good, bad, or even absent—had the potential to agitate both Christians and Muslims.[65] News that alarmed the Algerians had an inverse effect on Christian captives, who dreamed of Spanish conquest and liberation. For example, Colom reported the arrival in the city on April 13, 1604, of a Slovenian merchant, an acquaintance of many captives in Algiers. At first he provoked the authorities' fears, as they suspected he had come to spy on behalf of the Spaniards. But as the alarm dissipated, public opinion changed radically: "And with that the Turks were extremely pleased and the Christian [captives] greatly upset as their great hopes fell apart."[66] In either direction, exchange of information affected these connected communities in a reciprocal manner.

VALUABLE INFORMERS, RELIABLE NEWS

In Europe information-hungry state officials established institutionalized intelligence networks with armies of agents on the payroll. Evaluating news meant determining the significance of the transmitted information and how to respond to it.[67] In the western Mediterranean, where many of the information providers were ad hoc agents, the first step in assessing the quality and implications of news was to establish the informer's reliability. Eyewitnessing in itself did not automatically ensure reliability. The ideal informers had a reputation for trustworthiness.[68]

One example illustrates the need for an informer to be of good repute. Francisco Juan de Torres, who had been nominated viceroy of the Balearic Islands in 1618, sent word to the Council of State on October 9, 1618, that only a few Algerian ships were currently at sea but warned that soon, once "the Muslims' Lent," meaning Ramadan, was over, thirty ships would leave Algiers and head to Spain. Torres's informer had added that "the [Algerians] frequently discussed the armada the Spanish gathered to attack them and [the Algerians] say it is like a dog whose bark was worse than his bite."[69] However, the informer, who perhaps was trying to incite the Spaniards to take action, added that since the Algerians took no defensive measures, the conquest of Algiers would be an easy task. The viceroy made sure to indicate how novel this news was and how reliable his informer had proved to be—"a native of this kingdom who arrived last night, and has been out of Algiers since the first [days] of the last [month] . . . enslaved there for seven or eight years, and is a man of good judgment."[70] The description adopts nearly all the evaluative parameters for the trustworthiness of an informant: it establishes his nativity as an islander; his knowledge of the city; the age of the news; and, finally, that the informer is "de buena razón," or that one can trust his assessment.

"Oral accounts" (*relaciones de palabra*), the interviews that state officials conducted with captives, and the reports officials compiled on their basis reveal criteria employed to assess the quality of information and knowledge. Officials interviewed friars, consuls, merchants, and ship captains and their crews, as well as redeemed Christians and Muslim captives. But captives outnumbered the other groups and were typically better informed because they had spent long periods in Algiers. A report, probably from 1604, sent from Majorca to the Council of State synthesizes information received from the Majorcan captain Juan Maltés with information from Muslim captives Maltés had taken in Delis, sixty miles west of Algiers. According to the report, the Muslim captives recounted that "they have seen the army that left Algiers in order to go to the mountain of Cuco . . . and that Janissaries and Moors from [the garrisons of] Delis and Tamagot left to join the said force, which should include . . . around 1,500 men."[71] When Jewish and Muslim informers were evoked, even if the operator described them as "confidant," corroboration by a Christian source was deemed desirable. For example, in 1627, in one of his frequent updates to the Council of War about news received from Algiers, the Marquis of Velada, Antonio Sancho Dávila, passed on information he had received from a confidant Moor. Despite his positive evaluation of his source, he added that the Franciscan Melchor de Zúñiga, an expert on the area according to the marquis, had corroborated every aspect of the information delivered by the Moor. Most reports focused on statements from Christian captives, who were thought to be loyal to the Spanish crown.

Another example reveals operators seeking to verify the trustworthiness of their informants. On July 12, 1596, the new viceroy of Majorca, Fernando Zanoguera, wrote to the king about Miguel Rovira's recent achievements. A couple of weeks earlier, Rovira had left Majorca for Algiers on a mission to ransom his brother, father, and other Majorcans. He not only succeeded in this goal but also smuggled aboard a large number of Majorcan, Sicilian, Genovese, and Nicean captives. Zanoguera interviewed them all, but he found the testimonies of some more valuable than others for the report he was compiling. He was especially fond of the testimony of Antonio de Villafranca de Nice, who had served as head shipwright to the governor of Algiers. This position, which the latter had probably secured as a result of professional skills acquired in the shipyards of Nice, meant that de Villafranca had been able to move around in the city—mobility was one of the privileges that came with the office of shipwright—had worked hand in hand with corsairs, and might have had amicable relations with the pasha; he could therefore have gathered knowledge to which no other captive had access. He was precisely the kind of source that the viceroy sought as he composed such accounts: individuals who had either held positions of relative power in Algiers or spent many years in captivity and, by learning Arabic or Turkish, gained access to secret information. De Villafranca proved the most useful informer, but he was by no means the only informer among this group. As a way of authenticating his account, the viceroy indicated that in addition to the testimony of the Nicean, the report drew from the accounts of "the more intelligent among the others."[72]

In a way, that was reminiscent of Inquisitors seeking to authenticate the identity of authors of letters of support written for renegades (Chapter 4) or of the officials of the Council of War seeking more information to verify the claims of captives requesting assistance (Chapter 3). Spanish military officials were also mostly dependent on captives and others arriving from the Maghrib for information of all sorts. In order to verify the news these informants delivered, they coaxed more information from all possible sources, thus generating loops of production and transmission of further information that did not always succeed in eliminating doubt regarding the news that initiated the loop and yet reproduced the links that facilitated the transmission of information. Using trusted captives to validate the truthfulness of information sourced elsewhere was common. When the French consul in Algiers was sent to Majorca on March 22, 1604, to negotiate the ransom of several Muslim captives, he found himself accused of espionage. Qualms in Majorca were allayed, however, by "the good [things] about [the consul] the redemptors and others in Algiers wrote to the viceroy and what other ransomed captives who arrived from there declared [about him]."[73] Determining the reliability of the consul and his claims required turning to the place from which the consul had arrived: Algiers. Thus captives did more than simply produce and circulate information. Thanks to their knowledge of the field and the inability of government organs to assess other information from Algiers, captives were in charge of adjudicating the veracity of claims about identity, status, and intentions made by all sorts of informants posted to the Maghrib and by Maghribi officials. Similarly, when the Marquis of Villamizar, the viceroy of Valencia, received a letter from the pasha of Algiers on September 4, 1604—one of a few letters the pasha exchanged with the viceroy at the time—the viceroy turned to "many" captives for confirmation that the letter had indeed been written by the pasha.[74] In the service of Spanish officials, captives fulfilled a role as verifiers of questionable material that had often originated with Muslims or foreign agents, like the French consul in Algiers, who were suspected of cooperating with Muslims. That detainees were recruited to play this part suggests that even during their captivity, and even while serving as slaves, captives maintained a legal subjectivity acknowledged in Spain that could be employed to vouch for different kinds of claims in various administrative and legal contexts. At the same time, their role is indicative of the limits of the Spanish state's knowledge of the Maghrib and its constrained ability to control such information.

The very movements of those who carried news could help legitimate the relevance and timeliness of the information they transported. To indicate currency and hence applicability, Majorcan viceroys listed how information traveled across space and recorded whether it had originated from interrogations, personal letters, or intelligence reports. On October 5, 1604, the viceroy of Majorca sent the Council of War updates about Algiers that he had received from Charles Cochon, a French ship patron recently arrived from Algiers. The letter opens by mentioning Cochon's arrival date in Majorca and when he had left Algiers: "Last night a French settee [*saetia*] entered [the port]. It [arrived] from Algiers which it left five days ago."[75] Cochon reported that a new governor, Cader Pasha, had arrived in Algiers, that the Algerians were suffering hunger, and that the new pasha was seeking peace with the Kingdom of Cuco. Cochon had received this information from three ransomed Majorcan captives who had all left Algiers at the same time as he had but on a different settee. In most cases the viceroy would have interviewed the captives on their arrival, synthesized the information that they provided with that given by Cochon, and then sent a verified report on to the peninsula. But as the ship with the captives was late, and fearing that the news might turn into no news, the viceroy delivered Cochon's insights to the king and only later sent an update based on the information the captives provided.[76]

News might age after it had been delivered into official hands, getting lost on trails both physically and bureaucratically complex. Even information that seemed to have a relatively simple journey to make might face unexpected twists and turns. For example, on January 18, 1637, an elderly resident of Alicante who had been held captive in Algiers asked a fellow captive who had just been redeemed to deliver a letter to Murcian council members and a second lieutenant of the Murcian militia.[77] But the former captive brought the letter to the viceroy of Valencia, who instead of sending it 110 miles south to Murcia dispatched it north to Catalonia and up the chain of command to the Council of Aragon. The counselors ultimately had the missive sent to Murcia, but only after the information it contained had traveled across the Spanish Levant and then returned to its original destination. A letter sent in 1656 by an unidentified captive in Algiers to the Marquis of San Román, governor of Oran, crossed the Mediterranean twice before arriving at its intended destination.[78] The letter, which contained pressing information about an English-Algerian plan to take over Oran, had traveled more than five hundred miles to make the two-hundred-mile trip from Algiers to Oran. Distance, the availability of routes, and administrative protocols were often responsible for compromising the currency and relevance of news.[79]

CONCLUSION

Though the treatises that Mármol Carvajal, de Torres, and de Sosa penned are evidence of the pivotal role captives played in producing and circulating information, this was a process in which they participated alongside innumerable other reporters, chroniclers, letter writers, and interviewees. When well-known published works are lined up alongside other modes of knowledge transmission and circulation, the resulting picture suggests continuity in Spanish interest in the Maghrib, rather than rupture caused by the signing of the peace treaty of 1581 by the Ottomans and the Spanish Habsburgs. The continuity was both temporal and material since, desirous of information about the Mediterranean and North Africa, Spanish officials did not cease to draw from a variety of sources, printed, manuscript, and oral.

Additionally, when we view the violent practice of captive-taking alongside the production and circulation of strategic knowledge about the Maghrib, we can see how maritime contacts and links connecting Spain, Algiers, and Morocco enabled the production and circulation of representations of conflict and disunity at the very same time those links and contacts created and sustained an information system. This tension was reproduced in Spanish officials' attitudes toward captive informants, whom they deemed as both valuable and suspect. Imperial administrators distrusted captives and the information they provided but were simultaneously fully aware that captives were their best source for news and information from North Africa and about North Africa's relations with other European powers. This tension put news-providing captives under the microscope, with other captives tasked with authenticating the information and vouching for the informant.

CHAPTER 7

The Political Economy of Ransom

We return to the captivities of Fatima, Diego de Pacheco, the Trinitarians, and Muhammad Bey that opened this book. In early March 1609, Trinitarian friars Bernardo de Monroy, Juan del Águila, and Juan de Palacios departed the Valencian port of Denia, in charge of a ransom expedition to Algiers.[1] Although Monroy had never led such an endeavor before, de Palacios and del Águila knew about and had experience following the proper procedures: de Palacios had made two prior trips, and del Águila had spent seven years in Algiers, from 1595 to 1602, redeeming captives for his order. Corsairs who stopped them as they journeyed respected the safe conducts they produced, issued by the governor of Algiers, and left untouched the goods they had brought to trade. The friars landed at Algiers on April 1, 1609.[2] By mid-May, they had used the profits they had made from trading to ransom 130 captives and were ready to return to Spain. The Trinitarians had followed all customary procedures and had no reason to expect that this enterprise would be different from their previous experiences. On May 13, however, just minutes before they were to join the former captives onboard the ships that were to take them to Spain, they were detained on the orders of the divan.

The arrest had nothing to do with the behavior of the Trinitarians or the situation of the captives they had redeemed but was a cause and effect of a sequence of Mediterranean events beyond their control. It was also an example of the potential for reciprocity and vengeance across the sea that I discussed in Chapter 5. The divan's action was taken in retaliation for an injustice suffered by Mehmet Axá, a

Janissary and the commander of Annaba, a town east of Algiers and under that city's control.[3] A few months earlier, Genoese naval forces had stopped an Algerian vessel and had found onboard the children of a number of Algerian high officials, one of whom was Fatima, Axá's daughter.[4] The Genoese took their captives to Livorno, and from there the captives were able to contact their parents.[5] Their families commissioned a Corsican merchant who traded regularly with Algiers to ransom them.[6] The Grand Duke of Tuscany, who controlled Livorno, granted the merchant a pass that allowed him to travel to Algiers with the redeemed children.[7] The ransomer left Livorno with the captives he had ransomed, but a short time later their ship stopped at Calvi, a port town in northwest Corsica (then under the rule of the Republic of Genoa), where the bishop of Saona forced thirteen-year-old Fatima to convert to Christianity and baptized her as "Madalena."[8] Recognizing that the bishop would not permit him to take Madalena to Algiers, the merchant left Calvi for Algiers without her. Infuriated by the news carried by the ransomer, Axá went to the Algerian divan and demanded redress. By arresting the Trinitarian expedition led by Monroy, de Palacios, and del Águila, the Algerians were hoping to pressure Philip III of Spain to use his influence to ensure Fatima was repatriated to Algiers.

Immediately upon the arrest of the Trinitarians, the Spanish king asked Genoa to send an emissary to Calvi. At the king's behest, Muslim slaves questioned Fatima about her conversion and sent a report to Algiers and to Rome, from which Spain had also requested assistance.[9] The testimonies, compiled in Arabic, indicated that the girl had converted of her own free will and wished to keep living among Christians.[10] When Philip III learned that Fatima-Madalena had indeed been baptized, and as a faithful Christian, he could not require her return, lest he lose his authority as a defender of the faith, he ordered all ecclesiastic ransom operations in Algiers to be halted until the Trinitarians and the captives they had redeemed were freed.[11] However, Axá and the divan refused to retreat from the conditions set in 1609—Axá's daughter was to be exchanged for the Trinitarians and redeemed captives.

Departing from an analysis of this entangled case, this chapter reconstructs on an intimate scale the intertwined histories of these victims of maritime piracy and the equally complex negotiations over their exchange. In so doing we revisit many of the themes previous chapters have highlighted, such as the interdependence of the captivities of Muslims and Christians, the relations between commerce and redemption, the role of violence against captives in generating communication, and the informational networks the world of ransom engendered. This case thus illuminates on an intimate scale a core argument of this book: captivity and ransom in the early modern Mediterranean are best understood as a transnational political economy, the result of the interaction of market, politics, social obligation, and conversion.

Spanish, Algerian, and Moroccan political actors, ecclesiastic ransom institutions, Jewish and Muslim merchants, and captives all shaped the political economy of ransom of the early modern Mediterranean as they collaborated and competed with one another in overlapping ransom procedures, the construction of captives' value, and the regulation of human traffic across the sea. This case, with its exceptionally substantial archival presence, exemplifies how interactions between these actors transformed both the actors themselves and the system in which they operated. This world of ransom entailed the regulation of exchange and mobility across the Mediterranean, and its history is thus crucial for the making and unmaking of the region during the period.

SEARCHING FOR A SOLUTION

The arrest of the friars was unexpected, and not only because they had followed standard procedures. Ecclesiastic redemption expeditions frequented Algiers every few years, and a number of friars were posted to the city for long stretches of time. Trinitarians had redeemed 225 captives from Algiers in 1595 and 250 in 1599. The arrests evidently violated custom as well as the terms of the safe conducts. In Monroy's telling, when the Algerians imprisoned the friars, they were following the eye-for-an-eye code that governed Mediterranean cross-confessional violence.[12] According to this unwritten protocol, ecclesiastics would pay for violence directed by priests or Inquisitors at Muslims or renegades. Monroy recounted that the people of Algiers had been provoked by word from the Corsican merchant that the papists (papeçes) of Calvi had held Fatima in order to "turn her into a Christian." The Algerians began to spread the idea that the Trinitarians were papists too and therefore accountable for Fatima's return.

One of the earliest recorded Spanish responses to the arrests of Monroy, de Palacios, and del Águila testifies to the power of violent reciprocity. In a letter to Philip III dated October 15, 1609, the Valencian viceroy, the marquis of Caracena, lamented that Valencia had no debt to Algerians or Algerian sureties it could confiscate, which could be used to pressure Algiers to free the prisoners. And yet, he warned, if Spain punished Algerians enslaved in Valencia, Algiers might respond by punishing the many Christians captive in Algiers.[13] Whether the marquis was responding to a question from the Council of War or preempting it is unclear. Certainly the marquis was not the only Spaniard who pondered possible action and reaction. Nine years later, with the Trinitarians still in captivity, the viceroy of Sicily, then the Duke of Osuna, suggested all slave swapping be put on hold as a means of coaxing Algiers to release the Trinitarians. The plan was rejected.[14]

In addition, an imperial logic was at work, by which we can make sense of the Algerian decision to detain Spanish, rather than French or Italian, priests. At the time, Corsica was under the dominion of the Republic of Genoa, which from 1528 on was itself a Spanish satellite. Genoese bankers financed Spanish wars around the globe, the republic's fleet patrolled the Spanish Mediterranean, and Genoese merchants provisioned the Spanish Italian territories.[15] Monroy had warned the Algerians that Spain had no jurisdiction over Genoa, and his arrest was therefore futile. Technically, with Genoa not part of the Spanish Empire, he was right. But Genoese and Spanish reciprocal dependence gave the Spanish king power over Genoa.

In the following years, several failed attempts to free Fatima, Monroy, del Águila, de Palacios, and the captives they had redeemed were negotiated by the pasha of Algiers, grandees of the Spanish Empire, Jewish and Muslims intermediaries, the Trinitarians, other captives and their kin, the Queen Consort of France, the Grand Duke of Tuscany, the Republics of Venice and Genoa, the pope, and even the Ottoman sultan.[16] It became an affair of truly international scope, attracting attention from across Europe and the Mediterranean. First, in 1612, on behalf of the Spanish monarch, Jews from Spanish Oran contacted the Ottoman sultan Ahmed I and implored him to intervene. The sultan ordered the release of Monroy, but the Algerians had become accustomed to selective obedience to orders from Istanbul, and the directive went unheeded.[17] In 1617, the newly commissioned pasha of Algiers carried a similar order from the sultan, but it, too, was not obeyed.[18] In 1613 the governor of Oran had plotted to smuggle Monroy out of Algiers to Oran but was unsuccessful. In

1621, his envoy offered ten thousand ducats, to be paid by one of the leading Jewish families of Oran, but the captors remained unmoved. None of the Trinitarians was to be ransomed at any price until Fatima was returned.[19]

From the Christian perspective, her conversion had made Fatima inalienable. When Axá spurned the testimony of her Christian faith that Muslim slaves from Calvi had compiled, the Republic of Genoa, under pressure from Spain, offered him and four of his men a yearlong safe conduct with which to travel to Calvi, where he could verify his daughter's desire to stay among Christians. Axá refused.[20] Even when the safe pass was expanded to include his wife and six additional men, Axá insisted on meeting his daughter in person at Tabarka, a Genoese island located near Tunis and a few hundred miles east of Algiers; he promised to drop the matter if he thereby ascertained for himself that she was a Christian. "If she was a Christian he would leave her, and if a Moor, he would take her with him," declared Axá.[21] The Christians refused to cooperate with the Tabarka meeting, presumably recognizing that Axá was likely to take his daughter home regardless of what he heard from her. Even if the prospect of returning Fatima to Axá made some sense during the early stages of the affair, as time passed this solution became increasingly less feasible. By 1618, Fatima was married to a Corsican Christian, although the record does not say whether the couple had children.[22]

To overcome the impasse and secure the liberty of Monroy, del Águila, and de Palacios, the Spaniards sought to negotiate their exchange for Muslim captives. An opportunity seemed to have presented itself early in 1614 when a Spanish Sicilian squadron captured Muhammad, bey of Alexandria, and one of his wives, as well as some of their servants.[23] The bey offered the Sicilian viceroy twenty thousand ducats for his freedom. Three of the six members of the Council of State had favored releasing him without ransom as a gesture of generosity, owing to his age and ill health—and because as a younger man he had already been a captive of the Spaniards.[24] He almost regained his liberty when Monroy and others lobbying for the release of the Trinitarians intervened, hoping to strike a deal— the Trinitarians and the captives in return for the bey and his entourage.[25] The Ottoman sultan thought the deal advantageous, and in July 1614 he sent a messenger to Algiers to effect the trade.[26] The Trinitarian notary in Algiers ratified an agreement in the city's *bagno* (prison) in August 1614, with three captives serving as witnesses. The pact stipulated that the Spaniards would send the bey to Tabarka, the Ottoman messenger would arrange for the sultan to issue a manumission letter for the Trinitarians and the redeemed captives, and, once these Christian captives were free, the governor of Tabarka would let the bey and his entourage leave.

But Monroy was not the only contender for the bey. As alluded to in this book's introduction, another parent seeking his child, the Marquis of Villena, whose son Diego de Pacheco had been taken captive and sold in Algiers in 1609, was pulling strings in Madrid's political corridors.[27] At this point, Monroy and the sultan were competing with the Marquis de Villena and the Duke of Osuna, but as Algiers still refused to release the Trinitarians for anyone but Fatima, neither coalition across the religious divide won out. Diego de Pacheco was taken to Istanbul in 1610. He converted or was forced to convert in 1614 and died in 1619.[28] The bey died in a Sicilian prison cell in 1616. Juan de Águila, Juan de Palacios, and Bernardo Monroy died in Algiers in 1613, 1616, and 1622, respectively. The archive provides no further evidence of Fatima's fate, but it seems likely that she remained among Christians under her baptismal name Madalena.

Beyond the fact that they all failed, the efforts to ransom these victims also point to a broader picture, in which for every ransom deal executed, often several others were imagined or negotiated but ultimately remained unrealized.[29] Each scheme combined a different set of moves of redistribution, reciprocity, and exchange. Apart from the personal dimension of these failures, disastrous for the captives involved and their kin, these arrangements had political import, for they were representations of power in relationships in and between Spanish and Maghribi political hubs. The negotiating parties sought to impose on their counterparts a value, inflated or deflated, they attributed to a particular captive. In other words, regardless of the outcome of the negotiations, the parties involved—Maghribi Jews and Muslims, the Church and a host of political actors—had an opportunity to demonstrate, assess, and augment their political power. "Failure" does not tell the whole story, as each episode also revealed and molded mechanisms of exchange, the construction of value, and the prestige of slave traders and redeemers.

CONVERSION AND INALIENABILITY

Fatima's conversion was controversial in Spain as well as in Algiers. After all, how could a thirteen-year-old girl—described by some of the sources as eight or nine years old—imprisoned hundreds of miles away from her home and family and surrounded by people with whom she did not share a language take such a decision? Could she have converted of her own volition? Behind closed doors, Spaniards entertained the possibility that her conversion had been forced. In 1610, Madrid had addressed the pope, hoping to obtain a dispensation to permit her return, but he declined, perhaps anticipating outcry.[30] A captain in the Spanish Atlantic fleet held captive in Algiers opined about the affair in a letter he sent the Council of State in August 1617: "Even if the girl was Christianized by force, as they [the Algerians] claim, they could consider . . . that among [the Muslims] it is customary to turn young children into Moor by force. But their arrogance knows no par and they cannot keep their word."[31] The Spanish official acknowledged univocally the mutual nature of Mediterranean religious violence. The problem, as he saw it, was not that a thirteen-year-old girl had been forced to convert but, rather, that the Algerians refused to acknowledge that both parties practiced forced conversions and that Madalena's conversion—whether forced or voluntary—was a fait accompli. He also pointed out that since the Genoese had effected the conversion, the Algerians should take issue with them instead of with Spain.

The captain's letter is an example of how the conversion of enslaved captives removed them from economic exchange networks to place them instead in reciprocity-based networks. By converting or being converted, Diego de Pacheco and Fatima-Madalena entered a new religious value regime from which their kin could not redeem them, whatever their political power.[32] They were now members of a new confessional community and were protected or trapped (depending on perspective) by their new coreligionists, even though their kin persisted in arguing that forced conversion was invalid. Both the Marquis de Villena and Axá were politically powerful, but conversion made it impossible for them to deploy that power. In his attempts to obtain Muhammad and exchange him for his son, the Marquis de Villena argued that de Pacheco had been converted by force, implying that he still deserved to be redeemed. This framing of his son's conversion was an attempt to introduce mitigating circumstances and also underscored that de Pacheco's conversion had made it harder for the marquis to assert a claim to the bey. Similarly, the pressure exerted by Axá led to the arrest of the Trinitarians and the redeemed captives but failed to retrieve his daughter.

Scholars have addressed the influence on captives' value played by age, status, gender, profession, and kin's ability and will to provide ransom money.[33] But as objects of exchange in the political economy of ransom, captives had a value that was vulnerable to manipulation and they were capable of manipulating their own value in ways that made them inalienable. The Mediterranean world of ransom was based on mechanisms that enabled the violent insertion of people into exchange networks, but it allowed for complementary procedures for the removal of victims from the system. These mechanisms were rigid to the degree that redeeming a Christian who had "turned Turk" or a Muslim who had been baptized was nearly impossible. The system's inflexibility, or rather its efficiency, was predicated upon the membership of the "commodities" in question in distinct and mutually exclusive confessional communities. Captives who were familiar with the system might have threatened to convert in order to pressure the friars to ransom them, effectively subverting the economic logic of the market.[34] Primarily concerned with the salvation of Christian souls in danger, rather than with the termination of the trials of captivity, friars were vulnerable to such coercion.

Conversion left the convert inalienable: the convert's home community was not interested in the captive's ransom (Fatima's parents kept trying to arrange her return because they believed she had been forced to convert), while the convert's new religious community was unwilling to sell the captive back. As Fatima's case demonstrates, inalienability could lead to decommoditization through manumission. Her case, though, appears exceptional in that after her conversion Fatima lived as a free person who by 1618 was married to a Christian. More commonly, inalienability was socially and religiously oriented and did not necessarily lead to release from slavery. While conversion could eventually lead to manumission, slave owners whose slaves converted could still, and often did, sell them to other members of their confession. In other words, while inalienability meant that the convert could not be sold back to members of his or her original confessional community, he or she could still move between owners as a commodity. The unique commodity that slaves were, at once objects and subjects, points out the limits of these commercial networks for exchanging slaves and of the application of economic terminology to Mediterranean bondage.

DOING THINGS WITH WRITING

Spending many hours writing each day, Monroy became a hub of information. He pleaded with high officials in Spain and in Algiers, gathered and transmitted news (for example, about the capture of the bey and his quickly deteriorating health), and interacted with mediators. He also spent a good deal of time advancing his own ransom and that of others. He failed to free himself but succeeded in freeing children, women, and men in Algiers and neighboring cities. The Spanish priest Juan Fiol, who was held captive in Algiers at the same time as Monroy, testified that Monroy "never stopped encouraging others with letters, conversations, and advice."[35] From his prison cell, Monroy dispatched hundreds of notes and orders to captives, renegades, and Muslims in Algiers. He exchanged letters with captives in Tunis, communicated with the Trinitarian provincial of Castile and other friars in Spain, and corresponded with governors in Oran and Valencia and with the Spanish state councils in Madrid, as well as with Tuscan authorities in Livorno.[36] For Monroy, as for all captives, writing was a way not only of communicating with others but also of connecting them—and potentially of having people and objects moved across space.

While his efforts to pressure the Spanish authorities to search for ways to bypass the constraints imposed by Fatima's conversion never produced his own freedom, Monroy did succeed in convincing them to try. In a suggestive letter from 1610 to the Valencian viceroy, Monroy complained how senseless it was for the friars and the captives they had freed to suffer so much because of a thirteen-year-old girl who had been forced to convert.[37] In 1617, Monroy begged the king to accede to Axá's request and bring Fatima to Tabarka to meet with him, implying he was willing to see her repatriated even though she had converted.[38] In other words, more than once he had entertained the possibility of allowing Fatima to return to her parents despite her conversion, a plan that would have entailed challenging and potentially changing the system's conversion and forced mobility protocols.

Even when in solitary confinement in one of the city's towers, Monroy could collect money and link creditors, captives, slave owners, and intermediaries who could transfer captives back to their

homeland. He developed a reputation as an expert who knew everything about captives in Algiers. Merchants and captives' kin who
arrived in the city to ransom a captive would often turn to him for
advice.[39] In orchestrating efforts to bring about his ransom as well as
that of others, Monroy commissioned Jews, Muslims, and Moriscos,
acknowledging and asserting the growing importance these groups
were gaining in the Algerian ransom market at the expense of the
friars. While Monroy did not promote only these schemes and eventually they came to nothing, his attempts demonstrate the system's
flexibility and thus its potential for ongoing change.

Monroy and other Trinitarians also played an important role in
the social and spiritual life of captives in the city. Monroy sought
to provide comfort through handwritten notes to captives promising them they would be free soon. Other enslaved Trinitarians routinely preached, held religious services for the captives, encouraged
them, and provided them with medical care. They even established a
hospital in the main prison of Algiers, where they attended sick and
elderly captives.[40] Toward these ends they negotiated with the Algerian authorities, collected alms, and ordered liturgical and devotional
objects from Spain and Sicily. Trinitarian Simón Rojas shipped clothing and medications from Madrid for the hospital, as well as chalices,
patens, altars, and missals for the cult and cases full of rosaries, medals and prints of the Virgin, saints' lives, and Bibles for captives.[41] The
Trinitarians consoled captives in face-to-face interactions, but Monroy, who could not leave the *bagno*, did so with handwritten notes.

Monroy became a celebrity of sorts. He reported his miseries and
good works to the Trinitarian provincial of Castile, a close friend, and
to fellow Trinitarians. His letters to colleagues were published as pamphlets or in longer accounts of the affair, mostly in the original Spanish but occasionally in French or Portuguese.[42] In his letters Monroy
recounted the friars' encouragement of religious discipline among the
community of Christians in Algiers. He also celebrated the creation of
the hospital and described the ending of a long drought as the result
of the Trinitarians' prayers and godly intervention, adding that the
Muslims had been astonished by the results of the pious efforts of the
Christians. In their letters to him, the Trinitarians sought to console
and encourage Monroy, but their words disclose that they perceived
his suffering as martyrdom. For them captivity was an opportunity
God had offered the captive Trinitarians, for they might become martyrs for their faith, a living example of the Christian truth. After his

death, Monroy's published letters and the translated accounts of his travails served as initial steps toward his recognition as a Christian martyr. The testimonies of captives who knew him also became part of his canonization dossier, established for an ultimately unsuccessful process that might have culminated in Monroy's beatification, canonization, and sanctification (Chapter 4).

Until 1617, Monroy was allowed to move around the city of Algiers with relative freedom during the day and spent his nights at the city's main *bagno*. In 1617, the Algerians moved him to solitary confinement in a small, dark, and humid cell at the castle known as the "Emperor's Castle."[43] Captives bribed the guard of the tower to allow them to visit Monroy on a regular basis, communicate news, and receive letters, which they later delivered. In Madrid, Monroy's fellow Trinitarians framed the worsening conditions of his imprisonment as part of a providential plan to create a saint. Monroy also described the move to the emperor's castle as God's will but for a different reason: his transfer allowed him to collect information about the castle and its guards that he could then send on to Madrid and thus enabled him to serve his king.[44] Indeed, he provided military intelligence in the form of detailed accounts of the physical features of the structure, the number of guards and their arms, the best way to seize the castle, and the presence of a "pasha" who was a fellow prisoner. He also informed the king about the capture and arrival at Algiers of 480 Spanish soldiers who had been on their way to Italy.[45] In another note, from 1618, he reported the news Algiers had received about the Spanish armada's presence in Naples and the fears it had produced.[46] At some point, Madrid asked Monroy to provide information about Maties Murillo, the Catalan who had told the crown he could produce a renegade Janissary who wanted to return to Spain and would therefore help them take over the city (see Chapter 6). Monroy was asked for his opinion about both the plan's viability and the planner's credibility.

Monroy's agency stands out especially in comparison to Fatima's silence, and this difference is reflective of how little is known about female captives. Given the strict physical constraints he experienced, Monroy's activities and the transformations he went through as a result of his arrest exemplify captives' agency and the malleability of the world of ransom. In addition to becoming the captives' good shepherd and redeemer and a potential martyr and saint, Monroy also fashioned himself as a spy. While Monroy was held under the

most restrictive conditions, following her conversion Fatima became
a free person. And yet no record of her writing remains, and her story
is always summarized by men—her father, officials, friars, pam-
phleteers, and Christian and Muslim slaves. While being trapped in
Algiers as a captive must have been physically and emotionally pain-
ful for Monroy, it permitted him, together with others, to create his
own, exceptionally rich archive; in contrast, soon after her conversion, Fatima disappeared from the archive.

THE ALGERIAN PERSPECTIVE

Let us examine how the affair transformed relations between rulers,
friars, and merchants. In Chapter 2 we saw how Algerian, Moroccan,
and Spanish Jewish and Muslim merchants had previously collaborated with the friars, lodging them, serving as translators, negotiating
better prices, and redeeming slaves on their behalf. More important
than this involvement was their significant role in the Maghribi cross-
regional trade. When the friars traveled to Tétouan in Morocco but
not to Algiers, local Maghribi merchants bought Christian captives
in Algiers and traveled hundreds of miles west to Morocco, where
they delivered the captives to the friars. Maghribi authorities were less
than enthusiastic about this cross-regional trade, which they tried to
prevent, because while Algerian and Moroccan rulers had full control
over the friars, who were dependent upon them, and had to accept
their conditions and the prices they demanded, they had only limited
control over local merchants, who thanks to their local contacts and
mastery of the necessary languages evaded attempts to regulate the
ransom market.

On December 12, 1607, the Spanish spy Juan Bautista Soriano
described the arrival at Algiers of an English ship from Tétouan with
Turkish, Moorish, and Jewish merchants onboard who had come to
redeem captives.[47] Negotiations took some time, but he reported that
three and a half months later, the merchants had obtained a number
of Christian captives for exchange in Tétouan.[48] Through their services, the friars could take credit for ransoming captives from several
cities for the price of a single redemption expedition. On September
2, 1608, Bautista Soria recorded the divan's attempt to forbid the
practice whereby merchants brought captives to Tétouan, saying that
because of it, the friars were not paying the pasha's fees: "The galliot of . . . Marja Mamí . . . left for Tétouan. . . . Under the threat of

death, the Divan ordered him [Marja Mamí] not to take to Tétouan under any circumstances Christian [captives], neither the ones bought by the merchants nor [captives] owned by Algerians. *Because [the merchants] are the reason that the Spanish Trinitarians and Mercedarians do not arrive in this city [Algiers] and that the pasha is losing his fees.*"[49] This form of collaboration, then, was a routine matter. This time the ship scheduled to depart for Tétouan was Algerian and not English and was owned by a successful Algerian corsair, Marja Mami, a member of the Taifa, the corsairs' corporation.[50] This incident reveals that Algerian corsairs also participated in the redistribution of captives across the Maghrib, in violation of the divan's rulings. Moreover, the divan pointed an accusatory finger at the merchant go-betweens, explicitly linking their trade with Tétouan to the loss of revenue that the Algerian authorities had suffered. The Spanish undercover agent's repeated recital of incidents of cross-regional trade of captives suggests that the pasha and the divan failed to regulate actors other than the friars in the market, or at least came to accept their limited involvement. The very reasons that Jews and Muslims were desirable allies for the orders were also the very reasons that they were competitors for the pasha.

While neither Spain nor Algiers ever articulated a Mediterranean agenda as such, the decisions and actions of the two states are indicative of such politics. First, the Spanish king never officially permitted the friars to collaborate with non-Spanish Jews and Muslims, who theoretically could not set foot on Spanish soil. But by turning a blind eye to their presence, the king tacitly approved the alliance. Unspoken collaboration with intermediaries seemed an efficient communicative and commercial model for the Spanish crown.[51] In contrast, Algiers (together with the Moroccans and Tunisians) tried actively to control the trade. They preferred face-to-face—or as unmediated as possible—relations with the Spanish crown, selling captives directly to ransom agents authorized by the Spanish government. The Spanish king's decision not to limit the alliance between friars and Maghribi Jews suggests that go-betweens participated in only a small percentage of ransoming transactions. Algerian pashas came to accept the intermediaries' participation in the market, probably on the same grounds of their limited presence. Maghribi and Spanish Mediterranean agendas differed, but neither party felt an acute need to impose its own agenda. Both powers ultimately identified in intermediaries and in the Trinitarians and Mercedarians complementary means to achieving their goals.

CONTROVERSY IN ALGIERS

Fatima's conversion and the arrest of the Trinitarians divided the main political actors in Algiers. Spanish documents suggest that the Spanish crown believed the Algerians formed a united front on the matter, but in fact Algerian actors were motivated by contrasting and divisive interests.[52] Since 1587, the Ottoman sultan had nominated Algerian pashas for renewable triennial mandates. Nominees perceived their North African "exile" as an opportunity to make a fortune before they returned as wealthy men to Istanbul.[53] In contrast, the office of the Aga, the head of the Janissary militia who presided over the meetings of the divan, was elective, and in the seventeenth century each Aga held office for two lunar months.[54] The pasha, Aga, and fleet admiral made decisions about matters of state at the divan along with senior officers of the Janissaries, the leadership of the Taifa, and the mufti (Islamic jurist), cadi (Islamic judge), and secretaries. Throughout the seventeenth century, pashas gradually lost power, and Janissaries and the Taifa became the main political actors. The role of the pashas, who had lost much of their authority, was limited to mitigating tensions between the corsairs and the Janissaries.[55] This process was also indicative of the growing autonomy of Algiers, where the influence of the sultan diminished. No single event was responsible for this shift, which should be understood instead as a process that perhaps began in 1581 when the Spaniards and Ottomans signed a peace agreement that did not apply to Algerian corsairs, who formally were subjects of the sultan, and it was further articulated through various incidents involving Algerian privateering.[56] The conversion of Fatima and arrest of the Trinitarians was one such incident, extending the political schism in the Ottoman province and heightening the sultan's loss of power.[57]

According to Spanish spies reporting from Algiers, the discord between the pasha and the Aga on how to terminate the affair was to some degree related to political tensions over the Janissaries' salaries. Axá was a Janissary, and the Janissary militia members sought to protect his right to seek his daughter's return by refusing to ransom Monroy and the others. But the pasha was supposed to pay them every two lunar months, and as a result of difficulties in finding the necessary funds, he often withheld payment. The archival record reveals repeated discussions that tied the payment of the soldiers' salaries to the affair or to the reopening of commerce in captives in the city.[58]

On September 14, 1613, for example, in response to the Janissaries' complaint about a delay in satisfying their wages, the pasha replied that he could not pay until the Janissaries freed Monroy and the others and allowed unrestricted trade in captives. Several days later, the Janissaries still held the Trinitarians and the ransomed captives but had consented to the second part of the pasha's demand. Four months later, the pasha tried again, insisting he could not pay the Janissaries without the funds that would be gained from a deal with the Trinitarians. A month later, on February 7, 1614, the pasha made the same request. When the Janissaries demanded they first be paid, the pasha responded that "he had already dealt and cut [an agreement] with the [Trinitarian] fathers allowing them to leave; and in order to finalize it, he wants [the Janissaries] to give him their word that they will not hinder [the deal] but would rather let the fathers and the Christian [captives they had ransomed] go free."[59] The Aga implied he might relent, but on March 3, 1614, another heated divan meeting on the matter ended in tumultuous disaster. A French renegade pleaded with the members not to release the Trinitarians. The Janissaries began shouting their approval of the French renegade, and instead of bending, some soldiers threatened to slash the pasha's throat if he continued to withhold their pay over the matter.[60] A letter Suleyman Pasha wrote on February 23, 1618, to the Duke of Osuna, viceroy of Naples at the time, resonates with the continuous tensions generated by Fatima's conversion and the Trinitarians' arrest. The pasha, who had known Osuna for years and had communicated and exchanged gifts with him when Osuna was viceroy of Sicily and Suleyman Pasha of Tunis, lamented the situation, promising he was doing all he could to resolve it. Unfortunately, he added, "these *signori* of the Divan [the Janissaries] are being obstinate in their insistence on not liberating the Trinitarians unless the said girl [Fatima] is brought to Tabarka."[61] In these discussions, the effect of local relations and reciprocity on the wider network becomes evident.

The reciprocity the Janissaries sought to enforce, predicated upon a professional fraternity among the militia's members, shows how complex the political game was. On the one hand, different parties in Spain and in Algiers were divided over the measures to be taken to regain the status quo. On the other hand, the affair created ad hoc coalitions that crossed religious and political boundaries. The actions of Spaniards, their Jewish subjects in Oran, the Ottoman sultan, and the Algerian pasha were intended to bring about Monroy's release and restart state-regulated commerce in captives; the Aga and the Janissaries—former Christians from various communities of origin who had converted to Islam—objected to a compromise.

RANSOM OUTSOURCING

The arrest of the Trinitarians led Philip III to formalize the collaboration between the friars and Jewish and Muslim ransomers, transforming Jews and Muslims into imperially sanctioned ransom agents. The process began with the king's order that all Trinitarian and Mercedarian ransom operations in Algiers be halted until the detained Trinitarians and the redeemed captives were freed.[62] Since the prohibition did not prevent Algerian corsairs from capturing Spaniards, redeemers began searching for ways to circumvent the prohibition. Merchants had been buying captives in Algiers and selling them to the orders for years. The orders could continue working with these intermediaries, but given that the king now forbade them to rescue captives directly from Algiers, they had to rely entirely on the merchants' participation, for which royal assent was required. Moreover, captives' kin were exerting pressure on the orders to rescue their dear ones. A Mercedarian friar claimed that "many important people from this court have asked [him] to ransom captives who at present are in Algiers and offered [him] alms and *adjutorios* for that matter."[63] On March 3, 1612, the Mercedarians petitioned Philip III to formalize their collaboration with Jewish and Muslim ransomers; the king's endorsement was soon received.[64] The friars were licensed to commission a captain in Ceuta, which was a Spanish garrison,[65] or in Gibraltar to sail with North African Muslim or Jewish merchants to Algiers, where the captain would use the merchants' trading contacts to ransom the Spaniards, return them to Ceuta, and hand them over to the friars.[66] Similar petitions were submitted and permits issued continually. The Mercedarians returned to Algiers on a regular basis only after 1627 and with one exception the Trinitarians only after 1652.[67] During this period, the Spanish crown formally relied principally on Maghribis to rescue its subjects held captive in Algiers.

Formalizing working relations with North Africans by granting royal licenses had somewhat contradictory effects on the crown, the orders, and Maghribi middlemen. Nonetheless, it had long-reaching effects on both the ransom system and the Spanish state itself. In commissioning non-Habsburg subjects to execute the work of the friars, the crown achieved two objectives simultaneously, obviating the inherent risk of sending the orders to Algiers at the same time as ransoming its own subjects. Moreover, in compelling the orders to apply for a license to be allowed to follow a procedure that deviated from the crown's instructions, the king reaffirmed and strengthened his control over the orders. In this sense, the affair illuminates the complexity of political centralization in early modern imperial Spain. To date, scholars have read the crown's monopolization of the redemptive labor of the orders as part of state formation, centralization, and bureaucratization.[68] The crown's policy following the imprisonment of the Trinitarians in 1609 makes evident that the processes that composed redemption were often predicated upon the externalization of power and decentralization.[69] Scholars of political history have criticized the image of early modern Spain as an absolutist monarchy from nearly every angle, stressing the weakness of the political metropole in relation to its peripheries, historical territories such as Catalonia or Naples, cities, and corporations. As my discussion has illuminated, decentralization extended beyond imperial boundaries to involve former subjects previously expelled and now resident in enemy polities. Political processes shaped the political economy of ransom, but in turn ransom-making influenced state-making.

By repeatedly guaranteeing such permits, the crown was legitimizing the outsourcing of the ransoming of captives from Algiers in the context of the wider geopolitical and confessional stakes of the early seventeenth century. The documentation around the Monroy-Fatima affair testifies to how the Spanish king increasingly relied on non-Spaniards, and non-Christians, to protect his subjects.[70] Increasing royal involvement in ransom, a policy geared toward ensuring as many Spanish subjects as possible were rescued, to saving Christian souls in danger, and to forging the Catholic image of the monarchy, entailed more than the decentralization of political power. Royal participation also subverted royal ideologies, for increased efforts to redeem Christians from the Islamic world led to the establishment of new bonds and working relations with Jews and Muslims precisely as Philip III ordered the expulsion of the Moriscos, between 1609 and 1614, the descendants of the Muslim population of Spain who had been perceived as a "fifth column" and a threat.[71] The possibility of expulsion had been circulating in Spanish political corridors for decades. Historians have suggested that Spain executed the expulsion in 1609 to compensate for Spain's loss of international prestige, having signed a truce with the Dutch Republic in the Dutch wars of independence.[72] In the contemporary economy of religious prestige, the cleansing of the crown's territory of the Moriscos could compensate for the formation of new contractual relations between Spain and North African Muslims and Jews.

The affair also affected Maghribi Jewish and Muslim merchants. Once they had been *formally* tasked with negotiating and executing ransoms in Algiers on behalf of Trinitarians and Mercedarians, these merchants came to control a greater portion of all ransom deals. In the process, however, the king pressed his own ransom agenda. The royal decree halting all ransoming in Algiers by the religious orders had increased the volume of the trafficking of captives through Muslim-Jewish networks, but the existing vibrancy and potency of the networks had allowed the king to suspend redemptive expeditions to Algiers in the first place. The friars expressed their frustration at the middlemen's growing influence. Referring to Moroccan Jewish merchants, one Mercedarian wrote in 1618, "It does not seem advisable, nor will it ever be, that the redemptions be executed by intermediaries, especially not by Jews."[73] Nevertheless, he knew that he and his fellow Mercedarians were incapable of ransoming captives without precisely this kind of help.

TIGHTENING REGULATION AND FAILED MONOPOLIZATION

The Mercedarians were not alone in their dissatisfaction with the growing power of the intermediaries. The merchants' involvement may have solved a Spanish problem, but it also made the authorities in Tétouan and in Algiers unhappy. If prior to the cessation of direct ransoming from Algiers they had suspected that local merchants' profiting from ransoms came at their expense, now they harbored no doubts. It was not only Maghribi Jews and Muslims who were contracted by the king of Spain; once the ransoming of Spaniards held in Algiers had been outsourced, other merchants also began purchasing captives in Algiers and traveling with them to Tétouan.[74] From the Moroccan perspective, the Algerians and all these merchants were taking over their share of the ransom. When a Mercedarian expedition arrived in Ceuta in December 1614, the friar leading it immediately commissioned a French captain to sail to Algiers, the merchant Hamad Bordan from Tétouan to negotiate ransoms in Algiers, and the Jewish merchant Moises Mexia, a Tétouanite who constantly crisscrossed the short distance separating Tétouan from Ceuta to guarantee the transactions. According to the agreement, the friars would wait for the captives to arrive in Tétouan from Algiers. The Mercedarians met Amu Ben Amar, governor of Tétouan, and explained that they intended to use their funds first to ransom captives sent to Tétouan from Algiers.[75] Upset, the governor refused to help the friars unless they first spent their money on captives owned by Tétouanites. His people, he explained, were dissatisfied with the ransomers' plan, and he feared a rebellion.[76] Similar circumstances occurred three years later. The Tétouanite governor forbade the Mercedarians from contacting foreign merchants before they had bought captives he and his men owned.[77] Eventually, Tétouanite Jews mediated an agreement according to which the friars would spend some of their funds on the governor's captives and some on captives they commissioned from Algiers.[78]

The Algerians had opposed mediation even before the arrest of Monroy, his fellow friars, and the captive they had ransomed, but this episode now made them more active in their attempts to exclude local intermediaries from the ransom market. They were especially reluctant to sell the imprisoned Trinitarians and the captives they had redeemed. In September 1614, a Muslim merchant left Algiers with a frigate and thirty-three Christian captives he had intended to sell in Tétouan. Approximately a league from Algiers, however, the merchant's ship dropped anchor and took onboard three more Christians, who had been among the 130 Spaniards the Trinitarians had ransomed in 1609, right before they were detained. The Algerians stopped the frigate and strangled the merchant to death at the exact spot where he had picked up the three captives.[79]

The evidence shows clearly that the Algerians strictly forbade intermediaries from selling captives to Mercedarians in 1613 and also to Trinitarians in 1618.[80] Spanish reliance on Maghribi ransom agents, then, not only reduced the involvement of the friars but also compelled the Algerians and Moroccans to harden their policies. Ironically, the Spanish politics of ransom united Algerian pashas and Moroccan governors in an informal coalition, unbeknownst to its members; they never negotiated its terms or formally agreed to collaborate. If anything, after years of Algerian attempts to conquer Morocco, Algerians and Moroccans had perceived themselves as rivals.[81] Moreover, they sold the same commodity and competed for the same buyers. And yet, despite being diametrically opposed in their goals, they had a common interest in disempowering the go-betweens and negotiating ransom directly with the orders of redemption.

Whereas before Fatima's conversion and the imprisonment of the redeemers, the rulers of the western Mediterranean had perceived ransoming merchants and redeeming friars as complementary options, now these political powers actively pursued exchange and communication agendas that previously had remained only vaguely articulated. Philip III officially commissioned intermediaries as his ransom agents; the ransom agents in turn gained power and prominence and in practice monopolized the ransom of captives from Algiers. In response, both Algerian pashas and Moroccan governors employed all available methods to prevent these go-betweens from disrupting the existing political economy. The affair, then, resignified the relations between merchants, friars, and rulers, between commerce, redemption, and politics. Now, ransom via the orders and ransom via intermediaries were no longer two sides of one coin but instead different currency. Tensions between Spain, on one hand, and the Algerians and the Moroccans, on the other, increased as a result.

CONCLUSION

The last archival trace left by Fatima was made when she married a Christian in Calvi in 1616. The Corsican authorities' refusal to return her to her homeland and the deaths of the Trinitarians in Algiers continued, however, to trouble Spaniards, Algerians, and Moroccans for decades. In 1648, a former Spanish captive who had established strong friendship ties with his Algerian captors wrote to the latter and asked an Algerian envoy present in Madrid at the time to transport the letters. The former captive informed his former captors of his efforts to help the Algerian envoy convince the Spaniards to restore Trinitarian redemption expeditions to Algiers. As he explained, however, decision makers in Madrid feared a new Monroy affair and therefore preferred to send the friars to Tétouan and Salé, even though ransom was cheaper in Algiers.[82] That the ghosts of Fatima and the friars still haunted political players in 1648 within the context of Algerian lobbying to send more redemption expeditions to Algiers is an indication that the political economy of ransom was shaped not by the Spanish king or by the orders of redemption as discrete bodies but by the interactions of actors from all sides of the sea.

The conversion of Fatima and the detention of the Trinitarians were exceptional in the wealth of documentation they left behind. Similar kidnapings, forced conversions, violations of ransom agreements, detention of friars, and attempts, both successful and unsuccessful, to remove slaves from exchange networks were common, if less well-documented, throughout the early modern period.[83] The history of Mediterranean ransom clearly did not begin and end with the Fatima affair. The richness of the record for that episode sheds much light, however, on the dynamics that shaped Mediterranean ransom agendas and procedures from the later sixteenth century and up into the eighteenth century and, more broadly, on region formation in the western half of the Great Sea. The reconfiguring of social and spatial boundaries in North Africa and southern Europe was in part the product of a communicative network forged by ransoming whose density, protocols, and procedures heightened fluidity and connectedness.

The study of the trafficking of humans engendered by piracy and corsairs, a phenomenon that ranged from the trivial to the spectacular, requires a shifting analytical frame that combines attention to different value regimes on various geopolitical and social scales. These include a regional scale (the western Mediterranean) and a local scale (Majorca or Algiers) and how they were linked, and another that examines interimperial tensions (between Majorca and Madrid or Algiers and Istanbul) and transimperial relations (between Spain, Morocco, and the Ottoman Empire). Such a perspective focuses on a region-formation process—the degree to which the region cohered or disintegrated as a result of the interactions between competing imperial projects and cross-boundary maritime practices—such as the exchanges between Maghribi Jews and Muslims.

Conclusion

Maritime regions like the Mediterranean, populated by a host of political formations, underwent processes of region formation, of integration and disintegration. The suspension of the Spanish and Ottoman military projects in 1581 put in motion a process that the empires did not design and that contradicted any formal policies to give priority to northern or eastern concerns. Rather than leading to the sea's disintegration, the process initiated by the 1581 truce increased the intensity of cross-boundary maritime practices—such as captivity, enslavement, ransom, and commerce—created new information networks, and made old webs denser, thereby connecting North Africa and southern Europe in unintended and unexpected ways.

When imperial fleets cleared out of the Mediterranean, corsairs quickly filled the vacuum. As a result, the number of captives from both sides of the sea increased, and the patterns of their capturing were transformed—corsairs took fewer captives more often and took them from the middle of the sea as well from its edges. Rulers, corsairs, slave traders, friars, and kin developed ransom mechanisms and exchange enclaves in order to free these captives. Markets and politics as well as religious and social protocols shaped the political economy of ransoming that arose in the emergent region. Competing interests and interpretative frameworks were at play: captives' kin sought to reunite with their loved ones; church orders hoped to save souls from damnation but also to gain a monopoly over ransom; merchants were eager to reap easy profits; and kings and pashas, in addition to making profits, used ransom to consolidate their rule and constitute themselves as spiritual guardians.

Thinking about ransom as a transimperial political economy enacted between individual and institutional actors reveals the relevance of Molly Greene's critique of the modernizing force of the "northern invasion."[1] According to the "northern invasion" thesis, between the defeat of the Spanish armada in 1588 and the signing of the Twelve Years' Truce between Spain and the United Provinces in 1609 the Mediterranean became an economic sphere rather than one where religious enmity dominated. English, French, and Dutch merchants and corsairs did become a common presence on the sea and in its ports at that time, giving new form to age-old social and economic structures. However, the examination of the political economy of ransom makes clear that invaders from the north did not displace social obligation, religious mechanisms, imperial politics, or local actors when the sea allegedly withered away at the turn of the seventeenth century, becoming an internationalized economic sphere. The northerners doubtless reworked Mediterranean economic structures, and yet, in their turn, local actors continued to play a role in determining Spanish and European identities—for example, when Jews and Muslims were in charge of saving Christian souls and bodies—and in participating in state-formation processes. Insofar as captivity and ransom formed the main interface linking Morocco, Algiers, and Spain, analyzing their entangled history reveals their role in shaping and reshaping the early modern period.

The reconstruction of the communication networks and interactions engendered by the political economy of ransoming forces us to revise another story historians tell about the early modern western Mediterranean. According to this story, known as the "forgotten frontier," during the sixteenth century the Braudelian Mediterranean withered away and the sea turned into a sterile, segregated space.[2] This book showed how ransom moved people across religious and political boundaries and homogenized populations by returning Christians to Christendom and Muslims to the Muslim world. And yet the redemption of captives also led to the establishment of endless new entanglements of Spain, Morocco, and Ottoman Algiers. Ransom greased and turned the wheels of commerce and linked and remodeled families, villages, and confessional communities, as well as political institutions. Ransom boosted commerce and intensified exchanges between the northern and southern banks of the sea, as merchants and friars exported bullion and goods to North Africa and imported other staples from there to Spain. Captivity split up families and communities, and yet the efforts to plan and execute ransom extended family and communal links across the sea while reconstituting gender relations between kinsmen. Ransom required the exchange of information and enabled Spaniards, Algerians, and Moroccans violently torn away from their homes to continue to act as community members during their captivity—becoming the new fringes of their communities. In their letters, captives claimed their rulers' protection, informed home institutions about the changing status of other captives and issues related to political threats, and maintained affective ties with relatives. Rather than separating political and confessional subjects and communities, ransom established new and unforeseen links between them. Despite the violence that characterized relations between Islam and Christianity, the North African shores came to form an affective horizon for Spaniards, while Iberian regions operated similarly for Algerians and Moroccans.

Turning the gaze away from region making—that is, specific imperial projects such as Spanish early sixteenth-century attempts to conquer the Maghrib—toward region formation—the interaction between competing imperial projects and other actors interfering in their competition—allows a refocusing on the major role that ordinary people played in the intensification of movements and relations across the sea.[3] Captives and slaves from across the religious divide, as well as their humble wives and mothers, exchanged messages and coaxed rulers to act in their favor or, alternatively, to suspend action. Without ever intending it, their behavior resulted in intense diplomatic exchange between polities that had no formal peace agreements during this period. Moreover, the communication channels that people on the margins employed transformed the people into a major source of political information for the state. Similarly, petty merchants from the Maghrib redeemed Spaniards on behalf of their kin and the Spanish crown. In so doing, they were not only subverting Spanish ideologies of religious purity but also participating, again without ever planning to do so, in processes of state formation and in the centralization of royal power. Reconstructing the drama of captives' attempts to reunite with their kin and the machinations of the small-scale agents who assisted them in this endeavor reveals how fractured political power in early modern empires was. It shows, in other words, how much imperial politics was the result of competition and negotiation among a host of actors.

In the second half of the seventeenth century, relations between the political and religious forces whose interactions this book has described underwent a transformation that eventually changed the nature of region formation. In Morocco, the rising Alaouite dynasty (1631–present) united and pacified the country for the first time since the death of Saadian sultan Ahmad al-Mansūr in 1603. The Alaouites imposed their rule over Salé and Tétouan, which had been corsair cities up to that point, independent of the sultanate. The Alaouites restricted privateering, forced Algiers to acknowledge Moroccan independence, and extended legitimate economic activities.[4] A stronger Morocco, then, existed partly at the expense of Algiers, which suffered other blows as well. From the 1660s the English and the French began developing powerful fleets. This allowed the former in the 1670s and the latter in the 1680s to use gunpowder to impose peace agreements on the Ottoman regencies, which consequently vouched for free trade and prevented captive-taking.[5] Spain benefited neither from the rise of Morocco nor from that of England and France. To the contrary, powerful Alaouite sultan Mawlāy Ismāʿīl conquered Spanish Mehdya (la Mamora) and el Araich (Larache) in 1681 and 1689, respectively, and Algiers took over Spanish Oran in 1708. The constant presence of the hostile French fleet and French corsairs meant that Spanish corsairs were busy preying on French vessels more than on Maghribi shipping.[6] The English further debilitated Spanish Mediterranean power. In 1661 they obtained Tangiers, in 1704 Gibraltar, and in 1708 Balearic Mahon, controlling the straits and securing English trade in the Mediterranean.

These processes gradually led to the decline of piracy, captivity, and redemption. On the one hand, once Algiers could no longer prey on English, French, and Dutch subjects, it concentrated its naval attention on Spaniards and continued capturing and enslaving them throughout the eighteenth century, though in numbers smaller than in the seventeenth century. On the other hand, the peace agreements between the Ottoman regencies and England, France, and the United Provinces led to the integration of the Ottoman regencies into the European economy (a process the Alaouites initiated independently) and significantly weakened their naval power. By the second half of the eighteenth century, Spain was strong enough in relation to Maghribi polities to seek a similar line of action. It signed a peace treaty with Morocco in 1767 and sent the last church redemption mission, codirected by the Trinitarians and the Mercedarians, in 1768–69. In 1775 and 1784 it bombarded Algiers but failed to force a peace agreement. The attack did, however, convince Tripoli to sign an agreement in 1785. But the relations between Spain and Algiers were muddier as both competed for control over Oran, which Spain besieged and recaptured in 1732. In 1790 Algiers besieged Oran until a massive earthquake destroyed the city the following year. The earthquake convinced the Spaniards to leave the city and let Algiers take it over.[7] The only towns Spain maintained in North Africa were Ceuta and Melilla.

The region formation this book has studied was generated by a factor external to it: the temporary exit of Spanish and Ottoman power from the Mediterranean. Similarly, the end of the Thirty Years' War (1618–48) allowed the English and French to develop their fleets and transform the power balance at sea. While Spain never returned to rule the sea, in the eighteenth century it formed a stronger fleet in comparison to Algiers's reduced and by now mostly commercial fleet. Piracy, captivity, and redemption continued on a smaller scale until the end of the first third of the nineteenth century, when the French used these activities as an excuse to conquer and "civilize" Algiers.[8] These events and processes transformed once again the mobility regimes and forms of communication across the sea this book has explored.

By the mid-seventeenth century people living on opposite shores of the Mediterranean were better informed about each other than those who had lived there a century earlier. Rather than becoming a sterile space, the Ibero-Maghribi maritime frontier was traversed by three maritime communication and trade corridors that connected North Africa and Spain's Mediterranean territories: a western corridor stretched between Christian and Muslim cities in Atlantic and Mediterranean Morocco, on one side, and southern Andalusia and Sanlúcar de Barrameda in Atlantic Spain, on the other; a central corridor connected Ottoman Algiers, Spanish Oran, the Balearic Islands, and Catalonia; and an eastern corridor ran from Ottoman Tunis to Spanish Sicily and Malta. These corridors allowed ordinary Christians and Muslims to communicate on a regular basis, and information constantly flew across the sea. For those living around its shores, the region became a palpable scale linked to the local, the imperial, and the transimperial. Algiers for Majorcans and Andalusians and Andalusia and the Balearics for Algerians or Moroccans became part of their social horizon, even if feared and often detested. And that horizon, of which they were constantly informed, was connected to their present and home.

The intertwined histories of Spain, Ottoman Algiers, and Morocco raise questions that go beyond the specificity of the relations and exchanges that shaped these histories. They invite us to reevaluate early modern imperial projects of ethnic cleansing and religious unification, as well as modern national narratives of unity and sameness. This holds true in regard to Spanish attempts to constitute Spain as a nation purely Catholic and cleansed of Jewish and Muslim stains.[9] While the Spanish monarchy successfully unified Spain by expelling the Jews (1492) and the Moriscos (1609–14), it failed to eradicate from the Iberian landscape all signs of Muslim and Arab otherness.[10] In the last decade or so, the groundbreaking work of scholars like Mercedes García Arenal, Fernando Mediano, and others have demonstrated this incompleteness by exploring the continual and renewed interest of early modern Spanish humanists and ecclesiastics in Arabic and Islamic culture.[11] At the turn of the seventeenth century, Arabic served these scholars as a key to Spanish and Christian history. The process this book has charted suggests that the presence of Arabic and Islam had been much more pervasive than thus far noted, going beyond the realm of the learned and at times informing what the learned knew and had access to. Islam and Arabic manifested themselves in at least three forms in post-expulsion Spain: in communities of enslaved Muslims, who communicated with their kin and authorities at home and demanded and often received the privilege to practice their religion, bury their dead according to custom, and even establish mosques; in interaction, exchange, and informal agreements between Spanish, Moroccan, and Algerian authorities; and in the presence of thousands of ransomed captives, many of whom were fluent in or had mastered to some degree Arabic and Ottoman Turkish. Like Muslims enslaved in Spain, these former captives and captives' kin communicated with the Maghrib, not only with relatives but also, in some cases, with their previous captors. To be sure, in the seventeenth century Spain was far more homogeneous than ever before, and yet it remains to reconstruct and study the "refractory imprint of

the native counterclaim," as well as how this imprint evaded register-
ing in the archives.[12]

In a like manner, social imbrication and silenced histories of Christianity can be traced in the Maghrib. Jocelyne Dakhlia has suggested
that twentieth-century Maghribi historians shied away from discussing the history of the lingua franca, the Romance language spoken
across the Mediterranean and especially in North Africa, because
mentioning it threatened the project of crafting national history after
decolonization.[13] Beyond language, the rich material culture of Catholic Christianity also had a significant and continual presence in the
early modern Maghrib. Liturgical and devotional objects—missals,
chalices, ornaments, images, medals, rosaries with indulgences, devo-
tionals, chasubles and albs (liturgical vestments), frontals in all colors
(altar clothes), crosses, and small and large paintings and sculptures of
Christ and the Virgin—were shipped to the Maghrib by the thousands,
and a few were brought to Muslim cities by corsairs who snatched
them from churches in the villages they looted. These objects served
individual captives and adorned the walls of the numerous churches
and chapels in cities such as Algiers, Tunis, and Meknes.[14] Moreover,
in Morocco and in Tunis Moriscos—former Spanish subjects, many
of whom had previously lived as Christians—as well as renegades
played a key role in producing and circulating Muslim polemic literature.[15] The reconstruction and analysis of the exchanges and relations
across the Mediterranean promise to shed further light on this forgotten North African chapter in the history of early modern Christianity.

Seventeenth-century Spain continued to be a Mediterranean
empire even after it expelled its Moriscos and turned much of its
political attention to the Atlantic world. That it was a Mediterranean
empire does not imply it engaged in peaceful Christian-Muslim religious and intellectual exchanges reminiscent of images of medieval
convivencia. As a Mediterranean empire it was inherently bellicose
and transgressive. Maritime violence in the form of piracy, human
trafficking, and plunder in which Spanish subjects engaged as perpetrators and victims, so far perceived as symptomatic of the withering
away of the region, proved conducive of unexpected social, political,
and religious links and thus had an integrative power. Acknowledging
Spain's Mediterraneanness means giving full account of these forms
of violence and exchanges, official as well as other forms enacted by
small-scale actors.

INTRODUCTION

1. Salvatore Bono, "Slave Histories and Memoirs in the Mediterranean World: A Study of the Sources (Sixteenth–Eighteenth Centuries)," in *Trade and Cultural Exchange in the Early Modern Mediterranean, Braudel's Maritime Legacy*, ed. Maria Fusaro, Colin Heywood, and Mohamed-Salah Omro (London: Tauris Academic Studies, 2010), 105; Alessandro Stella, *Histoires d'esclaves dans la Péninsule Ibérique* (Paris: Ed. de L'Ecole des Hautes Etudes en Sciences Sociales, 2000), 78–79; Raffaella Sarti, "Bolognesi schiavi dei 'turchi' e schiavi 'turchi' a Bologna tra cinque e settecento: Alterità etnico-religiosa e riduzione in schiavitù," *Quaderni Storici* 107 (2001): 450; Michel Fontenay, "Il mercato maltese degli schiavi al tempo dei Cavalieri di San Giovanni (1530–1798)," *Quaderni Storici* 107 (2001): 397; Robert Davis, "Counting European Slaves on the Barbary Coast," *Past and Present* 172 (2001): 87–124.

2. Robert Davis estimated that 2–4 percent of all Christian slaves in North Africa were rescued and returned home; see Robert Davis, *Christian Slaves, Muslim Masters: White Slavery in the Mediterranean, the Barbary Coast, and Italy, 1500–1800* (Houndmills, Basingstoke, Hampshire: Palgrave Macmillan, 2003), 19–21. However, in the past decade, scholars have found more and more evidence of ransomed captives, and that figure must be higher. Alessandro Stella has suggested that the percentage of emancipated Muslim slaves in Iberia fluctuated between 5 and 20 depending on the decade and city; see Stella, *Histoires d'esclaves dans la Péninsule Ibérique*, 157.

3. Molly Greene, "The Ottomans in the Mediterranean," in *The Early Modern Ottoman Empire: A Reinterpretation*, ed. V. Aksan and D. Goffman (Cambridge: Cambridge University Press, 2007), 104–16.

4. Fernand Braudel, *The Mediterranean and the Mediterranean World in the Age of Philip II* (New York: Harper and Row, 1976); Peregrine Horden and Nicholas Purcell, *The Corrupting Sea: A Study of Mediterranean History* (Oxford: Blackwell, 2000); Michael McCormick, *Origins of the European Economy: Communication and Commerce, AD 300–900* (Cambridge: Cambridge University Press, 2002).

5. M. I. Finley, *Ancient Slavery and Modern Ideology* (New York: Viking Press, 1980), 75; Orlando Patterson, *Slavery and Social Death: A Comparative Study* (Cambridge, Mass.: Harvard University Press, 1982), 5.

6. The scholarship on slavery in Iberia is rapidly growing. For a useful guide, see William D. Phillips, *Slavery in Medieval and Early Modern Iberia* (Philadelphia: University of Pennsylvania Press, 2014). In contrast to the Atlantic world, slavery in the Indian Ocean is so varied and consists of so many different models that any attempt to compare it with other bondage systems risks reifying a multifaceted system; see Edward Alpers, Gwyn Campbell, and Michael Salman, eds., *Slavery and Resistance in Africa and Asia* (New York: Routledge, 2005). However, another study suggests that alienation seems to have been common in most South Asian forms of slavery; see Indrani Chatterjee and Richard M. Eaton, eds., *Slavery and South Asian History* (Bloomington: Indiana University Press, 2006), 3.

7. In Algiers and elsewhere in the Maghrib, the Christians had hospitals established by Trinitarians; see Ellen G. Friedman, "Trinitarian Hospitals in Algiers: An Early Example of Healthcare for Prisoners of War," *Catholic Historical Review* 66 (1980): 551–64. See also Guillaume Calafat and Cesare Santus, "Les avatars du 'Turc': Esclaves et commerçants musulmans à Livourne (1600–1750)," in *Les musulmans dans l'histoire de l'Europe*, vol. 1, *Une intégration invisible*, ed. Jocelyne Dakhlia and Bernard Vincent (Paris: Albin Michel, 2011), 477, 490–95; Salvatore Bono, *Schiavi musulmani nell'Italia moderna: Galeotti, vu' cumprà, domestici* (Naples: Edizioni Scientifiche Italiane, 1999), 241–52; Bernard Vincent, "Musulmanes y conversión en España en el siglo XVII," in *El río morisco* (Valencia: University of Valencia, 2006), 80; and Maximiliano Barrio Gozalo, "Esclaves musulmans en Espagne au XVIIIe siècle," *Cahiers de la Méditerranée* 87 (2013): 41–42. For the royal order regarding burial spaces, see Archivo de la Corona de Aragón (hereafter ACA), *Consejo de Aragón*, Leg. 672, fol. 39.

8. Cf. Michel Fontenay, "Esclaves et/ou captifs: Préciser les concepts," in *Le commerce des captifs: Les intermédiaires dans l'échange et le rachat des prisonniers en Méditerranée, XVe–XVIIIe siècle*, ed. Wolfgang Kaiser (Rome: École Française de Rome, 2008), 15–24. On the distinction in Roman, Christian, and Jewish traditions, see Andrés Díaz Borrás, *El miedo al Mediterráneo: La caridad popular valenciana y la redención de cautivos bajo poder musulmán 1323–1539* (Barcelona: Consejo Superior de Investigaciones Científicas, Institución Milá y Fontanals, Departamento de Estudios Medievales, 2001), 5–18. Algerian sources use the word "slave" ('abd) exclusively to refer to blacks. Enslaved European captives were referred to as "captive" (asîr), "Christian" (naçrâni), or "European" ('llj); see Lemnouar Merouche, *Recherches sur l'Algérie à l'époque ottoman*, vol. 1, *Monnaies, prix et revenus, 1520–1830* (Paris: Bouchene, 2002), 211; Nabil Matar, *Britain and Barbary, 1589–1689* (Gainesville: University Press of Florida, 2005), 114–15. Géza Dávid and Pál Fodor, introduction to *Ransom Slavery Along the Ottoman Borders (Early Fifteenth–Early Eighteenth Centuries)*, ed. Géza Dávid and Pál Fodor (Leiden: Brill, 2007), xiv.

9. Karl Polanyi, "The Economy as Instituted Process," in *Trade and Market in the Early Empires: Economies in History and Theory*, ed. Karl Polanyi, Conrad M. Arensberg, and Harry W. Pearson (Chicago: Henry Regnery, 1971), 243–70; Leor Halevi, "Religion and Cross-Cultural Trade: A Framework for Interdisciplinary Inquiry," in *Religion and Trade: Cross-Cultural Exchanges in World History, 1000–1900*, ed. Francesca Trivellato, Leor Halevi, and Cátia Antunes (Oxford: Oxford University Press, 2014), 24–61.

10. Peregrine Horden and Nicholas Purcell have recently introduced the distinction between "history in the Mediterranean" and "history of the Mediterranean." The first examines a small area and a short time span and is only contingently related to its geographical setting; the second is of the "whole Mediterranean or of one aspect of it to which the whole is an indispensable framework"; see Horden and Purcell, *The Corrupting Sea*, 2, 9.

11. The temporal axis has a spatial variant, according to which the eastern Mediterranean was a space of exchange and communication, whereas the western Mediterranean was dominated by religious hatred; see Adam G. Beaver, "The Renaissance Mediterranean Revisited: Christian Iberia and Muslim Egypt, ca. 1250–1517," in *Mapping the Medieval Mediterranean, ca. 300–1550: An Encyclopedia of Perspectives in Research*, ed. Amity Law (Leiden: Brill, forthcoming).

12. On the Mediterranean as a frontier, see Andrew C. Hess, *The Forgotten Frontier: A History of the Sixteenth Century Ibero-African Frontier* (Chicago: University of Chicago Press, 1978). Similarly, Robert Davis characterized North African sea roving as motivated by religious passion and a spirit of a jihad; see Davis, *Christian Slaves, Muslim Masters*, xxv. The original frontier scholar in the context of the Mediterranean is Henry Pirenne; see Henry Pirenne, *Mohammed and Charlemagne* (London: Unwin University Books, 1968).

13. Braudel, *The Mediterranean and the Mediterranean World in the Age of Philip II*, 14. On the oppositional aspect of Braudel's work and its intellectual sources, see E. Paris, *La genèse intellectuelle de l'œuvre de Fernand Braudel: La Méditerranée et le Monde Méditerranée à l'époque de Philippe II (1923–1947)* (Athens: Fides, 2002), 70–75.

14. Braudel, *The Mediterranean and the Mediterranean World in the Age of Philip II*, 615–42.

15. For an enlightening critique, see Molly Greene, "Beyond the Northern Invasion: The Mediterranean in the 17th Century," *Past and Present* 174 (2002): 42–47, and Molly Greene, *Catholic Pirates and Greek Merchants: A Maritime History of the Mediterranean* (Princeton, N.J.: Princeton University Press, 2010).

16. Faruk Tabak, *The Waning of the Mediterranean, 1550–1870: A Geohistorical Approach* (Baltimore: Johns Hopkins University Press, 2008), 8. See also Maria Fusaro, "After Braudel: A Reassessment of Mediterranean History Between the Northern Invasion and the Caravane Maritime," in *Trade and Cultural Exchange in the Early Modern Mediterranean, Braudel's*

Maritime Legacy, ed. Maria Fusaro, Colin Heywood, and Mohamed-Salah Omro (London: Tauris Academic Studies, 2010), 1–5.

17. For recent reviews of this emerging field, see Michele Bosco, "Il commercio dei captivi nel Mediterraneo di età moderna (secc. XVI–XVIII): Orientamenti e prospettive attuali di ricerca," *Cromohs* 18 (2013): 57–82; M'hamed Oualdi, "D'Europe et d'Orient, les approches de l'esclavage des chrétiens en terres d'Islam," *Annales. Histoires et sciences sociales* 4 (2008): 829–43; and Daniel Hershenzon, "Towards a Connected History of Bondage in the Mediterranean: Recent Trends in the Field," *History Compass* 15 (2017): 1–13.

18. Ellen G. Friedman, *Spanish Captives in North Africa in the Early Modern Age* (Madison: University of Wisconsin Press, 1983); José Antonio Martínez Torres, *Prisioneros de los infieles: Vida y rescate de los cautivos cristianos en el Mediterráneo musulmán (siglos XVI–XVII)* (Barcelona: Edicions Bellaterra, 2004).

19. On English captives, see Matar, *Britain and Barbary, 1589–1689*; Nabil I. Matar, "English Accounts of Captivity in North Africa and the Middle East: 1577–1625," *Renaissance Quarterly* 54, no. 2 (2001): 553–72; and Linda Colley, *Captives, Britain, Empire and the World, 1600–1850* (New York: Anchor, 2007). On French captives, see Gillian Lee Weiss, *Captives and Corsairs: France and Slavery in the Early Modern Mediterranean* (Stanford, Calif.: Stanford University Press, 2011). On Algerian captives, see Moulay Belhamissi, *Les captifs algériens et l'Europe chrétienne (1518–1830)* (Alger: L'Entreprise Nationale du Livre, 1988). More broadly, on North African captives, see Nabil I. Matar, "Piracy and Captivity in the Early Modern Mediterranean: The Perspective from Barbary," in *Pirates? The Politics of Plunder, 1550–1650*, ed. Claire Jowett (Basingstoke: Palgrave Macmillan, 2007), 56–73.

20. Wolfgang Kaiser, "L'Économie de la rançon en Méditerranée occidentale (XVIe–XVIIe siècle)," *Hyphothèses* 10, no. 1 (2007): 360; Wolfgang Kaiser and Guillaume Calafat, "The Economy of Ransoming in the Early Modern Mediterranean: A Form of Cross-Cultural Trade Between Southern Europe and the Maghreb (Sixteenth to Eighteenth Centuries)," in *Religion and Trade: Cross-Cultural Exchanges in World History, 1000–1900*, ed. Francesca Trivellato, Leor Halevi, and Catia Antunes (Oxford: Oxford University Press, 2014).

21. While the term "the economy of ransom" does not necessarily reduce the field to economics, some of the scholars who focused on economy have not always been sufficiently sensitive to the role of politics, religion, and society in the shaping of that economy; see Miguel Ángel Bunes Ibarra, *La imagen de los musulmanes y del norte de África en la España de los siglos XVI y XVII: Los caracteres de una hostilidad* (Madrid: Consejo Superior de Investigaciones Científicas, 1989), 142. The work of Ambrus and Chaney, focused on the Trinitarians and Mercedarians rather than ransoming merchants, also reduces ransom to a question of transaction costs: Attila Ambrus, Eric Chaney, and Igor Salitskiy, "Pirates of the Mediterranean: An Empirical Investigation of Bargaining with Transaction Costs" (Economic Research

Initiatives at Duke [ERID], Working Paper No. 115), http://scholar.harvard.edu/chaney/publications/pirates-mediterranean-empirical-investigation-bargaining-transaction-costs-0, accessed January 19, 2016. This perspective resonates with the reconceptualization of the Mediterranean offered by Horden and Purcell, which provokes a similar problem. In characterizing piracy and slavery as forms of redistribution, the authors remain blind to the process this book analyzes; see Horden and Purcell, *The Corrupting Sea*. For further critique of this and other aspects of Horden and Purcell's model, see Gadi Algazi, "Diversity Rules: Peregrine Horden and Nicholas Purcell's *The Corrupting Sea*," *Mediterranean Historical Review* 20 (2005): 227–45. More broadly, on problems in economizing perspectives and a useful discussion of the alternatives, see Halevi, "Religion and Cross-Cultural Trade."

22. For a theorization of the concept of transimperial subjects, see E. Natalie Rothman, *Brokering Empire: Trans-Imperial Subjects Between Venice and Istanbul* (Ithaca, N.Y.: Cornell University Press, 2012).

23. For an illuminating discussion of the perspective of region formation in the context of the historical anthropology of Sicily and Tunis, see Naor Ben-Yehoyada, *The Mediterranean Incarnate: Region Formation Between Tunisia and Sicily Since WWII* (Chicago: University of Chicago Press, 2017). See also Sebastian Conrad, *What Is Global History?* (Princeton, N.J.: Princeton University Press, 2017).

24. Julia A. Clancy-Smith, *Mediterraneans: North Africa and Europe in an Age of Migration, c. 1800–1900* (Berkeley: University of California Press, 2011).

25. To these one may add lateral corridors, for example, one running between the Spanish Levant and Catalonia west to the Spanish territories in Italy, and another running along the North African shores connecting Tunis, Algiers, and Morocco.

26. Conrad, *What Is Global History?*

27. Despite having lost its central place, the sea continued to play an important role in the world economy up until the eighteenth century. See Molly Greene, "The Early Modern Mediterranean," in *A Companion to Mediterranean History*, ed. Peregrine Horden and Sharon Kinoshita (West Sussex: Wiley Blackwell, 2014), 91–106.

28. At Lepanto, the Holy League captured over 3,000 Muslims, while 15,000 Christian slaves were rescued; when the Ottomans reconquered Tunis from the Spaniards in 1574 they captured thousands of imperial soldiers; and in Alcazarquivir, or the Battle of the Three Kings, in 1578, Ahmad al-Mansūr, new sultan of Morocco, took captive 14,000 Portuguese—almost the entire Portuguese nobility. On Lepanto, see Manuel Rivero Rodríguez, *La batalla de Lepanto: Cruzada, guerra santa e identidad confesional* (Madrid: Sílex, 2008), 366; on Alcazarquivir, see Mercedes García Arenal, *Ahmad al-Mansur: The Beginning of Modern Morocco* (New York: Oneworld Publications, 2012), 7; cf. Lucette Valensi, *Fables de la mémoire: La glorieuse bataille des Trois Rois, 1578: Souvenirs d'une grande tuerie chez les chrétiens, les juifs & les musulmans* (Paris: Chandeigne, 2009), 141; on Tunis and la Goleta, see Davis, *Christian Slaves, Muslim Masters*, xiv. To

contextualize these numbers, estimates of the number of Christians held captive at Algiers, the city that boasted the largest numbers in captivity, varied greatly between 5,000 and 30,000; see Davis, "Counting European Slaves on the Barbary Coast."

29. Lemnouar Merouche, *Recherches sur l'Algérie à l'époque ottoman*, vol. 2, *La course, mythes et réalité* (Paris: Bouchene, 2007), 213–15.

30. Wolfgang Kaiser, "La excepción permanente: Actores, visibilidad y asimetrías en los intercambios comerciales entre los países europeos y el Magreb (siglos XVI–XVII)," in *Circulación de personas e intercambios en el Mediterráneo y en el Atlántico (siglos XVI, XVII, XVIII)*, ed. José Antonio Martínez Torres (Madrid: Consejo Superior de Investigaciones Científicas, 2008), 171–89.

31. Tal Shuval, "Cezayir-I Garp: Bringing Algeria Back into Ottoman History," *New Perspectives on Turkey* 22 (2000): 87.

32. Leïla Maziane, *Salé et ses corsairs (1666–1727): Un port de course marocain au XVIIe siècle* (Caen: Presses Universitaires de Caen, 2007), 16–17; García Arenal, *Ahmad al-Mansur*, 144; Daniel J. Schroeter, *The Sultan's Jews, Morocco and the Sephardi World* (Stanford, Calif.: Stanford University Press, 2002), xiii.

33. Abdelhamid Henia, "Archives ottomans en Tunisie et histoire régionale," in *Les Ottomans au Maghreb à travers les archives locales et méditerranéennes*, ed. Abdelhamid Henia, Abderrahman el Moudden, and Abderrahim Benhadda (Rabat: Jāmiʿat Muḥammad al-Khāmis, Kullīyat al-Ādāb wa-al-ʿUlūm al-Insānīyah, 2005), 246–47.

34. Fatiha Loualich, "In the Regency of Algiers: The Human Side of the Algerine Corso," in *Trade and Cultural Exchange in the Early Modern Mediterranean, Braudel's Maritime Legacy*, ed. Maria Fusaro, Colin Heywood, and Mohamed-Salah Omro (London: Tauris Academic Studies, 2010), 69–96. See also her study of female black slaves: "Emancipated Female Slaves in Algiers: Marriage, Property, and Social Advancement in the Seventeenth and Eighteenth Centuries," in *Subalterns and Social Protest: History from Below in the Middle East and North Africa*, ed. Stephanie Cronin (New York: Routledge, 2012), 200–209. Another notable exception is the work of Lemnouar Merouche on the economic history of Algiers; see Lemnouar Merouche, *Recherches sur l'Algérie à l'époque ottoman*, vol. 1, *Monnaies, prix et revenus, 1520–1830* and vol. 2, *La course, mythes et réalité*. For a description of the early modern holdings of the Algerian Ottoman archives, see the appendices in the works of Loualich and Merouche.

CHAPTER 1

1. Jerónimo de Pasamonte, *Autobiografía*, ed. Miguel Ángel Bunes Ibarra (Seville: Ediciones Espuela de Plata, 2006), 39.

2. Ibid., 73–74.

3. Between the Middle Ages and the eighteenth century, more Muslims from the Maghrib were enslaved in Spain than any other ethnoreligious group; see Aurelia Martín Casares, "Evolution of the Origin of Slaves Sold in Spain

from the Late Middle Ages till the 18th Century," in *Schiavitù e servaggio nell'economia europea, secc. XI–XVIII: Atti della "Quarantacinquesima Settimana di studi," 14–18 aprile 2013*, ed. Simonetta Cavaciocchi (Florence: Florence University Press, 2014), 409–30. Data for black slaves in Algiers, Tunis, and Libya before the eighteenth century are limited; current estimates suggest that the total number of black slaves in Algiers and Tunis during the eighteenth century and in Libya between 1550 and 1699 (for which we possess information) was about 865,000. Since these estimates exclude sub-Saharan slavery in Morocco, most likely in the early modern Maghrib more sub-Saharans were enslaved than Europeans; see Ralph A. Austen, "The Mediterranean Islamic Slave Trade out of Africa: A Tentative Census," *Slavery and Abolition* 13 (1992): 214–48, and Ralph A. Austen, "The Trans-Saharan Slave Trade: A Tentative Census," in *The Uncommon Market: Essays in the Economic History of the Atlantic Slave Trade*, ed. Henry A. Gemery and Jan S. Hogendorn (New York: Academic Press, 1979), 23–76.

4. According to Paul Lovejoy, between 1450 and 1700 some 2,235,000 Africans were enslaved in the Atlantic; see Paul Lovejoy, "The Volume of the Atlantic Slave Trade: A Synthesis," *Journal of African History* 23 (1982): 494–500. A recent study offers the smaller figure of 1,884,200; see Alex Borucki, David Eltis, and David Wheat, "Atlantic History and the Slave Trade to Spanish America," *American Historical Review* 120 (2015): 433–61.

5. Bono, "Slave Histories and Memoirs in the Mediterranean World," 78–79; Sarti, "Bolognesi schiavi dei 'turchi' e schiavi 'turchi' a Bologna tra cinque e settecento"; Fontenay, "Il mercato maltese degli schiavi al tempo dei Cavalieri di San Giovanni," 397; Davis, "Counting European Slaves on the Barbary Coast."

6. These figures also exclude nearly a million black slaves from sub-Saharan Africa enslaved in Iberia and a similar or larger number of sub-Saharan Africans enslaved in the Maghrib during the early modern period. See Stella, *Histoires d'esclaves dans la Péninsule Ibérique*.

7. Aurelia Martín Casares, "Esclavage et rapports sociaux de sexe: Contribution méthodologique," *Cahiers des Anneux de la Mémoire* 5 (2003): 83–99.

8. On the notion of "bureaucratic autobiography," see James Amelang, "L'autobiografia popolare nella Spagna moderna: Osservazioni generali e particolari," in *Memoria, famiglia, identità tra Italia ed Europa nell'età moderna*, ed. Giovanni Ciappelli (Bologna: Il Mulino, 2009), 115–16; Rosa María Gregori Roig, "Representación pública del individuo: Relaciones de méritos y servicios en el Archivo General de Indias, siglos XVII–XVIII," in *El legado de Mnemosyne: Las escrituras del yo a través del tiempo*, ed. A. Castillo Gómez and V. Sierra Blas (Gijón: Trea, 2007), 355–79; and Victoria Sandoval Parra, *Manera de galardón: Merced pecuniaria y extranjería en el siglo XVII* (Madrid: Fondo de Cultura Económica), 206–24, 308–51.

9. João de Mascarenhas, *Esclave à Alger: Recit de captivité de João Mascarenhas (1621–1626)*, trans. Teyssier Paul (Paris: Chandeigne, 1999), 50–51.

10. Daniel Panzac, *Barbary Corsairs: The End of a Legend, 1800–1820* (Leiden: Brill, 2005), 21–25. On Maghribi corsairs, see also Maziane, *Salé et ses corsairs*, and Luis Fernando Fé Cantó, "El corso magrebí en España en los años centrales del siglo XVIII," *Clio and Crimen* 11 (2004): 209–26.

11. Fernando Jiménez de Gregorio, "'Relación de Orán,' por el Vicario D. Pedro Cantero Vaca (1631–1636)," *Hispania: Revista Española de Historia* 85 (1962): 109–10.

12. Weiss, *Captives and Corsairs*, 17.

13. On Majorcans, see Natividad Planas, "Pratiques de pouvoir au sein d'une société frontalière: Le voisinage du Royaume de Majorque et ses îles adjacentes avec les terres d'Islam au XVIIe siècle" (PhD diss., European University Institute, 2000); on Valencians, see Vicente Graullera Sanz, "La esclavitud en Valencia en los siglos XVI y XVII (causas de caída en cautiverio)," in *Primer congreso de historia del país valenciano, celebrado en Valencia del 14 al 18 de abril de 1971* (Valencia: University of Valencia, 1976), 3:239–50; on corsairs from Cartagena, see José Javier Ruiz Ibáñez and Vicente Montojo Montojo, *Entre el lucro y la defensa: Las relaciones entre la monarquía y la sociedad mercantil cartagenera: Comerciantes y corsarios en el siglo XVII* (Murcia: Real Academia Alfonso X El Sabio, 1998). On the Knights of Saint John, see Greene, *Catholic Pirates and Greek Merchants*; on the knights of Saint Stephen, see Luca Lo Basso, "Schiavi, forzati e buonevoglie: La gestione dei rematori delle galere dell'Ordine di Santo Stefano e della Repubblica di Venezia Modelli a confronto," in *L'Ordine di Santo Stefano e il mare* (Pisa: ETS, 2001), 169–232.

14. In a letter that the Duke of Maqueda, governor of Oran (1616–1625), wrote to Philip III on September 30, 1619, he claimed that under his predecessor, the Count Aguilar, 161 soldiers had defected; during his own term as a governor, the duke recorded, 52 soldiers had defected; see Archivo General de Simancas (hereafter AGS), *Estado*, Leg. 495, 9.28.1619, 9.30.1619. On these defectors during the eighteenth century, see Luis Fernando Fé Cantó, "La población de Orán en siglo XVIII, y el fenomeno de la deserción: Las sombras del discurso oficial," in *Orán: Historia de la corte chica*, ed. Miguel Ángel Bunes Ibarra and Beatriz Alonso Acero (Madrid: Ediciones Polifemo, 2011), 369–99. On the establishment of the Spanish garrisons and their portrayal as places of misery, see Fernand Braudel, "Les Espagnols et l'Afrique du Nord," *Revue Africaine* 69 (1928): 184–233, 351–428. For a recent critique of Braudel's portrayal of the garrisons as penal colonies, see Jean-Frédéric Schaub, *Les juifs du roi d'Espagne* (Paris: Hachette Littératures, 1999).

15. AGS, *Estado*, Leg. 198.

16. António de Almeida Mendes, "Musulmans et *mouriscos* du Portugal au XVIe siècle," in *Les musulmans dans l'histoire de l'Europe*, vol. 1, *Une intégration invisible*, ed. Jocelyne Dakhlia and Bernard Vincent (Paris: Albin Michel, 2011), 149.

17. AGS, *Guerra y Marina*, cartas, Leg. 1600, 10.3.1645 and Leg. 1598, 10.12.1645.

18. Beatriz Alonso Acero, *Orán-Mazalquivir, 1589–1639: Una sociedad española en la frontera de Berbería* (Madrid: Consejo Superior de Investigaciones Científicas, 2000), 273–79.

19. Phillips, *Slavery in Medieval and Early Modern Iberia*, 83–85.

20. Aurelia Martín Casares, "Maghrebian Slaves in Spain: Human Trafficking and Insecurity in the Early Modern Western Mediterranean," in *Mediterranean Slavery Revisited, 500–1800/Neue Perspektiven auf mediterraner Sklaverei, 500–1800*, ed. S. Hanß and J. Schiel (Zurich: Chronos Verlag, 2014), 109–11; Martín Casares, *La esclavitud en la Granada del siglo XVI: Género, raza y religion* (Granada: Editorial Universidad de Granada, Campus Universitario de Cartuja, 2000), 161–70.

21. Biblioteca Zabálburu, *Colección Altamira*, D. 1–20, 22. Similarly, the parochial baptism books of Oran record a higher number of female than male slaves baptized; see Juan Jesús Bravo Caro, "El reflejo de la esclavitud del Mediterráneo en los registros parroquiales oraneses," in *Orán: Historia de la corte chica*, ed. Miguel Ángel Bunes Ibarra and Beatriz Alonso Acero (Madrid: Ediciones Polifemo, 2011), 143–72.

22. Of the 3,886 captives registered in the notarial acts of the French consulate in Tunis, which document ransom deals concluded between 1591 and 1700, only 131 were women; see Leîla Blili, "Course et captivité des femmes dans la régence de Tunis aux XVIe et XVIIe siècles," in *Captius i esclaus a l'antiguitat i al món modern: Actes del XIX colloqui internacional del GIREA Organizat Pel Departament de Ciències Històriques i Teoria de les Arts, Universitat de les Illes Balears, Palma de Mollorca, 2–5 Octobre 1991*, ed. María Luisa Sánchez León and Gonçal López Nadal (Naples: Jovene, 1996), 260. Of the 6,690 captives Spanish Trinitarians and Mercedarians ransomed from North Africa at large between 1574 and 1692 only 36 were women; see Martínez Torres, *Prisioneros de los infieles*, 42–43.

23. Martínez Torres, *Prisioneros de los infieles*, 130–32; Blili, "Course et captivité des femmes dans la régence de Tunis."

24. For two notable exceptions, see Linda Colley, *The Ordeal of Elizabeth Marsh: A Woman in World History* (New York: Anchor, 2007), and Jocelyne Dakhlia, "Défenses et stratégies d'une captive hollandaise au Maroc: Un témoignage transgressif?" in *Le lien social revisité: Etudes et travaux de l'école doctorale de Toulouse-Le Mirail*, special volume edited by Natividad Planas, 8 (2006): 19–26.

25. Antonio de Sosa, *Topography of Algiers* in *An Early Modern Dialogue with Islam: Antonio de Sosa's Topography of Algiers (1612)*, ed. María Antonia Garcés (Notre Dame, Ind.: University of Notre Dame Press, 2011), 157.

26. Salvatore Bono, *Les corsaires en Méditerranée* (Paris: CNRS éditions, 1999), 193–201. On Algiers, see Sosa, *Topography of Algiers*, 158, and Laugier de Tassy, *Histoire du royaume d'Alger: Avec l'état présent de son gouvernement, de ses forces de terre et de mer, de ses revenus, police, justice, politique et commerce: Un diplomate français à Alger en 1724* (Paris: Loysel, 1992), 164. On Spain, see Barrio Gozalo, "Esclaves musulmans en Espagne au XVIIIe siècle," 43. On Malta, see Anne Brogini, *Malte, frontière*

de la chrétienté (1530–1670) (Rome: Publications de l'École Française de Rome, 2013).

27. Sosa, *Topography of Algiers*, 144.

28. Emanuel d'Aranda, *Les captifs d'Alger: Relation de la captivité du sieur Emanuel d'Aranda*, ed. Latifa Z'Rari Latifa (Paris: J. P. Rocher, 1998).

29. For example, d'Aranda, *Les captifs d'Alger*, 32–33, and Mascarenhas, *Esclave à Alger*, 56–57.

30. Amelang, "L'autobiografia popolare nella Spagna moderna."

31. Cristóbal de Villalón and Fernando G. Salinero, eds., *Viaje de Turquía; (La Odisea De Pedro De Urdemalas)* (Madrid: Cátedra, 1980), 139.

32. Mascarenhas, *Esclave à Alger*, 55. Elsewhere, he characterized captivity as the effacement of all racial and social marks (47).

33. Barrio Gozalo, "Esclaves musulmans en Espagne au XVIIIe siècle," 37.

34. Igor Kopytoff, "The Cultural Biography of Things: Commoditization as Process," in *The Social Life of Things: Commodities in Cultural Perspective*, ed. Arjun Appadurai (Cambridge: Cambridge University Press, 1986), 64–94.

35. Carlos Javier Garrido García, "La esclavitud en el reino de Granada en el último tercio del siglo XVI: El caso de Guadix y su tierra" (PhD diss., University of Granada, 2011), 278–86. On the Moriscos and the Second War of Granada, see L. P. Harvey, *Muslims in Spain, 1500 to 1614* (Chicago: University of Chicago Press, 2005), 204–37.

36. Pedro de Montaner, "Aspectos de la esclavitud en Mallorca durante la edad moderna," *Bolletí de la societat arqueològica lul·liana* 37 (1980): 327.

37. Phillips, *Slavery in Medieval and Early Modern Iberia*, 30–31.

38. Archivo Histórico Nacional (hereafter AHN), *Inquisición*, Lib. 862, fols. 81L–83, 5.4.1634. This text was recently published; see Onofre Vaquer Bennasar, *Captius i renegats al segle XVII: Mallorquins captius entre musulmans. Renegats davant la inquisició de Mallorca* (Mallorca: El Tall, 2014), 167–68.

39. AHN, *Inquisición*, Leg. 1706, carpeta 2, 19V–20R, 12.1689; AHN, *Inquisición*, Leg. 1711, carpeta 1, 33V–34R, 12.1689. For a published transcription of the trial's summary, see Vaquer Bennasar, *Captius i renegats al segle XVII*, 230–31.

40. Y. Hakan Erdem, *Slavery in the Ottoman Empire and Its Demise, 1800–1909* (Basingstoke, Hampshire: Palgrave, 2001), 15; Halil İnalcik, "Servile Labor in the Ottoman Empire," in *The Mutual Effects of the Islamic and Judeo-Christian Worlds: The East European Pattern*, ed. Abraham Ascher, Tibor Halasi-Kun, and Béla K. Király (Lanham, Md.: University Press of America, 1986), 28. For a detailed discussion of this system within the context of the maritime slave labor in Istanbul, see Nur Sobers-Khan, "Slaves Without Shackles: Forced Labour and Manumission in the Galata Court Registers, 1560–1572" (PhD diss., Pembroke College, 2012), 82–85, 182–208. Beyond the socioeconomic aspects of the system, Muslim slave owners who manumitted their slaves followed Koranic recommendations;

see Bernard Lewis, *Race and Slavery in the Middle East: An Historical Enquiry* (New York: Oxford University Press, 1990), 6.

41. Debra Blumenthal, *Enemies and Familiars: Slavery and Mastery in Fifteenth-Century Valencia* (Ithaca, N.Y.: Cornell University Press, 2009), 73–76.

42. Pasamonte, *Autobiografía*; Mascarenhas, *Esclave à Alger*; Diego Galán, *Relación del Cautiverio y Libertad de Diego Galán, Natural de la Villa de Consuegra y Vecino de la Ciudad de Toledo*, ed. Miguel Ángel de Bunes and Matías Barchino (Seville: Espuela de Plata, 2011).

43. Blumenthal, *Enemies and Familiars*, 72–73.

44. Stella, *Histoires d'esclaves dans la Péninsule Ibérique*, 463–64.

45. Walter Johnson, *Soul by Soul: Life Inside the Antebellum Slave Market* (Cambridge, Mass.: Harvard University Press, 1999).

46. Other slaves also found themselves forming part of an inheritance. Solimán, a Sardinian renegade, enslaved Jiovanni-Battista Castellano, a Sicilian mariner and later a Christian corsair, in the last years of the sixteenth century. After twenty years of service, Castellano, along with the rest of Solimán's household, became the property of one of Solimán's sons, following his father's death. Bartolomé Bennassar and Lucile Bennassar, *Los cristianos de Alá: La fascinante aventura de los renegados* (Madrid: Nerea, 1993), 133–34.

47. Ibid., 55.

48. In other cases, slaves were exchanged for goods or services. Guillermo Roger, as the records call this Englishman, testified in his trial by the Inquisition that the "Turk" who bought him in 1633 in Salé held him for six months and then bartered him ("le trocó") for a Morisco from Algiers. AHN, *Inquisición*, Lib. 862, fol. 368, 1642.

49. Giving gifts to recently manumitted slaves was not unusual. In 1636, the late Ottoman admiral Mohammad b. 'Abdullâh manumitted seven of his former slaves (six men and at least one Christian woman) and bequeathed them a large house with six rooms near the vegetable market. Loualich, "In the Regency of Algiers," 80–81.

50. Bennassar and Bennassar, *Los cristianos de Alá*, 57. This relationship recalls Kopytoff and Miers's portrayal of West African slavery, in which realms of kinship and slavery were intertwined. "This chattellike position" of the slaves, they have argued, "nevertheless lay on a continuum of marginality whose progressive reduction led in the direction of quasi kinship and, finally, kinship." Igor Kopytoff and Suzanne Miers, introduction to *Slavery in Africa: Historical and Anthropological Perspectives*, ed. Igor Kopytoff and Suzanne Miers (Madison: University of Wisconsin Press, 1977), 24. Erdem, who writes not on war captives but on the more structured systems of Ottoman slavery, characterizes Ottoman slavery as an open system in which slaves were finally incorporated into society; see Erdem, *Slavery in the Ottoman Empire and Its Demise*, 20. For a critique of Kopytoff and Miers's "absorptionist" model, see Frederick Cooper, "The Problem of Slavery in African Studies," *Journal of African History in Africa* 20 (1979): 103–25.

51. For a Mediterranean overview, see Michel Fontenay, "L'esclave galérien dans la Méditerranée des temps modernes," in *Figures de l'esclave au Moyen-âge et dans le monde moderne: Actes de la table ronde organisée les 27 et 28 octobre 1992 par le Centre d'Histoire Sociale et Culturelle de l'Occident de l'Université de Paris-X Nanterre*, ed. Henri Bresc (Paris: L'Harmattan, 1996), 116–25, and Alessandro Stella, "Les galères dans la Méditerranée (XVe–XVIIIe siècles): Miroir des mises en servitude," in *Esclavage et dépendances servils: Histoire comparée*, ed. Myriam Cottias, Alessandro Stella, and Bernard Vincent (Paris: L'Harmattan, 2007), 271. Algerian and other North African corsair fleets were the first to upgrade from the galley to the round ship propelled by sail alone between 1615 and 1625. Spain stopped using galleys only in 1748, but it had significantly cut back its Mediterranean fleet over the seventeenth century. The French, by contrast, built a large galley fleet during the seventeenth century, requiring armies of oar-pulling slaves.

52. On the sailing season and maritime routes, see Horden and Purcell, *The Corrupting Sea*, 137–43.

53. Sosa, *Topography of Algiers*, 151–52.

54. For a detailed analysis of the French galley fleet and the transformations it experienced out of the sailing season, see André Zysberg, *Les Galériens du roi—vies et destins de 60 000 forçats sur les galères de France: 1680–1748* (Paris: Seuil, 1987), 126–47.

55. Anne Brogini, "Une activité sous contrôle: L'esclavage à Malte à l'époque moderne," *Cahiers de la Méditerranée* 78 (2013): 49–61.

56. Sosa, *Topography of Algiers*, 153.

57. ACA, *Consejo de Aragón*, Leg. 911, fol. 106.

58. Tassy, *Histoire du royaume d'Alger*, 61–62.

59. Ibid., 65–66.

60. Ibid., 165. For an example of artisans and owners of small workshops in the Maghrib who hired slaves, see AHN, *Inquisición*, Lib. 863, fols. 294–295v, 1652.

61. Miguel de Cervantes, *Don Quixote*, trans. Edith Grossman and Harold Bloom (New York: Ecco, 2015), 1:343.

62. Ibid.

63. Davis, *Christian Slaves, Muslim Masters*, 73.

64. *Vogavan*, the term in the Mediterranean lingua franca, originated from the French *vogue-avant*; see ibid., 80–81. The *bogavante* sat on the aisle with the second, third, and fourth rowers next to him on the bench; see Augustin Jal, *Glossaire nautique: Répertoire polyglotte de termes de marine anciens et modernes* (Paris: Chez Firmin Didot Fréres, Libraires-Editeurs, Imprimeurs de l'Institut de France, 1848). For more on the work of galley slaves in the Mediterranean, see Fontenay, "L'esclave galérien dans la Méditerranée des temps modernes."

65. Galán, *Relación*, 76.

66. José Tamayo y Velarde, *Memorias del cautiverio y costumbres, ritos y gobiernos de Berbería, según el relato de un jesuita del siglo XVII*, ed. Felipe Maíllo Salgado (Oviedo: University of Oviedo, 2017), 202–12.

67. Villalón and Salinero, *Viaje de Turquía*, 151.

68. AGS, *Guerra y Marina*, Leg. 1858, 8.30.1645.

69. Zysberg, *Les Galériens du roi*, 140–43, 154.

70. Sosa, *Topography of Algiers*, 125. On the trope of diversity in descriptions of the Mediterranean, see E. Natalie Rothman, "Conceptualizing 'the Mediterranean': Ethnolinguistic Diversity and Early Modern Imperial Governmentality" (paper presented at the Mediterranean Criss-Crossed and Constructed Conference, Weatherhead Center, Harvard University, April 29–31, 2011).

71. The term *elche* was also used in early modern Granada to refer to Christians who had converted to Islam.

72. For a new study dedicated to the role of renegades in the Ottoman administration, mostly in the eastern half of the Mediterranean, see Tobias P. Graf, *The Sultan's Renegades: Christian-European Converts to Islam and the Making of the Ottoman Elite, 1575–1610* (Oxford: Oxford University Press, 2017).

73. For a discussion of the cultural specificity of the category of sincerity, and thus of its applicability to non-Protestant, non-elite contexts, see Talal Asad, "Comments on Conversion," in *Conversion to Modernities: The Globalization of Christianity*, ed. Peter Van der Veer (New York: Routledge, 1996), 263–73; Webb Keane, "From Fetishism to Sincerity: Agency, the Speaking Subject, and Their Historicity in the Context of Religious Conversion," *Comparative Studies in Society and History* 39 (1997): 674–93; Rothman, *Brokering Empire*; and Ryan Szpiech, *Conversion and Narrative: Reading and Religious Authority in Medieval Polemic* (Philadelphia: University of Pennsylvania Press, 2013).

74. Fernando Rodríguez Mediano, "Les conversions de Sebastião Pes de Vega, un Portugais au Maroc sa'dien," in *Conversions islamiques: Identités religieuses en Islam méditerranéen*, ed. Mercedes García Arenal (Paris: Maisonneuve et Larose, 2002), 173–92.

75. Bravo Caro, "El reflejo de la esclavitud del Mediterráneo en los registros parroquiales oraneses."

76. Vincent, "Musulmanes y conversión en España en el siglo XVII." On Jesuit mission among slaves, see Emanuele Colombo, "'Infidels' at Home: Jesuits and Muslim Slaves in Seventeenth-Century Naples and Spain," *Journal of Jesuit Studies* 1 (2014): 192–211, and Francois Soyer, "The Public Baptism of Muslims in Early Modern Spain and Portugal: Forging Communal Identity Through Collective Emotional Display," *Journal of Religious History* 39 (2015): 506–23.

77. Phillips, *Slavery in Medieval and Early Modern Iberia*, 93–96.

78. Laurent d'Arvieux, *Mémoires du chevalier d'Arvieux: Voyage à Tunis*, ed. Jacques de Maussion de Favières (Paris: Editions Kimé, 1994), 44–45.

79. Tassy, *Histoire du royaume d'Alger*, 62.

80. AGS, *Estado*, Leg. 210, 2.10.1608. See also Friedman, *Spanish Captives in North Africa in the Early Modern Age*, 88–90.

81. Brogini, "Une activité sous contrôle," 55.

82. On peace agreements between the French and the Ottomans during the seventeenth century, see Weiss, *Captives and Corsairs*, 82–87. On the relations of France and other Christian powers with the Maghribi polities, see Bono, *Les corsaires en Méditerranée*, 32–40. More broadly on these peace agreements, see Guillaume Calafat, "Ottoman North Africa and *Ius Publicum Europaeum*: The Case of the Treaties of Peace and Trade (1600–1750)," in *War, Trade, and Neutrality: Europe and the Mediterranean in the Seventeenth and Eighteenth Century*, ed. Antonella Alimento (Milano: FrancoAngeli, 2011), 171–87.

83. AHN, *Inquisición*, Lib. 862, fol. 92V. A similar story was told by Abrahán Clemente or Suliman; ibid., 10.29.1634.

84. Brogini, "Une activité sous contrôle," 55; Barrio Gozalo, "Esclaves musulmans en Espagne au XVIIIe siècle," 42; Colombo, "'Infidels' at Home."

85. Soyer, "The Public Baptism of Muslims in Early Modern Spain and Portugal," 516. On assimilation, the formation of new social ties, and the maintenance of older bonds in the case of converts in early modern Venice, see E. Natalie Rothman, "Becoming Venetian: Conversion and Transformation in the 17th Century Mediterranean," *Mediterranean Historical Review* 21 (2006): 39–75.

86. D'Arvieux, *Mémoires du chevalier d'Arvieux*, 39.

87. Beatriz Alonso Acero, *Sultanes de Berbería en tierras de la cristiandad: Exilio musulmán, conversión y asimilación en la Monarquía hispánica, siglos XVI–XVII* (Barcelona: Ediciones Bellaterra, 2006); Emanuele Colombo, "A Muslim Turned Jesuit: Baldassarre Loyola Mandes (1631–1667)," *Journal of Early Modern History* 17 (2013): 479–504.

88. Jocelyne Dakhlia, "'Turcs de profession'? Réinscriptions lignagères et redéfinitions sexuelles des convertis dans les cours maghrébines (XVIe–XIXe siècles)," in *Conversions islamiques: Identités religieuses en Islam méditerranéen*, ed. Mercedes García Arenal (Paris: Maisonneuve et Larose, 2002), 151–71.

89. Archivo del Mueso Canario, *Inquisición*, Leg. CXIX-21, 1667–71.

90. For examples, see Vaquer Bennasar, *Captius i renegats al segle XVII*, 124, 126, 128, 130, 150–51, 165–66, 174–75, 193, 194, 225, 235.

91. Blili, "Course et captivité des femmes dans la régence de Tunis," 270.

92. Martínez Torres, *Prisioneros de los infieles*, 123.

93. Dakhlia, "'Turcs de profession,'" 157.

94. Vincent, "Musulmanes y conversión en España en el siglo XVII."

95. Dakhlia, "'Turcs de profession,'" 157.

96. For examples of exchange of letters, see AHN, *Inquisición*, Leg. 1711/1/6, 6.10.1634 and AHN, *Inquisición*, Leg. 1711/1/8, 11.28.1689.

97. AHN, *Consejos*, Leg. 7050, 9.22.1589. For these visits and meetings between renegades and their kin, see AGS, *Estado*, Leg. 1950, 1.14.1619 and AHN, *Inquisición*, Leg. 1714, 1668–70.

98. AGS, *Guerra Antigua*, Leg. 316, fol. 209.

99. Miquel Llot de Ribera, *Verdadera relación de la vitoria y libertad que alcançaron quatrocientos christianos captivos de Hazan Baxá, almirante y capitán general del mar del gran turco, con dos galeras suyas que levantaron* (Barcelona: Casa De Sanson Arbus, 1590).

100. AGS, *Guerra Antigua*, Leg. 315, fol. 150.

101. On multilingualism and the lingua franca as crucial in facilitating communication between and among Muslims and Christians, see Eric Dursteler, "Speaking in Tongues: Language and Communication in the Early Modern Mediterranean," *Past and Present* 217 (2012): 47–77; Jocelyne Dakhlia, *Lingua franca: Histoire d'une langue métisse en Méditerranée* (Arles: Actes Sud, 2008); and Karla Mallette, "Lingua Franca," in *A Companion to Mediterranean History*, ed. Sharon Kinoshita and Peregrine Horden (Chichester: Wiley Blackwell, 2014), 330–44.

102. AGS, *Guerra Antigua*, Leg. 315, fol. 109.

CHAPTER 2

1. Jean-Claude Laborie, "Les ordres rédempteurs et l'instrumentalisation du récit de captivité: L'exemple des trinitaires entre 1630 et 1650," in *Captifs en Méditerranée (XVIe–XVIIIe siècles): Histoires, récits, et légendes*, ed. François Moureau (Paris: Presses de l'Université Paris-Sorbonne, 2008), 93–102.

2. On La Cuadra and on the circumstances in which the relief was commissioned, see Juan Agapito y Revilla, *Catálogo de la sección de escultura* (Valladolid: Imp. E. Zapatero, 1916), 39–40.

3. Pedro de la Cuadra, *La redención de cautivos*, 1599, Museo Nacional de Escultura, Valladolid.

4. Diego de Haedo, *Topografía e historia general de Argel* (Valladolid: Diego Fernandez De Cordoua y Ouiedo, 1612), 100. On Sosa, Haedo, and the true identity of the author of that text, see Camamis George, *Estudios sobre el cautiverio en el Siglo de Oro* (Madrid: Editorial Gredos, 1977), and María Antonia Garcés, introduction to *An Early Modern Dialogue with Islam: Antonio de Sosa's Topography of Algiers (1612)*, ed. María Antonia Garcés (Notre Dame, Ind.: University of Notre Dame Press, 2011), 1–78.

5. For the political uses of ransom in the French case, see Weiss, *Captives and Corsairs*, 52–71.

6. Magnus Russel, "The North European Way of Ransoming: Explorations into an Unknown Dimension of the Early Modern Welfare State," *Historical Social Research* 35 (2010): 128. In the Spanish context, this holds true when examined from a long-term perspective.

7. Friedman, *Spanish Captives in North Africa in the Early Modern Age*; Martínez Torres, *Prisioneros de los infieles*.

8. The sources indicate that the Order of Saint James of the Sword (La Ordem de Santiago da Espada) and the Dominican Order rescued captives occasionally; see Díaz Borrás, *El miedo al Mediterráneo*, 35, and Jarbal Rodriguez, *Captives and Their Saviors in the Medieval Crown of Aragon* (Washington, D.C.: Catholic University of America Press, 2007), 141. On the Congregation of the Holy Christ of Burgos in the seventeenth century and the Third Order of San Francisco in the eighteenth century and their involvement in the ransom of captives, see Friedman, *Spanish Captives in North Africa in the Early Modern Age*, 107.

9. Yvonne Friedman, *Encounter Between Enemies: Captivity and Ransom in the Latin Kingdom of Jerusalem* (Leiden: Brill, 2002), 87.

10. Díaz Borrás, *El miedo al Mediterráneo*, 39–41. On the medieval history of the order and more particularly on the establishment of the first houses, see James William Broadman, *Ransoming Captives in Crusader Spain: The Order of Merced on the Christian-Islamic Frontier* (Philadelphia: University of Pennsylvania Press, 1986), 15–26.

11. On land gifts and acquisition by the Mercedarians and on the leasing of land in the thirteenth century, see Broadman, *Ransoming Captives in Crusader Spain*, 78–94. On the property of the Mercedarians in Valencia from the fourteenth to the sixteenth century, see Díaz Borrás, *El miedo al Mediterráneo*, 49–51.

12. Díaz Borrás, *El miedo al Mediterráneo*, 51; Rodriguez, *Captives and Their Saviors in the Medieval Crown of Aragon*, 162–64, 170–71.

13. Rodriguez, *Captives and Their Saviors in the Medieval Crown of Aragon*, 182–83.

14. Broadman, *Ransoming Captives in Crusader Spain*, 66, 135.

15. Díaz Borrás, *El miedo al Mediterráneo*, 51–52.

16. Rodriguez, *Captives and Their Saviors in the Medieval Crown of Aragon*, 144.

17. The Trinitarian Alonso de San Antonio compiled some of the records that supported the Trinitarian case; see Alonso de San Antonio, *Primacia de redentorade cavtibos de la sagrada Orden de la SSma Trinidad, en las coronas de Castilla, Aragón y Nauarra, contra la illvstre Orden de Nuestra Sa. de la Merced* (Madrid, 1651–52).

18. María Teresa Ferrer i Mallol, "La redempció de captius a la corona catalano-aragonesa (segle XIV)," *Anuario de estudios medievales* 15 (1985): 271.

19. Ibid.

20. On the conquest of the city and the political, social, and linguistic changes it underwent in the following century, see David Coleman, *Creating Christian Granada: Society and Religious Culture in an Old World Frontier City, 1492–1600* (Ithaca, N.Y.: Cornell University Press, 2003), and Claire Gilbert, "A Grammar of Conquest: The Spanish and Arabic Reorganization of Granada After the 1492," *Past and Present* (2018).

21. For a brief discussion of this history with a helpful annotated bibliography, see James Amelang, *Historias paralelas: Judeoconversos y moriscos en la España moderna* (Madrid: Akal, 2012).

22. Braudel, "Les Espagnols et l'Afrique du Nord."

23. John H. Pryor, *Geography, Technology, and War-Studies in the Maritime History of the Mediterranean, 649–1571* (Cambridge: Cambridge University Press, 1988), 153. On "the second brilliant age of Algiers," see Braudel, *The Mediterranean and the Mediterranean World in the Age of Philip II*, 882–86. For an overview of the rise of Algiers during the sixteenth century to become a Mediterranean power, see María Antonia Garcés, *Cervantes en Argel: Historia de un cautivo* (Madrid: Gredos, 2005). On Maltese *corso*, especially in relation to its Greek victims, see Greene, *Catholic Pirates and Greek Merchants*.

24. Braudel, *The Mediterranean and the Mediterranean World in the Age of Philip II*, 865, 882.

25. Merouche, *Recherches sur l'Algérie à l'époque ottomane*, vol. 2, *La course, mythes et réalité*, 213–15.

26. Alms collected in Spanish America by the Mercedarians formed another important source of funding for the rescue of captives from North Africa; see Karen Melvin, "Charity Without Borders: Alms-Giving in New Spain for Captives in North Africa," *Colonial Latin American Review* 18 (2009): 75–97.

27. Martínez Torres, *Prisioneros de los infieles*, 85, 94–97; Friedman, *Spanish Captives in North Africa in the Early Modern Age*, 107–17; Maximiliano Barrio Gozalo, *Esclavos y cautivos: Conflicto entre la cristianidad y el Islam en el siglo XVIII* (Valladolid: Junta De Castilla y León, Consejería De Cultura y Turismo, 2006), 231.

28. Friedman, *Spanish Captives in North Africa in the Early Modern Age*, 107–8, 129–30.

29. The scribe had to prepare three copies of his books: one for the friar leading the expedition; one to be deposited at the order's archive; and one to be submitted for royal inspection "in order that the [Royal Council] will know and understand [how many] *maravedis* you had in your hands and will be used for the said redemption." Guillermo Gozalbes Busto, *Los Moriscos en Marruecos* (Granada: T. G. Arte, 1992), 283.

30. AGS, *Estado*, Leg. 3832, fol. 323, 12.19.1633.

31. Jean Andalousies, "Presencia cristiana en Argelia y Túnez del siglo XII al XIX," in *El cristianismo en el norte de África*, ed. Ramón Lourido Díaz and Henry Teissier (Madrid: Fundación MAPFRE, 1993), 64–66.

32. Philip II was highly invested in orchestrating the implementation of the Tridentine decrees and in the process solidified his political power and his control over the church in his vast territories; see R. Po-Chia Hsia, *The World of Catholic Renewal, 1540–1770* (New York: Cambridge University Press, 2005), 42, 46–53. Such gains for the political authority were pronounced in Spain but were not unique, for the Counter-Reformation enhanced a process that had begun nearly a century earlier as royal rulers appropriated ecclesiastical jurisdiction previously in papal hands. An important stage in that process had come in 1523, when Pope Adrian VI conceded the Patronato Real (a form of control the crown had over the church) to the emperor; see John Lynch, "Philip II and the Papacy," *Transactions of the Royal Historical Society* 11 (1961): 24. More successful than other rulers in this regard, Philip II came to hold immense rights over the church, nominating bishops, prelates, and heads of religious orders and benefiting from ecclesiastical revenues. Po-Chia Hsia, *The World of Catholic Renewal*, 47–48. The regulation and funding of ecclesiastical ransom, then, were part of a larger moral, disciplinary, and institutional reform of the orders that was in turn part of the implementation of the Tridentine decrees. For a thorough analysis of the religious reform of the Order of Our Lady of Mercy, see Bruce Taylor, *Structures of Reform: The Mercedarian Order in the Spanish Golden Age* (Leiden: Brill, 2000).

33. Russel, "The North European Way of Ransoming."

34. Cecilia Tarruell, "Circulations entre Chrétienté et Islam: Captivité et esclavage des serviteurs de la monarchie hispanique (ca. 1574–1609)" (PhD diss., EHESS-UAM, 2015).

35. Rodriguez, *Captives and Their Saviors in the Medieval Crown of Aragon*, 120.

36. Díaz Borrás, *El miedo al Mediterráneo*, 65.

37. On the ransom of Muslim captives in medieval Valencia, see Kathryn A. Miller, "Reflections on Reciprocity: A Late Medieval Islamic Perspective on Christian-Muslim Commitment to Captive Exchange," in *Religion and Trade: Cross-Cultural Exchanges in World History, 1500–1900*, ed. Francesca Trivellato, Leor Halevi, and Catia Antunes (Oxford: Oxford University Press, 2014), 131–49, and the appendix in Díaz Borrás, *El miedo al Mediterráneo*, 287–368. On the envisionings of Muslim captives in Andalusian fatwas, see Francisco Vidal Castro, "El cautivo en el mundo islámico: Cisión y vivencia desde el otro lado de la frontera andalusí," in *II Estudios de la frontera: Actividad y vida en la Frontera*, Congreso celebrado en Alcalá la Real, 19–22 de noviembre de 1997 (Jaén: Diputación Provincial de Jaén, 1998), 771–800; and Milouda Hasnaoui, "La ley Islámica y el rescate de los cautivos según las fetwas de al-Wanšarīsī e Ibn Tarkā," in *La liberazione dei "captivi" tra Cristianità e Islam: Oltre la crociata el il ǧihās: Tolleranza e servizio umanitario*, ed. Giulio Cipollone (Vatican: Archivio Segreto Vaticano, 2000), 549–58. See also Matar, "Piracy and Captivity in the Early Modern Mediterranean."

38. Ferrer i Mallol, "La redempció de captius a la corona catalano-aragonesa," 267.

39. These intermediaries charged 10 percent of the ransom as their fee, or a golden coin when Muslim captives were exchanged for Christians. In addition, the relatives of the captives had to pay their travel expenses; see Ferrer i Mallol, "La redempció de captius a la corona catalano-aragonesa," 262.

40. Another result of these geopolitical shifts was that the office of municipal ransomer nearly disappeared. There were exceptions to this rule. Cities that suffered from piracy on a regular basis, for example, Calpe, which was located in Spanish Levant between Valencia and Alicante, and the Balearic Islands, continued to employ *alfaqueques* or local independent ransomers; see AGS, *Guerra Antigua*, Leg. 1541, 9.19.1644. On the Balearic Islands, see Natividad Planas, "La frontière franchissable: Normes et pratiques dans les échanges entre le royaume de Majorque et les terres d'Islam au XVIIe siècle," *Revue d'histoire moderne et contemporaine* 48, no. 2 (2001): 123–47. On Morisco ransomers, see Miguel de Epalza, "Moriscos y Andalusíes en Túnez durante el siglo XVII," *Al-Andalus* 34, no. 2 (1969): 262–69. On consuls, see Erica Heinsen-Roach, "Consuls-of-State and the Redemption of Slaves: The Dutch Republic and the Western Mediterranean, 1616–1651," *Itinerario* 39 (2015): 69–90, and Niels Steensgaard, "Consuls and Nations in the Levant from 1570 to 1650," *Scandinavian Economic History Review* 15 (1967): 13–55.

41. Roberto Blanes Andrés, *Valencia y el Magreb: Las relaciones comerciales marítimas (1600–1703)* (Barcelona: Ediciones Bellaterra, 2010); Eloy

Martín Corrales, *Comercio de Cataluña con el Mediterráneo musulmán (siglos XVI–XVIII): El Comercio con los "enemigos de la fe"* (Barcelona: Ediciones Bellaterra, 2001).

42. Kaiser, "La excepción permanente."

43. Rafael Benítez, "La tramitación del pago de rescates a través del reino de Valencia: El último plazo del rescate de Cervantes," in *Le commerce de captifs: Les intermédiaires dans l'échange et le rachat des prisonniers en Méditerranée, XVe–XVIIIe siècle,* ed. Wolfgang Kaiser (Rome: École Française de Rome, 2008), 193–217.

44. A description that applies, for example, to Juan Lucas, resident of Tarragona (ACA, *Consejo de Aragón,* Leg. 728, 9.13.1650), and Gaspar de los Reyes, from the Canary Islands (AHN, *Inquisición,* Leg. 1824-2, 1670).

45. One of Malaqui's Muslim associates, the merchant Hamad Madan from Fez, stayed in Spain as a hostage, guaranteeing the agreements until at least 1595. AGS, *Guerra Antigua,* Leg. 448, fol. 206, 10.23.1595. At the same time, Malaqui also invested in mining in Spain, and the hostages he provided, who were experts on mining—"two Moors of Barbary who understand a lot [in mining]"—worked for him in this field. Julio Sánchez Gómez, *De minería, metalúrgica y comercio de metales* (Salamanca: Ediciones Universidad de Salamanca, 1989), 2:640. On Malaqui's son, see AGS, *Guerra Antigua,* Leg. 316, fol. 426. This strategy was not exceptional. In his *Les juifs du roi d'Espagne,* Schaub discusses the case of Felipe Moscoso, the son of Jacob Sasportas, one of the leaders of the Jewish community in Oran. Moscoso, who converted to Christianity, lived in Madrid and Alicante and served his family's interests at the court there; see Jean-Frédéric Schaub, *Les juifs du roi d'Espagne* (Paris: Hachette Littératures, 1999), 98–100. For Moscoso commercial correspondence, see Vicente Montojo Montojo, ed., *Correspondencia mercantile en el siglo XVII: Las cartas del mercader Felipe Moscoso (1660–1685)* (Murcia: University of Murcia, 2013).

46. AGS, *Guerra Antigua,* Leg. 271, fol. 304, 1589.

47. Ibid.

48. Traces of Malaqui and his involvement in the ransom market disappear in 1595, but mention of his name in an Inquisition case in 1600 suggests that at some point he converted to Christianity and moved to the peninsula; see Sebastián Cirac Estopañán, *Los procesos de hechicerías en la Inquisición de Castilla la Nueva* (Madrid: Diana, 1942), 70–71.

49. Crudo had commercial relations with Sima di Giuseppe Levi, a Jewish merchant active in Algiers and Livorno at the turn of the century, whom he met in Annaba; see Vittorio Salvadorini, "Traffici e schiavi fra Livorno e Algeria nella prima decade del '600," *Bollettino Storico Pisano* 51 (1982): 88.

50. AGS, *Guerra Antigua,* Leg. 487, fols. 213–15, 15.7.1597.

51. "[Y] vuelto en esta ciudad anda en habito de cristiano y trata y contrata en ella con mucha publicidad de que ha dado mucho escándalo." AHN, *Inquisición,* Leg. 2952, 5.8.1597.

52. The most complete study on this community is Schaub, *Les juifs du roi d'Espagne.* For a general survey of the Jewish population who lived at

the Spanish forts in North Africa, see Jonathan Israel, "The Jews of Spanish North Africa, 1600–1669," *Transactions of the Jewish Historical Society of England* 26 (1979): 71–86. For a general study of Oran in this period, see Alonso Acero, *Orán-Mazalquivir, 1589–1639*. The Mercedarians in Oran felt so indebted to members of the Çaportas family that in 1653 friars of the Mercedarian convent in town faked municipal documents in an attempt to help the family in its struggles against the governor-general, probably as a sign of gratitude for the favors family members had granted Christian captives; see Schaub, *Les juifs du roi d'Espagne*, 94–95.

53. The Çaportas had better links in Fez and Marrakesh, the Cansino in Tlemcen, and even in Algiers; see Schaub, *Les juifs du roi d'Espagne*, 55, 78, 89.

54. In some cases, these intermediaries openly competed against the orders. For the case of Yehuda Malaqui, a Jewish merchant form Tétouan and a supplier of the Spanish fort of the Peñón de Vélez in Morocco, see AGS, *Guerra Antigua*, Leg. 271, fol. 304, 1589.

55. For example, ACA, *Consejo de Aragón*, Leg. 743, 9.9.1659.

56. Ibid.

57. ACA, *Consejo de Aragón*, Leg. 607, fol. 41, 7.24.1660.

58. Horden and Purcell, *The Corrupting Sea*, 387–88.

59. Benítez, "La tramitación del pago de rescates a través del reino de Valencia," 197–98, 205.

60. Kaiser and Calafat, "The Economy of Ransoming in the Early Modern Mediterranean," 120–21.

61. Díaz Borrás, *El miedo al Mediterráneo*, 45.

62. Gabriel de la Asunción, *Memorial del General de la orden descalços de la Santísima Trinidad, redención de cautivos, contra el arbitrio dado por el capitán Guillermo Garret, sobre la erección de una escuadra de seis navíos, que guarden las costas que miran a Berbería, y preserven estos reinos y sus habitadores, del cautiverio de los moros, convirtiendo en el apresto y sustento desta escuadra, lo que se gasta en redención de cautivos, por medio de las ordenes de la Trinidad, y Merced, y diversas dotaciones*, in *Papeles de mi archivo, Relaciones de África (Marruecos)*, ed. Ignacio Bauer Landauer (Madrid: Editorial Ibero-Africano-Americana, 1922–23), 2:59.

63. Reciprocity is understood here, following Polanyi, as "movements between correlative points of symmetric groupings." Polanyi, "The Economy as Instituted Process," 250–53.

64. Such associations also characterized organized redemption institutions elsewhere in the Christian world. In Italy, each city-state had its own ransom institution; see Davis, *Christian Slaves, Muslim Masters*, 149–69.

65. Miller, "Reflections on Reciprocity."

66. Natividad Planas, "Conflicts de competence aux frontiers: Le contrôle de la circulation des homes et des marchandises dans le royaume de Majorque au XVIIe siècle," *Cromohs* 8 (2003): 1–14.

67. Kaiser, "La excepción permanente"; Kaiser, "L'Économie de la rançon en Méditerranée occidentale (XVIe–XVIIe siècle)"; Daniel Hershenzon, "Las redes de confianza y crédito en el Mediterráneo

occidental: Cautiverio y rescate, 1580–1670," in *Les Esclavages en Méditerranée: Espaces et dynamiques économiques*, ed. Fabiana Guillén and Salah Trabelsi (Madrid: Casa de Velázquez, 2012).

68. French envoys to the Maghrib claimed more than once that the friars depicted the living conditions of the slaves as worse than they were in order to justify their own labor. In his account of a 1666 voyage to Tunis, French emissary Laurent d'Arvieux accused the friars of spreading "pious lies" about tortured captives to encourage the faithful to give alms to be used for their redemption. And in his 1724 account of his mission to Algiers, diplomat Laugier de Tassy blamed Spanish redeemers for the terrible reputation of Muslims in Europe; see d'Arvieux, *Mémoires du chevalier d'Arvieux*, 44–45, and Tassy, *Histoire du royaume d'Alger*, 10. Such accusations allowed French royal envoys to claim expertise on the Maghrib at the expense of the friars, but these emissaries also had a point. In their exchanges with the Council of State and Council of War, the friars repeatedly insisted that their treatment and the treatment of Christian slaves by the North African rulers were more than fair (see Chapter 5 for more on the working relations between the friars and the Algerian authorities). In any case, these critics wrote in French and addressed a French audience, probably decision makers, and thus their attacks had little impact on the Spanish orders of redemption.

69. Miguel Martínez del Villar, *Discurso acerca de la conquista de los reynos de Argel y Bugia, en que se trata de las razones que ay para emprendela, respondiendo a las que se hazen en contrario* (Madrid: Luis Sánchez, 1619), Biblioteca Nacional de España (hereafter BNE), R/11834.

70. On Salé, see Maziane, *Salé et ses corsairs*. On the plans to attack Algiers, see Miguel Ángel Bunes Ibarra, "Felipe III y la defensa del Mediterráneo: La conquista de Argel," in *Guerra y sociedad en la monarquía hispánica: Política, estrategia, y cultura en la Europa moderna (1500–1700)*, vol. 1, ed. Enrique García Hernán and David Maffi (Madrid: Laberinto, 2006), 921–46.

71. Magnus Russel and Cornel Zwierlein, "The Ransoming of North European Captives from North Africa: A Comparison of Dutch, Hanseatic, and English Institutionalization of Redemption from 1610–1645," in *Seeraub im Mittelmeerraum: Piraterie, Korsarentum und maritime Gewalt von der Antike bis zur Neuzeit*, ed. Nikolas Jaspert and Sebastian Kolditz (Paderborn: Verlag Ferdinand Schöningh, 2014), 377–406.

72. Taylor, *Structures of Reform*, 361.

73. "Copia de una carta original del Duque de Osuna á S.M. fecha en Palermo á 31 de mayo de 1612," *Colección de documentos inéditos para la historia de España* (hereafter CODOIN), 44:285.

74. Martínez del Villar, *Discurso acerca de la conquista de los reynos de Argel y Bugia*.

75. On early modern Spanish perceptions of Muslim masculinity, see Mar Martínez-Góngora, *Los espacios coloniales en las crónicas de Berbería* (Madrid: Iberoamericana, 2013), 181–98.

76. A pamphlet published in 1628 summarized Garrett's arguments and the response of the General of the Discalced Trinitarians; see Gabriel de la Asunción, *Memorial del General*, 2:53–86.

77. Tirso de Molina, the dramatist, poet, and member of the Mercedarian order, described this dynamic in his history of the Mercedarians; see Tirso de Molina, *Historia general de la orden de nuestra señora de las mercedes (1568–1639)*, vol. 2, ed. Manuel Penedo Rey (Madrid: Provincia de la Merced de Castilla, 1974), 493–94.

78. Replies were composed in 1627 by Pedro de Merino, the Mercedarian provincial of Castile, in 1628 by Gabriel de la Asunción, general of the order of the Discalced Trinitarians, and in 1631 by the Portuguese Mercedarian Serafín de Freitas; see Anita Gonzales-Raymond, "Le rachat des chrétiens en terres d'Islam: De la charité chrétienne à la raison d'état: Les éléments d'une controverse autour des années 1620," in *Chrétiens et musulmans a la Renaissance, Actes du 37e colloque international de CESR, 1994*, ed. Bartolomé Bennassar and Robert Sauzet (Paris: H. Champion, 1998), 371–89; Gabriel de la Asunción, *Memorial del General de la orden descalços de la Santísima Trinidad*; Taylor, *Structures of Reform*, 364.

79. Tirso de Molina, *Historia general de la orden de nuestra señora de las mercedes*, 551–52. On Olivares's reforms, see John Elliott, *Richelieu and Olivares* (Cambridge: Cambridge University Press, 1984), 60–85.

80. For his discussion of the topic, see Tamayo y Velarde, *Memorias del cautiverio y costumbres*, 193–203.

81. AGS, *Estado*, Leg. 2672, 5.11.1654; Calafat, "Ottoman North Africa and *Ius Publicum Europaeum*."

82. Bartolomé Garcés Ferrá, "Propuesta de armada contra los piratas berberiscos entre Holanda y España a mediados del siglo XVII," *Hispania* 8, no. 32 (1948): 403–33.

83. Barrio Gozalo, *Esclavos y cautivos*, 232–33.

84. Gabriel de la Asunción, *Memorial del General*, 2:84.

85. Martín Corrales, *Comercio de Cataluña con el Mediterráneo musulmán*, 71.

86. ACA, *Consejo de Aragón*, Leg. 592, 7.7.1631. Similarly, in 1668, the skipper Già exported tar to Algiers on behalf of a mercantile company from Majorca but was arrested and sentenced by the Majorcan Inquisition upon his return; see AHN, *Inquisición*, Leg. 1714, carpeta 7. The Inquisition based its right to interfere on matters of commerce with Muslims on a papal bull that prohibited such trade. But Già's attorney claimed the bishop had annulled the bull and hence the matter fell under episcopal rather than Inquisitorial jurisdiction. We do not know the bishop's response, but the lawyer's claim points to how interactions with Maghribi fell under a multiplicity of competing jurisdictions, a situation the parties involved employed to their favor; see Planas, "Conflicts de competence aux frontiers."

87. Blanes Andrés, *Valencia y el Magreb*, 203.

88. Ibid., 182.

89. The following argument is based on Planas, "La frontière franchissable."

90. Friedman, *Spanish Captives in North Africa in the Early Modern Age*, 107–8, 129–30. On the various taxes and tolls the orders had to pay in

North Africa, see Kaiser and Calafat, "The Economy of Ransoming in the Early Modern Mediterranean," 116–17.

91. Gillian Weiss, "Ransoming 'Turks' from France's Royal Galleys," *African Economic History* 42 (2014): 37–58.

92. Apart from official efforts, Maghribis relied on Christian, Jewish, and Muslim merchants to help them reunite with their enslaved kin; see Epalza, "Moriscos y Andalusíes en Túnez durante el siglo XVII," 262–69. Algerian Moriscos also ransomed Muslims; see Vaquer Bennasar, *Captius i renegats al segle XVII*, 145–46. For other examples of Muslim merchants who engaged in ransoming Muslim slaves, see Panzac, *Barbary Corsairs*, 23–24. On Jews who ransomed Muslims, see Renzo Toaff, "Schiavitù e schiavi nella Nazione Ebrea di Livorno nel Sei e Settecento," *La Rassegna Mensile di Israel* 51 (1985): 92–94.

93. AGS, *Estado*, Leg. 246, 5.12.1612.

94. AGS, *Estado*, Leg. 992, 10.30.1629.

95. Aldo Gallotta, "Diplomi turchi dell'Archivio di Stato di Firenze: Lettere da Algeri ai Granduchi di Toscana (secolo XVII)," *Studi Magrebini* 11 (1979): 167–205 and facsimiles I–XII.

96. AGS, *Estado*, Leg. 3446, 3.21.1633.

97. Miriam Hoexter, *Endowments, Rulers and Community: Waqf al Haramayn in Ottoman Algiers* (Leiden: Brill, 1998), 27, 158; Panzac, *Barbary Corsairs*, 24–25. The practice of using *waqf* funds to redeem captives has older roots; see Ahmad ibn Yahyā al-Wansharīsī, *La pierre de touche des fétwas de Ahmad al-Wanscharīsī*, in *Archives Marocaines: Publication de la mission scientifique du Maroc*, vol. 13, ed. and trans. Émile Amar (Paris: E. Leroux, 1908–9), 384, 394.

98. Panzac, *Barbary Corsairs*, 22–24.

99. Peter Kitlas, "Al-Miknāsī's Mediterranean Mission: Negotiating Moroccan Temporal and Spiritual Sovereignty in the Late Eighteenth Century," *Mediterranean Studies* 23 (2015): 179–88.

100. For documents and more about this case, see J. Vernet, "La embajada de al-Gassani (1690–1691)," *Al-Andalus* 18 (1953): 109–31; Tomás García Figueras and Carlos Rodríguez Joulia Saint-Cyr, *Larache: Datos para su historia en el siglo XVII* (Madrid: Instituto de Estudios Africanos, CSIC, 1973), 319–27; Mariano Arribas Palau, "De nuevo sobre la embajada de al-Gassani (1690–1691)," *Al-Qantara* 6 (1985): 199–289; and Ubaldo de Casanova y Todolí, "Algunas anotaciones sobre el comportamiento de los esclavos moros en Mallorca durante el siglo XVII y un ejemplo de intercambio con cautivos cristianos," *Bolletí de la Societat Arqueològica Lul·liana: Revista d'estudis històrics* 41 (1985): 323–32. For documents and study of the ransom of Moroccans and Algerians in the second half of the eighteenth century orchestrated by Sultan Muhammad ibn 'Abdallāh al-Khaṭīb, see Ramón Lourido Díaz, "La obra redentora del sultán marroquí Sīdī Muḥammad b. 'Abd Allāh entre los cautivos musulmanes en Europa (siglo XVIII)," *Cuadernos de Historia del Islam* 11 (1984): 138–83, and Mariano Arribas Palau, "Argelinos cautivos en España, rescatados por el sultán de Marruecos," *Boletín de la Asociación Española de Orientalistas* 26 (1990): 23–54.

101. Barrio Gozalo, *Esclavos y cautivos*, 315. More specifically, on fatwas on the issue of captives and the obligation to ransom them, see Matar, "Piracy and Captivity in the Early Modern Mediterranean"; Vidal Castro, "El cautivo en el mundo islámico"; and Hasnaoui, "La ley Islámica."

102. Panzac, *Barbary Corsairs*, 24.

103. Barrio Gozalo, *Esclavos y cautivos*, 310–20.

104. Pascual Saura Lahoz, "Los Franciscanos en Marruecos: Relación inédita de 1685," *Archivo Ibero-Americano* 17 (1921): 79–100.

105. Friedman, *Spanish Captives in North Africa in the Early Modern Age*, 142–44.

106. Similar arguments were advanced by Martin I of Aragon (r. 1396–1409). Ferrer i Mallol, "La redempció de captius a la corona catalano-aragonesa," 274.

CHAPTER 3

1. Early modern Mediterranean merchants found varied solutions. The Venetians employed family members and could count on their republic and its banks; see Frederic C. Lane, "Family Partnerships and Joint Ventures in the Venetian Republic," *Journal of Economic History* 4 (1944): 178–96. The Genoese developed shared property rights that bound even unknown parties together; see Ricardo Court, "'Januensis Ergo Mercator': Trust and Enforcement in the Business Correspondence of the Brignole Family," *Sixteenth Century Journal* 35 (2004): 987–1003. In contrast to these commercial contexts, the commodities in ransom agreements were themselves party to the deals; once a deal had taken place, the commodity disappeared, as captives gained their liberty.

2. Pasamonte, *Autobiografía*, 73.

3. Galán, *Relación*, 95.

4. Friedman, *Spanish Captives in North Africa in the Early Modern Age*, 147.

5. James Casey, *Early Modern Spain: A Social History* (London: Routledge, 1999), 26.

6. Davis, *Christian Slaves, Muslim Masters*, 147; Martínez Torres, *Prisioneros de los infieles*, 144–45; Kaiser and Calafat, "The Economy of Ransoming in the Early Modern Mediterranean," 113–14.

7. The list includes captives captured between 1760 and 1772; see A. de Voulx, ed. and trans., *Tachrifat, Recueil de notes historiques sur l'administration de l'ancienne régence d'Alger* (Algiers: Impr. du Gouvernement, 1852), 88–89.

8. Ambrus, Chaney, and Salitskiy, "Pirates of the Mediterranean."

9. Jerónimo Gracián, *Tratado de la redención de cautivos: En que se cuentan las grandes miserias que padecen los cristianos que están en poder de infieles, y cuán santa obra sea la de su rescates*, ed. Miguel Ángel Bunes Ibarra and Beatriz Alonso Acero (Seville: Ediciones Espuela de Plata, 2006), 98. See also d'Arvieux, *Mémoires du chevalier d'Arvieux*, 41.

10. "Libro de la Redención que se ha hecho en Argel este año de 1679, siendo redentores el padre maestro fray Lorenzo Mayers y el padre presentado fray Francisco de Tineo," BNE, Mss. 2974, fol. 5.

11. Daniel Carpi, "The Activities of the Officials of the Sephardic Jewish Congregation in Venice for the Redemption of Captives (1654–1670) [Hebrew]," *Zion* 68 (2003): 201.

12. "But the Spaniards, who would not let go their solemnity, prefer to stay slaves for long time periods and even die there than to lower themselves. They loudly say they are gentlemen, rich and that their parents who are great lords will not stand their being slaves and that soon they would send considerable sums of money for their ransom." D'Arvieux, *Mémoires du chevalier d'Arvieux*, 267–68.

13. Ambrus, Chaney, and Salitskiy, "Pirates of the Mediterranean."

14. In a letter from November 6, he wrote that he planned to approach the pasha, saying, "You see that much [money, it's yours] if you want [it], if not, stay with me as your captive." Jerónimo Gracián, *Cartas, Monumenta historica Carmeli Teresiani*, ed. Juan Luis Astigarraga (Rome: Teresianum, 1989), 6.11.1594. A month later, he wrote to Andreas de Córdoba, an auditor in the Roman Curia, telling him that when Ottoman officeholders end their terms, "they have appetite for money and they take anything" (7.6.1594).

15. For an early modern chronology of plagues in Tunis and the rest of the Maghrib, see Édouard Bloch, "La peste en Tunisie (aperçu historique et epidémiologique)" (PhD diss., Impr. J. Aloccio, 1929), 3–11.

16. Weiss, *Captives and Corsairs*, 83.

17. Mascarenhas, *Esclave à Alger*, 160.

18. D'Aranda, *Les captifs d'Alger*, 132.

19. Ibid. See also Tamayo y Velarde, *Memorias del cautiverio y costumbres*, 205.

20. Jean-Baptiste Gramaye, *Alger, XVIe–XVIIe siècle: Journal de Jean-Baptiste Gramaye, "évêque d'Afrique,"* trans. Abd El Hadi Ben Mansour (Paris: Éd. du Cerf, 1998), 309.

21. Tunis to Juana Dantisco, his mother, 7.6.1594; Gracián, *Cartas, Monumenta historica Carmeli Teresiani*, 169.

22. Letter to Andreas de Cordoba, 7.6.1594, Gracián, *Cartas, Monumenta historica Carmeli Teresiani*, 166–67.

23. Gracián, *Tratado de la redención de cautivos*, 117.

24. Ibid., 95.

25. On Bourdieu's notion of *hexis* and the manner in which social structures are inculcated and written onto bodies, see Pierre Bourdieu, *The Logic of Practice* (Stanford, Calif.: Stanford University Press, 1990), 66–79.

26. D'Aranda, *Les captifs d'Alger*, 52–53. For further analysis of the interaction, see Jocelyne Dakhlia, "Ligne de fuite: Impostures et reconstructions identitaires en Méditerranée musulmane à l'époque moderne," in *Gens de passage en Méditerranée de l'Antiquité à l'époque modern: Procédures de contrôle et d'identification. L'atelier Méditerranéen*, ed. Wolfgang Kaiser and Claudia Moatti (Paris: Maisonneuve et Larose, 2007), 427–58.

27. D'Aranda, *Les captifs d'Alger*, 52.

28. D'Arvieux, *Mémoires du chevalier d'Arvieux*, 5:267; AHN, *Inquisición*, Lib. 862, fol. 92V.

29. *Relación verdadera embiada de la ciudad de Argel, dando cuenta de los alborotos y ruidos, que aquellos barbaros tienen entre sí . . . y el sucesso que ha tenido la redempción de los religiosos de Nuestro Señora de la Merced* (Madrid: Iulian de Paredes, 1661); ACA, *Consejo de Aragón*, Leg. 607, fol. 41, 7.24.1660.

30. Tassy, *Histoire du royaume d'Alger*, 169.

31. See also Tamayo y Velarde's critique in *Memorias del cautiverio y costumbres*, 193–203.

32. AGS, *Guerra Antigua*, Leg. 268, fol. 200, 1.3.1589.

33. For example, in 1664, when the Spanish captain Francisco Villanueva took over a Muslim galley, he captured its sixty-two Muslim crew members and released twenty-five Christian oarsmen. AGS, *Estado*, Leg. 3287, fol. 25, 3.7.1664.

34. Juan Márquez, *Vida del venerable P. Fr. Alonso de Orozco, Religioso de la Orden de N. P. S. Agustin, y Predicador de las Catolicas Magestades de Carlos V y Felipe II* (Madrid: Iuan Sánchez, 1648). I thank Andrea Celli for pointing out to me this source, which he analyzes in his forthcoming book chapter on the biblical narrative of Hagar; see Andrea Celli, "The Early-Modern Invention of 'Abrahamic Religions': An Overview of Baroque Approaches to the Hagar Narrative," in *Legacies, Transfers & Polemics: Interactions Between Judaism, Christianity and Islam from Late Antiquity to the Present*, ed. Alexander Dubrau, Davide Scotto, and Ruggero Vimercati Sanseverino (Tübingen: Mohr Siebeck, forthcoming).

35. ACA, *Consejo de Aragón*, Leg. 993, fol. 49, 3.9.1692.

36. For example, Martín de Medina asked the king to pass the salary owed him for his military service to Agustín García, a resident of Cadiz with trading contacts in Algiers (AGS, *Guerra Antigua*, Leg. 1541, 3.4.1644). On these petitions, see Sandoval Parra, *Manera de galardón*, 163–92.

37. Wolfgang Kaiser, "Les mots du rachat: D'Action et rhétorique dans les procédures de rachat de captifs en Méditerranéen, XVIe–XVIIe siècles," in *Captifs en Méditerranée (XVIe–XVIIIe siècles): Histoires, récits, et légendes*, ed. François Moureau (Paris: PUPS, 2008), 103–17.

38. AHN, *Consejos*, Leg. 6902, 5.25.1672.

39. ACA, *Consejo de Aragón*, Leg. 993, fol. 30, 4.28.1692 and Chapter 6.

40. AGS, *Guerra Antigua*, Leg. 442, fol. 46, 4.22.1594.

41. AGS, *Guerra Antigua*, Leg. 768, fol. 3, 10.12.1612.

42. Beatriz Carceles de Gea, "La 'justicia distributiva' en el siglo XVII (Aproximación politico-constitucional)," *Chronica Nova* 14 (1984–85): 93–122.

43. Amelang, "L'autobiografia popolare nella Spagna moderna," 115–16; Natalie Zemon Davis, *Fiction in the Archives: Pardon Tales and Their Tellers in Sixteenth-Century France* (Stanford, Calif.: Stanford University Press, 1987).

44. AHN, *Inquisición*, Leg. 933-2, 11.13.1655.

45. For example, in the 1580 petition from Catalina Gutiérrez regarding her son's captivity in Istanbul, the magistrates indicated that Gutiérrez

"presented a summarized interrogation of witnesses [*información*] and a letter which she says is from the said captive" (AHN, *Consejos*, Leg. 7045, 7.29.1580). The members of the Council of Castile and of the Council of War almost always commented on their minutes on the submitted evidence: "Presents an interrogation of witnesses [*información*] by which what he claims in his petition is proved" (AHN, *Consejos*, Leg. 7045, 6.5.1580).

46. AHN, *Consejos*, Leg. 7048, 12.4.1587.

47. AGS, *Guerra Antigua*, Leg. 274, fol. 116, 9.20.1589.

48. D'Aranda, *Les captifs d'Alger*, 44.

49. Pancracio Celdrán Gomariz, ed., *Judíos, moros y cristianos en la ciudad de Argel (según un manuscrito inédito de Melchor de Zúñiga, 1639)* (Madrid: Ediciones del Orto, 2012), 149–50.

50. "Donnez deux mille patagons à Livourne ou quinze cents ici." Ibid.

51. Carpi, "The Activities of the Officials of the Sephardic Jewish Congregation," 190–91.

52. Diego Suárez Montañés, *Historia del Maestre último que fue de Montesa y de su hermano Don Felipe de Borja: La manera como gobernaron las memorables plazas de Orán y Mazalquivir, Reinos de Tremecén y Ténez, en África*, ed. Miguel Ángel Bunes Ibarra and Beatriz Alonso Acero (Valencia: Institució Alfons El Magnànim, 2005), 173.

53. ACA, *Consejo de Aragón*, Leg. 993, fol. 8, 12.27.1665.

54. AGS, *Guerra Antigua*, Leg. 487, fol. 142, 7.13.1597.

55. For example, in December 1664 Rabbi Abraham Cansino, one of three leaders of the Jewish community of Oran and a slave trader, negotiated an agreement with fifty-year-old Jalifa ben Brahem, who arranged for two hostages to stay in the city while she left to arrange her ransom fee; see Biblioteca Zabálburu, *Colección Altamira*, D. 52, 12.21.1664. Athman, another slave who arrived in the city as a hostage, was sent to Madrid as a slave in September 1661, probably because the slave in exchange for whom he remained hostage did not pay his or her debt; see Biblioteca Zabálburu, *Colección Altamira*, D. 52, 9.27.1661.

56. Cf. Dakhlia, "Défenses et stratégies d'une captive hollandaise au Maroc." For other examples of the practice, see AHN, *Consejos*, Leg. 7048, 8.21.1587; AGS, *Guerra Antigua*, Leg. 262, fol. 140, 4.17.1589; AHN, *Consejos*, Leg. 6900, 9.20.1591; AGS, *Guerra Antigua*, Leg. 833, 2.11.1617; Archivo Histórico de la Catedral de Burgos (hereafter AHCB), Reg. 81, fols. 256–57, 12.11.1628; AHN, *Consejos*, Leg. 7055, 10.7.1667, Leg. 6902, fol. 2, 5.25.1672; AHCB, Reg. 87, fol. 490, 2.12.1676; AHN, *Consejos*, Leg. 6903, 11.15.1677, Leg. 6902, carpeta 5, fol. 6. 4.20.1674, Leg. 6904, November 1684; and AHCB, Reg. 89, fols. 413–14, 1.29.1685.

57. AGS, *Cámara de Castilla*, Leg. 683, fol. 42, 5.10.1588; AHN, *Consejos*, Leg. 7046, 6.16.1581.

58. AGS, *Guerra Antigua*, Leg. 274, fol. 116, 9.20.1589.

59. For example, in 1625, the Mercedarians carried with them two Muslims whom they exchanged for a Christian child and a woman; *Memorial del General de la orden descalços de la Santísima Trinidad*, 2:85. Similarly, among the Christians whom the friars ransomed from Morocco in 1661 was

one who was exchanged for a Muslim slave; see *Relación nueva de las cosas más notables, que han sucedido a los padres redemptores del orden de la santísima trinidad calçados de las provincias de Castilla, y Andaluzia, en la redempción que han hecho en Arcila, Alcaçar, Zalé, Fez, y otras ciudades de África, sacando 136 cautivos christianos del poder de infieles*, BNE, Mss. 2388, fols. 189–201.

60. Diego Díaz Hierro, *Historia de la Merced de Huelva: Hoy catedral de su diócesis* (Huelva: Imp. Guillermo Martín, 1975).

61. Barrio Gozalo, *Esclavos y cautivos*, 309–10.

62. AGS, *Guerra y Marina*, Lib. 305, fol. 136, 10.1675.

63. Celdrán Gomariz, *Judíos, moros y cristianos en la ciudad de Argel*, 228–29.

64. Tamayo y Velarde, *Memorias del cautiverio y costumbres*, 197.

65. Ahmad ibn Yahyā al-Wansharīsī, *La pierre de touche des fétwas de Ahmad al-Wanscharīsī*, in *Archives Marocaines: Publication de la mission scientifique du Maroc*, vol. 12, ed. and trans. Émile Amar (Paris: E. Leroux, 1908–9), 235.

66. AGS, *Guerra Antigua*, Leg. 272, fols. 162–63, 1.15.1589.

67. AGS, *Guerra Antigua*, Leg. 442, fol. 46, 4.23.1594.

68. On April 17, 1616, for example, Prince Philibert of Savoy, captain general of the Spanish Mediterranean fleet between 1612 and 1624, issued an order to the generals of the squadrons. He referred to his earlier permitting of such exchanges, permission that was annulled by the king's order; AGS, *Guerra Antigua*, Leg. 812, 4.17.1616.

69. AGS, *Guerra y Marina*, Leg. 3362, Cartas-M, 4.1.1654.

70. Juana de los Santos argued in her petition that the captain who caught Hamad Musa lied when he listed him as a *ra'īs*—"and the captain who captured him, in order to increase his benefits, despite the fact he [the Muslim] was someone else, handed him to them [galley's officers] as an *ra'īs*." AGS, *Guerra Antigua*, Leg. 274, fol. 116, 9.20.1589.

71. See, for example, the depositions of former Christian captives and Muslim slaves regarding the status of Muhammad Ibn 'Abdallāh, a potter from Fez captured by the Spaniards on July 31, 1586, AGS, *Guerra Antigua*, Leg. 220, fols. 175–79. Juana de los Santos provided a declaration from witnesses who swore that Hamad Musa, the Muslim slave de los Santos requested from the crown, was "of no importance [*baxo*]." The *adelantado* denied her the slave she needed for the ransom of her husband nonetheless. In her petition to the crown, she complained that the *adelantado* was "always looking for excuses and not feeling the sufferings of the Christian captives" (AGS, *Guerra Antigua*, Leg. 274, fol. 116). In other words, royal writs ordering the fleet officers to hand over slaves to petitioners were not always sufficient, and officers along the chain of command could prevent the execution of such exchanges. Isabel Hernández, Antón Rodriguez's wife, claimed that "even though she went to the *adelantado* with the two said writs [*cedula*], he refused to give her the said Turk whom she demanded." AGS, *Guerra Antigua*, Leg. 272, fol. 56.

72. AGS, *Guerra Antigua*, Leg. 1541, 4.18.1644.

73. "Libro de quenta y razón cargo y descargo del padre maestro fray Francisco de Benavides y del p. maestro fray Gaspar Núñez redentores de la orden de nuestra señora de la merced por las provincias de Castilla y Andaluzia en este rescate que ban a hazer de los cautibos de Zale en el reyno de Fez este presente año de mill y seiscientos y veynte y quarto." BNE, Mss. 3634. In his history of the Mercedarian order, a work that lists all the early modern expeditions the order sent, the names of redeemers, and the number of captives ransomed, José Antonio Gari y Siumell embellishes the bravery of the friars and describes how in 1624 they supposedly combed the prisons of Tétouan and Salé for Spanish captives. See José Antonio Gari y Siumell, *La orden redentora de la Merced ó sea historia de las redenciones de cautivos cristianos realizadas por los hijos de la orden de la Merced* (Barcelona: Imprenta De los Herederos de la Viuda Pla, 1873), 294.

74. In the sixteenth century, Trinitarians and Mercedarians had often embezzled contributions they had collected from the faithful for the payment of ransoms. Royal reform eliminated this practice, and in the seventeenth century, in only one case, in 1627, was a Mercedarian accused of defrauding captives and their supporters; see Taylor, *Structures of Reform*, 358–65.

75. "Que de otra manera piérdense los dineros que se dan a mercaderes demás de los intereses que por ellos llevan." Gracián, *Cartas, Monumenta historica Carmeli Teresiani*, 6.7.1594.

76. "Y por experiencia sé que ningún daño mayor ay para los cautiverios que dar dineros a mercantes, que por el mesmo caso ay innumerables captivos que nunca salen de cautiverio." Gracián, *Cartas, Monumenta historica Carmeli Teresiani*, 11.25.1594.

77. Pasamonte, *Autobiografía*, 80.

78. AHN, *Inquisición*, Leg. 1824-2, carpeta 14.

79. BNE, Mss. 5065, carpeta 1.

80. On Margliani and his mission in Istanbul, see Braudel, *The Mediterranean and the Mediterranean World in the Age of Philip II*, 1152–65.

81. AGS, *Estado*, Leg. 491, 11.1579.

82. Ibid.

83. Pasamonte, *Autobiografía*, 80.

84. For example, the lease from 1615; see AGS, *Estado*, Negociaciones de Sicilia, Leg. 1169, fols. 18–20.

85. Philippe Gourdin, *Tabarka (15–18. siècle): Histoire et archéologie d'un présidе espagnol et d'un comptoir génois en terre africaine* (Rome: École Française de Rome, 2008), 245–69.

86. AGS, *Estado*, Leg. 1416, fol. 138.

87. Díaz Hierro, *Historia de la Merced de Huelva*.

88. AHN, *Inquisición*, Leg. 933-2, 11.13.1655.

89. D'Aranda, *Les captifs d'Alger*, 44.

90. AGS, *Estado*, Leg. 1094, fol. 239, 1595.

91. AGS, *Guerra Antigua*, Leg. 478, fol. 268, 12.17.1596.

92. AHN, *Consejos*, Leg. 6900, 1.25.1591. Pedro de Prado, from Ibiza, captured by corsairs during his military service, managed to borrow money and return home. Unable to pay the debt, he was imprisoned. In the petition he

sent the crown in 1590 he stated, "In consideration that he was captured while in the service of his majesty, he petitions that for the love of God, [his majesty] help him with alms to help and pay his ransom, [and] in consideration that he is a very poor soldier and in charge of children and the authorities imprison him in order to force him to pay the said ransom and he does not have anyone to support him." AGS, *Guerra Antigua*, Leg. 305, fol. 31, 7.17.1590.

93. Martínez Torres, *Prisioneros de los infieles*, 99–105.

94. AHN, *Códices*, Lib. 148, fols. 119–20, 1718.

95. Bonifacio Porres Alonso, *Libertad a los cautivos: Actividad redentora de la Orden Trinitaria* (Córdoba: Secretariado Trinitario, 1997), 249–50.

96. Mercedes García Arenal, Fernando Rodríguez Mediano, and Rachid El Hour, eds., *Cartas marruecas: Documentos de Marruecos en archivos españoles (siglos XVI–XVII)*, Estudios árabes e islámicos, Monografías 3 (Madrid: Consejo Superior de Investigaciones Científicas, 2002), 222–23.

97. AHN, *Inquisición*, Leg. 1952, 7.25.1607; cf. Martínez Torres, *Prisioneros de los infieles*, 120.

98. Gracián, *Tratado de la redención de cautivos*, 75–76. See also his description of these events in his *Peregrinación de Anastasio*, in Jerónimo Gracián, *Peregrinación de Anastasio: Obras del P. Jerónimo Gracián de la Madre de Dios*, ed. P. Silverio de Santa Teresa (Burgos: Tipografía De "El Monte Carmelo," 1932–33), 3:120–21. On the history, function, and increase in the power of the qadi in the Ottoman legal system during the sixteenth and seventeenth centuries, see Haim Gerber, *State, Society, and Law in Islam: Ottoman Law in Comparative Perspective* (Albany: State University of New York Press, 1994), 66–71.

99. "Y porque le pedían les pagase, se fue a cassa de la duana donde gobierna Haziali . . . y le dijo que quería renegar de la ley de dios y volverse moro, y el dicho Haziali le respondió que pagara primero a quien devía y que luego se volviera moro." AHN, *Inquisición*, Leg. 1824-2, carpeta 14.

100. In his *Crónica de Almançor*, the Portuguese António de Saldaña describes how al-Mansūr asked the European merchants in his realm to write home telling "how well he treated them" (*o bom trato lhes fazia*). This policy "provoked the arrival in Marrakech of many Italians, Spaniards, French, English and Flemish that filled those kingdoms with such a quantity of commodities" (*que foi ocasito de se irem pera Marrocos muitos italianos, espanhois, franceses, ingreses e framengos que encheram aqueles reinos de todas as mercadorias em tanta cantidade*). António de Saldanha, *Crónica de Almançor, sultão de Marrocos (1578–1603)*, ed. António Dias Farinha (Lisbon: Instituto de Investigação Científica Tropical, 1997), 31. On the measures al-Mansūr took to attract merchants to Morocco, see García Arenal, *Ahmad al-Mansur*, 111–15.

101. García Arenal, Mercedes, and El Hour, *Cartas marruecas*.

102. Gracián, *Tratado de la redención de cautivos*, 76.

103. AHN, *Clero*, Leg. 3821, lib. VI.

104. Lauren A. Benton, *Law and Colonial Cultures: Legal Regimes in World History, 1400–1900*, Studies in Comparative World History (New York: Cambridge University Press, 2002).

CHAPTER 4

1. Gonçal Artur López Nadal, *El corsarisme mallorquí a la Mediterrània occidental, 1652–1698: Un comerç forçat* (Palma de Mallorca: Conselleria D'Educació i Cultura Del Govern Balear, 1986), 533–34.

2. AHN, *Inquisición*, Leg. 1824-2.

3. Gracián, *Cartas, Monumenta historica Carmeli Teresiani*, "A Dª Juana Dantisco, su madre, Túnez, 11.6.1594." Gracián was not the only captive to provide such services. Emanuel d'Aranda mentions a captive from Brabant, François l'Étudiant, who in the 1640s provided scribal services for captives from Dunkirk; see d'Aranda, *Les captifs d'Alger*, 45.

4. AHN, *Inquisición*, Leg. 1824-2.

5. On captivity narratives as a way of working through trauma, see Garcés, *Cervantes en Argel*.

6. Luis Alberto Anaya Hernández, "Voces del cautiverio: Las cartas de los esclavos canarios desde Berbería (siglos XVI–XVII)," in *XVIII Coloquio de historia Canario-americana (2008)*, ed. Francisco Morales Padrón (Las Palmas de Gran Canaria: Casa de Colón, 2010), 1202; AHN, *Inquisición*, Leg. 1824-2.

7. Brendan Maurice Dooley, introduction to *The Dissemination of News and the Emergence of Contemporaneity in Early Modern Europe*, ed. Brendan Maurice Dooley (Burlington, Vt.: Ashgate, 2010), 1–19.

8. Tamar Herzog, *Defining Nations: Immigrants and Citizens in Early Modern Spain and Spanish America* (New Haven, Conn.: Yale University Press, 2003), 7.

9. Pierre Bourdieu, "Le langage autorisé: Note sur les conditions sociales de l'efficacité du discours ritual," *Actes de la recherche en sciences sociales* 5–6 (1975): 183–90. On how nonhumans, letters in this case, participate in the construction of the self, see Colin Jerolmack and Iddo Tavori, "Molds and Totems: Nonhumans and the Constitution of the Social Self," *Sociological Theory* 32 (2014): 64–77.

10. Historians of gossip and rumors must look to an eclectic body of sources that runs from learned treatises to Inquisitorial records or court cases; see, for example, Elizabeth Horodowich, "The Gossiping Tongue: Oral Networks, Public Life and Political Culture in Early Modern Venice," *Renaissance Studies* 19 (2005): 22–45, and Chris Wickham, "Gossip and Resistance Among the Medieval Peasantry," *Past and Present* 100 (1998): 3–24.

11. These letters have been little examined. A notable exception is Fiume's study, which sheds light on both the stylistic features of such letters and their content; see Giovanna Fiume, "Lettres de Barbarie: Esclavage et rachat de captifs siciliens (XVIe–XVIIIe siècle)," *Cahiers de la Méditerranée* 87 (2013): 229–54. On prisoners' letters in other contexts, see Elizabeth Foyster, "Prisoners Writing Home: The Functions of Their Letters c. 1680–1800," *Journal of Social History* 47 (2014): 943–67. On merchant letters, see the illuminating work of Francesca Trivellato, *The Familiarity of Strangers: The Sephardic Diaspora, Livorno, and Cross-Cultural Trade in the Early Modern Period* (New Haven, Conn.: Yale University Press, 2009), 177–93, and Peter

N. Miller, *Peiresc's Mediterranean World* (Cambridge, Mass.: Harvard University Press, 2015), 54–142.

12. For instance, in a letter he wrote his wife from Marrakesh in 1570, Antonio Delgado reported "that up to date, he had written [. . .] and sent many letters for which he had received no answer"; see Anaya Hernández, "Voces del cautiverio," 1206. Nearly a century later, Lucas Delgado informed his wife at the beginning of a letter he wrote her from Algiers on July 14, 1668, that "up to this date, I received three of yours (letters) dated October fourth," suggesting that she had sent three copies with three couriers and that Delgado was aware that she might have sent more letters with other messengers who had not yet arrived (ibid., 1209). In a letter from Algiers written in 1641, friar Gaspar Merino reported he had already sent his addressee ten letters (ibid., 1208).

13. AHN, *Inquisición*, Leg. 933-2, October 1655.

14. Luis Alberto Anaya Hernández, "Repercusiones del corso berberisco en Canarias durante el siglo XVII: Cautivos y renegados canaríes," in *V Coloquio de Historia Canario-Americana* (1982), vol. 2, ed. Francisco Morales Padrón (Las Palmas de Gran Canaria: Excmo. Cabildo Insular de Gran Canaria, 1985), 177.

15. Ibid.

16. AHN, *Inquisición*, Leg. 1706-2, carpeta 12, fol. 7v. See also AHN, *Inquisición*, Leg. 1824-2 and Mascarenhas, *Esclave à Alger*, 110.

17. ACA, *Consejo de Aragón*, Leg. 933, fol. 49.

18. Carmen Barceló and Ana Labart, eds., *Archivos moriscos: Textos árabes de la minoría islámica Valenciana, 1401–1608* (Valencia: University of Valencia, 2009), 292–93.

19. AHN, *Inquisición*, Lib. 862, fols. 189–95.

20. Anaya Hernández, "Voces del cautiverio," 1208-9.

21. In the diocesan archive of Gran Canaria this information was kept in the section covering marriage, bachelor/spinsterhood (*solterías*), and widowhood. The section covering concessions (for marriage) at the diocesan archive of Majorca contains hundreds of pieces of information from the seventeenth century, with testimonies submitted by captives and freed captives about deaths in captivity; see Vaquer Bennasar, *Captius i renegats al segle XVII*, 68–120.

22. Alyson M. Poska, "When Bigamy Is the Charge: Gallegan Women and the Holy Office," in *Women in the Inquisition: Spain and the New World*, ed. Mary E. Giles (Baltimore: Johns Hopkins University Press, 1999), 189–208.

23. Vaquer Bennasar, *Captius i renegats al segle XVII*, 172–73.

24. David E. Vassberg, "The Status of Widows in Sixteenth Century Rural Castile," in *Poor Women and Children in the European Past*, ed. John Henderson and Richard Wall (London: Routledge, 1994), 180–95.

25. Vidal Castro, "El cautivo en el mundo islámico," 782–83.

26. Loualich, "In the Regency of Algiers," 76–78.

27. Ibid., 87–88.

28. AHN, *Inquisición*, Leg. 1824-2.

29. Bennassar and Bennassar, *Los cristianos de Alá*, 171–89.

30. Herzog, *Defining Nations*, 64–93, 119–40.

31. Archivo del Mueso Canario, *Inquisición*, Leg. CXIX-21, 1667–71.

32. Galán, *Relación*, 54.

33. Anaya Hernández, "Voces del cautiverio," 1207.

34. Luis Alberto Anaya Hernández, *Moros en la costa: Dos siglos de corsarismo berberisco en las islas canarias (1569–1749)* (Las Palmas de Gran Canaria: Gobierno de Canarias, Consejería de Educación, Cultura y Deportes, Dirección General de Universidades e Investigación, 2006), 127.

35. A renegade whose name the sources do not disclose mediated the ransom of a certain Bautista Fernandez in 1589. The latter was ordered by the renegade to pay his debt to the renegade's mother, to whom Bautista's relative provided guarantees; see AHN, *Consejos*, Leg. 7050, 9.22.1589.

36. AGS, *Estado*, Leg. 1950, 1.14.1619.

37. Benítez, "La tramitación del pago de rescates a través del reino de Valencia."

38. Similarly, the Andalusian Lorenzo Jiménez testified in late 1669 at the Inquisitorial trial of a merchant accused of selling materials of war to Algiers that in 1665 he had returned to Algiers, where he had previously been held captive. He explained that he went to give a gift to his former owner and his owner's wife, Catalina Bruna, a convert to Islam, who had treated him very well during his captivity. Jiménez added, perhaps because he was testifying in an Inquisition trial and did not want to become a suspect himself, that the wife was secretly Christian and that he had hoped to return to Spain with her. AHN, *Inquisición*, Leg. 1714, 1668–70.

39. Eric Dursteler, "Where Is Cigala? Rumor, Report and the Flow of Information in the Late Sixteenth-Century Mediterranean" (paper presented at "The Informational Fabric of the Premodern Mediterranean, 1400–1800," 14th Mediterranean Research Meeting, European University Institute, Mersin, Turkey, March 2013).

40. For more on this episode and more broadly on Cigala, see Evrim Türkçelik, "Cigalazade Yusuf Sinan Pasha y el Mediterráneo entre 1591–1606" (PhD diss., Autonomous University of Madrid, 2012).

41. For the summary of his Inquisitorial trial, see Vaquer Bennasar, *Captius i renegats al segle XVII*, 233–34.

42. AHN, *Inquisición*, Leg. 1711-1, carpeta 8, 11.28.1689.

43. Ibid.

44. AHN, *Inquisición*, Leg. 1711-1, carpeta 6, 2.5.1644.

45. Ibid.

46. Ibid.

47. A function Max Gluckman has assigned to gossip; see Max Gluckman, "Gossip and Scandal," *Current Anthropology* 4 (1963): 307–16.

48. Gracián, *Peregrinación de Anastasio*, 130. See also the Franciscan account from Morocco: Saura Lahoz, "Los Franciscanos en Marruecos."

49. Gracián, *Tratado de la redención de cautivos*, 45.

50. For an analysis that examines the connections between the characters in the comedy and individuals that Cervantes met during his captivity

in Algiers, see Jaime Oliver Asín, "La Hija de Agi Morato en la obra de Cervantes," *Boletín de la Real Academia Española* 27 (1947–48): 245–339.

51. Miguel de Cervantes, *"The Bagnios of Algiers" and "The Great Sultana": Two Plays of Captivity*, trans. and ed. Barbara Fuchs and Aaron J. Ilika (Philadelphia: University of Pennsylvania Press, 2010), 14.

52. Ibid.

53. The records of the Inquisitorial tribunal at Majorca reveal several such cases. In 1626, the Genovese renegade Juan Bautista Brea presented the island's Inquisitors with a letter in Italian, written on his behalf by a captive in Algiers, asking a resident of Ibiza to assist him. In 1632 the French renegade Vileta Guirau from Languedoc presented his Inquisitors with a letter an ecclesiastic in Algiers had written for him in which the author testified to the favors Guirau had done for Christians. In 1634, the French renegade Jacobo de Maqueda described how he got a letter of recommendation "given by the captives, members of religious orders, who were in Tunis at the time." In 1635, two renegades presented the Inquisitors with letters in Latin written for them in Algiers by a Dominican friar; the letters testified to the renegades' beliefs and their intention to return to Christendom. In 1644, the renegade Miguel Nicolau presented two letters written for him in the prison in Algiers by enslaved ecclesiastics. The same year, the renegade Adrián de Rivas presented a note in his favor, claiming he was a good Christian. In 1648, the German renegade Pedro Castriana presented a letter in which priests in Algiers asserted that they had absolved him for his conversion. For these sources, see Vaquer Bennasar, *Captius i renegats al segle XVII*, 158, 160, 167–68, 175–76, 198–200, 207–9. On *relaciones de causa*, see Jean-Pierre Dedieu, "The Archives of the Holy Office of Toledo as a Source for Historical Anthropology," in *The Inquisition in Early Modern Europe: Studies on Sources and Methods*, ed. Gustav Henningsen, John A. Tedeschi, and Charles Amiel (Dekalb: Northern Illinois University Press, 1986), 158–89.

54. AHN, *Inquisición*, Lib. 862, fols. 83v–84v, 4.1634.

55. Ibid.

56. AHN, *Inquisición*, Leg. 933-2, 10.28.1655.

57. Miguel de Cervantes, *Obras completas* (Madrid: Editorial Aguilar, 1962), 1213, emphasis added.

58. Gracián, *Tratado de la redención de cautivos*, 71–72.

59. Andrés del Mármol, *Excelencias, vida y trabaios del Padre Gerónimo Gracián de la Madre de Dios Carmelita* (Valladolid: Francisco Fernández de Cordoua, 1619), cap. IX.

60. Juan Martínez Ruiz, "Cautivos precervantinos: Cara y cruz del cautiverio," *Revista de filología española* 50 (1967): 239.

61. Patterson, *Slavery and Social Death*.

62. On the importance of martyrdom in the post-Tridentine Catholic and specifically Hispanic world, see Alejandro Cañeque, "Mártires y discurso martirial en la formación de las fronteras misionales jesuitas," *Relaciones* 145 (2016): 13–61.

63. For example, captives took parts of the body of Josep Moranta, burned in Algiers in 1643, and buried his body, with the intention of shipping it at some

point to Spain. For testimonies, see M. Carme Coll Font, "Josep Moranta, frare predicador captiu a Alger (1635–43): Relat de les seves conversions i el seu martiri," *Bolletí de la societat arqueològica lul·liana* 65 (2009): 271–84.

64. Bonifacio Porres Alonso, *Testigos de Cristo en Argel: Bernardo de Monroy, Juan del Águila, and Juan de Palacios, Trinitarios* (Córdoba: Secretariado Trinitario, 1994), 133–35.

65. Ibid. See also *Relación de la cruelissima muerte, que en la ciudad de Argel ha padecido el muy reverendo Padre Fr. Francisco Cirano, Religioso del orden de nuestro seráfico padre San Francisco* (Lima, 1667).

66. When Christians in Marrakesh sought body parts of the Franciscan Juan de Prado, who had been burned to death on May 24, 1631, local renegades pressured the Muslim authorities not to give permission, warning that the relics would serve a cult dishonoring Islam; see Matías de San Francisco, *Relación del viage espiritual que hizo a Marruecos el beato Juan de Prado, primer provincial de la provincial Franciscana de Andalucía, restaurador de las misiones franciscanas de Marruecos en 1630*, ed. José López (Tangier: Tipografia Hispano-Arábiga De La Misión Católica, 1945), 102.

67. On the procedures for and problems of authenticating relics in the Mediterranean, see A. Katie Harris, "Gift, Sale, and Theft: Juan de Ribera and the Sacred Economy of Relics in the Early Modern Mediterranean," *Journal of Early Modern History* 18 (2014): 193–226, and Katrina B. Olds, "The Ambiguities of the Holy: Authenticating Relics in Seventeenth-Century Spain," *Renaissance Quarterly* 65 (2012): 135–84.

68. As, for example, in the case of the remains of seven Portuguese, Spanish, and French martyrs who died in Morocco in 1585; see António da Conceição, *A relação da vida e morte dos sete mártires de Marrocos de fr. António da Conceição*, ed. Domingos Maurício Gomes dos Santos (Coimbra: Associação Portuguesa para o Progresso das Ciências, 1957).

69. Porres Alonso, *Testigos de Cristo en Argel.*

70. Ibid., 138–39.

71. Simon Ditchfield, "How Not to Be a Counter-Reformation Saint: The Attempted Canonization of Pope Gregory X, 1622–45," *Papers of the British School at Rome* 60 (1992): 381.

72. Ibid.

73. Similarly, the account prepared by António da Conceição on behalf of seven Iberian and French martyrs was also based on interviews with other captives; see *A relação da vida e morte dos sete mártires de Marrocos de fr. António da Conceição.*

74. Peter Burke, "How to Be a Counter-Reformation Saint," in *The Historical Anthropology of Early Modern Italy: Essays on Perception and Communication* (Cambridge: Cambridge University Press, 1987), 48–62.

75. Ditchfield, "How Not to Be a Counter-Reformation Saint," 381.

76. Giovanna Fiume, *Schiavitù mediterranee: Corsari, rinnegati e santi di età moderna* (Milan: Bruno Mondadori, 2009), 326–30.

77. Alternatively, María Antonia Garcés has read the Cervantine corpus as a continuous attempt by its author to work through the trauma he had experienced in Algiers; see Garcés, *Cervantes en Argel.*

78. Benedict Anderson, *Imagined Communities: Reflections on the Origins and Spread of Nationalism* (London: Verso, 2006); Herzog, *Defining Nations*.

CHAPTER 5

1. AGS, *Estado*, Leg. 198, 12.13.1603.
2. Ibid.
3. Matar, "Piracy and Captivity in the Early Modern Mediterranean," 62.
4. William Ian Miller, "Threat," in *Feud, Violence and Practice: Essays in Medieval Studies in Honor of Stephen D. White*, ed. Belle S. Tuten and Tracey L. Billado (Farnham, Surrey: Ashgate, 2010), 9–14.
5. "An Account of the Rigorous Martyrdom of the Father Friar Ioan de Prado" described the life and death in Marrakesh of the Franciscan Juan de Prado, whose only sin was his refusal to convert to Islam; see *Relación de el riguroso martyrio que el padre fr. Ioan de Prado de la provincial de San Diego de Sevilla, que es de frailes descalços Franciscos: Padeció en la ciudad de Marruecos por mano y orden de el rey de la dicha ciudad, la qual relación embió el governador, de Marzagan, a el excelentíssimo señor duque de Medina Sydonia*, in *Papeles de mi archivo, Relaciones de África (Marruecos)*, vol. 2, ed. Ignacio Bauer Landauer (Madrid: Editorial Ibero-Africano-Americana, 1922–23), 249–52. On descriptions of violence, see Enrique Fernández, "El cuerpo torturado en los testimonies de los corsarios berberiscos (1500–1700)," *Hispanic Review* 71 (2003): 51–66. The most famous example of such captivity narratives is Sosa's *Diálogo de los mártires de Argel*, which offers its reader a catalogue of atrocities Christians suffered in Algiers before they were finally killed. Trinitarians and Mercedarians included in the pamphlets that they circulated references to Muslims' violence against Christian captives or members of the orders on ransom missions. For several examples, see the collection of early modern pamphlets related to Algiers: Ignacio Bauer Landauer, *Papeles de mi archivo: Relaciones de África (Argel)*, vol. 4 (Madrid: Editorial Ibero-Africano-Americana, 1922–23). Many of the captives who recounted their captivity in autobiographies include similar descriptions; for an example, see Mascarenhas, *Esclave á Alger*, 119. At other points in his autobiography, however, Mascarenhas also captured the reciprocal nature of such violent moments; see ibid., 113–16.
6. Martínez Torres, *Prisioneros de los infieles*. Another possible reason for scholars of captivity to ignore these texts is that they also operated as ammunition in a battle between Catholics and Protestants over sanctity and sainthood. As Protestant reformers were criticizing the canonization of saints, they invested time and energy in forming their own cadre of martyrs, who died as witnesses of their faith and whose stories were published in printed collections. Maghribi martyr stories formed a Catholic response to Protestant efforts, and in some cases Catholic authors and publishers went as far as to make use of woodcuts Protestant artists designed; see José María Parreño, "Experiencia y literatura en la obra de Antonio de Sosa,"

in Antonio de Sosa, *Diálogo de los mártires de Argel*, ed. Emilio Sola (Madrid: Hiperión, 1990), 9–23; Emilio Sola, "Renacimiento, contrarreforma y problema morisco en la obra de Antonio de Sosa," in Antonio de Sosa, *Diálogo de los mártires de Argel*, ed. Emilio Sola (Madrid: Hiperión, 1990), 27–52; and Eva Belén Carro Carbajal, "España y el mundo mediterráneo: Advocaciones y milagros en las relaciones poéticas de martirios a finales del siglo XVI," in *España y el mundo mediterráneo a través de las relaciones de sucesos: Actas del IV Coloquio Internacional sobre Relaciones de Sucesos: (Paris, 23–25 de septiembre de 2004)*, ed. Pierre Civil, Françoise Crémoux, and Jacobo S. Sanz Hermida (Salamanca: Ediciones Universidad de Salamanca, 2008), 55–67.

7. In contrast to Spain, France was already negotiating and signing peace agreements with Algiers in the seventeenth century. These treaties specified the privileges slaves deserved and the conditions under which France and Algiers had to liberate their Muslim and Christian slaves; see Weiss, *Captives and Corsairs*.

8. AGS, *Estado*, Leg. 198, 8.19.1602.

9. Ibid., 1.8.1603.

10. Ibid., 1.25.1603.

11. Ibid.

12. Ibid., 5.18.1603.

13. D'Arvieux, *Mémoires du chevalier d'Arvieux*, 44.

14. AGS, *Estado*, Leg. 198, 1.8.1602.

15. Ibid., 8.3.1602, 8.7.1602, 8.18.1602.

16. AGS, *Estado*, Leg. 198, 5.1.1603, 5.3.1603.

17. AHN, *Inquisición*, Leg. 861, fols. 142–143V, 9.4.1617.

18. On the logic of challenge and riposte, see Pierre Bourdieu, "The Sentiment of Honor in Kabyle Society," in *Honour and Shame: The Values of Mediterranean Society*, ed. J. G. Peristiany (Chicago: University of Chicago Press, 1966), 191–241. A similar logic governed medieval blood feuds in Iceland; see William Ian Miller, *Bloodtaking and Peacemaking: Feud, Law, and Society in Saga Iceland* (Chicago: University of Chicago Press, 1990), 182–87.

19. Melvin, "Charity Without Borders."

20. For an illuminating discussion and theorization of the competition between different intermediaries and experts on the orient, see Gil Eyal, *The Disenchantment of the Orient: Expertise in Arab Affairs and the Israeli State* (Stanford, Calif.: Stanford University Press, 2006).

21. ACA, *Consejo de Aragón*, Leg. 607, fol. 33, 1.1663.

22. Ibid.

23. AGS, *Guerra Antigua*, Leg. 1541, 3.9.1644.

24. On the Mercedarians and Trinitarians, see Friedman, *Spanish Captives in North Africa in the Early Modern Age*; Barrio Gozalo, *Esclavos y cautivos*; and Martínez Torres, *Prisioneros de los infieles*. On Italian ransom institutions, see Davis, *Christian Slaves, Muslim Masters*.

25. On such networks, see the articles in Wolfgang Kaiser, ed., *Le commerce des captifs: Les intermédiaires dans l'échange et le rachat des*

prisonniers en Méditerranée, XVe–XVIIIe siècle (Rome: École Française de Rome, 2008).

26. ACA, *Consejo de Aragón*, Leg. 993, fol. 30, 4.28.1692. For more related documents and analysis of other aspects of this affair, see Juan Vernet Ginés, *El rescate del arraez argeli Bibi, prisionero en Mallorca* (Tétouan: Impr. del Majzen, 1952).

27. ACA, *Consejo de Aragón*, Leg. 993, fol. 30, 4.28.1692.

28. Ibid.

29. Ibid.

30. Ibid.

31. Muhammad's second letter, in Arabic, survived: ACA, *Consejo de Aragón*, Leg. 993, fol. 37, 7.26.1692.

32. AHN, *Estado*, Leg. 670, 5.1696.

33. Gracián, *Tratado de la redención de cautivos*, 18. Gracián was not alone. In the Mercedarian account of the 1639 ransom expedition to Algiers, a similar accusation was made; see Gari y Siumell, *La orden redentora de la Merced*, 311.

34. Chapter 7 of this book also expands on Fatima's case. On the 1658 Algerian letters, see AGS, *Estado*, Leg. 2675. On the converted Algerian girl in 1668, see AGS, *Estado*, Leg. 2688 and AHN, *Códices*, Lib. 142B. On the killing of the Turks in Ibiza, see AHN, *Estado*, Leg. 670. On the eight Algerian children, see Haci Ahmed bin al-Haci's letter to the Grand Duke of Livorno in Gallotta, "Diplomi turchi dell'Archivio di Stato di Firenze," 200–205. Such incidents and accusations were not limited to the western Mediterranean. For an example from the Venetian-Ottoman border, see E. Natalie Rothman, "Conversion and Convergence in the Venetian-Ottoman Borderlands," *Journal of Medieval and Early Modern Studies* 41 (2011): 601–33.

35. Friedman, *Spanish Captives in North Africa in the Early Modern Age*, 135–36.

36. On Christians who converted to Islam, see Bennassar and Bennassar, *Los cristianos de Alá*, and Rodríguez Mediano, "Les conversions de Sebastião Pes de Vega."

37. The Sūrat al-Baqara (2:256) states "there shall be no compulsion in the religion. The right course has become clear from the wrong," namely that individuals should convert only if the right path is clear to them. On canon law and Christian theological objection to forced conversion, see Seth Kimmel, *Parables of Coercion: Conversion and Knowledge at the End of Islamic Spain* (Chicago: University of Chicago Press, 2015), 17–42.

38. AGS, *Estado*, Leg. 210, 2.10.1608. See also Friedman, *Spanish Captives in North Africa in the Early Modern Age*, 88–90.

39. D'Arvieux, *Mémoires du chevalier d'Arvieux*.

40. AHN, *Estado*, Leg. 670, 5.1696.

41. Ibid.

42. Bono, *Schiavi musulmani nell'Italia moderna*, 241–52. See also the case of French Marseille; Régis Bertrand, "Les cimetières des 'esclaves turcs' des arsenaux de Marseille et de Toulon au XVIIIe siècle," *Revue des mondes musulmans et de la Méditerranée* 99–100 (2002): 205–17.

43. The letter was published in Franceso Pera, *Curiosità livornesi inedite o rare* (Livorno: U. Bastogi, 1971), 117–18. On the Muslims in Livorno, see Calafat and Santus, "Les avatars du 'Turc.'"

44. For more about this event, see Stephanie Nadalo, "Negotiating Slavery in a Tolerant Frontier: Livorno's Turkish *Bagno* (1547–1747)," *Mediavalia* 32 (2011): 302–4.

45. AHN, *Inquisición*, Leg. 3733, fol. 301. The document is undated, but the friars it mentions were active in Algiers in the 1720s and 1730s. Bernard Vincent mentions the episode in his "Musulmanes y conversión en España en el siglo XVII." On Muslims in Spain and more broadly in Europe in the early modern period, see Jocelyne Dakhlia and Bernard Vincent, eds., *Les musulmans dans l'histoire de l'Europe*, vol. 1, *Une intégration invisible* (Paris: Albin Michel, 2011); and Jocelyne Dakhlia and Wolfgang Kaiser, eds., *Les musulmans dans l'histoire de l'Europe*, vol. 2, *Passages et contacts en Méditerranée* (Paris: Albin Michel, 2013).

46. ACA, *Consejo de Aragón*, Leg. 672, fol. 39, 8.7.1696.

47. Marshall Sahlins, *Stone Age Economics* (Chicago: Aldine-Atherton, 1972), 95–96.

48. Gadi Algazi, "Some Problems with Reciprocity," *Endoxa, Series Filosoficas* 15 (2002): 43–50.

49. Juan Pérez de Montalván, "El valiente más dichoso, Don Pedro Guiral," in *Segundo tomo de las Comedias del doctor Juan Pérez de Montalván* (Madrid: Impresor del Reyno, 1638), fols. 225v–249.

50. Memorial Luis Guiral Carvajal submitted to the Cortes of Castile on July 16, 1627, in *Actas de las Cortes de Castilla . . . desde el día 8 de junio de 1627 hasta el 8 de junio de 1628* (Madrid: Impresores de la Casa Real, 1928), 46:85–86.

51. AGS, *Estado*, Leg. 3444, fols. 107, 112, 2.6.1631.

52. Copy of a letter from Isidro del Castillo y Aguilera to Cid Ali Hache Catalán, Real Academia de la Historia (hereafter RAH), *Colección de Don Luis Salazar y Castro*, Leg. 38, carpeta 5, 11.18.1648.

53. Celdrán Gomariz, *Judíos, moros y cristianos en la ciudad de Argel*, 229–30.

54. On the early modern history of Tétouan, see Gozalbes Busto, *Los Moriscos en Marruecos*; Abderrahim Yebbur Oddi, *El gobierno de Tetuán por la familia Al-Naqsis (1597–1673)* (Tétouan: Imprenta del Majzen, 1955); Jean-Louis Miège, "Consuls et négociants à Tétouan, 1681–1727," in *Titwan hilal al-qarnayn 16 wa-17: Àmal Nadwat Titwan Hilal al-Qarnayn 16 wa-17: 9, 10, 11 mars 1995* (Titwan: Kulliyat al-Adab wa-l-'Ulum al-Insaniya: Al-Magmùa al-Hadariya li-Madinat Titwan, 1996), 109–49; and Jean-Louis Miège, M'hammad Benaboud, and Nadia Erzini, *Tétouan: Ville andalouse marocaine* (Paris: CNRS Editions, 1996), 12–73.

55. AGS, *Guerra Antigua*, Leg. 247, fol. 141, 10.4.1589.

56. Ibid.

57. AGS, *Guerra Antigua*, Leg. 423, fol. 71.

58. On "diplomacy from below" involving other powers separated by a body of water, see Renaud Morieux, "Diplomacy from Below and Belonging:

Fishermen and Cross-Channel Relations in the Eighteenth Century," *Past and Present* 202 (2009): 83–125. Morieux examines neutrality agreements between the French and the English, which are distinct from the interactions analyzed here. He claims, however, that the "originality" of the agreements he has studied lies in their survival throughout the century, and yet the agreements examined here survived at least through the seventeenth century and perhaps for a good few decades into the eighteenth.

CHAPTER 6

1. Lisa Voigt has explored the role Portuguese, Spanish, and English captives played in knowledge production and their crucial part in imperial expansion. However, Voigt focuses on captivity in the Americas and bases her analysis almost exclusively on published captivity narratives, which provide limited information about the mechanics and context of these processes or the reception of this knowledge. See Lisa Voigt, *Writing Captivity in the Early Modern Atlantic: Circulations of Knowledge and Authority in the Iberian and English Imperial Worlds* (Chapel Hill: University of North Carolina Press, 2009). Additionally, such narratives were exceptional, for very few captives were literate, and of the literate only a small minority wrote about their experiences. In contrast, the seventeenth-century Mediterranean, where captives arrived in port cities almost daily, provides an excellent setting for an examination of captives' roles in the production and circulation of information.

2. On the position that Spain had lost interest in Islam after negotiating a truce with the Ottomans, see Mercedes García Arenal, introduction to Diego de Torres, *Relación del origen de los xarifes y del estado de los reinos de Marruecos, Fez, y Tarudante*, ed. Mercedes García Arenal (Madrid: Siglo Veintiuno, 1980), 2; Mercedes García Arenal, "Spanish Literature on North Africa in the XVI Century: Diego de Torres," *Maghreb Review* 8, no. 1–2 (1983): 53–59; Mar Martínez-Góngora, "El discurso africanista del Renacimiento en *La primera parte de la descripción general de África* de Luis del Mármol Carvajal," *Hispanic Review* 77 (2009): 175–77; and Bunes Ibarra, *La imagen de los musulmanes*, 3–6. Cf. Bunes Ibarra, "Felipe III y la defensa del Mediterráneo."

3. For an excellent recent discussion and theorization of the relations between printed information and information circulating in manuscript form, see Johann Petitjean, *L'Intelligence des choses: Une histoire de l'information entre Italie et Méditerranée (XVIe–XVIIe siècles)* (Rome: École Française de Rome, 2013).

4. Luis del Mármol Carvajal, *Descripción general de África*, vol. 1 (Madrid: Instituto de Estudios Africanos del Patronato Diego Saavedra Fajardo del CSIC, 1953); Diego de Torres, *Relación del origen de los xarifes y del estado de los reinos de Marruecos, Fez, y Tarudante*, ed. Mercedes García Arenal (Madrid: Siglo Veintiuno, 1980); Haedo, *Topografía e historia general de Argel*.

5. Natalie Zemon Davis, *Trickster Travels: A Sixteenth Century Muslim Between Worlds* (New York: Hill and Wang, 2007).

6. In 1805, al-Wazzan's work was also translated into German. On the history and politics of the publication of al-Wazzan's *Description of Africa*, see Zhiri Oumelbanine, "Leo Africanus, Translated and Betrayed," in *The Politics of Translation in the Middle Ages and the Renaissance*, ed. Renate Blumenfeld-Kosinski, Luise von Flotow, and Daniel Russell (Ottawa: University of Ottawa Press, 2001), 161–74.

7. On Mármol's use of al-Wazzan and on the differences between the works, see Martínez-Góngora, "El discurso africanista del Renacimiento." On how de Torres used Mármol and others, see García Arenal, introduction, 11–14. Other Portuguese authors also wrote on the Maghrib, and on the Portuguese defeat in 1578 at the Battle of the Three Kings in particular, but I am unable to include them in my discussion here; see García Arenal, introduction.

8. On the life of Mármol, see Agustín González de Amezúa, "Prólogo," in Luis del Mármol Carvajal, *Descripción general de África*, ed. Agustín González de Amezúa (Madrid: CSIC, 1953). Amezúa claimed that Mármol Carvajal's imprisonment was "a providential captivity" as it allowed the future author to master Arabic and the "African" language and accumulate direct experience with regions from Morocco to Egypt, about which he later wrote; see ibid., 13–14.

9. Diego de Torres, *Relación del origen de los xarifes*, 150.

10. Garcés, introduction, 58–59.

11. Ibid., 50.

12. González de Amezúa, "Prólogo." For more on the way Mármol frames his work within an imperial context, see Martínez-Góngora, "El discurso africanista del Renacimiento."

13. Following the death of King Don Sebastian, de Torres's widow replaced the original dedication with one to Philip II; see García Arenal, introduction, 16–21. On de Torres's colonial agenda, see Rica Amiran, "Ceuta en la relación de Diego de Torres," in *España y el mundo Mediterráneao a través de las relaciones de sucesos (1500–1750): Actas del IV coloquio internacional sobre Relaciones de Sucesos (París, 23–25 de septiembre de 2004)*, ed. Pierre Civil, Françoise Crémoux, and Jacobo Sanz (Salamanca: Ediciones Universidad de Salamanca, 2010).

14. Garcés, introduction, 36.

15. Andrew C. Hess, "The Battle of Lepanto and Its Place in Mediterranean History," *Past and Present* 57 (1972): 53–73.

16. González de Amezúa, "Prólogo," 22.

17. Only three years saw no increase: 1582, 1593, and 1594. See Alexander S. Wilkinson, *Iberian Books: Books Published in Spanish or Portuguese or on the Iberian Peninsula Before 1601* (Leiden: Brill, 2010), xiv.

18. Ibid.

19. Luis del Mármol Carvajal, *Historia del [sic] rebelión y castigo de los moriscos del Reino de Granada* (Alicante: Biblioteca Virtual Miguel de Cervantes, 2001).

20. García Arenal, "Spanish Literature on North Africa in the XVI Century," 53–59.

21. García Arenal, introduction, 3–4, 9.

22. On the history of the scholarly debate regarding the identity of the author of the *Topografía*, see Garcés, introduction, 65–66.

23. Garcés, introduction, 51–54.

24. Haedo, *Topografía e historia general de Argel*.

25. Among those who owned a copy of this work were one of the king's secretaries, an accountant, a general, a knight in the Order of Santiago, a knight in the Order of Calatrava, and the queen's glove maker; see José Manuel Prieto Bernabé, *Lectura y lectores, la lectura del impreso en el Madrid del Siglo de Oro (1550–1650)* (Mérida: Junta de Extremadura, 2004), 2:41, 62, 80, 195, 202, 419. Forty-three copies of the first part of the book, published in 1573, are extant, and nineteen of the second part, published in 1599; see Wilkinson, *Iberian Books*, 488.

26. Contemporary British historian Joseph Morgan reproduced entire sections of de Sosa's work in his history of the Maghrib; see Joseph Morgan, *A Compleat History of the Present State of War in Africa, Between the Spaniards and Algerines: Giving a Full and Exact Account of Oran and Al-Mursa; Compiled from the Best Approved Spanish Writers; the Author's Twenty Years Knowledge of the Country; and from Diverse Late Conferences with Haj Mahammed, the Algerine Envoy and Haj Ali, His Excellency's Secretary, Now Here Resident; with a New Map of the Kingdom of Algiers; and Several Useful Annotations* (London: Printed for W. Mears, at the Lamb in the Old Bailey, 1732).

27. Wilkinson, *Iberian Books*, 724. A search on Google Books, likely not exhaustive but still indicative, shows no early modern works in Spanish that refer to Torres.

28. Bunes Ibarra, "Felipe III y la defensa del Mediterráneo."

29. Parreño, "Experiencia y literatura en la obra de Antonio de Sosa," 20–21. On Galán, see Matías Barchino, introduction to *Edición crítica de Cautiverio y trabajos de Diego Galán*, ed. Matías Barchino (Cuenca: Ediciones de la Universidad de Castilla la Mancha, 2001), 29.

30. Martínez del Villar, *Discurso acerca de la conquista de los reynos de Argel y Bugia*.

31. For example, Francisco Antonio Silvestre, *Fundacion historica de los hospitales que la religion de la Santissima Trinidad, redempcion de cautivos, de calçados, tiene en la ciudad de Argel. . . . El Maestro Fr. Francisco Antonio Silvestre, administrador general de dichos hospitales* (Madrid: Iulian De Paredes, 1690).

32. AGS, *Estado*, Leg. 198, Valencia, 9.4.1604.

33. ACA, *Consejo de Aragón*, Leg. 715, fol. 15, 3.20.1637.

34. For three notable exceptions, see Bunes Ibarra, "Felipe III y la defensa del Mediterráneo"; Carlos Rodriguez Joulia Saint-Cyr, *Felipe III y El rey de Cuco* (Madrid: Instituto de Estudios Africanos, 1953); and Henry Lapeyre, "Du Nouveau sur Simon Danzer," in *Miscellanea offerts à Charles Verlinden à l'occasion de ses trente ans de professorat: Miscellanea Aangeboden aan Charles Verlinden ter Gelegenheid van Zijn Dertig Jaar Professoraat* (Gent, 1975), 335–40.

35. Blanes Andrés, *Valencia y el Magreb*, 237–38.

36. AGS, *Estado*, Leg. 210, 10.24.1608.

37. Carlos Rodriguez, *Felipe III y El rey de Cuco*; Pierre Boyer, "Espagne et Kouko: Les négociations de 1598 et 1610," *Revue de l'Occident Musulman et de la Méditerranée* 8 (1970): 25–40; Natividad Planas, "Diplomacy from Below or Cross-Confessional Loyalty? The 'Christians of Algiers' Between the Lord of Kuko and the King of Spain in the Early 1600s," *Journal of Early Modern History* 19 (2015): 153–73.

38. Carlos Rodríguez, *Felipe III y El rey de Cuco*, 84.

39. While Brussels was the center of imperial intelligence within Spain's European territories during Philip II's final years and the early portion of the reign of his son, Philip III, Naples was the epicenter of information for the Habsburgs in the Mediterranean, and Venice also played an important role. See the articles by Lucien Bély, "Espions et ambassadeurs à l'époque moderne," 21–30, Miguel Ángel Bunes Ibarra, "Avis du Levant," 223–40, and Raphael Carrasco, "L'espionnage espagnol du Levant au XVIe siècle d'après la correspondance des agents espagnols en poste à Venise," 202–23, in the volume edited by Béatrice Perez, *Ambassadeurs, apprentis espions et maitres comploteurs: Les systèmes de renseignement en Espagne à l'époque moderne* (Paris: Presses de l'Université Paris-Sorbonne, 2010). As this chapter demonstrates, in the seventeenth century Majorca was an important hub for information about the Maghrib.

40. AGS, *Estado*, Leg. 1102, fol. 88, 4.28.1605. Emrah Gürkan has meticulously studied sixteenth-century Mediterranean networks of spies; see Emrah Safa Gürkan, "Espionage in the 16th Century Mediterranean: Secret Diplomacy, Mediterranean Go-Betweens and the Ottoman Habsburg Rivalry" (PhD diss., Georgetown University, 2012); Emrah Safa Gürkan, "The Efficacy of Ottoman Counter-Intelligence in the 16th Century," *Acta Orientalia Academiae Scientiarum Hungaricae* 65 (2012): 1–38; and Emrah Safa Gürkan, "Fooling the Sultan: Information, Decision-Making and the 'Mediterranean Faction' (1585–1587)," *Journal of Ottoman Studies* 45 (2015): 57–96. See also Genarro Varriale, "La capital de la frontera Mediterránea: Exiliados, espías y convertidos en la Nápoles de los virreyes," *Estudis* 38 (2012): 303–21.

41. Gardens play a pivotal role in almost all genres of text involving captives. Many captives and ex-captives in Istanbul had to take care of their owners' gardens and summerhouses, a responsibility that they might exploit.

42. AGS, *Estado*, Leg. 1103, fol. 115, 6.22.1605. See a similar story in the petition submitted by Juan Domínguez from Caceres in Extremadura in April 1595, AGS, *Guerra Antigua*, Leg. 443, fol. 89, 4.10.1595.

43. AGS, *Guerra Antigua*, Leg. 782, 6.21.1613.

44. AGS, *Estado*, Leg. 210.

45. Ibid.

46. AGS, *Estado*, Leg. 210.

47. AGS, *Estado*, Leg. 198.

48. Topographic narratives were not the only kind of description of North Africa that captives compiled. For example, in 1592, Francisco de Narváez

authored a long text recounting the history of the kingdom of Cuco and its relations with its neighbors and the Spanish Empire. AGS, *Guerra Antigua*, Leg. 364, fol. 405.

49. AGS, *Estado*, Leg. 1950.
50. AGS, *Estado*, Leg. 1952.
51. Ibid.
52. Ibid.
53. Ibid., 1.6.1615.
54. AGS, *Estado*, Leg. 1948, fol. 230, 5.8.1615.
55. Ibid.
56. AGS, *Estado*, Leg. 1950.
57. Ibid.
58. Here, Pardo adds information to what de Sosa had written years earlier. See Sosa, *Topography of Algiers*, 112.
59. Garcés, introduction, 45.
60. AHN, *Inquisición*, Leg. 1824-2, carpeta 14.
61. AGS, *Estado*, Leg. 263, 10.13.1617.
62. Joulia Saint-Cyr, *Felipe III y El rey de Cuco*, 83.
63. This kind of information fascinated Spaniards of all classes. The Catalan chronicler Jeroni Pujades recorded such curiosity when, in August 1601, he documented the arrival at Barcelona of a Majorcan ship patron who had just returned from Algiers, where he had ransomed captives; patron and former captives alike assured the Catalans that "in Algiers no one talked about nor knew anything about the [Spanish] armada." Jeroni Pujades, *Dietari de Jeroni Pujades*, ed. Josep M.a Casas Homs (Barcelona: Fundació Salvador Vives Casajuana, 1975), vol. 1, 8.31.1601.
64. AGS, *Estado*, Leg. 298, 4.9.1604.
65. AGS, *Estado*, Leg. 198.
66. Ibid.
67. Christopher Storrs, "Intelligence and Formulation of Policy and Strategy in Early Modern Europe: The Spanish Monarchy in the Reign of Charles II (1665–1700)," *Intelligence and National Security* 21 (2006): 493–519.
68. Arndt Brendecke, "Informing the Council: Central Institutions and Local Knowledge in the Spanish Empire," in *Empowering Interactions: Political Cultures and the Emergence of the State in Europe, 1300–1900*, ed. Wim Blockmans, André Holenstein, and Jon Mathieu (London: Routledge, 2016), 235–52.
69. AGS, *Estado*, Leg. 1950, 10.9.1618.
70. Ibid.
71. AGS, *Estado*, Leg. 198, undated.
72. AGS, *Guerra Antigua*, Leg. 457, fol. 187.
73. AGS, *Estado*, Leg. 198, 3.22.1604.
74. AGS, *Estado*, Leg. 198, 4.9.1604.
75. AGS, *Estado*, Leg. 198, 10.5.1604.
76. Ibid.
77. ACA, *Consejo de Aragón*, Leg. 715, fol. 15, 3.20.1637.
78. ACA, *Consejo de Aragón*, Leg. 902, fol. 139, 12.20.1656.

79. Sylvia Sellers-García, *Distance and Documents at the Spanish Empire's Periphery* (Stanford, Calif.: Stanford University Press, 2014).

CHAPTER 7

1. Benítez, "La tramitación del pago de rescates a través del reino de Valencia."

2. Porres Alonso, *Libertad a los cautivos*, 341.

3. Gramaye, *Alger, XVIe–XVIIe siècle*, 357.

4. This reconstruction is based on an account Monroy sent the Council of War a few months after his arrest, a French recounting of the events dated 1613, and a Spanish account from the eighteenth century: AGS, *Estado*, Leg. 1661, 9.17.1609; Dominique Gaspard, *Histoire véritable de ce qui s'est passé en Turquie pour la délivrance et rédemption de chrétiens captifs depuis l'année 1609 et des sécheresses extraordinaires advenues en Alger l'an passe, pendant lesquelles arriva una pluie miraculeuse par l'intercession de trois religieux de l'ordre de la Sainte Trinite de la rédemption des captifs* (Paris, 1613), reprinted in H. Ternaux Compans, ed., *Archives des voyages ou collection d'anciennes relations* (Paris, 1840–41), 2:442–64; and Francisco de la Vega y Toraya, *Chrónica de la provincia de Castilla, León y Navarra del Orden de la Santíssima Trinidad* (Madrid: La Imprenta Real, 1720), 66. For a detailed study dedicated exclusively to the Trinitarians and the affair, see Porres Alonso, *Testigos de Cristo en Argel*.

5. Fatima was sold to Sima and Dianora Levi; see Archivio di Stato di Livorno, *Capitano, poi Governatore ed Auditore*, Leg. 2602, "Suppliche," fol. 597, no. 308. I thank Guillaume Calafat for this reference.

6. The Corsican merchant, Manfredino de Manfredi, had two brothers, one of whom was a renegade living in Algiers; see Vega y Toraya, *Chrónica de la provincia de Castilla*, 66. Manfredino traded various goods and often ransomed captives, both Muslim and Christian. In October 1609, for example, a few months after the Trinitarians and the ransomed captives were detained, Manfredino arrived in Livorno having ransomed three Christian captives in Algiers; see Vittorio Salvadorini, "Traffici e schiavi fra Livorno e Algeria nella prima decade del '600," 72.

7. ACA, *Consejo de Aragón*, Leg. 604, fol. 39, 6.15.1609.

8. AGS, *Estado*, Leg. 1882, fol. 273. Most of the documents on which this chapter is based claim that Fatima was thirteen years old when she was captured. However, a few claim she was only eight or nine years old at the time.

9. Archivio di Stato di Genova, *Senato*, Senarega-Collegii diversorum, Leg. 38, 1612.

10. Vega y Toraya, *Chrónica de la provincia de Castilla*, 87, 91.

11. AGS, *Guerra Antigua*, Leg. 767, 3.9.1612.

12. AGS, *Estado*, Leg. 1661, 9.17.1609.

13. AGS, *Estado*, Leg. 217, 10.15.1609.

14. AGS, *Estado*, Leg. 1882, fol. 270, undated document but probably from 1618.

15. On the relations between Genoa and the Spanish Empire, see Céline Dauverd, *Imperial Ambition in the Early Modern Mediterranean: Genoese Merchants and the Spanish Crown* (New York: Cambridge University Press, 2015); Thomas Allison Kirk, *Genoa and the Sea: Policy and Power in an Early Modern Maritime Republic, 1559–1684* (Baltimore: Johns Hopkins University Press, 2005); and Manuel Herrero Sánchez, "La república de Génova y la monarquía hispánica (siglos XVI–XVII)," *Hispania* 65, no. 219 (2005): 9–20.

16. On the exchange between the Republic of Genoa and the Spanish ambassador there, see AGS, *Estado*, Leg. 346, 10.4.1609, 10.24.1609; AGS, *Estado*, Leg. 1434, fol. 238, 11.19.1609. For the efforts of the Spanish ambassador in France, see AGS, *Estado*, Leg. 246, 1.5.1610. On exchanges with the Spanish ambassador in Venice on the matter, see AHN, *Estado*, Lib. 346, 1.5.1610. On attempts to gain assistance from the pope, see Archivo General del Ministerio de Asuntos Exteriores, *Santa Sede*, Leg. 55, fol. 238, 6.23.1610. On the involvement of the Grand Duke of Tuscany via his governor of Livorno, see Archivio di Stato di Livorno, *Capitano, poi Governatore ed Auditore*, Leg. 2602, "Suppliche," fol. 597, no. 308.

17. AGS, *Guerra Antigua*, Leg. 772, 11.21.1612. On the rift between the sultan and the Algerian authorities, see Calafat, "Ottoman North Africa and *Ius Publicum Europaeum*."

18. AGS, *Estado*, Leg. 263, 10.13.1617. Writing in 1619, Gramaye mentioned another instance in which the sultan ordered the release of Monroy; see Gramaye, *Alger, XVIe–XVIIe siècle*, 357.

19. AGS, *Guerra Antigua*, Leg. 785, 4.19.1613; AGS, *Estado*, Leg. 190, 7.17.1621, 10.16.1621.

20. Archivio di Stato di Genoa, *Senato*, Senarega-Collegii diversorum, Leg. 38, 1612.

21. AGS, *Estado*, Leg. 1882, fol. 245, 8.1.1617. On Tabarka and its importance as a meeting point for ransomers and slave traders, see Gourdin, *Tabarka*, 538–43, and Ildefonso Pulido Bueno, *Guerra y riqueza en Berbería: La corona española y sus posesiones de Maçal-Arez y Tabarka cedidas en enfiteusis al linaje Lomellini (1540–1742): De solución a problema para la hacienda real* (Huelva: Ildefonso Pulido Bueno, 2015).

22. The viceroy of Valencia indicated Fatima's married status in a letter to the Council of State from October 29, 1618; AGS, *Estado*, Leg. 1882, fol. 266, 10.29.1618.

23. AGS, *Estado*, Leg. 495, 6.5.1614; *CODOIN*, 44:547–52.

24. On the bey's offer, see AGS, *Estado*, Leg. 1168, 7.25.1614; on the votes of the counselors, see *CODOIN*, 44:549–52.

25. AGS, *Estado*, Leg. 495, 7.19.1614.

26. AGS, *Estado*, Leg. 259, 11.20.1614.

27. For a testimony on the capture of Diego de Pacheco, see AGS, *Estado*, Leg. 1949, fols. 133, 136, 3.24.1613. On the marquis's attempts to exchange de Pacheco for the bey, see AGS, *Estado*, Leg. 1168, fol. 171, 12.14.1613 and fol. 206, 10.5.1614.

28. AGS, *Estado*, Leg. 1949, fol. 133, 3.24.1613; AGS, *Estado*, Leg. 1167, fol. 45, 5.11.1614; AGS, *Estado*, Leg. 1892, fol. 37, 7.23.1619.

29. The case of *ra'īs* Ali, or Francesco Guicciardo, from Ferrara was, like Fatima's case, thoroughly documented. Guicciardo was taken captive in his youth and converted to Islam. He gained a reputation as a Tunisian corsair but was captured by Alvarao Baçan, the marquis of Santa Cruz, who submitted him to the Sicilian tribunal of the Inquisition in 1624. While more than a dozen witnesses disagreed, he insisted that he had been born Muslim. As with the taking of Fatima, his arrest led to the detention of recently redeemed captives. Over the course of fifteen years there were at least two near-agreements for his return, both of which failed. On Guicciardo's capture, see *Copia de una carta que de la ciudad de Palermo embió el capitán Francisco Ruiz Díaz de Villegas . . . en que se haze relación de la gran vitoria que Don Alvaro Baçan, Marqués de Santa Cruz, general de las galeras de Sicilia, tuvo con quatro navíos de guerra de enemigos . . . con el cosario Sanson, por otro nombre llamado Ali Arraez . . . de Palermo, 1. Iulio de 1624,* in *Papeles de mi archivo, Los turcos en el Mediterráneo (relaciones),* vol. 5, ed. Ignacio Bauer Landauer (Madrid: Editorial Ibero-Africano-Americana, 1922–23), 141–47. For a description and analysis of the Inquisition trial, see Bennassar and Bennassar, *Los cristianos de Alá,* 89–124. On the request of Carmelite priests to be exchanged for Guicciardo, see AHN, *Inquisición,* Lib. 1252, fols. 129V–130, 7.3.1642. On the attempts of Doria, previous doge of the Republic of Genoa, to cook up a ransom deal, see AGS, *Estado,* Leg. 3482, fol. 148, 8.26.1639. For the arguments raised by the parties, Inquisitors, and others, see AHN, *Inquisición,* Lib. 897, fol. 166; AHN, *Inquisición,* Lib. 1252, 7.3.1642; and AHN, *Estado,* Lib. 454D, fol. 1.

30. Archivo General del Ministerio de Asuntos Exteriores, *Santa Sede,* Leg. 55, fol. 238, 6.23.1610; AGS, *Estado,* Leg. 1950, 7.17.1621.

31. AGS, *Estado,* Leg. 1882, fol. 273, 8.14.1617.

32. On "regimes of value," see Arjun Appadurai, "Introduction: Commodities and the Politics of Value," in *The Social Life of Things: Commodities in Cultural Perspective,* ed. Arjun Appadurai (Cambridge: Cambridge University Press, 1986), 3–63. More specifically, on people moving between different regimes of value, see Kopytoff, "The Cultural Biography of Things."

33. Davis, *Christian Slaves, Muslim Masters,* 147; Martínez Torres, *Prisioneros de los infieles,* 144–45; Kaiser, "L'Économie de la rançon"; Kaiser and Calafat, "The Economy of Ransoming in the Early Modern Mediterranean."

34. *Relación verdadera embiada de la ciudad de Argel dando cuenta de los alborotos, y ruidos, que aquellos barbaros tienen entre sí,* BNE, VE 57-17.

35. Porres Alonso, *Testigos de Cristo en Argel,* 109.

36. For letters, copies of letters, or references to letters by Monroy, see AGS, *Estado,* Leg. 1661, 9.17.1609; AGS, *Estado,* Leg. 2640, fol. 195, 2.11.1610; AGS, *Guerra Antigua,* Leg. 772, 11.21.1612; AGS, *Guerra Antigua,* Leg. 785, 2.28.1613; AGS, *Guerra Antigua,* Leg. 786, 6.25.1613; AGS, *Estado,* Leg. 495, 6.5.1614, 6.30.1614, and 7.19.1614; AGS, *Estado,* Leg. 259, 11.20.1614; AGS, *Estado,* Leg. 1952, 12.18.1614, 11.6.1618; AGS, *Estado,* Leg. 1951, 8.30.1617; and AGS, *Estado,* Leg. 1882, 8.17.1617. For

copies of letters written to Monroy, see BNE, Mss. 185/8/1, 7.15.1616; Mss. 185/8/2, 7.3.1617; Mss. 20213/24, 5.11.1617; Mss. 20209/19, 1616.

37. AGS, *Estado*, Leg. 2640, fol. 195, 2.11.1610.

38. AGS, *Estado*, Leg. 1882, fol. 271, 8.17.1617.

39. AGS, *Estado*, Leg. 1952, 12.18.1614.

40. Friedman, "Trinitarian Hospitals in Algiers."

41. Porres Alonso, *Testigos de Cristo en Argel*, 112.

42. For example, see *Relación de la carta que el padre fray Bernardo de Monroy, administrador general de la redención de cautivos de la orden de la Santissima Trinidad de la provincia de Castilla, embió de Argel al padre provincial de su provincia* (Mallorca, 1612) (AGS, *Estado*, Leg. 255). The letter was reprinted in 1613 in Barcelona at the Casa de la viuda Dotil (Biblioteca Nacional de Portugal, Res. 254, fols. 23–24). For a full bibliography, see Porres Alonso, *Testigos de Cristo en Argel*, 17–21.

43. It was also known as "Fort of Hasan Pasha."

44. AGS, *Estado*, Leg. 1951, fols. 95–96, 8.30.1617.

45. Ibid.

46. AGS, *Estado*, Leg. 1952, 11.6.1618.

47. AGS, *Estado*, Leg. 210, 12.14.1607.

48. AGS, *Estado*, Leg. 210, 3.25.1608.

49. AGS, *Estado*, Leg. 210, 9.2.1608, my emphasis.

50. On the Taifa, see Ciro Manca, *Il modello di sviluppo economico delle città marittime barbaresche dopo Lepanto* (Napoli: Gianinin, 1982), 41–57.

51. The market did not impose this agenda on the king of Spain; in fact, working with Maghribi intermediaries seems to have been a more expensive solution. See the copy of a letter from Isidro del Castillo y Aguilera to Cid Ali Hache Catalán, RAH, *Colección de Don Luis Salazar y Castro*, Leg. 38, carpeta 5, 11.18.1648.

52. Unfortunately, no minutes of the divan meetings survive. In general, Ottoman Algerian archives hold very few documents for this period. See Loualich, "In the Regency of Algiers," 93–96, and Merouche, *Recherches sur l'Algérie à l'époque ottoman*, vol. 2, *La course, mythes et réalité*.

53. John B. Wolf, *The Barbary Coast: Algiers Under the Turks, 1500 to 1830* (New York: Norton, 1979), 82.

54. Ibid., 76; Farid Khiari, *Vivre et mourir en Alger, L'Algérie Ottomane aux XVIe–XVIIe siècles: Un destin confisqué* (Paris: L'Harmattan, 2002), 199–200.

55. R. Mantran, "North Africa in the Sixteenth and Seventeenth Centuries," in *The Cambridge History of Islam*, vol. 2A, ed. P. M. Holt, Ann K. S. Lambton, and Bernard Lewis (Cambridge: Cambridge University Press, 1977), 254–55; Jamil M. Abun-Nasr, *A History of the Maghrib in the Islamic Period* (Cambridge: Cambridge University Press, 1987), 158–59; Khiari, *Vivre et mourir en Alger*, 199, 204; Merouche, *Recherches sur l'Algérie à l'époque ottoman*, vol. 2, *La course, mythes et réalité*, 152–53. The negotiations between the king of France, the Ottoman sultan, and the governors of the Ottoman regencies in the Maghrib suggest the same standing for the pasha; see Weiss, *Captives and Corsairs*, 13.

56. Merouche, *Recherches sur l'Algérie à l'époque ottoman*, vol. 2, *La course, mythes et réalité*, 141.

57. The capture of Venetian ships by Tunisian and Algerian corsairs in 1624 was another transformative incident; see Joshua M. White, "Shifting Winds: Piracy, Diplomacy, and Trade in the Ottoman Mediterranean, 1624–1626," in *Well-Connected Domains: Towards an Entangled Ottoman History*, ed. Pascal W. Firges, Tobias P. Graf, Christian Roth, and Gülay Tulasğlu (Leiden: Brill, 2014), 37–53.

58. The source of this information is the report of an anonymous spy-cum-captive from Denia (on the shoreline about sixty miles south of Valencia) that was sent to the viceroy of Majorca. The detailed description of the meetings provided by the anonymous Valencian suggests that he was either present in person or had a valuable informer. His account covers almost every day between September 1613 and March 1614. AGS, *Estado*, Leg. 255, 9.14.1613.

59. AGS, *Estado*, Leg. 255, 2.7.1614.

60. Ibid.

61. AGS, *Estado*, Leg. 1881, fol. 32, 4.14.1618.

62. AGS, *Guerra Antigua*, Leg. 767, 3.9.1612.

63. Ibid. The second lieutenant Domingo Pérez petitioned the Council of War to help him ransom his nephew from Algiers; see AGS, *Guerra Antigua*, Leg. 768, 11.9.1612. María de Hierro, possibly following instructions from Medina, specifically petitioned the council to allow Medina to execute his plans. She was hoping to ransom her husband, who was held captive in Algiers; see AGS, *Guerra Antigua*, Leg. 767, 4.2.1612.

64. AGS, *Guerra Antigua*, Leg. 767, 3.9.1612. For the crown's approval, see AGS, *Guerra Antigua*, Leg. 764, 4.16.1612.

65. A former Portuguese garrison, Ceuta had become Spanish with the Spanish-Portuguese union of 1580.

66. The license the Trinitarians received two years later allowed that "a captain from Gibraltar, Ceuta or Tangiers could go with his ship to Algiers, taking with him a few Jewish or Muslim merchants who have contacts among the Muslim merchants of Algiers, to execute the said ransom." Porres Alonso, *Libertad a los cautivos*, 345. Many of the captives ransomed in this expedition were brought to Tétouan from Algiers. See *Trinitarios calzados. Libro de la redención de cautivos de Tetuán, Fez y Marruecos. Resultado de las comisiones de fray Jerónimo Fernández y fray Antonio de Madrid. Año 1614*, AHN, *Códices*, Lib. 124. For the 1617 Mercedarian expedition to Algiers and its reliance on local merchants, see Gari y Siumell, *La orden redentora de la Merced*, 280–86.

67. In 1618, the Spaniards tried using the services of a Valencia-based French trader to buy Spanish soldiers held captive in Algiers. The Algerians refused, however, to sell the Frenchman captives unless Trinitarian friars were present. Eventually, and despite his own veto on sending redeemers to the city, Philip III ordered the Trinitarians to travel to Algiers and join the French merchant. This exception was deemed necessary because the captives were soldiers whose return to military service was a royal necessity. On this

ransom expedition, see AHN, *Códices*, Lib. 125, fols. 7r and 22–27v (first foliation) and fol. 56v (second foliation). On the commercial activities of the French merchant Antoine Masued (or Masuer or Massuer), see Alvaro Castillo Pintado, *Tráfico marítimo y comercio de importación en Valencia a comienzos del siglo XVII* (Madrid, 1967), 85, 99, and Benítez, "La tramitación del pago de rescates a través del reino de Valencia," 201, 203, 215.

68. Martínez Torres, *Prisioneros de los infieles*, 24, 77.

69. For an elucidating recent discussion of the problem from the perspective of the political economy of the Spanish Empire, see Regina Grafe, *Distant Tyranny: Markets, Power and Backwardness in Spain, 1650–1800* (Princeton, N.J.: Princeton University Press, 2012). For a useful discussion, see James Amelang, "The Peculiarities of the Spaniards: Historical Approaches to the Early Modern State," in *Public Power in Europe: Studies in Historical Transformations*, ed. James Amelang and Siegfried Beer (Pisa: Pisa University Press, 2006), 40–57.

70. On membership in the community, see Herzog, *Defining Nations*.

71. Andrew Hess, "The Moriscos: An Ottoman Fifth Column in Sixteenth Century Spain," *American Historical Review* 74 (1968): 1–25.

72. For a discussion of the debates about the expulsion and the ways in which it strengthened Spain's image as defending the faith, see Antonio Feros, *El Duque de Lerma, realeza y privanza en la España de Felipe III* (Madrid: Marcial Pons, 2002), 353–72.

73. Gari y Siumell, *La orden redentora de la Merced*, 287–88.

74. AGS, *Guerra Antigua*, Leg. 783, 10.13.1613.

75. Gozalbes Busto, *Los Moriscos en Marruecos*, 278.

76. For a description of the uproar that erupted in 1614 once the Mercedarians' plans became public and its threat to the friars' lives, see BNE, Mss. 12078, fol. 160.

77. Gari y Siumell, *La orden redentora de la Merced*, 283.

78. Very little has been published on the early modern history of the Jewish community of Tétouan; see Juan Bautista Villar Ramírez, *Tetuán en el resurgimiento judío contemporáneo (1850–1870): Aproximación a la historia del judaísmo norte africano* (Caracas: Editorial Arte, 1985), 15–33, and *La judería de Tetuán, 1489–1860* (Murcia: Universidad de Murcia, 1969), 15–39.

79. AGS, *Estado*, Leg. 255, 9.20.1614.

80. AGS, *Guerra Antigua*, Leg. 786, 6.25.1613, and *Trinitarios calzados. Libros de la redención de cautivos en Tetuán, Fez y Marruecos. Resultado de las comisiones de fray Andrés de Mancera y fray Pedro de Castillo. Años 1617–1618*, AHN, *Códices*, Lib. 125.

81. There is very little research on Ottoman-Moroccan relations during the seventeenth century. On Ottoman attempts to intervene in Moroccan politics, see Auguste Cour, *L'Établissement des dynasties des Chérifs au Maroc et leur rivalité avec les Turcs de la régence d'Álger 1509–1830* (Saint Denis: Bouchene, 2004), and Abderrahmane El Moudden, "Sharifs and Padishahs: Moroccan-Ottoman Relations from the Sixteenth Through

the Eighteenth Centuries: Contribution to the Study of a Diplomatic Culture" (PhD diss., Princeton University, 1992), 149–50.

82. Copy of a letter from Isidro del Castillo y Aguilera to Cid Ali Hache Catalán, RAH, *Colección de Don Luis Salazar y Castro*, Leg. 38, carpeta 5, 11.18.1648.

83. Smaller-scale entanglements that created similar ad hoc ransom coalitions and oppositions were common in the early modern period. For other examples, see Daniel Hershenzon, "'[P]ara que me saque cabesa por cabesa . . .': Exchanging Muslim and Christian Slaves Across the Mediterranean," *African Economic History* 42 (2014): 11–36.

CONCLUSION

1. Greene, "Beyond the Northern Invasion."

2. The power this story holds stands out when comparing the dearth of studies dedicated to the seventeenth-century western Mediterranean to the wealth of scholarly work on Istanbul and Venice, and more broadly on the eastern Mediterranean in the same time period.

3. Ben-Yehoyada, *The Mediterranean Incarnate*, 232–36.

4. Weiss, *Captives and Corsairs*, 92–118; Friedman, *Spanish Captives in North Africa in the Early Modern Age*, 29.

5. Panzac, *Barbary Corsairs*, 31–38.

6. Planas, "Pratiques de pouvoir au sein d'une société frontalière."

7. These tumultuous relations are reflected in Algerian censuses listing the number of slaves in Algiers according to their nationality. The number of Spaniards rose and fell in tandem with the events discussed; see de Voulx, *Tachrifat*, 86–88.

8. Weiss, *Captives and Corsairs*, 156–69.

9. In the past decade, leading scholars on Morisco history began using the term "ethnic cleansing" to describe this process that culminated in the expulsion of the Moriscos; see Mercedes García Arenal and Gerard Wiegers, introduction to *Los moriscos: Expulsión y diaspora*, ed. Mercedes García Arenal and Gerard Wiegers (Valencia: University of Valencia, 2013), 11–24; Trevor J. Dadson, *Los moriscos de Villarrubia de los Ojos (Siglos XV–XVIII)* (Madrid: Iberamericana Editorial, 2007); and Amelang, *Historias paralelas*.

10. For a theorization of the idea that "the process of replacement maintains the refractory imprint of the native counter-claim," see Patrick Wolfe, "Settler Colonialism and the Elimination of the Native," *Journal of Genocide Research* 8 (2006): 389. See also Caroline Elkins and Susan Pederson, introduction to *Settler Colonialism in the Twentieth Century: Projects, Practices, Legacies*, ed. Caroline Elkins and Susan Pederson (New York: Routledge, 2005), 1–20, and Gerald Sider, "When Parrots Learn to Talk, and Why They Can't: Domination, Deception, and Self-Deception in Indian-White Relations," *Comparative Studies in Society and History* 29 (1987): 3–23.

11. Mercedes García Arenal and Fernando Rodríguez Mediano, *The Orient in Spain: Converted Muslims, the Forged Lead Books of Granada, and the Rise of Orientalism* (Leiden: Brill, 2013).

12. Wolfe, "Settler Colonialism and the Elimination of the Native," 389. On the invisibility of Muslim slaves in Spanish, especially Majorcan, archives, see Natividad Planas, "Musulmans invisibles? Enquête dans les territoires insulaires du roi d'Espagne (XVIe–XVIIe siècle)," in *Les musulmans dans l'histoire de l'Europe*, vol. 1, *Une intégration invisible*, ed. Jocelyne Dakhlia and Bernard Vincent (Paris: Albin Michel, 2011), 558–92.

13. Jocelyne Dakhlia, "Lingua Franca: A Non Memory," in *Remembering Africa*, ed. E. Mudimbe-Boyi (Portsmouth: Heinemann, 2002), 234–44.

14. Clara Ilham Álvarez Dopico, "The Catholic Consecration of an Islamic House: The St. John de Matha Trinitarian Hospital in Tunis," in *Sacred Precincts: The Religious Architecture of Non-Muslim Communities Across the Islamic World*, ed. Mohammad Gharipour (Leiden: Brill, 2015), 291–307.

15. Gerard A. Wiegers, "European Converts to Islam in the Maghrib and the Polemical Writings of the Moriscos," in *Conversions islamiques: Identités religieuses en Islam méditerranéen*, ed. Mercedes García Arenal (Paris: Maisonneuve et Larose, 2002), 207–23. On the role of converts in processes of confessionalization in the Ottoman Empire, see Tijana Krstic, "Illuminated by the Light of Islam and the Glory of the Ottoman Sultanate: Self-Narratives of Conversion to Islam in the Age of Confessionalization," *Comparative Studies in Society and History* 51 (2009): 35–63.

MANUSCRIPT AND ARCHIVAL SOURCES

Archivio di Stato di Genoa

Senato: Senarega-Collegii diversorum, Leg. 38

Archivio di Stato di Livorno

Capitano, poi Governatore ed Auditore:
Leg. 2602

Archivo de la Corona de Aragón

Consejo de Aragón: Leg. 592, 604, 607, 672, 715, 728, 743, 902, 911, 933, 993

Archivo del Museo Canario

Inquisición: Leg. CXIX-21

Archivo Ducal de Medina Sidonia

Leg. 4407

Archivo General de Simancas

Cámara de Castilla: Leg. 683
Cámara y Juntas de Hacienda: Leg. 683
Estado: Leg. 190, 192, 198, 210, 217, 246, 255, 259, 263, 298, 346, 491,

495, 992, 1094, 1102, 1103, 1167, 1168, 1169, 1416, 1434, 1661, 1881,
1882, 1892, 1948, 1949, 1950, 1951, 1952, 2640, 2672, 2675, 2688,
3287, 3444, 3446, 3482, 3832
Guerra Antigua: Leg. 220, 247, 262, 268, 271, 272, 274, 305, 315, 316, 364,
423, 442, 443, 448, 457, 478, 487, 764, 767, 768, 772, 782, 783, 785,
786, 808, 812, 833, 1541
Guerra y Marina: Leg. 1598, 1600, 1858, 3362
Lib. 305

Archivo General del Ministerio de Asuntos Exteriores

Santa Sede: Leg. 55

Archivo Histórico de la Catedral de Burgos

Reg. 81, 87, 89

Archivo Histórico Nacional

Clero: Leg. 3821, Lib. VI
Códices: Lib. 124, 125, 142B, 148
Consejos: Leg. 6900, 6902, 6903, 6904, 7045, 7046, 7048, 7050, 7055
Estado: Leg. 670
Lib. 346, 454D
Inquisición: Leg. 861, 933, 1592, 1706, 1711, 1714, 1824, 1952, 2952, 3733
Lib. 862, 863, 897, 1252

Biblioteca Nacional de España

Sala de Cervantes: VE 57-17
R/11834
Mss. 185, 2388, 2974, 3634, 5065, 12078, 20209, 20213

Biblioteca Nacional de Portugal

Res. 254

Biblioteca Zabálburu

Colección Altamira: 275, D. 1–22, 52, 64
52, D.

Museo Nacional de Escultura, Valladolid

De la Cuadra, Pedro. *La redención de cautivos*, 1599.

Newberry Library, Chicago

San Antonio, Alonso de. *Primacia de redentora de cavtibos de la sagrada Orden de la SSma Trinidad, en las coronas de Castilla, Aragón y Nauarra, contra la illvstre Orden de Nuestra Sa. de la Merced*. Madrid, 1651–52.

Real Academia de la Historia

Colección de Don Luis Salazar y Castro: Leg. 38

PRINTED SOURCES

Actas de las Cortes de Castilla . . . desde el día 8 de junio de 1627 hasta el 8 de junio de 1628. Vol. 46. Madrid: Impresores de la Casa Real, 1928.

Anaya Hernández, Luis Alberto. "Repercusiones del corso berberisco en Canarias durante el siglo XVII: Cautivos y renegados canarios." In *V Coloquio de Historia Canario-Americana* (1982). Vol. 2, ed. Francisco Morales Padrón. 123–78. Las Palmas de Gran Canaria: Excmo. Cabildo Insular de Gran Canaria, 1985.

———. "Voces del cautiverio: Las cartas de los esclavos canarios desde Berbería (siglos XVI–XVII)." In *XVIII Coloquio de historia Canario-americana 2008*, ed. Francisco Morales Padrón. Las Palmas de Gran Canaria: Casa de Colón, 2010.

Aranda, Emanuel d'. *Les captifs d'Alger: Relation de la captivité du sieur Emanuel d'Aranda*. Ed. Latifa Z'Rari Latifa. Paris: J. P. Rocher, 1998.

Arribas Palau, Mariano. "Argelinos cautivos en España, rescatados por el sultán de Marruecos." *Boletín de la Asociación Española de Orientalistas* 26 (1990): 23–54.

———. "De nuevo sobre la embajada de al-Gassani (1690–1691)." *Al-Qantara* 6 (1985): 199–289.

Arvieux, Laurent d'. *Mémoires du chevalier d'Arvieux: Voyage à Tunis*. Ed. Jacques de Maussion de Favières. Paris: Editions Kimé, 1994.

———. *Mémoires du chevalier d'Arvieux Envoyé Extraordinaire Du Roy À La Porte, Consul D'alep, D'alger, De Tripoli, & Autres Echelles Du Levant. Contenant Ses Voyages À Constantinople, Dans L'asie, La Syrie, La Palestine, L'egypte, & La Barbarie, La Description De Ces Païs, Les Religions, Les Moeurs, Les Coûtumes, Le Négoce De Ces Peuples, & Leurs Gouvernemens, L'histoire Naturelle & Les Événemens Les Plus*

Considerables, Recüeillis De Ses Mémoires Originaux, & Mis En Ordre Avec Des Réfléxions. Vol. 5. Paris: Charles-Jean-Baptiste Delespine le Fils, Libraire, 1735.

Asunción, Gabriel de la. *Memorial del General de la orden descalços de la Santísima Trinidad, redención de cautivos, contra el arbitrio dado por el capitán Guillermo Garret, sobre la erección de una escuadra de seis navíos, que guarden las costas que miran a Berbería, y preserven estos reinos y sus habitadores, del cautiverio de los moros, convirtiendo en el apresto y sustento desta escuadra, lo que se gasta en redención de cautivos, por medio de las ordenes de la Trinidad, y Merced, y diversas dotaciones.* In *Papeles de mi archivo. Relaciones de África (Marruecos),* Vol. 2, ed. Ignacio Bauer Landauer. 53–86. Madrid: Editorial Ibero-Africano-Americana, 1922–23.

Barceló, Carmen, and Ana Labart, eds. *Archivos moriscos: Textos árabes de la minoría islámica Valenciana, 1401–1608.* Valencia: University of Valencia, 2009.

Bauer Landauer, Ignacio. *Papeles de mi archivo: Relaciones de África (Argel).* Vol. 4. Madrid: Editorial Ibero-Africano-Americana, 1922–23.

Celdrán Gomariz, Pancracio, ed. *Judíos, moros y cristianos en la ciudad de Argel (según un manuscrito inédito de Melchor de Zúñiga, 1639).* Madrid: Ediciones del Orto, 2012.

Cervantes, Miguel de. *"The Bagnios of Algiers" and "The Great Sultana": Two Plays of Captivity.* Trans. and ed. Barbara Fuchs and Aaron J. Ilika. Philadelphia: University of Pennsylvania Press, 2010.

———. *Don Quixote.* Trans. Edith Grossman and Harold Bloom. New York: Ecco, 2015.

———. *Obras completas.* Madrid: Editorial Aguilar, 1962.

Coll Font, M. Carme. "Josep Moranta, frare predicador captiu a Alger (1635–43): Relat de les seves conversions i el seu martiri." *Bolletí de la societat arqueològica lul·liana* 65 (2009): 271–84.

Conceição, António da. *A relação da vida e morte dos sete mártires de Marrocos de fr. António da Conceição.* Ed. Domingos Maurício Gomes dos Santos. Coimbra: Associação Portuguesa para o Progresso das Ciências, 1957.

"Copia de una carta original del Duque de Osuna á S. M. fecha en Palermo á 31 de mayo de 1612." In *Colección de documentos inéditos para la historia de España.* 44:285. Madrid: Imprenta de la Viuda de Galero, 1864.

Copia de una carta que de la ciudad de Palermo embió el capitán Francisco Ruiz Díaz de Villegas . . . en que se haze relación de la gran vitoria que Don Alvaro Baçan, Marqués de Santa Cruz, general de las galeras de Sicilia, tuvo con quatro navíos de guerra de enemigos . . . con el cosario

Sanson, por otro nombre llamado Ali Arraez . . . de Palermo, 1. Iulio de 1624. In *Papeles de mi archivo, Los turcos en el Mediterráneo (relaciones).* Vol. 5, ed. Ignacio Bauer Landauer. 141–47. Madrid: Editorial Ibero-Africano-Americana, 1922–23.

Díaz Hierro, Diego. *Historia de la Merced de Huelva: Hoy catedral de su diócesis.* Huelva: Imp. Guillermo Martín, 1975.

Galán, Diego. *Relación del cautiverio y libertad de Diego Galán, natural de la villa de Consuegra y vecino de la ciudad de Toledo.* Ed. Miguel Ángel de Bunes and Matías Barchino. Seville: Espuela de Plata, 2011.

Gallotta, Aldo. "Diplomi turchi dell'Archivio di Stato di Firenze: Lettere da Algeri ai Granduchi di Toscana (secolo XVII)." *Studi Magrebini* 11 (1979): 167–205 and facsimiles I–XII.

García Arenal, Mercedes, Fernando Rodríguez Mediano, and Rachid El Hour, eds. *Cartas marruecas: Documentos de Marruecos en archivos españoles (siglos XVI–XVII).* Estudios árabes e islámicos. Monografías 3. Madrid: Consejo Superior de Investigaciones Científicas, 2002.

Gari y Siumell, José Antonio. *La orden redentora de la Merced ó sea historia de las redenciones de cautivos cristianos realizadas por los hijos de la orden de la Merced.* Barcelona: Imprenta De los Herederos de la Viuda Pla, 1873.

Gaspard, Dominique. *Histoire véritable de ce qui s'est passé en Turquie pour la délivrance et rédemption de chrétiens captifs depuis l'année 1609 et des sécheresses extraordinaires advenues en Alger l'an passe, pendant lesquelles arriva une pluie miraculeuse par l'intercession de trois religieux de l'ordre de la Sainte Trinite de la rédemption des captifs.* Paris, 1613. Reprinted in *Archives des voyages, ou, Collection d'anciennes relations inédites ou très-rares de lettres, mémoires, itineraires et autres documents relatifs à la géographie et aux voyages.* Vol. 2, ed. H. Ternaux Compans. Paris: Arthus Bertrand, 1845.

Gozalbes Busto, Guillermo. *Los Moriscos en Marruecos.* Granada: T. G. Arte, 1992.

Gracián, Jerónimo. *Cartas, Monumenta historica Carmeli Teresiani.* Ed. Juan Luis Astigarraga. Rome: Teresianum, 1989.

———. *Peregrinación de Anastasio: Obras del P. Jerónimo Gracián de la Madre de Dios.* Vol. 3, ed. P. Silverio de Santa Teresa. Burgos: Tipografía De "El Monte Carmelo," 1932–33.

———. *Tratado de la redención de cautivos: En que se cuentan las grandes miserias que padecen los cristianos que están en poder de infieles, y cuán santa obra sea la de su rescates.* Ed. Miguel Ángel Bunes Ibarra and Beatriz Alonso Acero. Seville: Ediciones Espuela de Plata, 2006.

Gramaye, Jean-Baptiste. *Alger, XVIe–XVIIe siècle: Journal de Jean-Baptiste*

Gramaye, *"évêque d'Afrique."* Trans. Abd El Hadi Ben Mansour. Paris: Éd. du Cerf, 1998.

Haedo, Diego de. *Topografía e historia general de Argel.* Valladolid: Diego Fernandez De Cordoua y Ouiedo, 1612.

Jiménez de Gregorio, Fernando. "'Relación de Orán,' por el Vicario D. Pedro Cantero Vaca (1631–1636)." *Hispania: Revista Española de Historia* 85 (1962): 81–117.

Llot de Ribera, Miquel. *Verdadera relación de la vitoria y libertad que alcançaron quatrocientos christianos captivos de Hazan Baxá, almirante y capitán general del mar del gran turco con dos galeras suyas que levantaron.* Barcelona: Casa De Sanson Arbus, 1590.

López Nadal, Gonçal Artur. *El corsarisme mallorquí a la Mediterrània occidental, 1652–1698: Un comerç forçat.* Palma de Mallorca: Conselleria D'Educació i Cultura Del Govern Balear, 1986.

Lourido Díaz, Ramón. "La obra redentora del sultán marroquí Sīdī Muḥammad b. 'Abd Allāh entre los cautivos musulmanes en Europa (siglo XVIII)." *Cuadernos de Historia del Islam* 11 (1984): 138–83.

Mármol, Andrés del. *Excelencias, vida y trabaios del Padre Gerónimo Gracián de la Madre de Dios Carmelita.* Valladolid: Francisco Fernández De Cordona, 1619.

Mármol Carvajal, Luis del. *Descripción general de África.* Vol. 1. Madrid: Instituto de Estudios Africanos del Patronato Diego Saavedra Fajardo del CSIC, 1953.

———. *Historia del [sic] rebelión y castigo de los moriscos del Reino de Granada.* Alicante: Biblioteca Virtual Miguel de Cervantes, 2001.

Márquez, Juan. *Vida del venerable P. Fr. Alonso de Orozco, religioso de la orden de N. P. S. Agustin, y predicador de las Catolicas Magestades de Carlos V y Felipe II.* Madrid: Iuan Sánchez, 1648.

Martínez del Villar, Miguel. *Discurso acerca de la conquista de los reynos de Argel y Bugia, en que se trata de las razones que ay para emprendela, respondiendo a las que se hazen en contrario.* Madrid: Luis Sánchez, 1619.

Martínez Ruiz, Juan. "Cautivos precervantinos: Cara y cruz del cautiverio." *Revista de filología española* 50 (1967): 203–56.

Martorell Téllez-Girón, Ricardo, ed. *Anales de Madrid de León Pinelo, reinado de Felipe III, años 1598 a 1621: Edición y estudio crítico del manuscrito número 1.255 de la Biblioteca Nacional.* Madrid: Estanislao Maestre, 1931. Ed. facs. Valladolid: Maxtor, 2003.

Mascarenhas, João de. *Esclave à Alger: Recit de captivité de João Mascarenhas (1621–1626).* Dossiers Historique & Iconographique. Trans. Teyssier Paul. Paris: Chandeigne, 1999.

Molina, Tirso de. *Historia general de la orden de nuestra señora de las mercedes (1568–1639)*. Vol. 2, ed. Manuel Penedo Rey. Madrid: Provincia de la Merced de Castilla, 1973.

Montalván, Juan Pérez de. *Segundo tomo de las comedias del doctor Juan Pérez de Montalván*. Madrid: Impresor del Reyno, 1638.

Montaner, Pedro de. "Aspectos de la esclavitud en Mallorca durante la edad moderna." *Bolletí de la societat arqueològica lul·liana* 37 (1980): 289–328.

Montojo Montojo, Vicente, ed. *Correspondencia mercantile en el siglo XVII: Las cartas del mercader Felipe Moscoso (1660–1685)*. Murcia: University of Murcia, 2013.

Morgan, Joseph. *A Compleat History of the Present State of War in Africa, between the Spaniards and Algerines: Giving a Full and Exact Account of Oran and Al-Mursa; Compiled from the Best Approved Spanish Writers; the Author's Twenty Years Knowledge of the Country; and from Diverse Late Conferences with Haj Mahammed, the Algerine Envoy and Haj Ali, His Excellency's Secretary, Now Here Resident; with a New Map of the Kingdom of Algiers; and Several Useful Annotations*. London: Printed for W. Mears, at the Lamb in the Old Bailey, 1732.

Pasamonte, Jerónimo de. *Autobiografía*. Ed. Miguel Ángel Bunes Ibarra. Seville: Ediciones Espuela de Plata, 2006.

Pera, Franceso, ed. *Curiosità livornesi inedite o rare*. Livorno: U. Bastogi, 1971.

Pujades, Jeroni. *Dietari de Jeroni Pujades*. Vol. 1, ed. Josep M.a Casas Homs. Barcelona: Fundació Salvador Vives Casajuana, 1975.

Relación de el riguroso martyrio que el padre fr. Ioan de Prado de la provincial de San Diego de Sevilla, que es de frailes descalços Franciscos: Padeció en la ciudad de Marruecos por mano y orden de el rey de la dicha ciudad, la qual relación embió el governador, de Marzagan, a el excelentíssimo señor duque de Medina Sydonia. In *Papeles de mi archivo, Relaciones de África (Marruecos)*. Vol. 2, ed. Ignacio Bauer Landauer. 249–52. Madrid: Editorial Ibero-Africano-Americana, 1922–23.

Relación de la carta que el padre fray Bernardo de Monrroy, administrador general de la redención de cautivos de la orden de la Santissima Trinidad de la provincia de Castilla, embió de Argel al padre provincial de su provincia. Mallorca, 1612.

Relación de la carta que el padre fray Bernardo de Monrroy, administrador general de la redención de cautivos de la orden de la Santissima Trinidad de la provincia de Castilla, embió de Argel al padre provincial de su provincia. Barcelona: Viuda de Dotil, 1613.

Relación de la cruelissima muerte, que en la ciudad de Argel ha padecido el muy reverendo Padre Fr. Francisco Cirano, religioso del orden de nuestro seráfico padre San Francisco. Lima, 1667.

Relación verdadera embiada de la ciudad de Argel, dando cuenta de los alborotos y ruidos, que aquellos barbaros tienen entre sí . . . y el sucesso que ha tenido la redempción de los religiosos de Nuestro Señora de la Merced. Madrid: Iulian de Paredes, 1661.

Saldanha, António de. *Crónica de Almançor, sultão de Marrocos (1578– 1603).* Ed. António Dias Farinha. Lisbon: Instituto de Investigação Científica Tropical, 1997.

San Francisco, Matías de. *Relación del viage espiritual que hizo a Marruecos el beato Juan de Prado, primer provincial de la provincial Franciscana de Andalucía, restaurador de las misiones franciscanas de Marruecos en 1630.* Ed. José López. Tangier: Tipografia Hispano-Arábiga De La Misión Católica, 1945.

Saura Lahoz, Pascual. "Los Franciscanos en Marruecos: Relación inédita de 1685." *Archivo Ibero-Americano* 17 (1921): 79–100.

Silvestre, Francisco Antonio. *Fundacion historica de los hospitales que la religion de la Santissima Trinidad, redempcion de cautivos, de calçados, tiene en la ciudad de Argel. . . . El Maestro Fr. Francisco Antonio Silvestre, administrador general de dichos hospitales.* Madrid: Iulian De Paredes, 1690.

Sosa, Antonio de. *Topography of Algiers* in *"An Early Modern Dialogue with Islam: Antonio de Sosa's Topography of Algiers (1612),"* ed. María Antonia Garcés. Notre Dame, Ind.: University of Notre Dame Press, 2011.

Suárez Montañés, Diego. *Historia del Maestre último que fue de Montesa y de su hermano Don Felipe de Borja: La manera como gobernaron las memorables plazas de Orán y Mazalquivir, Reinos de Tremecén y Ténez, en África.* Ed. Miguel Ángel Bunes Ibarra and Beatriz Alonso Acero. Valencia: Institució Alfons El Magnànim, 2005.

Tamayo y Velarde, José. *Memorias del cautiverio y costumbres, ritos y gobiernos de Berbería, según el relato de un jesuita del siglo XVII.* Ed. Felipe Maíllo Salgado. Oviedo: University of Oviedo, 2017.

Tassy, Laugier de. *Histoire du royaume d'Alger: Avec l'état présent de son gouvernement, de ses forces de terre et de mer, de ses revenus, police, justice, politique et commerce: Un diplomate français à Alger en 1724.* Paris: Loysel, 1992.

Torres, Diego de. *Relación del origen de los xarifes y del estado de los reinos de Marruecos, Fez, y Tarudante.* Ed. Mercedes García Arenal. Madrid: Siglo Veintiuno, 1980.

Vaquer Bennasar, Onofre. *Captius i renegats al segle XVII: Mallorquins captius entre musulmans. Renegats davant la inquisició de Mallorca.* Mallorca: El Tall, 2014.

Vega y Toraya, Francisco de la. *Chrónica de la provincia de Castilla, León y Navarra del Orden de la Santíssima Trinidad*. Madrid: La Imprenta Real, 1720.

Vernet Ginés, Juan. *El rescate del arraez argeli Bibi, prisionero en Mallorca*. Tétouan: Impr. del Majzen, 1952.

Villalón, Cristóbal de, and Fernando G. Salinero, eds. *Viaje de Turquía; (La Odisea De Pedro De Urdemalas)*. Madrid: Cátedra, 1980.

Voulx, A. de, ed. and trans. *Tachrifat, Recueil de notes historiques sur l'administration de l'ancienne régence d'Alger*. Algiers: Impr. du Gouvernement, 1852.

Al-Wansharīsī, Ahmad ibn Yahyā. *La pierre de touche des fétwas de Ahmad al-Wanscharīsī*. In *Archives Marocaines: Publication de la mission scientifique du Maroc*. Vols. 12 and 13, ed. and trans. Émile Amar. Paris: E. Leroux, 1908–9.

SECONDARY SOURCES

Abun-Nasr, Jamil M. *A History of the Maghrib in the Islamic Period*. Cambridge: Cambridge University Press, 1987.

Agapito y Revilla, Juan. *Catálogo de la sección de escultura*. Valladolid: Imp. E. Zapatero, 1916.

Algazi, Gadi. "Diversity Rules: Peregrine Horden and Nicholas Purcell's *The Corrupting Sea*." *Mediterranean Historical Review* 20 (2005): 227–45.

———. "Some Problems with Reciprocity." *Endoxa, Series Filosoficas* 15 (2002): 43–50.

Almeida Mendes, António de. "Musulmans et *mouriscos* du Portugal au XVIe siècle." In *Les musulmans dans l'histoire de l'Europe*. Vol. 1, *Une intégration invisible*, ed. Jocelyne Dakhlia and Bernard Vincent. 143–58. Paris: Albin Michel, 2011.

Alonso Acero, Beatriz. *Orán-Mazalquivir, 1589–1639: Una sociedad española en la frontera de Berbería*. Madrid: Consejo Superior de Investigaciones Científicas, 2000.

———. *Sultanes de Berbería en tierras de la cristiandad: Exilio musulmán, conversión y asimilación en la Monarquía hispánica, siglos XVI–XVII*. Barcelona: Ediciones Bellaterra, 2006.

Alpers, Edward, Gwyn Campbell, and Michael Salman, eds. *Slavery and Resistance in Africa and Asia*. New York: Routledge, 2005.

Álvarez Dopico, Clara Ilham. "The Catholic Consecration of an Islamic House: The St. John de Matha Trinitarian Hospital in Tunis." In *Sacred Precincts: The Religious Architecture of Non-Muslim Communities*

Across the Islamic World, ed. Mohammad Gharipour. 291–307. Leiden: Brill, 2015.

Ambrus, Attila, Eric Chaney, and Igor Salitskiy. "Pirates of the Mediterranean: An Empirical Investigation of Bargaining with Transaction Costs." Economic Research Initiatives at Duke (ERID). Working Paper No. 115. http://scholar.harvard.edu/chaney/publications/pirates-mediterranean-empirical-investigation-bargaining-transaction-costs-o. Accessed January 19, 2016.

Amelang, James. "L'autobiografia popolare nella Spagna moderna: Osservazioni generali e particolari." In *Memoria, famiglia, identità tra Italia ed Europa nell'età moderna*, ed. Giovanni Ciappelli. 113–30. Bologna: Il Mulino, 2009.

———. *Historias paralelas: Judeoconversos y moriscos en la España moderna*. Madrid: Akal, 2012.

———. "The Peculiarities of the Spaniards: Historical Approaches to the Early Modern State." In *Public Power in Europe: Studies in Historical Transformations*, ed. James Amelang and Siegfried Beer. 40–57. Pisa: Pisa University Press, 2006.

Amiran, Rica. "Ceuta en la relación de Diego de Torres." In *España y el mundo Mediterráneo a través de las relaciones de sucesos (1500–1750): Actas del IV coloquio internacional sobre Relaciones de Sucesos (París, 23–25 de septiembre de 2004)*, ed. Pierre Civil, Françoise Crémoux, and Jacobo Sanz. Salamanca: Ediciones Universidad de Salamanca, 2008.

Anaya Hernández, Luis Alberto. *Moros en la costa: Dos siglos de corsarismo berberisco en las islas canarias (1569–1749)*. Las Palmas de Gran Canaria: Gobierno de Canarias, Consejería de Educación, Cultura y Deportes, Dirección General de Universidades e Investigación, 2006.

Andalousies, Jean. "Presencia cristiana en Argelia y Túnez del siglo XII al XIX." In *El cristianismo en el norte de África*, ed. Ramón Lourido Díaz and Henry Teissier. 57–71. Madrid: Fundación MAPFRE, 1993.

Anderson, Benedict. *Imagined Communities: Reflections on the Origins and Spread of Nationalism*. London: Verso, 2006.

Appadurai, Arjun. "Introduction: Commodities and the Politics of Value." In *The Social Life of Things: Commodities in Cultural Perspective*, ed. Arjun Appadurai. 3–63. Cambridge: Cambridge University Press, 1986.

Arribas Palau, Mariano. "De nuevo sobre la embajada de al-Gassani (1690–1691)." *Al-Qantara* 6 (1985): 199–289.

Asad, Talal. "Comments on Conversion." In *Conversion to Modernities: The Globalization of Christianity*, ed. Peter Van der Veer. 263–73. New York: Routledge, 1996.

Austen, Ralph A. "The Mediterranean Islamic Slave Trade out of Africa: A Tentative Census." *Slavery and Abolition* 13 (1992): 214–48.

———. "The Trans-Saharan Slave Trade: A Tentative Census." In *The Uncommon Market: Essays in the Economic History of the Atlantic Slave Trade*, ed. Henry A. Gemery and Jan S. Hogendorn. 23–76. New York: Academic Press, 1979.

Barchino, Matías. Introduction to *Edición crítica de Cautiverio y trabajos de Diego Galán*, ed. Matías Barchino. 11–64. Cuenca: Ediciones de la Universidad de Castilla la Mancha, 2001.

Barrio Gozalo, Maximiliano. "Esclaves musulmans en Espagne au XVIIIe siècle." *Cahiers de la Méditerranée* 87 (2013): 33–48.

———. *Esclavos y cautivos: Conflicto entre la cristiandad y el Islam en el siglo XVIII*. Valladolid: Junta De Castilla y León, Consejería De Cultura y Turismo, 2006.

Beaver, Adam G. "The Renaissance Mediterranean Revisited: Christian Iberia and Muslim Egypt, ca. 1250–1517." In *Mapping the Medieval Mediterranean, ca. 300–1550: An Encyclopedia of Perspectives in Research*, ed. Amity Law. Leiden: Brill, forthcoming.

Belhamissi, Moulay. *Les captifs algériens et l'Europe chrétienne (1518–1830)*. Alger: Enterprise Nationale du Livre, 1988.

Bély, Lucien. "Espions et ambassadeurs à l'époque moderne." In *Ambassadeurs, apprentis espions et maitres comploteurs: Les systèmes de renseignement en Espagne à l'époque moderne*, ed. Béatrice Perez. 21–30. Paris: Presses de l'Université Paris-Sorbonne, 2010.

Ben-Yehoyada, Naor. *The Mediterranean Incarnate: Region Formation Between Tunisia and Sicily Since WWII*. Chicago: University of Chicago Press, 2017.

Benítez, Rafael. "La tramitación del pago de rescates a través del reino de Valencia: El último plazo del rescate de Cervantes." In *Le commerce de captifs: Les intermédiaires dans l'échange et le rachat des prisonniers en Méditerranée, XVe–XVIIIe siècle*, ed. Wolfgang Kaiser. 193–217. Rome: École Française de Rome, 2008.

Bennassar, Bartolomé, and Lucile Bennassar. *Los cristianos de Alá: La fascinante aventura de los renegados*. Madrid: Nerea, 1993.

Benton, Lauren A. *Law and Colonial Cultures: Legal Regimes in World History, 1400–1900*. Studies in Comparative World History. New York: Cambridge University Press, 2002.

Bertrand, Régis. "Les cimetières des 'esclaves turcs' des arsenaux de Marseille et de Toulon au XVIIIe siècle." *Revue des mondes musulmans et de la Méditerranée* 99–100 (2002): 205–17.

Blanes Andrés, Roberto. *Valencia y el Magreb: Las relaciones comerciales marítimas (1600–1703)*. Barcelona: Ediciones Bellaterra, 2010.

Blili, Leîla. "Course et captivité des femmes dans la régence de Tunis aux XVIe et XVIIe siècles." In *Captius i esclaus a l'antiguitat i al món modern: Actes del XIX colloqui internacional del GIREA Organizat Pel Departament de Ciències Històriques i Teoria de les Arts, Universitat de les Illes Balears, Palma de Mollorca, 2–5 Octobre 1991*, ed. María Luisa Sánchez León and Gonçal López Nadal. 259–72. Naples: Jovene, 1996.

Bloch, Édouard. "La peste en Tunisie (aperçu historique et epidémiologique)." PhD diss. Impr. J. Aloccio, 1929.

Blumenthal, Debra. *Enemies and Familiars: Slavery and Mastery in Fifteenth-Century Valencia*. Ithaca, N.Y.: Cornell University Press, 2009.

Bono, Salvatore. *Les corsaires en Méditerranée*. Paris: CNRS éditions, 1999.

———. *Schiavi musulmani nell'Italia moderna: Galeotti, vu' cumprà, domestici*. Naples: Edizioni Scientifiche Italiane, 1999.

———. "Slave Histories and Memoirs in the Mediterranean World: A Study of the Sources (Sixteenth–Eighteenth Centuries)." In *Trade and Cultural Exchange in the Early Modern Mediterranean, Braudel's Maritime Legacy*, ed. Maria Fusaro, Colin Heywood, and Mohamed-Salah Omro. 97–115. London: Tauris Academic Studies, 2010.

Borucki, Alex, David Eltis, and David Wheat. "Atlantic History and the Slave Trade to Spanish America." *American Historical Review* 120 (2015): 433–61.

Bosco, Michele. "Il commercio dei captivi nel Mediterraneo di età moderna (secc. XVI–XVIII): Orientamenti e prospettive attuali di ricerca." *Cromohs* 18 (2013): 57–82.

Boubaker, Sadok. "Réseaux et techniques de rachat des captifs de la course à Tunis au XVII siècle." In *Le commerce des captifs: Les intermédiaires dans l'échange et le rachat des prisonniers en Méditerranée, XVe–XVIIIe siècle*, ed. Wolfgang Kaiser. 25–46. Rome: École Française de Rome, 2008.

Bourdieu, Pierre. "Le langage autorisé: Note sur les conditions sociales de l'efficacité du discours ritual." *Actes de la recherche en sciences sociales* 5–6 (1975): 183–90.

———. *The Logic of Practice*. Stanford, Calif.: Stanford University Press, 1990.

———. "The Sentiment of Honor in Kabyle Society." In *Honour and Shame: The Values of Mediterranean Society*, ed. J. G. Peristiany. 191–241. Chicago: University of Chicago Press, 1966.

Boyer, Pierre. "Espagne et Kouko: Les négociations de 1598 et 1610." *Revue de l'Occident Musulman et de la Méditerranée* 8 (1970): 25–40.

Braudel, Fernand. "Les Espagnols et l'Afrique du Nord." *Revue Africaine* 69 (1928): 184–233, 351–428.

———. *The Mediterranean and the Mediterranean World in the Age of Philip II.* New York: Harper and Row, 1976.

Bravo Caro, Juan Jesús. "El reflejo de la esclavitud del Mediterráneo en los registros parroquiales oraneses." In *Orán: Historia de la corte chica*, ed. Miguel Ángel Bunes Ibarra and Beatriz Alonso Acero. 143–72. Madrid: Ediciones Polifemo, 2011.

Brendecke, Arndt. "Informing the Council: Central Institutions and Local Knowledge in the Spanish Empire." In *Empowering Interactions: Political Cultures and the Emergence of the State in Europe, 1300–1900*, ed. Wim Blockmans, André Holenstein, and Jon Mathieu. 235–52. London: Routledge, 2016.

Broadman, James William. *Ransoming Captives in Crusader Spain: The Order of Merced on the Christian-Islamic Frontier.* Philadelphia: University of Pennsylvania Press, 1986.

Brogini, Anne. "Une activité sous contrôle: L'esclavage à Malte à l'époque moderne." *Cahiers de la Méditerranée* 78 (2013): 49–61.

———. *Malte, frontière de la chrétienté (1530–1670).* Rome: Publications de l'École Française de Rome, 2013.

Bunes Ibarra, Miguel Ángel. "Avis du Levant." In *Ambassadeurs, apprentis espions et maitres comploteurs: Les systèmes de renseignement en Espagne à l'époque moderne*, ed. Béatrice Perez. 223–40. Paris: Presses de l'Université Paris-Sorbonne, 2010.

———. "Felipe III y la defensa del Mediterráneo: La conquista de Argel." In *Guerra y sociedad en la monarquía hispánica: Política, estrategia, y cultura en la Europa moderna (1500–1700).* Vol. 1, ed. Enrique García Hernán and David Maffi. 921–46. Madrid: Laberinto, 2006.

———. *La imagen de los musulmanes y del norte de África en la España de los siglos XVI y XVII: Los caracteres de una hostilidad.* Madrid: Consejo Superior de Investigaciones Científicas, 1989.

Burke, Peter. *The Historical Anthropology of Early Modern Italy: Essays on Perception and Communication.* Cambridge: Cambridge University Press, 1987.

Calafat, Guillaume. "Ottoman North Africa and *Ius Publicum Europaeum*: The Case of the Treaties of Peace and Trade (1600–1750)." In *War, Trade, and Neutrality: Europe and the Mediterranean in the Seventeenth and Eighteenth Century*, ed. Antonella Alimento. 171–87. Milano: FrancoAngeli, 2011.

Calafat, Guillaume, and Cesare Santus. "Les avatars du 'Turc': Esclaves et commerçants musulmans à Livourne (1600–1750)." In *Les musulmans dans l'histoire de l'Europe.* Vol. 1, *Une intégration invisible,* ed. Jocelyne Dakhlia and Bernard Vincent. 471–522. Paris: Albin Michel, 2011.

Camamis, George. *Estudios sobre el cautiverio en el Siglo de Oro.* Madrid: Editorial Gredos, 1977.

Cañeque, Alejandro, "Mártires y discurso martirial en la formación de las fronteras misionales jesuitas." *Relaciones* 145 (2016): 13–61.

Carceles de Gea, Beatriz. "La 'justicia distributiva' en el siglo XVII (Aproximación político-constitucional)." *Chronica Nova* 14 (1984–85): 93–122.

Carpi, Daniel. "The Activities of the Officials of the Sephardic Jewish Congregation in Venice for the Redemption of Captives (1654–1670) [Hebrew]." *Zion* 68 (2003): 175–222.

Carrasco, Raphael. "L'espionnage espagnol du Levant au XVIe siècle d'après la correspondance des agents espagnols en poste à Venise." In *Ambassadeurs, apprentis espions et maitres comploteurs: Les systèmes de renseignement en Espagne à l'époque moderne,* ed. Béatrice Perez. 202–23. Paris: Presses de l'Université Paris-Sorbonne, 2010.

Carro Carbajal, Eva Belén. "España y el mundo mediterráneo: Advocaciones y milagros en las relaciones poéticas de martirios a finales del siglo XVI." In *España y el mundo mediterráneo a través de las relaciones de sucesos: Actas del IV Coloquio Internacional sobre Relaciones de Sucesos: (Paris, 23–25 de septiembre de 2004),* ed. Pierre Civil, Françoise Crémoux, and Jacobo S. Sanz Hermida. 55–67. Salamanca: Ediciones Universidad de Salamanca, 2013.

Casanova y Todolí, Ubaldo de. "Algunas anotaciones sobre el comportamiento de los esclavos moros en Mallorca durante el siglo XVII y un ejemplo de intercambio con cautivos cristianos." *Bolletí de la Societat Arqueològica Lul·liana: Revista d'estudis històrics* 41 (1985): 323–32.

Casey, James. *Early Modern Spain: A Social History.* London: Routledge, 1999.

Castillo Pintado, Alvaro. *Tráfico marítimo y comercio de importación en Valencia a comienzos del siglo XVII.* Madrid: Seminario de Historia Social y Económica de la Facultad de Filosofía y Letras de la Universidad de Madrid, 1967.

Celli, Andrea. "The Early-Modern Invention of 'Abrahamic Religions': An Overview of Baroque Approaches to the Hagar Narrative." In *Legacies, Transfers & Polemics: Interactions Between Judaism, Christianity and Islam from Late Antiquity to the Present.* Ed. Alexander Dubrau, Davide Scotto, and Ruggero Vimercati Sanseverino. Tübingen: Mohr Siebeck, forthcoming.

Chatterjee, Indrani, and Richard M. Eaton, eds. *Slavery and South Asian History.* Bloomington: Indiana University Press, 2006.

Cirac Estopañán, Sebastián. *Los procesos de hechicerías en la Inquisición de Castilla la Nueva.* Madrid: Diana, 1942.

Clancy-Smith, Julia A. *Mediterraneans: North Africa and Europe in an Age of Migration, c. 1800–1900.* Berkeley: University of California Press, 2011.

Coleman, David. *Creating Christian Granada: Society and Religious Culture in an Old World Frontier City, 1492–1600.* Ithaca, N.Y.: Cornell University Press, 2003.

Colley, Linda. *Captives, Britain, Empire and the World, 1600–1850.* New York: Anchor, 2007.

———. *The Ordeal of Elizabeth Marsh: A Woman in World History.* New York: Anchor, 2007.

Colombo, Emanuele. "'Infidels' at Home: Jesuits and Muslim Slaves in Seventeenth-Century Naples and Spain." *Journal of Jesuit Studies* 1 (2014): 192–211.

———. "A Muslim Turned Jesuit: Baldassarre Loyola Mandes (1631–1667)." *Journal of Early Modern History* 17 (2013): 479–504.

Conrad, Sebastian. *What Is Global History?* Princeton, N.J.: Princeton University Press, 2017.

Cooper, Frederick. "The Problem of Slavery in African Studies." *Journal of African History in Africa* 20 (1979): 103–25.

Cour, Auguste. *L'Établissement des dynasties des Chérifs au Maroc et leur rivalité avec les Turcs de la régence d'Álger 1509–1830.* Paris: Bouchene, 2004.

Court, Ricardo. "'Januensis Ergo Mercator': Trust and Enforcement in the Business Correspondence of the Brignole Family." *Sixteenth Century Journal* 35 (2004): 987–1003.

Dadson, Trevor J. *Los moriscos de Villarrubia de los Ojos (Siglos XV–XVIII).* Madrid: Iberamericana Editorial, 2007.

Dakhlia, Jocelyne. "Défenses et stratégies d'une captive hollandaise au Maroc: Un témoignage transgressif?" *Le lien social revisité: Etudes et travaux de l'école doctorale de Toulouse-Le Mirail,* special volume edited by Natividad Planas, 8 (2006): 19–26.

———. "Ligne de fuite: Impostures et reconstructions identitaires en Méditerranée musulmane à l'époque modern." In *Gens de passage en Méditerranée de l'Antiquité à l'époque modern: Procédures de contrôle et d'identification. L'atelier Méditerranée,* ed. Wolfgang Kaiser and Claudia Moatti. 427–58. Paris: Maisonneuve et Larose, 2007.

———. "Lingua Franca: A Non Memory." In *Remembering Africa,* ed. E. Mudimbe-Boyi. 234–44. Portsmouth: Heinemann, 2002.

———. *Lingua franca: Histoire d'une langue métisse en Méditerranée.* Arles: Actes Sud, 2008.

———. "Turcs de profession? Réinscriptions lignagères et redéfinitions sexuelles des convertis dans les cours maghrébines (XVIe–XIXe siècles)." In *Conversions islamiques: Identités religieuses en Islam méditerranéen,* ed. Mercedes García Arenal. 151–71. Paris: Maisonneuve et Larose, 2002.

Dakhlia, Jocelyne, and Vincent Bernard, eds. *Les musulmans dans l'histoire de l'Europe.* Vol. 1, *Une intégration invisible.* Paris: Albin Michel, 2011.

Dakhlia, Jocelyne, and Wolfgang Kaiser, eds. *Les musulmans dans l'histoire de l'Europe.* Vol. 2, *Passages et contacts en Méditerranée.* Paris: Albin Michel, 2013.

Dauverd, Céline. *Imperial Ambition in the Early Modern Mediterranean: Genoese Merchants and the Spanish Crown.* New York: Cambridge University Press, 2015.

Dávid, Géza, and Pál Fodor, eds. *Ransom Slavery Along the Ottoman Borders (Early Fifteenth–Early Eighteenth Centuries).* Leiden: Brill, 2007.

Davis, Robert. *Christian Slaves, Muslim Masters: White Slavery in the Mediterranean, the Barbary Coast, and Italy, 1500–1800.* Houndmills, Basingstoke, Hampshire: Palgrave Macmillan, 2003.

———. "Counting European Slaves on the Barbary Coast." *Past and Present* 172 (2001): 87–124.

Dedieu, Jean-Pierre. "The Archives of the Holy Office of Toledo as a Source for Historical Anthropology." In *The Inquisition in Early Modern Europe: Studies on Sources and Methods,* ed. Gustav Henningsen, John A. Tedeschi, and Charles Amiel. 158–89. Dekalb: Northern Illinois University Press, 1986.

Díaz Borrás, Andrés. *El miedo al Mediterráneo: La caridad popular valenciana y la redención de cautivos bajo poder musulmán 1323–1539.* Barcelona: Consejo Superior de Investigaciones Científicas, Institución Milá y Fontanals, Departamento de Estudios Medievales, 2001.

Ditchfield, Simon. "How Not to Be a Counter-Reformation Saint: The Attempted Canonization of Pope Gregory X, 1622–45." *Papers of the British School at Rome* 60 (1992): 379–422.

Dooley, Brendan Maurice. Introduction to *The Dissemination of News and the Emergence of Contemporaneity in Early Modern Europe,* ed. Brendan Maurice Dooley. 1–19. Burlington, Vt.: Ashgate, 2010.

Dursteler, Eric. "Speaking in Tongues: Language and Communication in the Early Modern Mediterranean." *Past and Present* 217 (2012): 47–77.

———. "Where Is Cigala? Rumor, Report and the Flow of Information in the Late Sixteenth-Century Mediterranean." Paper presented at the International Workshop "The Informational Fabric of the Premodern Mediterranean, 1400–1800." 14th Mediterranean Research Meeting, European University Institute, Mersin, Turkey, March 2013.

Elkins, Caroline, and Susan Pederson. Introduction to *Settler Colonialism in the Twentieth Century: Projects, Practices, Legacies*, ed. Caroline Elkins and Susan Pederson. New York: Routledge, 2005.

Elliott, John. *Richelieu and Olivares*. Cambridge: Cambridge University Press, 1984.

Epalza, Miguel de. "Moriscos y Andalusíes en Túnez durante el siglo XVII." *Al-Andalus* 34, no. 2 (1969): 247–327.

Erdem, Y. Hakan. *Slavery in the Ottoman Empire and Its Demise, 1800–1909*. Basingstoke, Hampshire: Palgrave, 2001.

Eyal, Gil. *The Disenchantment of the Orient: Expertise in Arab Affairs and the Israeli State*. Stanford, Calif.: Stanford University Press, 2006.

Fé Cantó, Luis Fernando. "El corso magrebí en España en los años centrales del siglo XVIII." *Clio and Crimen* 11 (2004): 209–26.

———. "La población de Orán en siglo XVIII, y el fenomeno de la deserción: Las sombras del discurso oficial." In *Orán: Historia de la corte chica*, ed. Miguel Ángel Bunes Ibarra and Beatriz Alonso Acero. 369–99. Madrid: Ediciones Polifemo, 2011.

Fernández, Enrique. "El cuerpo torturado en los testimonies de los corsarios berberiscos (1500–1700)." *Hispanic Review* 71 (2003): 51–66.

Feros, Antonio. *El Duque de Lerma, realeza y privanza en la España de Felipe III*. Madrid: Marcial Pons, 2002.

Ferrer i Mallol, María Teresa. "La redempció de captius a la corona catalano-aragonesa (segle XIV)." *Anuario de estudios medievales* 15 (1985): 237–97.

Finley, M. I. *Ancient Slavery and Modern Ideology*. New York: Viking Press, 1980.

Fiume, Giovanna. "Lettres de Barbarie: Esclavage et rachat de captifs siciliens (XVIe–XVIIIe siècle)." *Cahiers de la Méditerranée* 87 (2013): 229–54.

———. *Schiavitù mediterranee: Corsari, rinnegati e santi di età moderna*. Milan: Bruno Mondadori, 2009.

Fontenay, Michel. "L'esclave galérien dans la Méditerranée des temps modernes." In *Figures de l'esclave au Moyen-âge et dans le monde moderne: Actes de la table ronde organisée les 27 et 28 octobre 1992 par le Centre d'Histoire Sociale et Culturelle de l'Occident de l'Université de Paris-X Nanterre*, ed. Henri Bresc. 115–43. Paris: L'Harmattan, 1996.

———. "Esclaves et/ou captifs: Préciser les concepts." In *Le commerce des captifs: Les intermédiaires dans l'échange et le rachat des prisonniers en Méditerranée, XVe–XVIIIe siècle*, ed. Wolfgang Kaiser. 15–24. Rome: École Française de Rome, 2008.

————. "Il mercato maltese degli schiavi al tempo dei Cavalieri di San Giovanni (1530–1798)." *Quaderni Storici* 107 (2001): 391–413.

Foyster, Elizabeth. "Prisoners Writing Home: The Functions of Their Letters c. 1680–1800." *Journal of Social History* 47 (2014): 943–67.

Friedman, Ellen G. *Spanish Captives in North Africa in the Early Modern Age*. Madison: University of Wisconsin Press, 1983.

————. "Trinitarian Hospitals in Algiers: An Early Example of Healthcare for Prisoners of War." *Catholic Historical Review* 66 (1980): 551–64.

Friedman, Yvonne. *Encounter Between Enemies: Captivity and Ransom in the Latin Kingdom of Jerusalem*. Leiden: Brill, 2002.

Fusaro, Maria. "After Braudel: A Reassessment of Mediterranean History Between the Northern Invasion and the Caravane Maritime." In *Trade and Cultural Exchange in the Early Modern Mediterranean, Braudel's Maritime Legacy*, ed. Maria Fusaro, Colin Heywood, and Mohamed-Salah Omro. 1–22. London: Tauris Academic Studies, 2010.

Garcés, María Antonia. *Cervantes en Argel: Historia de un cautivo*. Madrid: Gredos, 2005.

————. Introduction to *An Early Modern Dialogue with Islam: Antonio de Sosa's Topography of Algiers (1612)*, ed. María Antonia Garcés. 1–78. Notre Dame, Ind.: University of Notre Dame Press, 2011.

Garcés Ferrá, Bartolomé. "Propuesta de armada contra los piratas berberiscos entre Holanda y España a mediados del siglo XVII." *Hispania* 8, no. 32 (1948): 403–33.

García Arenal, Mercedes. *Ahmad al-Mansur: The Beginning of Modern Morocco*. New York: Oneworld Publications, 2012.

————. Introduction to Diego de Torres, *Relación del origen de los xarifes y del estado de los reinos de Marruecos, Fez, y Tarudante*, ed. Mercedes García Arenal. Madrid: Siglo Veintiuno, 1980.

————. "Spanish Literature on North Africa in the XVI Century: Diego de Torres." *Maghreb Review* 8, no. 1–2 (1983): 53–59.

García Arenal, Mercedes, and Fernando Rodríguez Mediano. *The Orient in Spain: Converted Muslims, the Forged Lead Books of Granada, and the Rise of Orientalism*. Leiden: Brill, 2013.

García Arenal, Mercedes, and Gerard Wiegers. Introduction to *Los moriscos: Expulsión y diaspora*, ed. Mercedes García Arenal and Gerard Wiegers. 11–24. Valencia: University of Valencia, 2013.

García Figueras, Tomás, and Carlos Rodríguez Joulia Saint-Cyr. *Larache: Datos para su historia en el siglo XVII*. Madrid: Instituto de Estudios Africanos, CSIC, 1973.

Garrido García, Carlos Javier. "La esclavitud en el reino de Granada en el último tercio del siglo XVI: El caso de Guadix y su tierra." PhD diss., University of Granada, 2011.

Gerber, Haim. *State, Society, and Law in Islam: Ottoman Law in Comparative Perspective.* Albany: State University of New York Press, 1994.

Gilbert, Claire. "A Grammar of Conquest: The Spanish and Arabic Reorganization of Granada After 1492. " *Past and Present* (2018).

Gluckman, Max. "Gossip and Scandal." *Current Anthropology* 4 (1963): 307–16.

Gonzales-Raymond, Anita. "Le rachat des chrétiens en terres d'Islam: De la charité chrétienne à la raison d'état: Les éléments d'une controverse autour des années 1620." In *Chrétiens et musulmans à la Renaissance, Actes du 37e colloque international de CESR, 1994,* ed. Bartolomé Bennassar and Robert Sauzet. 371–89. Paris: H. Champion, 1998.

González de Amezúa, Agustín. "Prólogo." In Luis del Mármol Carvajal, *Descripción general de África,* ed. Agustín González de Amezúa. Madrid: CSIC, 1953.

Gourdin, Philippe. *Tabarka (15–18. siècle): Histoire et archéologie d'un préside espagnol et d'un comptoir génois en terre africaine.* 538–43. Rome: École Française de Rome, 2008.

Graf, Tobias P. *The Sultan's Renegades: Christian-European Converts to Islam and the Making of the Ottoman Elite, 1575–1610.* Oxford: Oxford University Press, 2017.

Grafe, Regina. *Distant Tyranny: Markets, Power and Backwardness in Spain, 1650–1800.* Princeton, N.J.: Princeton University Press, 2012.

Graullera Sanz, Vicente. "La esclavitud en Valencia en los siglos XVI y XVII (causas de caída en cautiverio)." In *Primer Congreso de historia del país valenciano, celebrado en Valencia del 14 al 18 de abril de 1971.* 3:239–50. Valencia: University of Valencia, 1976.

Greene, Molly. "Beyond the Northern Invasion: The Mediterranean in the 17th Century." *Past and Present* 174 (2002): 42–71.

———. *Catholic Pirates and Greek Merchants: A Maritime History of the Mediterranean.* Princeton, N.J.: Princeton University Press, 2010.

———. "The Early Modern Mediterranean." In *A Companion to Mediterranean History,* ed. Peregrine Horden and Sharon Kinoshita. 91–106. West Sussex: Wiley Blackwell, 2014.

———. "The Ottomans in the Mediterranean." In *The Early Modern Ottoman Empire: A Reinterpretation,* ed. V. Aksan and D. Goffman. 104–16. Cambridge: Cambridge University Press, 2007.

Gregori Roig, Rosa María. "Representación pública del individuo: Relaciones de méritos y servicios en el Archivo General de Indias, siglos XVII–XVIII." In *El legado de Mnemosyne: Las escrituras del yo a través del tiempo*, ed. A. Castillo Gómez and V. Sierra Blas. 355–79. Gijón: Trea, 2007.

Gürkan, Emrah Safa. "The Efficacy of Ottoman Counter-Intelligence in the 16th Century." *Acta Orientalia Academiae Scientiarum Hungaricae* 65 (2012): 1–38.

———. "Espionage in the 16th Century Mediterranean: Secret Diplomacy, Mediterranean Go-Betweens and the Ottoman Habsburg Rivalry." PhD diss., Georgetown University, 2012.

———. "Fooling the Sultan: Information, Decision-Making and the 'Mediterranean Faction' (1585–1587)." *Journal of Ottoman Studies* 45 (2015): 57–96.

Halevi, Leor. "Religion and Cross-Cultural Trade: A Framework for Interdisciplinary Inquiry." In *Religion and Trade: Cross-Cultural Exchanges in World History, 1000–1900*, ed. Francesca Trivellato, Leor Halevi, and Cátia Antunes. 24–61. Oxford: Oxford University Press, 2014.

Harris, A. Katie. "Gift, Sale, and Theft: Juan de Ribera and the Sacred Economy of Relics in the Early Modern Mediterranean." *Journal of Early Modern History* 18 (2014): 193–226.

Harvey, L. P. *Muslims in Spain, 1500 to 1614*. Chicago: University of Chicago Press, 2005.

Hasnaoui, Milouda. "La ley Islámica y el rescate de los cautivos según las fetwas de al-Wanšarīsī e Ibn Tarkā." In *La liberazione dei "captivi" tra Cristianità e Islam: Oltre la crociata el il ǧihās: Tolleranza e servizio umanitario*, ed. Giulio Cipollone. 549–58. Vatican: Archivio Segreto Vaticano, 2000.

Heinsen-Roach, Erica. "Consuls-of-State and the Redemption of Slaves: The Dutch Republic and the Western Mediterranean, 1616–1651." *Itinerario* 39 (2015): 69–90.

Henia, Abdelhamid. "Archives ottomans en Tunisie et historire régionale." In *Les Ottomans au Maghreb à travers les archives locales et méditerranéennes*, ed. Abdelhamid Henia, Abderrahman el Moudden, and Abderrahim Benhadda. 241–55. Rabat: Jāmiʿat Muḥammad al-Khāmis, Kullīyat al-Ādāb wa-al-ʿUlūm al-Insānīyah, 2005.

Herrero Sánchez, Manuel. "La república de Génova y la monarquía hispánica (siglos XVI–XVII)." *Hispania* 65, no. 219 (2005): 9–20.

Hershenzon, Daniel. "'[P]ara que me saque cabesa por cabesa . . .': Exchanging Muslim and Christian Slaves Across the Mediterranean." *African Economic History* 42 (2014): 11–36.

———. "Plaintes et menaces réciproques: Captivité et violence religieuses dans la Méditerranée du XVIIe siècle." In *Les musulmans dans l'histoire de l'Europe*. Vol. 2, *Passages et contacts en Méditerranée*, ed. Jocelyne Dakhlia and Wolfgang Kaiser. 441–60. Paris: Albin Michel, 2013.

———. "The Political Economy of Ransom in the Early Modern Mediterranean." *Past and Present* 231 (2016): 61–95.

———. "Las redes de confianza y crédito en el Mediterráneo occidental: Cautiverio y rescate, 1580–1670." In *Les Esclavages en Méditerranée: Espaces et dynamiques économiques*, ed. Fabiana Guillén and Salah Trabelsi. Madrid: Casa de Velázquez, 2012.

———. "Towards a Connected History of Bondage in the Mediterranean: Recent Trends in the Field." *History Compass* 15 (2017): 1–13.

Herzog, Tamar. *Defining Nations: Immigrants and Citizens in Early Modern Spain and Spanish America*. New Haven, Conn.: Yale University Press, 2003.

Hess, Andrew C. "The Battle of Lepanto and Its Place in Mediterranean History." *Past and Present* 57 (1972): 53–73.

———. *The Forgotten Frontier: A History of the Sixteenth Century Ibero-African Frontier*. Chicago: University of Chicago Press, 1978.

———. "The Moriscos: An Ottoman Fifth Column in Sixteenth Century Spain." *American Historical Review* 74 (1968): 125.

Hoexter, Miriam. *Endowments, Rulers and Community: Waqf al Haramayn in Ottoman Algiers*. Leiden: Brill, 1998.

Horden, Peregrine, and Nicholas Purcell. *The Corrupting Sea: A Study of Mediterranean History*. Oxford: Blackwell, 2000.

Horodowich, Elizabeth. "The Gossiping Tongue: Oral Networks, Public Life and Political Culture in Early Modern Venice." *Renaissance Studies* 19 (2005): 22–45.

Hsia, R. Po-Chia. *The World of Catholic Renewal, 1540–1770*. New York: Cambridge University Press, 2005.

İnalcık, Halil. "Servile Labor in the Ottoman Empire." In *The Mutual Effects of the Islamic and Judeo-Christian Worlds: The East European Pattern*, ed. Abraham Ascher, Tibor Halasi-Kun, and Béla K. Király. 25–52. Lanham, Md.: University Press of America, 1986.

Israel, Jonathan. "The Jews of Spanish North Africa, 1600–1669." *Transactions of the Jewish Historical Society of England* 26 (1979): 71–86.

Jal, Augustin. *Glossaire nautique: Répertoire polyglotte de termes de marine anciens et modernes*. Paris: Chez Firmin Didot Fréres, Libraires-Editeurs, Imprimeurs de l'Institut de France, 1848.

Jerolmack, Colin, and Iddo Tavori. "Molds and Totems: Nonhumans and the Constitution of the Social Self." *Sociological Theory* 32 (2014): 64–77.

Johnson, Walter. *Soul by Soul: Life Inside the Antebellum Slave Market*. Cambridge, Mass.: Harvard University Press, 1999.

Joulia Saint-Cyr, Carlos Rodriguez. *Felipe III y El rey de Cuco.* Madrid: Instituto de Estudios Africanos, 1953.

Kaiser, Wolfgang, ed. *Le commerce des captifs: Les intermédiaires dans l'échange et le rachat des prisonniers en Méditerranée, XVe–XVIIIe siècle.* Rome: École Française de Rome, 2008.

———. "L'Économie de la rançon en Méditerranée occidentale (XVIe–XVIIe siècle)." *Hyphothèses* 10, no. 1 (2007): 359–68.

———. "La excepción permanente: Actores, visibilidad y asimetrías en los intercambios comerciales entre los países europeos y el Magreb (siglos XVI–XVII)." In *Circulación de personas e intercambios en el Mediterráneo y en el Atlántico (siglos XVI, XVII, XVIII)*, ed. José Antonio Martínez Torres. 171–89. Madrid: Consejo Superior de Investigaciones Científicas, 2008.

———. "Les mots du rachat: D'Action et rhétorique dans les procédures de rachat de captifs en Méditerranéen, XVIe–XVIIe siècles." In *Captifs en Méditerranée (XVIe–XVIIIe siècles): Histoires, récits, et légendes*, ed. François Moureau. 103–17. Paris: PUPS, 2008.

Kaiser, Wolfgang, and Guillaume Calafat. "The Economy of Ransoming in the Early Modern Mediterranean: A Form of Cross-Cultural Trade Between Southern Europe and the Maghreb (Sixteenth to Eighteenth Centuries)." In *Religion and Trade: Cross-Cultural Exchanges in World History, 1000–1900*, ed. Francesca Trivellato, Leor Halevi, and Catia Antunes. 108–30. Oxford: Oxford University Press, 2014.

Keane, Webb. "From Fetishism to Sincerity: Agency, the Speaking Subject, and Their Historicity in the Context of Religious Conversion." *Comparative Studies in Society and History* 39 (1997): 674–93.

Khiari, Farid. *Vivre et mourir en Alger, L'Algérie Ottomane aux XVIe–XVIIe siècles: Un destin confisqué.* Paris: L'Harmattan, 2002.

Kimmel, Seth. *Parables of Coercion: Conversion and Knowledge at the End of Islamic Spain.* Chicago: University of Chicago Press, 2015.

Kirk, Thomas Allison. *Genoa and the Sea: Policy and Power in an Early Modern Maritime Republic, 1559–1684.* Baltimore: Johns Hopkins University Press, 2005.

Kitlas, Peter. "Al-Miknāsī's Mediterranean Mission: Negotiating Moroccan Temporal and Spiritual Sovereignty in the Late Eighteenth Century." *Mediterranean Studies* 23 (2015): 170–94.

Kopytoff, Igor. "The Cultural Biography of Things: Commoditization as Process." In *The Social Life of Things: Commodities in Cultural Perspective*, ed. Arjun Appadurai. 64–94. Cambridge: Cambridge University Press, 1986.

Kopytoff, Igor, and Suzanne Miers, eds. *Slavery in Africa: Historical and*

Anthropological Perspectives. Madison: University of Wisconsin Press, 1977.

Krstic, Tijana. "Illuminated by the Light of Islam and the Glory of the Ottoman Sultanate: Self-Narratives of Conversion to Islam in the Age of Confessionalization." *Comparative Studies in Society and History* 51 (2009): 35–63.

Laborie, Jean-Claude. "Les ordres rédempteurs et l'instrumentalisation du récit de captivité: L'exemple des trinitaires entre 1630 et 1650." In *Captifs en Méditerranée (XVIe–XVIIIe siècles): Histoires, récits, et légendes*, ed. François Moureau. 93–102. Paris: Presses de l'Université Paris-Sorbonne, 2008.

Lane, Frederic C. "Family Partnerships and Joint Ventures in the Venetian Republic." *Journal of Economic History* 4 (1944): 178–96.

Lapeyre, Henry. "Du Nouveau sur Simon Danzer." In *Miscellanea offerts à Charles Verlinden à l'occasion de ses trente ans de professorat: Miscellanea Aangeboden aan Charles Verlinden ter Gelegenheid van Zijn Dertig Jaar Professoraat*. 335–40. Gent, 1975.

Lewis, Bernard. *Race and Slavery in the Middle East: An Historical Enquiry.* New York: Oxford University Press, 1990.

Lo Basso, Luca. "Schiavi, forzati e buonevoglie: La gestione dei rematori delle galere dell'Ordine di Santo Stefano e della Repubblica di Venezia Modelli a confronto." In *L'Ordine di Santo Stefano e il mare*. 169–232. Pisa: ETS, 2001.

Loualich, Fatiha. "Emancipated Female Slaves in Algiers: Marriage, Property, and Social Advancement in the Seventeenth and Eighteenth Centuries." In *Subalterns and Social Protest: History from Below in the Middle East and North Africa*, ed. Stephanie Cronin. 200–209. New York: Routledge, 2012.

———. "In the Regency of Algiers: The Human Side of the Algerine Corso." In *Trade and Cultural Exchange in the Early Modern Mediterranean, Braudel's Maritime Legacy*, ed. Maria Fusaro, Colin Heywood, and Mohamed-Salah Omro. 69–96. London: Tauris Academic Studies, 2010.

Lovejoy, Paul. "The Volume of the Atlantic Slave Trade: A Synthesis." *Journal of African History* 23 (1982): 494–500.

Lynch, John. "Philip II and the Papacy." *Transactions of the Royal Historical Society* 11 (1961): 24.

Mallette, Karla. "Lingua Franca." In *A Companion to Mediterranean History*, ed. Sharon Kinoshita and Peregrine Horden. 330–44. Chichester: Wiley Blackwell, 2014.

Manca, Ciro. *Il modello di sviluppo economico delle città marittime barbaresche dopo Lepanto*. Napoli: Gianinin, 1982.

Mantran, R. "North Africa in the Sixteenth and Seventeenth Centuries." In *The Cambridge History of Islam*. Vol. 2A, ed. P. M. Holt, Ann K. S. Lambton, and Bernard Lewis. 254–55. Cambridge: Cambridge University Press, 1977.

Martín Casares, Aurelia. "Esclavage et rapports sociaux de sexe: Contribution méthodologique." *Cahiers des Anneux de la Mémoire* 5 (2003): 83–99.

———. *La esclavitud en la Granada del siglo XVI: Género, raza y religión*. Granada: Editorial Universidad de Granada, Campus Universitario de Cartuja, 2000.

———. "Evolution of the Origin of Slaves Sold in Spain from the Late Middle Ages till the 18th Century." In *Schiavitù e servaggio nell'economia europea, secc. XI–XVIII: Atti della "Quarantacinquesima Settimana di studi," 14–18 aprile 2013*, ed. Simonetta Cavaciocchi. 409–30. Florence: Florence University Press, 2014.

———. "Maghrebian Slaves in Spain: Human Trafficking and Insecurity in the Early Modern Western Mediterranean." In *Mediterranean Slavery Revisited, 500–1800/Neue Perspektiven auf mediterraner Sklaverei, 500–1800*, ed. S. Hanß and J. Schiel. 97–117. Zurich: Chronos Verlag, 2014.

Martín Corrales, Eloy. *Comercio de Cataluña con el Mediterráneo musulmán (siglos XVI–XVIII): El Comercio con los "enemigos de la fe."* Barcelona: Ediciones Bellaterra, 2001.

Martínez-Góngora, Mar. "El discurso africanista del Renacimiento en *La primera parte de la descripción general de África* de Luis del Mármol Carvajal." *Hispanic Review* 77 (2009): 171–95.

———. *Los espacios coloniales en las crónicas de Berbería*. Madrid: Iberoamericana, 2013.

Martínez Torres, José Antonio. *Prisioneros de los infieles: Vida y rescate de los cautivos cristianos en el Mediterráneo musulmán (siglos XVI–XVII)*. Barcelona: Edicions Bellaterra, 2004.

Matar, Nabil I. *Britain and Barbary, 1589–1689*. Gainesville: University Press of Florida, 2005.

———. "English Accounts of Captivity in North Africa and the Middle East: 1577–1625." *Renaissance Quarterly* 54, no. 2 (2001): 553–72.

———. "Piracy and Captivity in the Early Modern Mediterranean: The Perspective from Barbary." In *Pirates? The Politics of Plunder, 1550–1650*, ed. Claire Jowett. 56–73. Basingstoke: Palgrave Macmillan, 2007.

Maziane, Leïla. *Salé et ses corsairs (1666–1727): Un port de course marocain au XVIIe siècle*. Caen: Presses Universitaires de Caen, 2007.

McCormick, Michael. *Origins of the European Economy: Communication and Commerce, AD 300–900.* Cambridge: Cambridge University Press, 2002.

Melvin, Karen. "Charity Without Borders: Alms-Giving in New Spain for Captives in North Africa." *Colonial Latin American Review* 18 (2009): 75–97.

Merouche, Lemnouar. *Recherches sur l'Algérie à l'époque ottoman.* Vol. 1, *Monnaies, prix et revenus, 1520–1830.* Paris: Bouchene, 2002.

———. *Recherches sur l'Algérie à l'époque ottoman.* Vol. 2, *La course, mythes et réalité.* Paris: Bouchene, 2007.

Miège, Jean-Louis. "Consuls et négociants à Tétouan, 1681–1727." In *Titwan hilal al-qarnayn 16 wa-17: Àmal Nadwat Titwan Hilal al-Qarnayn 16 wa-17: 9, 10, 11 mars 1995.* Titwan: Kulliyat al-Adab wa-l-Ulum al-Insaniya: Al-Magmùa al-Hadariya li-Madinat Titwan, 1996.

Miège, Jean-Louis, M'hammad Benaboud, and Nadia Erzini. *Tétouan: Ville andalouse marocaine.* Paris: CNRS Editions, 1996.

Miller, Kathryn A. "Reflections on Reciprocity: A Late Medieval Islamic Perspective on Christian-Muslim Commitment to Captive Exchange." In *Religion and Trade: Cross-Cultural Exchanges in World History, 1500–1900,* ed. Francesca Trivellato, Leor Halevi, and Catia Antunes. 131–49. Oxford: Oxford University Press, 2014.

Miller, Peter N. *Peiresc's Mediterranean World.* Cambridge, Mass.: Harvard University Press, 2015.

Miller, William Ian. *Bloodtaking and Peacemaking: Feud, Law, and Society in Saga Iceland.* Chicago: University of Chicago Press, 1990.

———. "Threat." In *Feud, Violence and Practice: Essays in Medieval Studies in Honor of Stephen D. White,* ed. Belle S. Tuten and Tracey L. Billado. 9–27. Farnham, Surrey: Ashgate, 2010.

Morieux, Renaud. "Diplomacy from Below and Belonging: Fishermen and Cross-Channel Relations in the Eighteenth Century." *Past and Present* 202 (2009): 83–125.

Moudden, Abderrahmane El. "Sharifs and Padishahs: Moroccan-Ottoman Relations from the Sixteenth Through the Eighteenth Centuries: Contribution to the Study of a Diplomatic Culture." PhD diss., Princeton University, 1992.

Nadalo, Stephanie. "Negotiating Slavery in a Tolerant Frontier: Livorno's Turkish *Bagno* (1547–1747)." *Mediavalia* 32 (2011): 275–324.

Olds, Katrina B. "The Ambiguities of the Holy: Authenticating Relics in Seventeenth-Century Spain." *Renaissance Quarterly* 65 (2012): 135–84.

Oliver Asín, Jaime. "La Hija de Agi Morato en la obra de Cervantes." *Boletín de la Real Academia Española* 27 (1947–48): 245–339.

Oualdi, M'hamed. "D'Europe et d'Orient, les approches de l'esclavage des chrétiens en terres d'Islam." *Annales. Histoires et sciences sociales* 4 (2008): 829–43.

Oumelbanine, Zhiri. "Leo Africanus, Translated and Betrayed." In *The Politics of Translation in the Middle Ages and the Renaissance*, ed. Renate Blumenfeld-Kosinski, Luise von Flotow, and Daniel Russell. 161–74. Ottawa: University of Ottawa Press, 2001.

Panzac, Daniel. *Barbary Corsairs: The End of a Legend, 1800–1820.* Leiden: Brill, 2005.

Paris, E. *La genèse intellectuelle de l'œuvre de Fernand Braudel: La Méditerranée et le Monde Méditerranée à l'époque de Philippe II (1923–1947).* Athens: Fides, 2002.

Parreño, José María. "Experiencia y literatura en la obra de Antonio de Sosa." In Antonio de Sosa, *Diálogo de los mártires de Argel*, ed. Emilio Sola. 9–23. Madrid: Hiperión, 1990.

Patterson, Orlando. *Slavery and Social Death: A Comparative Study.* Cambridge, Mass.: Harvard University Press, 1982.

Petitjean, Johann. *L'Intelligence des choses: Une histoire de l'information entre Italie et Méditerranée (XVIe–XVIIe siècles).* Rome: École Française de Rome, 2013.

Phillips, William D. *Slavery in Medieval and Early Modern Iberia.* Philadelphia: University of Pennsylvania Press, 2014.

Pirenne, Henri. *Mohammed and Charlemagne.* London: Unwin University Books, 1968.

Planas, Natividad. "Conflicts de competence aux frontiers: Le contrôle de la circulation des hommes et des marchandises dans le royaume de Majorque au XVIIe siècle." *Cromohs* 8 (2003): 1–14.

———. "Diplomacy from Below or Cross-Confessional Loyalty? The 'Christians of Algiers' Between the Lord of Kuko and the King of Spain in the Early 1600s." *Journal of Early Modern History* 19 (2015): 153–73.

———. "La frontière franchissable: Normes et pratiques dans les échanges entre le royaume de Majorque et les terres d'Islam au XVIIe siècle." *Revue d'histoire moderne et contemporaine* 48, no. 2 (2001): 123–47.

———. "Musulmans invisibles? Enquête dans les territoires insulaires du roi d'Espagne (XVIe–XVIIe siècle)." In *Les musulmans dans l'histoire de l'Europe.* Vol. 1, *Une intégration invisible*, ed. Jocelyne Dakhlia and Bernard Vincent. 558–92. Paris: Albin Michel, 2011.

———. "Pratiques de pouvoir au sein d'une société frontalière: Le voisinage du Royaume de Majorque et ses îles adjacentes avec les terres d'Islam au XVIIe siècle." PhD diss., European University Institute, 2000.

Po-Chia Hsia, R. *The World of Catholic Renewal, 1540–1770.* New York: Cambridge University Press, 2005.

Polanyi, Karl. "The Economy as Instituted Process." In *Trade and Market in the Early Empires: Economies in History and Theory*, ed. Karl Polanyi, Conard M. Arensberg, and Harry W. Pearson. 243–70. Chicago: Henry Regnery, 1971.

Porres Alonso, Bonifacio. *Libertad a los cautivos: Actividad redentora de la Orden Trinitaria*. Córdoba: Secretariado Trinitario, 1997.

———. *Testigos de Cristo en Argel: Bernardo de Monroy, Juan del Águila, and Juan de Palacios, Trinitarios*. Córdoba: Secretariado Trinitario, 1994.

Poska, Alyson M. "When Bigamy Is the Charge: Gallegan Women and the Holy Office." In *Women in the Inquisition: Spain and the New World*, ed. Mary E. Giles. 189–208. Baltimore: Johns Hopkins University Press, 1999.

Prieto Bernabé, José Manuel. *Lectura y lectores, la lectura del impreso en el Madrid del Siglo de Oro (1550–1650)*. Vol. 2. Mérida: Junta de Extremadura, 2004.

Pryor, John H. *Geography, Technology, and War-Studies in the Maritime History of the Mediterranean, 649–1571*. Cambridge: Cambridge University Press, 1988.

Pulido Bueno, Ildefonso. *Guerra y riqueza en Berbería: La corona española y sus posesiones de Maçal-Arez y Tabarka cedidas en enfiteusis al linaje Lomellini (1540–1742): De solución a problema para la hacienda real*. Huelva: Ildefonso Pulido Bueno, 2015.

Rivero Rodríguez, Manuel. *La batalla de Lepanto: Cruzada, guerra santa e identidad confesional*. Madrid: Sílex, 2008.

Rodriguez, Jarbel. *Captives and Their Saviors in the Medieval Crown of Aragon*. Washington, D.C.: Catholic University of America Press, 2007.

Rodríguez Mediano, Fernando. "Les conversions de Sebastião Pes de Vega, un Portugais au Maroc sa'dien." In *Conversions islamiques: Identités religieuses en Islam méditerranéen*, ed. Mercedes García Arenal. 173–92. Paris: Maisonneuve et Larose, 2002.

Rothman, E. Natalie. "Becoming Venetian: Conversion and Transformation in the 17th Century Mediterranean." *Mediterranean Historical Review* 21 (2006): 39–75.

———. *Brokering Empire: Trans-Imperial Subjects Between Venice and Istanbul*. Ithaca, N.Y.: Cornell University Press, 2012.

———. "Conceptualizing 'the Mediterranean': Ethnolinguistic Diversity and Early Modern Imperial Governmentality." Paper presented at the Mediterranean Criss-Crossed and Constructed Conference. Weatherhead Center, Harvard University, April 29–31, 2011.

———. "Conversion and Convergence in the Venetian-Ottoman Borderlands." *Journal of Medieval and Early Modern Studies* 41 (2011): 601–33.

Ruiz Ibáñez, José Javier, and Vicente Montojo Montojo. *Entre el lucro y la defensa: Las relaciones entre la monarquía y la sociedad mercantil cartagenera: Comerciantes y corsarios en el siglo XVII.* Murcia: Real Academia Alfonso X El Sabio, 1998.

Russel, Magnus. "The North European Way of Ransoming: Explorations into an Unknown Dimension of the Early Modern Welfare State." *Historical Social Research* 35 (2010): 125–47.

Russel, Magnus, and Cornel Zwierlein. "The Ransoming of North European Captives from North Africa: A Comparison of Dutch, Hanseatic, and English Institutionalization of Redemption from 1610–1645." In *Seeraub im Mittelmeerraum: Piraterie, Korsarentum und maritime Gewalt von der Antike bis zur Neuzeit,* ed. Nikolas Jaspert and Sebastian Kolditz. 377–406. Paderborn: Verlag Ferdinand Schöningh, 2014.

Sahlins, Marshall. *Stone Age Economics.* Chicago: Aldine-Atherton, 1972.

Salvadorini, Vittorio. "Traffici e schiavi fra Livorno e Algeria nella prima decade del '600." *Bollettino Storico Pisano* 51 (1982): 67–104.

Sánchez Gómez, Julio. *De minería, metalúrgica y comercio de metales.* Vol. 2. Salamanca: Universidad de Salamanca, 1989.

Sandoval Parra, Victoria. *Manera de galardón: Merced pecuniaria y extranjería en el siglo XVII.* Madrid: Fondo de Cultura Económica, 2014.

Sarti, Raffaella. "Bolognesi schiavi dei 'turchi' e schiavi 'turchi' a Bologna tra cinque e settecento: Alterità etnico-religiosa e riduzione in schiavitù." *Quaderni Storici* 107 (2001): 437–74.

Schaub, Jean-Frédéric. *Les juifs du roi d'Espagne.* Paris: Hachette Littératures, 1999.

Schroeter, Daniel J. *The Sultan's Jew, Morocco and the Sephardi World.* Stanford, Calif.: Stanford University Press, 2002.

Sellers-García, Sylvia. *Distance and Documents at the Spanish Empire's Periphery.* Stanford, Calif.: Stanford University Press, 2014.

Shuval, Tal. "Cezayir-I Garp: Bringing Algeria Back into Ottoman History." *New Perspectives on Turkey* 22 (2000): 85–114.

Sider, Gerald. "When Parrots Learn to Talk, and Why They Can't: Domination, Deception, and Self-Deception in Indian-White Relations." *Comparative Studies in Society and History* 29 (1987): 3–23.

Sobers-Khan, Nur. "Slaves Without Shackles: Forced Labour and Manumission in the Galata Court Registers, 1560–1572." PhD diss., Pembroke College, 2012.

Sola, Emilio. "Renacimiento, contrarreforma y problema morisco en la obra de Antonio de Sosa." In Antonio de Sosa, *Diálogo de los mártires de Argel,* ed. Emilio Sola. 27–52. Madrid: Hiperión, 1990.

Soyer, Francois. "The Public Baptism of Muslims in Early Modern Spain and

Portugal: Forging Communal Identity Through Collective Emotional Display." *Journal of Religious History* 39 (2015): 506–23.

Steensgaard, Niels. "Consuls and Nations in the Levant from 1570 to 1650." *Scandinavian Economic History Review* 15 (1967): 13–55.

Stella, Alessandro. "Les galères dans la Méditerranée (XVe–XVIIIe siècles): Miroir des mises en servitude." In *Esclavage et dépendances servils: Histoire comparée*, ed. Myriam Cottias, Alessandro Stella, and Bernard Vincent. 265–82. Paris: L'Harmattan, 2007.

———. *Histoires d'esclaves dans la Péninsule Ibérique.* Paris: Ed. de L'Ecole des Hautes Etudes en Sciences Sociales, 2000.

Storrs, Christopher. "Intelligence and Formulation of Policy and Strategy in Early Modern Europe: The Spanish Monarchy in the Reign of Charles II (1665–1700)." *Intelligence and National Security* 21 (2006): 493–519.

Szpiech, Ryan. *Conversion and Narrative: Reading and Religious Authority in Medieval Polemic.* Philadelphia: University of Pennsylvania Press, 2013.

Tabak, Faruk. *The Waning of the Mediterranean, 1550–1870: A Geohistorical Approach.* Baltimore: Johns Hopkins University Press, 2008.

Tarruell, Cecilia. "Circulations entre Chrétienté et Islam: Captivité et esclavage des serviteurs de la monarchie hispanique (ca. 1574–1609)." PhD diss., EHESS-UAM, 2015.

Taylor, Bruce. *Structures of Reform: The Mercedarian Order in the Spanish Golden Age.* Leiden: Brill, 2000.

Toaff, Renzo. "Schiavitù e schiavi nella Nazione Ebrea di Livorno nel Sei e Settecento." *La Rassegna Mensile di Israel* 51 (1985): 82–95.

Trivellato, Francesca. *The Familiarity of Strangers: The Sephardic Diaspora, Livorno, and Cross-Cultural Trade in the Early Modern Period.* New Haven, Conn.: Yale University Press, 2009.

Türkçelik, Evrim. "Cigalazade Yusuf Sinan Pasha y el Mediterráneo entre 1591–1606." PhD diss., Autonomous University of Madrid, 2012.

Valensi, Lucette. *Fables de la mémoire: La glorieuse bataille des Trois Rois, 1578: Souvenirs d'une grande tuerie chez les chrétiens, les juifs & les musulmans.* Paris: Chandeigne, 2009.

Varriale, Genarro. "La capital de la frontera Mediterránea: Exiliados, espías y convertidos en la Nápoles de los virreyes." *Estudis* 38 (2012): 303–21.

Vassberg, David E. "The Status of Widows in Sixteenth Century Rural Castile." In *Poor Women and Children in the European Past*, ed. John Henderson and Richard Wall. 180–95. London: Routledge, 1994.

Vernet, J. "La embajada de al-Gassani (1690–1691)." *Al-Andalus* 18 (1953): 109–31.

Vidal Castro, Francisco. "El cautivo en el mundo islámico: Cisión y vivencia desde el otro lado de la frontera andalusí." In *II Estudios de la frontera: Actividad y vida en la Frontera*. Congreso Celebrado en Alcalá La Real, 19–22 de noviembre de 1997. 771–800. Jaén: Diputación Provincial de Jaén, 1998.

Villar Ramírez, Juan Bautista. *La judería de Tetuán, 1489–1860*. Murcia: Universidad de Murcia, 1969.

———. *Tetuán en el resurgimiento judío contemporáneo (1850–1870): Aproximación a la historia del judaísmo norte africano*. Caracas: Editorial Arte, 1985.

Vincent, Bernard. "Musulmanes y conversión en España en el siglo XVII." In *El río morisco*. 75–87. Valencia: University of Valencia, 2006.

Voigt, Lisa. *Writing Captivity in the Early Modern Atlantic: Circulations of Knowledge and Authority in the Iberian and English Imperial Worlds*. Chapel Hill: University of North Carolina Press, 2009.

Weiss, Gillian Lee. *Captives and Corsairs: France and Slavery in the Early Modern Mediterranean*. Stanford, Calif.: Stanford University Press, 2011.

———. "Ransoming 'Turks' from France's Royal Galleys." *African Economic History* 42 (2014): 37–58.

White, Joshua M. "Shifting Winds: Piracy, Diplomacy, and Trade in the Ottoman Mediterranean, 1624–1626." In *Well-Connected Domains: Towards an Entangled Ottoman History*, ed. Pascal W. Firges, Tobias P. Graf, Christian Roth, and Gülay Tulasğlu. 37–53. Leiden: Brill, 2014.

Wickham, Chris. "Gossip and Resistance Among the Medieval Peasantry." *Past and Present* 100 (1998): 3–24.

Wiegers, Gerard A. "European Converts to Islam in the Maghrib and the Polemical Writings of the Moriscos." In *Conversions islamiques: Identités religieuses en Islam méditerranéen*, ed. Mercedes García Arenal. 207–23. Paris: Maisonneuve et Larose, 2002.

Wilkinson, Alexander S. *Iberian Books: Books Published in Spanish or Portuguese or on the Iberian Peninsula Before 1601*. Leiden: Brill, 2010.

Wolf, John B. *The Barbary Coast: Algiers Under the Turks, 1500 to 1830*. New York: Norton, 1979.

Wolfe, Patrick. "Settler Colonialism and the Elimination of the Native." *Journal of Genocide Research* 8 (2006): 387–409.

Yebbur Oddi, Abderrahim. *El gobierno de Tetuán por la familia Al-Naqsis (1597–1673)*. Tétouan: Imprenta del Majzen, 1955.

Zemon Davis, Natalie. *Fiction in the Archives: Pardon Tales and Their Tellers in Sixteenth-Century France*. Stanford, Calif.: Stanford University Press, 1987.

———. *Trickster Travels: A Sixteenth Century Muslim Between Worlds*. New York: Hill and Wang, 2006.

Zysberg, André. *Les Galériens du roi—vies et destins de 60 000 forçats sur les galères de France: 1680–1748*. Paris: Seuil, 1987.

INDEX

Illustrations are indicated by italicized page numbers; tables are indicated by "t" following the page number.

ACKNOWLEDGMENTS

One way of conceiving a book project is thinking about it as an intellectual and emotional debt-accruing machine. This book has been
extremely efficient in this regard, and it is a great pleasure for me
to thank all who have made it possible. I am extremely grateful to
many friends and colleagues who read the manuscript at various
stages, helping me to make it better. I was especially lucky to think
and write together with Naor Ben-Yehoyada, Andrea Celli, Claire
Gilbert, Seth Kimmel, Jessica Marglin, Natalie Rothman, and Cor-
rey Tazzara. I am also extremely grateful for those who read various
parts of the manuscript, offering their thoughtful feedback, including
Danna Agmon, Tara Alberts, Pamela Ballinger, Agustin Casas, Javier
F. Castro Ibaseta, Brian Catlos, Adrien Delmas, Andrew Devereux,
Camilo Gómez-Rivas, Regina Grafe, Mayte Green-Mercado, Stefano
Gulizia, Yanay Israeli, Mahinder S. Kingra, Sharon Kinoshita, Ariel
Krill, Susan Slyomovics, Stefan Stantchev, Pier Mattia Tommasino,
Daniel Wasserman-Soler, and Claire Zimmerman.

I had and have the privilege of having brilliant, dedicated, and
inspiring mentors. I thank Diane Owen Hughes, who helped shape
the project in its initial stages, pushing me to sharpen questions and
arguments, Jonathan Sheehan, who in addition to providing precious criticism was there to (literally) tie knots at critical moments,
James Amelang and his marvelous bibliographical suggestions, Ryan
Szpiech, an exceptionally attentive reader, Antonio Feros for astute
suggestions and endless support, Gadi Algazi, whose research and
politics were and still are an inspiration, Enrique García Santo-
Tomás for the best professional advice, and Mercedes García Arenal for directing me toward rich sources and studies and for being
extremely generous with her time and intellect. I would also like to

thank Wolfgang Kaiser and Jocelyne Dakhlia for conversations without which the book would have never been written in this manner.

It is also a pleasure to thank friends and colleagues whose intellectual dynamism and ongoing support have contributed immensely to the book: Benjamin Arbel, Iván Armenteros Martínez, Costanza Beltrami, Guy Burak, Guillaume Calafat, Miri Eliav-Feldon, Hussein Fancy, Cornell H. Fleischer, Jorge Flores, Barbara Fuchs, Albert Garcia Balaña, William Granara, Molly Greene, Tom Green, Jean Hebrard, Michael Herzfeld, Stephen Jacobson, Peter F. Kitlas, Val Kivelson, Aviad Kleinberg, Manuel Lomas, Monica Lopez Lerma, Jackie Loss, Eloy Martín Corrales, Peter Miller, Luca Molà, Gustavo Nanclares, Natividad Planas, Helmut Puff, Oded Rabinovitch, Fernando Rodríguez Mediano, Roser Salicrú i Lluch, Jean-Frédéric Schaub, Jeffrey Shoulson, Cecilia Tarruell, Francesca Trivellato, Eduardo Urios-Aparisi, Bernard Vincent, Ittai Weinryb, and Amalia Zomeño Rodríguez. I owe a special thanks to Isabel Aguirre Landa, who initiated me to the captivating secrets of Simancas, as well as to the archivists of the Archivo Histórico Nacional, Archivo de la Corona de Aragón, Archivio di Stato di Genoa, Archivo General de Simancas, the special collections room of the Biblioteca Nacional de España, and the Biblioteca Zabálburu.

Various institutions generously funded my research. The bulk of my time in the archives was funded by fellowships from the Social Science Research Council, the Council for European Studies at Columbia, and the Program for Cultural Cooperation Between Spain's Ministry of Culture and U.S. Universities. Shorter archival visits were enabled by fellowships from the Casa de Velázquez in Madrid, the Newberry Library in Chicago, a National Endowment for the Humanities Summer Institute in Barcelona, a Franklin Research Grant from the American Philosophical Society, a Bernadotte Schmitt Research Grant from the American Historical Association, grants from the Department of History, the Medieval and Early Modern Studies Program, the Center for European Studies, the International Institute, and the Rackham School of Graduate Studies at the University of Michigan, and various grants from the University of Connecticut. Several yearlong fellowships provided precious writing time and complemented it with exciting and dynamic intellectual communities of fellow scholars: the Humanities Institute at the University of Michigan, the Max Weber Program at the European University Institute in Florence, a semester as a visiting scholar at the Bard Graduate Center, and the Humanities Institute at the University of Connecticut.

At the University of Pennsylvania Press, I am extremely grateful to Jerry Singerman for trusting in the project from an early stage. I also thank Hannah Blake, Gavi Fried, Erica Ginsburg, Tim Roberts, and Jenn Backer for leading me so smoothly through the publishing process. I also thank the press's anonymous readers for helping make the book better. Some parts of Chapters 2 and 7 have previously appeared in my article "The Political Economy of Ransom in the Early Modern Mediterranean," *Past and Present* 231 (2016): 61–95. Portions of Chapter 5 originally appeared in my contribution "Plaintes et menaces réciproques: Captivité et violence religieuses dans la Méditerranée du XVIIe siècle," which appeared in *Les Musulmans dans l'histoire de l'Europe*, vol. 2, *Passages et contacts en Méditerranée*, edited by Jocelyne Dakhlia and Wolfgang Kaiser (Paris: Albin Michel, 2013), 441–60. And a few sections of Chapter 3 appeared in my article "'[P]ara que me saque cabesa por cabesa . . .': Exchanging Muslim and Christian Slaves Across the Mediterranean," *African Economic History* 42 (2014): 11–36.

The book is dedicated to my parents, without whom the book would have never been written. I warmly thank my mother, Fanny Hershenzon, for endless loving support throughout the years. My father, José Hershenzon, who did not live to see this book, taught me much about intellectual conversation and history, and was and will always be an important and loved source of inspiration. I also thank my sister-in-law, Abigail Saggi, and my brother, Martin Hershenzon. Their encouragement took so many forms over the years, and this text would not have been written without their support.